D1112635

# NOTES ON ENGLAND

*Hippolyte Taine*

# TAINE'S
# Notes on England

TRANSLATED
WITH AN INTRODUCTION BY
EDWARD HYAMS

## London
THAMES AND HUDSON

*Translated from the French
'Notes Sur L'Angleterre'
by Hippolyte Taine, 1860—1870*

# CONTENTS

# LIST OF ILLUSTRATIONS

*Frontispiece:* Hippolyte Taine

## FROM 'PUNCH'

## FROM 'NOTES SUR L'ANGLETERRE'

## FROM 'GAVARNI IN LONDON'

## FROM 'THE ADVENTURES OF Mr VERDANT GREEN'

# INTRODUCTION

Hippolyte Taine was born at Vouziers in the Ardennes in 1828. His father was a lawyer; the family had long been settled in the region and had produced, in several generations, the kind of sound, sober bourgeois who fill municipal offices so usefully, and leave their sons a little better off, a little higher in the social scale, than they were themselves. Until the age of eleven Hippolyte lived at home; he was taught Latin by his father, with whom he used to go for long walks in the forests where he made the acquaintance of the shrewd and honest lumbermen of that region; and English by his uncle. He also attended a small local school run by a M. Pierson. Hippolyte was a remarkable child: he was brilliant, but he was also so reliable that, at ten years of age, the schoolmaster had no hesitation in leaving the boy in charge of the school when he himself was indisposed. Yet he does not seem to have been a prig, and from childhood until his death he attracted and held the affection as well as the trust of everyone excepting those political and ecclesiastical authorities he despised. That, at least, is the impression left by all three of his biographers, and by the sayings, letters and other writings of such friends as Guizot, Renan and Prévost-Paradol.

In 1839 M. Taine fell ill and Hippolyte was sent to a Church school at Rethel were he remained until his father died eighteen months later. Then, on the advice of the uncle who had taught him English, and who realised that the boy must be sent where he could develop his already remarkable character and his not less remarkable mind he went to the Institution Mathé, in Paris, a boarding establishment whose alumni attended lessons at the Collège Bourbon, at that time probably the best school in France.

Taine was not happy as a boarding-school boy. I have no doubt that he still remembered his own miseries at the age of twelve when, many years later, he visited Eton and Harrow and had occasion to compare the freedom, leisure and almost adult responsibility enjoyed by English school-boys with the prison-like conditions and Herculean tasks which French *collégiens* were subject to. In one of the last essays he ever wrote

Taine described the boarding-school life as "an anti-social and anti-natural regime", and animadverted against the life of a *collégien* who, he says, "lives, deprived of all initiative like a horse between the shafts of a cart." It was not so much the twelve-hour working day he objected to, although he thought it excessive, nor the additional homework, nor, perhaps, the entire absence of games, for he thought later that English boys gave too much time to them. He hated the cloistered atmosphere, and the constant surveillance in reaction against which the boys' imaginations became overheated, and they were led into an unwholesome sentimental precocity.

As a result of her son's unhappiness Mme Taine moved to Paris with her daughters, so that Hippolyte could live with them. It is very well known that Frenchmen are peculiarly devoted to their mothers: the relationship, at its best, has never been more movingly and charmingly depicted than by Stendhal, in the affectionate confidence between Lucien, and Mme Leuwen. Taine and his mother were on this footing throughout his lifetime, a fact which probably coloured the warm and pleasant picture he drew of French domestic life with which, at the end of his *Notes sur l'Angleterre,* he compared English domestic life unfavourably. His mother was, Taine said, "the unique friend, who occupied the first place in my heart". And after she died he wrote of her, "My mother's life was all devotion and all love ... no woman was ever so profoundly and so perfectly a mother."

Taine continued to attend the Collège Bourbon as a day-boy, and soon became its star pupil. From the age of fourteen he drew up a schedule of work and reading to be got through every day, and he adhered to it. The almost stolid faculty for sheer application rarely goes with brillance, but it certainly did in his case, and Giraud, his Swiss biographer, suggests that the quality was "racial", an idea he seems to have borrowed from some of Michelet's reflections on the peculiar character of France's north-eastern frontier people. Gerson, Mabillon and Turenne were born and bred in Taine's part of France and they too possessed a singular capacity for hard work soberly and methodically done, a quality more German than French. "Taine", wrote Emile Boutmy [*] "avait une imagination Germanique administrée et exploitée par une raison latine." That, of course, is not the same thing as Michelet had in mind; it is almost *au rebours*. It hardly matters

[*] *Taine, Schérer. Laboulaye, Paris 1901.*

x

which, if either, was true. The fact is that Taine had an enormous appetite for work.

His schedule allowed him twenty minutes a day for rest and recreation; one hour for piano practice, but that, too, he would have regarded as recreation for he adored music; the rest of the day was devoted to work. This enabled him to pursue a course of private reading as well as to get through his school work. It was as well that the success of these efforts was spectacular, for he paid a heavy price for them. "Every year," says Monod, "at the time of the annual examinations, leeches had to be applied to his head to prevent a cerebral congestion." As a result of this precaution, or in spite of it, Taine not only took all six first prizes in the class of Rhetoric, offered by his own school, but the prize of honour and three *proxime accessits* in the *concours* open to all colleges. Subsequently, in the class of Philosophy, he won all the Bourbon first prizes, three for natural sciences and two for *dissertation* and two second prizes in the *concours général*. In 1848 he passed into the Ecole Normale with two baccalaureat degrees, that is as a Bachelor of Letters, and of Science.

It is curious to find Taine's biographers, all men of his own or the next generation, quoting a list of names all forgotten by now excepting, perhaps, by a few specialists, in order to prove that the men of Taine's year at the Ecole Normale were an exceptionally brilliant lot. We are told of their achievements in literature, journalism, teaching and politics and it is clear that these were expected to be remembered. That they are forgotten is not to say that they were of no importance. How many journalists, how many teachers, are remembered after their generation? Yet the work they do is perhaps the most important of all: for the thinking of those rare geniuses who decide the way we are to go can have no consequences whatsoever if patient, skilful and able interpreters are lacking to persuade the rest of us to adopt the new idea. At all events Taine's contemporaries were struck by the fact that, brilliant as the other young men at the Ecole Normale were in 1848, Taine towered above them all. Of the three men who had most influence on him two were about his own age, and their names, indeed, still mean something: both Prévost-Paradol and Renan were his friends. The other was a generation older, Guizot, to whom Prévost-Paradol introduced Taine, and who took a great fancy to this brilliant student. We may suppose that, as the author of the *Histoire de la révolution anglaise* Guizot contributed to turning Taine's mind towards a study of English thought.

Like Renan, Taine was born a Catholic but it is impossible to discover whether he was early influenced in a sense hostile to that religion, perhaps by his father, or whether he arrived at hostility of his own volition and under the influence of the books he read. His experience in this respect may have been much like Renan's, but their conclusions were different.

It will be recalled that when Renan's quitting the Church was misunderstood and he was said to have gone the same way as Guizot, a fellow guest in a Paris drawing-room challenged him with, "I understand, M. Renan, that you have turned Protestant?" To which Renan replied, "Madame, I have lost my faith, but not my reason." It was an amusing, but certainly not a sensible answer for the author of the *Vie de Jésus* to have made; and Taine, for whom the *Vie de Jésus* was a great book, an enlightening book, would never have made it. In the first place he was no wit. But what is much more important, he would never have dismissed an important spiritual discipline merely because he personally thought it ill-founded. By the time he was twenty he could certainly not have accepted any God more formal than the metaphysical abstraction he found in Spinoza's *Ethics;* yet something rather more than respect for an immensely useful social instrument re-emerges in his praise of Anglicanism, in the *Notes.* He was readily moved by the idea of the individual conscience, the individual soul, face to face with the unknowable, elevating itself to a loftiness of feeling and behaviour by dwelling upon the idea of the Power which must lie beyond the mystery, the *au-delà.* His sympathy for English Protestantism constantly shows through the cloak of his pretence to analyse it merely in its social attributes.

Although Taine was an intellectual giant at the Ecole Normale, not indeed among pygmies, but among exceptionally well grown minds, he never sought to make his superiority felt. He was, on the contrary, remembered for his sweetness of temper, modesty, cheerfulness and kindness; he is even described as often gay. And, as regards the first four of these admirable qualities, he did not change: the man who wrote the *Notes* does not strike one as gay, but certainly he was kind and cheerful and modest, and his sweetness of temper is expressed in a sort of endearing simplicity: one wants, from time to time, to tell him that he is having his leg pulled; he had a taste for English humour, as he proved in the specimen of it which he chose to demonstrate it to his readers; but one has a feeling that he was not always and immediately aware of it.

At the Ecole Normale, we are told, he was regarded with "affectionate respect". It is a suitable feeling towards people of two kinds: venerable and sweet-natured elders; and holy innocents. And such, for all his intellectual stature, perhaps because of it, was Taine. Take, for example, his nick-name: his fellow-students called him *le grand bûcheron*. It was inspired partly by his physique, partly by the principal industry of his native mountains; but partly, surely, by his character. The ideas, or rather feelings, associated, however mistakenly, with the life of a woodman, are those of sober cheerfulness, candid simplicity. Knowing that he was so called we hardly need to be told that, for all he entered the Ecole Normale as an *érudit*, he worked as hard as if he knew nothing; and had not the slightest objection to his brains being picked not only by his fellow-students but, on occasion, by his professors.

It was at the Ecole Normale that Taine drew up the plan for his life to which he tried, with some success, to adhere. We have an account of it in a letter to Prévost-Paradol and I shall quote it in part because it reveals not only his appetite for work, and the disinterested loftiness of his ambition, but a shrewd foreknowledge, almost out of character, of how that freedom of thought which was, for him, a condition of self-respect, would be regarded by the authorities.

> March 20. 1849
>
> ... I have an immense volume of work before me. To begin with there is the work officially required of us in Greek, Latin, history and French; then the preparation for my *licence*, entailing the reading of the thirty of forty difficult authors we may be required to expound at the examination; and finally all my own private studies in literature, history and philosophy ... I have drawn up a big plan of study and it is my purpose to accomplish part of it during my three years here, and to complete it thereafter. I want to be a philisopher and, since you now understand the whole significance of that word, you will realise what a course of reflection and what a body of knowledge are essential to me. If I wanted to do no more than pass an examination, or

simply to occupy a Chair, I should not need to put myself to much trouble: a limited amount of reading would suffice, given an unquestioning loyalty to the professor's doctrine, and a total ignorance of what philosophy and modern science really mean ... As I study because I want to know, and not in order to make a living, I want my education to be thorough. That is why I am plunging into all kinds of research work and why I shall be forced, when I leave the Ecole, to add the social sciences, political economy, and the physical sciences, to my curriculum of study. But what takes up a great deal of my time is private reflection: to understand a thing one must discover it for oneself; to believe in philosophy one must re-make it for oneself, even if only to discover what others have already discovered.

Many young men and women make lists of books to read and sciences to study: Was there ever a case of such plan being adhered to? By all accounts Taine did precisely what he said he would do, and contrived to do it without appearing a prig. Here, at the end of his three years at the Ecole Normale, is what M. Vacherot, the Director of studies, wrote in his report on him:

The most industrious and distinguished student I have ever known at the Ecole. Prodigiously well-informed for his age. An ardour and avidity in search of knowledge such as I have never experienced. His mind is remarkable for its rapid grasp, and for the refinement, power and subtlety of his thinking. However, he seizes an idea, conceives a line of thought, judges, and formulates a conclusion too quickly. He is too fond of formulas and clear definitions, to which he is apt to sacrifice the real facts, but unwittingly for he is of the most perfect sincerity. Taine will be a very distinguished teacher; but, what is more, he will be a *savant* * of the highest order if his health allows him to accomplish a long career.

He has great sweetness of nature, an attractive appearance, and unconquerable strength of mind such that his thinking

* I have left the word in French because I do not know what M. Vacherot means. Before about 1840 *savant* meant what we mean by scholar. Now it *usually* means what we mean by scientist. About 1850 it was clearly being used in both senses. M. Vacherot may have been referring to Taine's promise in humanism; or to his eager interest and faith in the rising natural sciences.

E. H.

cannot be influenced by anyone. In fact he is not of this world *(n'est pas de ce monde:* "too good for this world"). His motto will be Spinoza's *"Live to think".* Conduct and bearing excellent. As for his morals, I believe that his nature, altogether exceptional, a *nature d'élite,* is innocent of all passion but a passion for truth. It has the advantage of placing him beyond temptation. In lectures and in examination this student is first, and that by a wide margin.

The France into which Taine emerged from the Ecole Normale was, like our own world a hundred years later, in a state of violent change. I am not referring to the superficial changes entailed in switching, every fifteen or twenty years, from a republican to a monarchical form of government, from monarchy back to republic, and from republic to empire. Something more than the name given to government was changing. As Taine himself was to put it later, the "reigning model" was being changed. In the 17th century that model had been *"l'honnête homme";* in the 18th, *"le philosophe";* in the early part of the 19th, it had been the romantic poet. Now the Hero was to be the *savant,* in the new sense, the scientist. It is odd that Giraud, in the 'nineties, was giving the new Hero half a century's innings starting in the 'forties: can he have supposed that the scientist would have had his day by 1900? Perhaps it was only the two German wars which gave him a much longer lease of life. At all events his first lease began when Taine was at the university. France, in the 'forties and 'fifties, was building railways, installing electric telegraphs, and inventing photography; physics, chemistry and astronomy were suddenly advancing with giant strides; Pasteur was in the offing. In 1840 Renan wrote his *Avenir de la science* (which was not published until 1890); in it he declared, *Science is a religion.* It was an idea which Renan, in common with Taine, had derived from Hegel, and it took just over a century for us to discover that it was one of the most tragic mistakes ever made by a thinker. Taine was one of the first of the immense swarm of people who were to repeat it. But at least the error, as made by him, had noble origins: as what one may perhaps call "pure enquiry" the natural sciences were a branch of philosophy. Philosophy was the only possible religion for an intelligent, educated, high-minded man, a man whose prophet was Spinoza. So, then, science *was*

the new religion and it was in the scientific spirit that history and literature must be approached.*

In view of the damage which has been done by this artificial elevation of the higher branches of useful mechanics to the status of philosophy, one can almost forgive those boards of examiners, and the clerical *éminences grises* who stood darkly behind them, for the way in which they ploughed Taine at his *agrégation* examination, and at his first attempt at a doctorate later. Almost, but not quite: it was not foresight but prejudice which animated them.

The astonishment at Taine's failure, and the scandal, says Monod, were great. "The young philosopher's reputation had spread beyond the Ecole. Everybody had expected him to pass first. His failure was attributed not to his papers, but to his doctrines."

Those doctrines had emerged in his answers; the answers were brilliant, but they made it clear that Taine was not impressed by the traditional proofs for the existence of God, that he did not regard philosophy as being a repetition, in more or less felicitous terms, of Victor Cousin's moral and religious bromides; and that he saw merit in a materialist, positivist approach even to religion. His aim, in presenting himself for *agrégation* was to get an appointment as a professor of philosophy, for, as he told Prévost-Paradol, he believed that the best way to learn was to teach.

---

* "Comme chaque nation d'ordinaire lie sa vie suprasensible en une gerbe spirituelle, qui est sa littérature ... la vraie psychologie de l'humanité consisterait surtout dans l'histoire des littératures. ... La vraie littérature d'un époque est celle qui la peint et l'exprime ... La critique a admiré jusqu'ici les chefs d'œuvres des littératures comme nous admirons les belles formes d'un corps humain. La critique de l'avenir les admirera comme l'anatomiste, qui perce ces beautés sensibles pour trouver au-delà, dans les secrets de l'organisation, un ordre de beauté mille fois supérieur."

Renan, *l'Avenir de la Science.*

But it was Taine who was to make a beginning on this *critique de l'avenir*, first in his *Essais de critique et d'histoire* and thereafter in his *Histoire de la littérature anglaise.* It is, of course, the ancestor of Marxist criticism. In Taine's case it was softened by his own resistance to spiritual scepticism. ("... *le doute, si ce n'est pas celui de Pascal, est une lacheté.*" And, again, *"la confiance absolue que j'ai dans le pouvoir de l'intelligence... je ressemble à un Catholique qui ne sait parler que de l'Eglise et de la foi."* (Quoted by E. Faguet in *Hippolyte Taine. Paris 1900.*) Taine made constant efforts to make purely intellectual responses to ideas and things do work which does not belong to the intellect at all. The results are sometimes curious, as in his ecstatic response to E. B. Browning's *Aurora Leigh,* see *Notes on England,* hereafter. E. H.

The board declared him incapable of teaching philosophy.

The consequent outcry among the learned, and the protests published by such journals as *Liberté de pensée* seem to have frightened the Minister for Education into destroying the board's report on Taine, and overruling the findings; and in 1851 Taine was appointed lecturer in philosophy at Toulon. As he did not want to go so far from his mother this was changed, at his own request, to Nevers. He took up his appointment with enthusiasm, free to develop, in his *Philosophie de l'art* and his *Histoire de la littérature anglaise,* the very ideas which had led the examining board to reject him, the ideas which gave rise to the theory of '*grace, mouvement, milieu*' for which he became famous.

In December 1851 Napoleon's first *coup d'Etat* was accomplished, and all university teachers were regarded by the new dictatorship with marked suspicion. Many were retired, some were dismissed; others, not waiting for the inevitable, resigned. In his argument with Prévost-Paradol, who proposed that they should both resign, Taine gives us a taste of his political attitude. The *coup d'Etat* had been confirmed by the overwhelming majority obtained by the Dictator-President in the plebiscite of December 10. The only authority for political power in France, said Taine, was universal suffrage, and universal suffrage had vindicated Napoleon. It was, therefore, one's plain duty to accept the *régime* in silence; any resistance offered to it was an act of insurrection, a small personal *coup d'Etat*. Taine wrote to his friend: "The crassest boor has a perfect right to dispose of his own field, his own private property, as he pleases, and similarly a nation of imbeciles has the right to dispose of itself, that is of the public property. One must either deny the sovereignty of the will of the people, and the whole nature of common law; or one must obey universal suffrage." A week later he again wrote to Prévost-Paradol: "Here is a peasant on his own land; being stupid he cultivates it badly. I, a scientist, come along and advise him, rightly, to do it some other way. He persists in his own way and ruins his harvest. But if I try to prevent him I commit an injustice. Here is a people deciding upon its government. Being stupid and ignorant, they entrust it to a man with an illustrious name but who has committed a wicked action and will lead them into the abyss. Moreover, in doing this they are stripping themselves of their liberties, guarantees, and of the means of improving and educating themselves. I am distressed and indignant; but in using my vote I did all I could against such a piece of brutality. The people belong to themselves, and if I go against that sacred and inviolable thing, the will of the people, I commit an injustice."

It is the attitude of Socrates in the *Phaedo,* refusing to save his life at the cost of breaking the law. And writing a month later Taine said, "... the man reigning over us has a good chance of lasting. He has ingeniously obtained the backing of universal suffrage; and universal suffrage will not ask him for liberty, but for well-being. He has the clergy and the army: add to that his uncle's name, the fear of socialism, and the divisions in the ranks of the opposition. It means that *political life is barred to us for, perhaps, ten years.*⁕ Our only way is pure science and pure literature."

This Socratic acceptance of the people's will was modified by some reservations in the matter of conscience. Taine did not concede the majority's right to do absolutely everything it liked. "There are certain things which are outside the social contract, which are therefore not part of the public domain, and consequently are not subject to public decisions ... for example, freedom of conscience, and all those rights and duties which come before the claims of the community."

Holding which opinion he, alone of the faculty at Nevers, refused to sign the document whereby university staffs were made to signify not merely their approval of, but their gratitude to the Dictator-President for the *coup d'Etat.* He said that if he signed it would be to forswear himself. He was black-marked as a revolutionary and transferred, despite a petition and protest by his students, to Poitiers, where he could be kept under the sharp supervision of the archbishop. Taine did his best to conform, even to the extent of attending religious services: for was not that what the will of the people required of him? But nothing could have whitewashed him: his dossier contained not only records of his dangerous thoughts, but a malicious libel in the form of a report, by a former pupil whom he had had to degrade from first to tenth place in class, and who was both noble, and Jesuit-trained, to the effect that Taine had praised Danton in the course of his lessons.

⁕ He was, of course, too optimistic: the dictatorship lasted, with some liberalisations more apparent than real, twenty years, until Prussia destroyed it.  E. H.

It was pure invention, but it sufficed. The political archbishop had already removed Taine's predecessor for the subversive crime of being a Jew; he removed Taine for no ostensible reason whatsoever. The Ministry, bound by a ten-year agreement, offered Taine the sixth form at Besançon *lycée*. Taine, of course, refused and demanded leave. It was granted by return, and prolonged, year after year, during the whole period of his appointment.

The foundation of those ideas which supported all Taine's major works were laid in the theses he wrote for his doctorate in 1852, one in French and one in Latin as was usual.

The French one was the first ripe fruit of his psychological work and was entitled *Les Sensations*. "It is", he wrote to Prévost-Paradol, "psychology and pure observation. For the fundamentals I have used Aristotle as my authority," — this, as he confessed later, was by way of being a sop to the examining professors — "I hope I may pass... I believe I have made several discoveries and produced a sound theory, especially several palpable facts on the nature of the soul. Will this be thought too bold?"

The thesis was one of the bases of his *De l'Intelligence*, published sixteen years later.

Taine realised that his *Sensations* would be offensive to the Faculty from the doctrinaire point of view. But he thought that the examiners could not fail to recognise its merits, and that they would be enabled to do so officially by a rule relating to the consideration of doctoral theses according to which the Faculty was declared not answerable for candidates' opinions. However, he was mistaken. His point of departure had indeed been Aristotle's $\overset{\prime}{\varepsilon}\nu\tau\varepsilon\lambda\varepsilon\chi\varepsilon\iota\alpha$, but he had set himself up in opposition to the received authorities, Reid for example; and he had "erected a system of relationships between the nervous system and the ego which, if not entirely materialist, was far from being orthodox".

His second attempt on a doctorate was made in 1853 with a Latin thesis entitled *De Personis platonicis* and a French one, *Essais sur les Fables de La Fontaine*. With some grumbling at his excessive respect for classical morality and too little regard for the Christian variety, and at the "philosophic poison" which, it was alleged by one professor, lurked in his *La Fontaine*, Taine was granted his degree.

Meanwhile he had been working at a long essay on Livy which

was, in fact, a theory of history. Having parted with the university but won his doctorate, he completed this and entered it at a *concours* of the Académie Française. It happened to fall to Guizot to report on this work, and Guizot urged it warmly on his fellow Immortals: they resisted. The young philosopher was learned certainly, brilliant no doubt, but he had too little respect for the role of great men in history (curious for an admirer of Carlyle), and entirely too much for the ideas of Michelet and Niebuhr. Even these misdemeanours might have passed; but to say of Bossuet that despite his good sense and grand style he wrote *history for children* was an insupportable outrage. The best that Guizot and Taine's other friends could do was to get the *concours* postponed in order to prevent the *couronnement* going to someone else. Taine modified the offending passages and in 1855 the work was *couronné*. Whereupon the young laureate printed it but with a small addition, a half-page preface as follows: "Man", says Spinoza, "is not in nature like an empire within an empire, but as a part in a whole; and the motions of the intelligent automaton which is our being are as subject to rule as are those of the material world in which it is included." The *Académie*, having thought it was crowning a work of literary and historical criticism, found itself sponsoring what, with this key provided, appeared as a work of determinist philosophy. In the following ten years they did not get over their annoyance.

At the beginning of 1854 Taine fell ill: he was subject to periods of nervous exaustion during which work, as he understood it, became impossible. During such terms, however, he was not idle. On this occasion he started to study medicine with his cousin Baillarger, the noted alienist. He read, by way of relaxation, Buchez and Roux on the French Revolution and was much struck by the intellectual mediocrity of the most famous men of that period. He stayed with his married sister in the country, observing and making notes on the peasantry, agriculture, and stock-raising. Finally, at the suggestion of the publisher Hachette, he went to the Pyrenees and there wrote his *Voyage aux Pyrenées*, surely one of the oddest travel books ever written. Exercising his gift for descriptive writing, he mixed in amusing sketches on rustic manners, historical anecdotes and satires on the fashionable watering-places. Illustrated by Gustav Doré, the book appeared in 1855. Taine did not regard it as an important piece of work, but the two principal features of his style are apparent in it: fresh and vivid description; and categorisation. Order was a mania with him, and that mania is behind his admiration for Macaulay. Of his own taste in this connection he wrote, "Guizot's History of Civilization and Jouffroy's lectures gave me my first strong feeling of literary pleasure, because of their progressive classifications."

His own style, he declared, would be based on an attempt to "substitute for intuition *insight* \*, for spontaneous abstraction *Vernunft*, analysis of the kind used in oratory." He used the method in his *Notes on England:* it is apt to creak. There were, he admitted, two gifts proper to a writer which he did not possess and which he regretted: he had not the art of telling a story; and he had not the art of creating live, active characters. And this, since he considered the novelist's art to be of the highest order, was hard. He did try to write a novel, but he gave it up short of a hundred pages, perceiving that it was dead under his hand. "I have", he wrote to a friend, "known real artists too well, real fertile minds capable of giving birth to living characters, to pretend to be one myself."

Nevertheless the years 1855 and 1856 were those during which his talent came to maturity and he acquired full confidence in it. He lived, during most of this time, with his mother and sister in the Ile St Louis, a cheerful, active, sensible life, seeing a great deal of his friends — Prévost, Planat, Renan, Havet, Sainte-Beuve. He went on with his medical studies and psychological researches, and a friendship with Franz Woepke opened the world of mathematics to his eager mind. At this time he began to contribute copiously to the *Journal de l'Instruction Publique, La Revue des Deux Mondes* and the *Journal des Débats,* mostly critical analyses of the work of men who interested him, Macaulay, Washington, Menandre, Saint-Simon and many others.

His *Histoire de la littérature anglaise* began to appear in the *Journal de l'Instruction publique* in 1856 and was transferred after that year to the *Revue des Deux Mondes.* At the same time he began publication of his *Philosophes français au XIXe Siècle.* He treated the philosophical pundits with scant respect, his style was vigorously agressive and his attack sharpened with irony. As a result he has been accused of a want of seriousness in treating this subject; but the fact is he did genuinely regard the philosophy of the Establishment as a serious bar to freedom of thought, and he set out to discredit it. His lack of reverence appears to have upset his biographers: I find them apt to apologise to their readers for this work, and to claim indulgence on the ground that Taine

\* See footnote on page xvi.

was only twenty-seven when he wrote it and that we should regard it as a sowing of wild oats.

There can be no doubt that the public thought, however, when the book appeared in volume form in 1857. It was an immediate and resounding success, so much so that Taine became famous over-night.

The object of this essay is not to present Taine's whole life, nor to give a catalogue of his works: it is to give the reader an idea of what kind of man he was whose impressions of England during the 1860s we are about to read. Having seen him into fame, therefore, it will be sufficient to say very little more concerning the rest of his life; and his mature work is part of our heritage.

As to his private life it appears to have been exceptionally calm and happy. He had never been poor; his success made him comparatively rich. In 1859 he paid his first, long visit to England, was greatly impressed by what he saw, and returned with full note-books. In 1868, at the age of forty, he married the daughter of a successful architect, a Mlle Denuelle. She appears to have made him an excellent wife, capable of sharing his life and taking an intelligent interest in his work, but principally occupied with their home and with their children who, if we are to believe his biographers, never caused him any feeling less satisfactory than pride and joy. About half the year was spent in Paris, among a large and agreeable circle of men of letters, scientists and artists, Renan, Gautier, Flaubert and the Goncourts among others, a circle whose powerful but unofficial patroness was the Princesse Mathilde. The other half of the year was spent in the country; after 1874 this was at Boringe, the country estate which Taine bought beside the Lake of Annecy. This calm and happiness were interrupted only once, by the public disaster of the Prussian War and the Commune. It was during the Commune, in 1871, that Taine paid his second *recorded* visit to England, in order to lecture at Oxford. The pleasant round of work and friendship and domesticity was then resumed until Taine died, at the age of 65, in 1893.

Although I can find no trace of it in the biographies, Taine would appear to have paid a third visit to England, between the other two, that is in 1862. I base this on the fact that he dated his MS June 1862 and on evidence which professional historians may regard with dubiety but which my horse-racing friends assure me is as sound as evidence can be: the *Notes* include an account of Taine's visit to the Derby; the winner — we do not gather that he backed it — was Caractacus. Caractacus won the Derby in 1862.

Now for a brief note of Taine's work during the rest of his life. It may best be considered under three main headings and a kind of appendix:

1. As a scientist, that is a psychologist, his ideas found their fullest expression in his *De l'Intelligence*, which appeared in 1870. All his psychological researches and all his philosophical reading since his twenties were tributary to this major work. A quarter of a century after its appearance a *savant* of consequence could write of it — "the subsequent discoveries of science have done no more than confirm Taine's work in all its parts".

2. As art historian and critic Taine published not only his great history of English literature, which is a work of philosophical determinism as well as literary criticism, but a whole series of *Philosophies* of art ... *La Philosophie de l'art*, 1865; *l'Idéale dans l'art*, 1867; *La Philosophie de l'art en Italie*, 1866; *La Philosophie de l'art dans les Pays Bas*, 1868; *La Philosophie de l'art dans la Grèce*, 1869. In each case a visit was paid to the principal art collections, monuments and churches of the countries concerned; Taine travelled a great deal, particularly in Italy, Germany and Flanders. All these books were republished as his *Philosophy of Art* in 1880.

3. Taine's third rôle was teaching — both in person and in such instructive books as his *Voyage en Italie*, *Notes sur l'Angleterre* and *Origines de la France moderne*. Despite his inauspicious beginning Taine held official appointments during about a third of his life, although determined efforts were made to have him removed from them. These failed because, little though the authorities relished his ideas, there was no getting over the fact that they had made a tremendous impression and that, barring Renan, Taine was regarded as the intellectual leader of the second half of the nineteenth century.* In 1862 he only just failed to get the Chair of literature at the Ecole Polytechnique. In 1863, at the instance of the Minister of Education himself, the military author-

* "Aucun écrivain n'a exercé en France dans la seconde moitié de ce siècle une influence égale la sienne, partout, dans la philosophie, dans l'histoire, dans la critique, dans le roman, dans la poésie même, on retrouve la trace de cette influence."

G. Monod in *Renan, Taine, Michelet*. De Margerie, and Giraud, in their respective studies of Taine's work, come to much the same conclusion. E. H.

ities appointed Taine examiner in History and German at Saint-Cyr. In the following year he replaced Viollet-le-Duc as professor of aesthetics and art history at the Ecole des Beaux Arts. These appointments were not made without fierce resistance from Taine's old enemy the Church. Monseigneur Dupanloup, a 'liberal' whose distinction it is to have become an almost legendary clerical reactionary, caused Taine's appointments (and Renan's to the Collège de France) to be suspended. Fortunately the Princesse Mathilde, who had much influence with her brother, the Emperor, took a hand, and the appointments were confirmed. But although he was the most distinguished man of letters in France with the one exception of his friend Renan, fifteen more years passed before Taine was elected to the Académie Française. He held his Chair at the Beaux Arts for twenty years. As he was only required to deliver twelve lectures a year, and as his work as examiner at Saint-Cyr only entailed three months' work a year, neither appointment interfered seriously with his other work.

In addition to all this, Taine did a certain amount of work in a rather lighter vein. The most important product of this light-heartedness was his *Vie et Opinions de Thomas Graindorge*, or *La Vie Parisienne*. It was a work of satirical observation, a critic-ism of Parisian *mœurs*, offered by Taine in the disguise of an American business man. I have not read it. It is said by some to be very witty and amusing, but his biographers tend to apologise for it and De Margeries says frankly that it is heavy-handed and ill-contrived.

Of his pleasures music was the greatest. A pianist himself he listened to music with intense delight, and his reaction to it was entirely characteristic of the man: the highest praise he could find for a Beethoven sonata which had left him *aux anges* was, *beauti-ful as a syllogism*. He read novels with enjoyment and admiration in several languages, his French favourite being Stendhal\*, his English, so far as I can judge, George Eliot. Musset was his poet,

\* In this connection and in view of Taine's own ideas, it is worth noting, in Stendhal's *Introduction de l'histoire de la peinture en Italie*, the following: *"Mon but est d'expliquer comment chaque civilization produit ses poètes."* And, again, *"Le climat tempéré et la monarchie font naître des admirateurs de Racine, l'orageuse liberté et les climats extrêmes produisent des enthou-siastes de Shakespeare."* But whereas Stendhal, as Faguet pointed out, did nothing with this idea, Taine developed it to its conclusions. E. H.

Marcus Aurelius his moralist, Michelet, Guizot and Macaulay his historians. He never lost his delight in Spinoza but acquired with age some reservations on the subject of Hegel whom he had formerly regarded as *sans pareil*. He began to find the German philosopher "vague and hypothetical". He kept his taste for country walks and he adored gardens, regarding the English as supreme in the art of making them.

Of the remaining means of estimating his character no doubt the opinions of those who had most to do with him are the most revealing. As a husband and father he was not merely respected, although one might expect that in the case of a man who did not marry until he was forty; he was loved and trusted. Renan, Guizot and other intimates of their calibre had great affection for the man and great admiration for his work. Sainte-Beuve, although a good friend, was more critical: "[There is is him] some intellectual violence or haughtiness, too much reliance on books and the written word; he puts too much assurance in the pen and its products." It was Sainte-Beuve's opinion that this fault was common among former students of the Ecole Normale, and Taine seems to have agreed with him: "One should certainly go to the Ecole," he was wont to say, 'but one should not stay there for ever." And whatever Sainte-Beuve might say, Taine learnt form Buckle and Stuart Mill to go to life for his material, as witness the *Notes*.

As for his critics, Schérer called him a positivist; Caro, champion of the eclectics, called him a materialist; Planche said he was a "spinozaist-pantheist". He was called a revolutionary and even a socialist. He was accused of "clothing Hegel's formulas in Diderot's naturalism", a considerable feat had it been true. But whoever now reads his life and some of his works can hardly fail to conclude that he is entitled to a remarkable distinction which none of his contemporaries were in a position to attribute to him. Hippolyte Taine was a very rare, possibly, unique, bird: undeniably French, he was yet, strikingly, an Eminent Victorian.

## The Notes

The only interesting travel writers are those who have a standard by which they insist on judging what they see and estimating the future of the land they are visiting. Other writers may provide us with some very pretty descriptive writing which is, however, apt to become tedious. Only the Doughtys and Polos, Livingstones and Douglases, with a large commercial, social, artistic or spiritual axe to grind, are consistently interesting. That is why many modern travel books are, in so far as they are not mere guide books, almost unreadable: we have lost our nerve, we no longer judge and compare; we merely observe passively.

From what state of mind did Taine perceive England, what were his 'reactions' to that country? First and foremost they were aesthetic: he was, after all, an historian of art. His descriptive passages are short, but they are extraordinarily vivid. Secondly, Taine was a categorisor, if there is such a word. His strongly scientific bent drove him to classify people into types, and since, on his own admission, he had failed to become a novelist, it is hardly surprising that his types are not very convincing: the various kinds of Englishmen he describes in jerky, rather slapdash passages, are caricatures. But a caricature serves a purpose: it emphasises the salient features. Consequently Taine's categories of English men and women and children are not without value, and they are certainly amusing. Moreover, in his descriptions of people and of interiors he uses a comparative method, he constantly refers to the nearest French equivalent, so that the differences between his own country and the one he was visiting emerge very sharply.

But Taine did not judge England merely as an aesthete, did not confine himself to word-pictures of misty landscapes with figures, of Stygian slums populated by pitiful grotesques, of dark, satanic mills and parks full of gigantic trees, brilliant flowers, and a grass so shrilly green that he never ceases to wonder at it. He was a man with a faith, perhaps the first of that line of materialist-optimists which ended when H. G. Wells, a few years before his death, wrote *Man at the end of his tether*. In England he saw the first practical application of the ideas which he had come to believe in; for the England of the mid-nineteenth century was trying to do what had not been done before in the history of mankind: run a community on entirely rational lines, without reference to anything which can properly be called religion, and with a respect for science which was new, and very much to Taine's taste. Taine was among the first of those men who believed that a strictly rational application of scientific thechniques to human problems would result in steady 'progress'. And presumably he was, unlike ourselves, able to believe that progress in material well-being would somehow entail moral and spiritual progress.

We know now, of course, that this is not so; true, most of us still act as if we still believed this, but only because we have left ourselves nothing else to believe. A faith which, in the 1860s, could be held by a man of Taine's integrity and intellectual stature, has now become no more than a slogan for popular journalists, industrialists and mechanics with a vested interest in the idea, and demagogues pretending to be statesmen. And in reading Taine's *Notes* it is possible to study the basis for this optimism, and possibly to see where we have gone wrong. For it does not follow that Taine and others like him were mistaken to believe and feel as they did: it is quite possible that their optimism has not been justified only because there has been a failure to fulfil some of the conditions for success in materialism. From the *Notes*, however, I am inclined to think that Taine himself, and men who thought as he did, made two gross blunders at the very beginning of the short career of good repute which the philosophy of materialism was, in the event, to enjoy. They failed, above all, to perceive that they must provide for the highest education for everybody, so that all men would be equipped with the tools necessary to make a life without religion. In default of this they failed to provide the only alternative to universal higher education in the kind of world they envisaged, an instrument for persuading the people to follow them, even though they did not fully understand why or where.

Taine was, of course, aware, in a general way, of the need for some such device. He seems to have thought that it was furnished, in England, by the Church of England. For over a thousand years the people of Europe had been persuaded to behave according to certain rules conceived by leaders who had been men of great spiritual power, by the rewards and punishments of the Catholic Church. But Taine found the beliefs and ceremonial of that Church degrading to the human mind. And he praises the reasonable and sensible and unmagical school of ethics which he found when he attended services in Anglican and Nonconformist places of worship. At the same time he did realise that the English approach to this problem would end, in his own words, "in German exegesis". His own personal religion was described by some among his enemies as 'spinozaist-pantheist': this is perfectly true, and it even falsified his taste in literature, as witness his altogether excessive admiration for *Aurora Leigh*. It certainly never occured to Taine that the substitution of dry ethical teaching and a vague intellectual pantheism, for a clear, simple, rewards-and-punishments religion, would leave the western world entirely without spiritual support.

Not that Taine was anything like uncritically admiring of all he saw in England. He was profoundly shocked by the plight of the working-class in the great industrial centres, and he was quick to see that the young trade union movement would be the salvation of the workers. The English quality which he admired above all, and in all classes, was that of self-help. Time and again he brings forward instances of reforms being pushed and wrongs righted not by political action, but by the coming together of men in groups to get certain things done, at the expense of their own time, labour and pockets. He was shocked, too, by the misery of the agricultural poor, and contrasts their lot unfavourably with that of the small-holding French peasantry. The three flaws which he finds in the English character are drunkenness, unthriftiness, and sexual brutality; but he recognises that the drunkenness is a product of the misery of the poor; and that the English have a substitute for thrift in their extraordinary capacity for long hours of very hard work. As for sexual brutality manifest in the enormous number, and degraded misery of prostitutes in England, it is at least to some extent offset by the English gift for romantic love, their faithfulness, and, in particular, the devotion of English women to their husbands.

Taine is not uncritical of the English system of justice but he is full of admiration for the integrity with which it is administered. For the political system he has nothing but praise. For Taine, as for Montesquieu before him, the English had obviously solved the problem of self-government. He foresees that the franchise will have to be progressively broadened, is quite certain that universal franchise is a gross error, (had it not elevated the wretched Napoleon III?), and believes that the English ruling class will know when, and to what extent, the franchise can safely be extended. He is impressed by the fact that the relatively new and rich industrialists are willing to leave government very much in the hands of the aristocracy for the excellent reason that aristocracy was a trained governing class, but he notes that these same new men will not tolerate dishonesty or ineffeciency: let the gentry continue to govern, but let them be men of ability.

He is astonished by the comfort and order of the English domestic interior, shocked by the inferior position of women before the law, and distressed by the want of strong family feeling and warm family confidence such as was common in French households. He admires the beauty of English children, but deplores the brutality of their education, and he is almost as greatly horrified by the fagging system in the great public schools, as by the industrial poverty. His English girls are either angelically beautiful, or they are grotesque, and in any case they have no style, no *savoir-vivre*, and no taste in clothes.

Taine is most interesting of all on the subject of English art and letters. These were subjects he had, of course, made his own, and the most entertaining passages in his *Notes* are those concerning the badness of English painting. The fact is, he tells us, the English ought never to try to paint, for they are such sublime poets that they should confine themselves to poetry, or to the novel, in the writing of which they are also supreme. Their painting is literary, and the literary content is often interesting and valuable: on the other hand their paintings are so hideous it is hardly possible to look at them. In music he finds the English even less apt than the French. The one plastic art, if one can call it that, in which they excel, is gardening, and on the gardens of England he is lyrical.

Foreignness, and the strangeness which makes it so interesting, is a quality conferred by distance, in space, but also in time. The England which Taine visited a hundred years ago is as alien to us now as it was to Taine in 1858. But only in the sense that our own youth is alien: to read his *Notes* is very like looking through a photograph album belonging to the period of our adolescence. We are surprised at our own superabundant energy, we blush for our past uncouthness and for the cruelty of which we are reminded by the awkward arrogance of our poses, and we smile indulgently over our former simplicity. The "youth" in question here was not, of course, national; it would be absurd to call mid-nineteenth-century England young. What *was* young was the new scientific-bourgeois-industrial system, which is now at its last gasp.

Today, in order to visit a country as foreign to us as England was to Taine in the 1860s, we should have to travel several thousand miles, and even then we could perhaps not manage it: the English sports which were like the curious athletic rites of a remote and barbarous people to Taine, are now played not merely by the French — and with what zeal! — but by Patagonians and Poles, Egyptians and, for all I know, Eskimos. Horribly revealing caricatures of the English Parliamentary system, which Taine admired so greatly and was so rightly sure could not be transplanted, are still to be found, on their last legs, from pole to pole. The splendid vulgarity of English women's clothes has gone, and been replaced by French good taste. Our food, perhaps, remains as nasty as Taine found it when he was here, but it is doubtful whether it is still as nourishing. The hideous poverty that shocked Taine in the industrial north and the London slums, something quite new to him, has almost gone; so has the festering sore of gin-drunkenness; so has the fabulous wealth of the English gentry. And with the disappearance of these three evils has gone the dramatic tension which goes with evil, and which has entailed the loss of spiritual power that gave rise to what Taine considered the most beautiful poetry in the world, beyond comparison. "Respectable" people no longer breed like rabbits; English painting, which Taine thought the ugliest ever perpetrated, is no longer so strikingly ugly; and the English, from being the least musical have become the most musical people in Europe.

In the only previous translation of the *Notes,* very badly done for serialisation in the *Daily News* in the 'seventies, a number of short passages, all dealing with the vulgarity of English design, all the footnotes, and one long passage, that which deals with the sexual life of the English, were suppressed. The present translation is, therefore, the first complete one. As I have said, I believe that by reading it we may be helped to see whether we are better or worse than we were, whether we are all at sea, or steering a steady course in a desirable direction. For Taine's book must surely the be the best documentary study of England in the 1860s, by an outsider, an England of arrogant wealth and degrading poverty, of religious faith and commercial enterprise, of vulgarity, honesty, earnestness, cruelty and charity ... in short, an alien England.

Reflecting upon what I had read and translated in the *Notes,* I tried to think of any social historian who has contrived to give us precisely Taine's picture. But the England which Taine visited, and described with such a stimulating mixture of liveliness and solemnity has, I think, best been summed up, and our own situation in relation to that strange land and people most wittily stated, not in thick volumes of social history but in a score of lines by Mr Evelyn Waugh...

It is Ambrose Silk talking, in *Put Out More Flags.* "The decline of England, my dear Geoffrey," he said, "dates from the day we abandoned coal fuel. No, I'm not talking about distressed areas, but about distressed *souls*, my dear. We used to live in a fog, the splendid, luminous, tawny fogs of our early childhood. The golden aura of the Golden Age ... We designed a city which was meant to be seen in fog. We had a foggy habit of life, and a rich, obscure, choking literature. The great catch in the throat of English lyric poetry is just *fog*, my dear, on the vocal chords. And out of the fog we could rule the world; we were a Voice of Sinai smiling through the clouds. Primitive peoples always choose a God who speaks from a cloud. ... *Then* some busybody invents electricity or oil fuel or whatever it is they use nowadays. The fog lifts, the world sees us as we are, and, worse still, we see ourselves as we are. It was a carnival ball, my dear, which, when the guests un-masked at midnight, was found to be composed entirely of im-postors. Such a *rumpus*, my dear."

Silk has a wit's licence: Taine, penetrating the fog, did not find impostors. But he certainly found men who spoke out of a fog, both literally and in Ambrose Silk's sense. The reek of coal in humid air under a lowering sky is sharp in Taine's book, the catch in the throat of English poetry receives his close attention and is found to have, indeed, the authentic note of prophecy. And his attribution of English strength to the very nature of mid-nine-teenth-century physical England is not far from being identical with Silk's epigrammatic analysis.

E. H.

# NOTES ON ENGLAND

# CHAPTER ONE

# APPEARANCES

*The Aproaches.*                                   *June 1862. At Sea.*
IT IS eleven o'clock. On the horizon Boulogne recedes and grows small. First the slender masts, then the hulls of ships in the port are swallowed in a vast darkness; now the lights are waning, and presently are no more than a constellation of pale stars on the horizon.

The sensation is strange and moving; the sea is silent, and a still mist hangs over it. Everything has vanished; only the revolving lighthouse on the horizon casts, from time to time, a gleam of light on a passing wave. It is as if we were entering upon a realm of void and silence, in a colourless and amorphous world of things which are not. Shadow, vast and vague, is everywhere. The ship cleaves it and is lost in it. A moment since, astern, a dark edge, the now distant land, was still perceptible; now only obscurity full of motion surrounds the vessel. Yet the ship advances within it, making, with a sure instinct, its way amidst the unseen. Like a laborious insect it moves its great limbs of steel, stirring a phosphorescent wake about its hull. The waves gleam with changing lights of opal and mother o' pearl. One follows their long undulations in the rise and fall of their soft luminescence. Diamonds shot with colour, leaping pearls gleam and turn in each hollow, each crest has a fringe of foam like an edge of dull silver; a frame, tortuously wrought and eternally weaving, to the nocturnal mirror.

*In the Thames.*
THE SUN has been up for half an hour but is not visible. There is a faint lightening towards the east: the rest of the sky is covered by clouds.

To the east, sea to the horizon, and there a clean line dividing pale calm from pale calm. To the left and right of the vessel, a fine, remote line is emerging from the water; it is land; through the mist its green unevenness becomes apparent.

We are going forward; but, in this immense estuary, land, so flat and low, appears as little more than a streak of mud; colour is drowned in humidity; all its shades are washed-out, faded; you might take it for a pale water colour on which a child had splashed drops of water from his fingers.

To the right, the coast draws nearer; here, already, is the true English landscape, such as I saw between Newhaven and London last year. Dull, green hills, broken up by hedges with here and there a single tree; a pasture enclosed by fences, then another, and still another, and cattle standing isolated. Another Belgium, but neither so flat nor so homogeneous, brilliant in sunshine, but very melancholy and very sombre when the sky is sodden with rain; and these skies are very often so!

The river is enormous, but soiled and darkened with livid, false tints. Pressed back by the flowing tide, it rolls between banks of mud which it covers and uncovers at each tide; its small, choppy waves have a lugubrious air beneath an atmosphere impregnated with water and coal-smoke. Livid, it flows, and foul, but useful, a worker, a carrier unique of its kind. Already its broad back is beginning to be covered with ships, sailing past in groups, most of them laden, great and small, of every shape and cut of rigging; the sailors, climbing among the rigging, look like spiders.

Conversation with an Englishman of the middle-classes, son of a merchant, as I suppose: he knows neither French, German nor Italian; he is not altogether a gentleman. Twenty-five years old, a decided, incisive, sardonic face. He has just completed a twelve months' journey, for pleasure and education, and is on his way back from Australia and India. Forty thousand miles in all. "In order to know peoples," he says, "one must see them."

He comes from Liverpool. There, with three or four hundred pounds sterling per annum, a family which keeps no carriage can live comfortably. He will of course, marry: that is "in nature"; he hopes to do so during the next two or three years. Better stay a bachelor if one does not meet the person with whom one would be ready to spend one's life. "But you always do meet her; the thing is, not to miss her." He has, when very young, already had such encounters; but his fortune was then inadequate; now being "independent", he will be on the look-out. A dowry is not necessary. It is natural, and even pleasant, to undertake the burden of a wife and family. "If your wife is good, and loves you, she is well worth that."

It is obvious to me that, for them, happiness consists in that state: home at six in the evening, an agreeable, faithful wife, tea, four or five children clambering over their knees, and respectful servants. Aboard the ship there is a family of four children, the eldest being four and a half, the mother twenty-three or -four. At seaside watering places, on the front, I have often seen whole broods, the father at their head; it is not unusual to encounter families of children in a rising scale from the infant at breast up to an eighteen-year-old daughter. The parents do not consider themselves overburdened by such families, or embarrased. According to my Englishman all they owe their children is an education: the daughters marry without a dowry, the sons do the best they can for themselves. I know a solicitor who makes a great deal of money and spends it all, excepting three or four hundred pounds a year, which he lays out in insurances for his children. At each new child, a new insurance to bring in £2000, payable to the child on the father's death. In this way, the child is provided for, and besides, trade and industry supply him with numerous opportunities which are not offered to the young Frenchman.

Of all the countries my Englishman has seen, England is "the most moral". Even so, in his opinion, the trouble with the country is "the want of morality". France he judges à l'Anglaise: "The women badly brought up, don't read the Bible, are too fond of dancing, interested in nothing but clothes. The men frequent cafés and keep mistresses; hence the number of unhappy households. It is not a matter of race, but of education. French women, reared in England, seriously, in the English manner, make very good wives in this country.

"Is everything good in your country?"

"No. The national, and terrible, vice is drunkenness. A man making twenty shillings a week, drinks ten. Add to that want of foresight, unemployment, and pauperism."

"But in extreme cases, you have your poor-houses, workhouses?"

"They won't go into them. They prefer to starve to death."

"Why?"

"For three reasons. Because they want to drink as they like. Because they hate being shut up. Because there are formalities: you have to prove you belong to the parish; but most of them don't know where they were born, or find it too difficult to get the necessary papers."

Very talkative and not in the least stiff. Two other Englishmen with whom I talked on board were the same: I have always found the English so. Probably the reason for their contrary reputation may be that, abroad, when obliged to speak a foreign language, they remain silent from shyness, and keep a watch on themselves in order not to lay themselves open. Speak their English badly, with a bad accent, and they shed their uneasiness, feel themselves superior. If, politely and gently, you ask them a question, or even to do you some small service, they are obliging and even anxious to help. This I have experienced a score of times, last year, in London and elsewhere.

Also noted aboard ship: two young couples sitting on deck, enveloped in rugs and protected by umbrellas; there was a prolonged downpour of rain, but they stayed where they were, until at last they were soaked to the skin: this, in order that husband and wife should not be separated by going below to the men's and women's saloons, respectively. A young woman very seasick: her husband, who appeared to be a commercial traveller, held her in his arms, supported her, tried to read to her, in short nursed her with complete freedom and infinite tenderness. Two girls between fifteen and sixteen, who spoke German and French very well and without accent: large, lively eyes, big, white teeth; chattered and laughed without reserve, and with an admirable vivacity of animal spirits; not a shade of coquetterie; nothing resembling our own carefully acquired and deliberately used little graces of manner; they had no thought of the gallery. A lady of forty, bespectacled, seated beside her husband; a threadbare dress, relics of some usual feminine ornaments, teeth like tusks — very serious and really excessively comical; a Frenchwoman, albeit of ripe years, never forgets to bear herself properly, or to give some attention to her dress. Noted also; patience and phlegm of a tall, lean Englishman who hardly moved from under the awning, took only one turn about the deck, spoke to nobody, was sufficient to himself. In contrast, three Frenchmen, who questioned everyone about everything and nothing, made wild assertions, grew impatient, gesticulated and cracked bad jokes: they seemed, beside the Englishman, like nice children.

Little by little the clouds have disappeared and the sky is radiant. To left and right we glide past small country houses,

*Fig. 1   London Docks*

pretty, neat and freshly painted: green lawns and, here and there, tall trees well grouped and placed. To the left, Gravesend, a pile of brown houses clustered about a grey-blue steeple. More and more ships and warehouses; one is aware of getting nearer to a great city. Small embarkation jetties, thrusting fifty paces out into the river above gleaming mud left high and dry by the ebb-tide. Every quarter of an hour, the mark and presence of man, the power with which he has transformed nature, become more obvious. Docks, warehouses, ship-building and repairing yards, workshops, dwelling houses, part-processed materials, accumulations of goods; to the right, we pass the iron carcase of a church, being made here for assembly in India. Astonishment at last gives way to indifference; it is too much. Above Greenwich the river becomes no more than a street, a mile and more wide, with an endless traffic of ships going up and down stream between two rows of buildings, interminable brick and tile files, a murky red, fenced behind huge piles driven into the mud for the mooring of ships which tie-up there to load or unload. More and more warehouses — for copper, stone, coal, ship's gear, and the rest; more and more great piles of bales, sacks being hoisted, barrels rolled, cranes turning and creaking, capstans squeaking. The sea reaches up to London by way of the river; it is a great port in the midst of the land. It is here that New York, Melbourne, Canton and Calcutta touch first. But what carries the impression it makes, to its zenith is the number of canals by which the docks open into

7

the body of the river; they are streets set at right-angles, but they are streets of ships; you suddenly come upon them — in an endless vista: from Greenwich, which I visited last year, going to the hill-top, the horizon is completely composed of masts and rope.

The manifold, the innumerable riggings, stretch a vast circle of spider-web all round the rim of the sky. This, surely, is one of the mighty spectacles of our planet; to see a comparable agglomeration of buildings, works, men, ships and trade, one would have to go to China.

To the west of us a forest of masts and rigging grows out of the river: ships coming, going, waiting, in groups, in long files, then in one continuous mass, at moorings, in among the chimneys of houses and the cranes of warehouses — a vast apparatus of un-ceasing, regular and gigantic labour. They are enveloped in a fog of smoke irradiated by light. The sun turns it to golden rain, and the water, opaque, shot with yellow, green and purple, gleams and glitters as its surface lifts and falls, with strange and brilliant lights. The atmosphere seems like the heavy, steamy air of a great hot-house. Nothing here is natural: everything is transformed, violently changed, from the earth and man himself, to the very light and air. But the hugeness of this accumulation of man-made things takes off the attention from this deformity and this artifice; in default of a wholesome and noble beauty, there is life, teeming and grandiose. The gleam of brown river water, the diffusion of light trapped in vapour, the white and rosy luminosity playing over all these colossal objects, spreads a kind of grace over the monstrous city — like a smile on the face of some dark and bristling Cyclops.

*First weeks.*

A wet Sunday in London: shops closed, streets almost empty; the aspect of a vast, and well-kept graveyard. The few people in this desert of squares and streets, hurrying beneath their um-brellas, look like unquiet ghosts; it is horrible.

I had had no conception of anything like this, and they say it is common in London. The rain is small, fine, close, pitiless: looking at it, there seems no reason why it should not last until the end of time. Feet clatter; there is water everywhere, dirty and impregnated with the smell of soot. A thick, yellow fog fills the air, sinks, crawls on the very ground; at thirty paces a house or a steam-ship look like ink-stains on blotting paper. * In the Strand, especially, and the rest of the City, after an hour's walking, one is possessed by spleen and can understand suicide. The tall, flat, straight façades are of dark brick; fog and soot have deposited their secretions on these surfaces. Monotony and silence. Only the brass and marble name-plates speak, indicating the absent master; an enormous bone-black factory, closed because of a death in the family.

A really frightful thing is, in the Strand, the enormous palace they call Somerset House. A massive and ponderous architecture, with every crevice inked in, porticos foul with soot, a simulacrum of a fountain, waterless in the midst of an empty courtyard, puddles of water on the flagstones, long ranks of blind windows; what can they do in such a catacomb? Even in the parks the livid, smoke-laden fog has fouled the very greenery. But, most afflicting of all to the eye are the colonnades, peristyles and Greek ornaments, the mouldings and garlands on the houses, all washed with soot; poor architecture of antiquity, what is it doing in such a climate as this! On the façades of the British Museum the fluting of the columns is full of greasy filth, as if sticky mud had been set flowing down them. St Paul's, a kind of Pantheon, has two storeys of columns, the lower ones all black, the top ones, recently scraped, still white, a glaring white, painful; but already coal smoke has fouled them with its leprosy.

These stains are dreary; they show the rotting of the stone. And then, those unclothed statues in memory of Greece! That Wellington, as an embattled hero, naked beneath the streaming trees in the park! † That hideous Nelson, planted upon his column, like a rat empaled on the end of a stick! Here, any classical form or idea is against the grain. Such a bog as this is, for the antique arts, a place of exile. When the Romans landed here they must have thought themselves in Homer's inferno, in the land of the Cimmerians. The vast space which, in the south, lies between earth and heaven, is missed, here, by the seeking eye; no more air, nothing but the flowing fog. In this livid smoke, objects are no more than phantoms and nature looks like a bad drawing in charcoal on which someone has rubbed his sleeve.

* No words can describe the fog in winter. There are days when, holding a man by the hand, one cannot see his face. See, in this connection, the picture drawn by the greatest contemporary English artist — Dickens. *Our Mutual Friend*, 111, ch. 1, p. 1.

† The Achilles statue! E. H.

9

I have just spent half an hour on Waterloo Bridge. 'Parliament House' *, indistinct, outline washed out, seems, in the distance, no more than a wretched huddle of scaffolding; nothing perceptible, above all nothing alive, except the small steam-boats moving on the river, black, smoky, indefatigable insects: a Greek, seeing their passengers embark and disembark, would have thought of the Styx. He would have considered that to live here was not to live at all; and, indeed, here men live otherwise than in Greece — the ideal has changed with the climate. The soul withdraws from the open, enters within itself, and there creates its own world. Here, it is necessary to have a well-kept 'home', clubs, associations, much business, a quantity of religious and moral pre-occupations. Above all, it is necessary to avoid abandoning oneself to outside impressions, and to shut the door on the melancholy influence of a hostile nature, to fill up the great void where melancholy and boredom could find lodgement. During the week there is work, assiduously done, the hard work by means of which a man defends himself and provides against the inclemency of things. But what is to be done on the day of rest? The public-house, or church; drunkenness or a sermon; deaden the mind, or use it. There is nothing else to do on such a Sunday as this; and by these means, either by taking thought or killing it, a man can withdraw, forget. I see a great number of half-open doors into gin-cellars; dismal, lifeless or savage faces entering or leaving. Next for the church.

I visit four, and hear two sermons, the first in a Nonconformist church in the Strand. The nave bare, cold, without ornament excepting for two allegorical figures at the far end. Tall, wooden pews, in which one is shut in up to the neck. These are not filled by the common people, but by respectable middle-class people very correctly dressed, and with serious, sensible faces. They are here for moral advice and to refurbish their principles. The preacher chose as his text, "Of one mind and one soul", and on its basis advised his congregation to be firm in their principles, but conciliatory towards all men. A good sermon, a little commonplace, but solid. It is quite obvious, from the numerous essays in English literature and, to-day, the "little morals" in the *Saturday Review* (?) that commonplaces do not bore them. Apparently they consider morality not an object of curiosity, but of use — a tool in daily requisition, so that, on Sundays, it needs sharpening.

* Where Taine uses English words, these are printed within single quotation marks thus 'home'. E. H.

10

Books set out on the rests in the pews: they are the *Psalms*, and the *Book of Common Prayer*, the Mass-book of England. A great deal of wordiness and a certain Hebraic grandiloquence in the style of Milton. No tenderness, no ecstasy, as in the *Imitation*. No flowers of rhetoric or gentle sentimentalities, as in our own pious tracts, but a tone which is imposing, passionate, and sometimes lyrical. The liturgy was composed during the Renaissance, and the accent of that period has been retained. A thing worth noting: the date and origin of each passage are given in a note; one piece may be from the sixth (sic) century; another, a prayer, was taken from the Apocrypha, but has been retained because of its elevated sentiments. By means of these notes, the faithful are educated, informed, in the criticism and history (of their religion). Consider Tillotson's and Barrow's sermons, contemporary with Bossuet, with Greek text and notes on grammatical sense. Given time, this is bound to lead to German exegesis.

Westminster Abbey: superb nave, admirable Gothic architecture — the only style which suits the climate: the jumble of shapes, the sinuous and roaring bones of the building, the profusion of fine sculpture are required to fill this sombre atmosphere, and people the vast formlessness of dark interiors. I spent some time there, looking at monuments to the dead, a great number of graceful 18th-century sculptures, others, cold and pedantic, belonging to our own time. Suddenly, voices were raised in song, not the monotonous psalmody of our own vespers, not a rude and monkish plain-chant, not the lines and responses uttered in what always seem to be the voices of sick monks, but beautiful songs, in parts, grave and noble recitatives, round and full, melodious, a style and harmony redolent of the best epoch. Then, after a reading on Sisera, the organ and choir, both boys' voices and bass voices, resumed — a motet, full and rich. All this music is a worthy accompaniment to the psalms and prayers I had just been reading. Realised in this sense, religion becomes the opera of the high-souled, serious believer. Nothing could be more important: a people's Church, and its services must be on a par with the feelings not merely of the common and unlettered people, but with those of the *élite*.

Visit to two other churches in the afternoon. Here, too, the hymns were fine, and the buildings were filled by people of the comfortable middle-class. The tall, closed pews and all the galleries were full of well-dressed worshippers; as many men as women, and many of them 'gentlemen'. Very different from our own congregations of women, aged dyspeptics, servants, working-class people. Of the three ministers I saw, one, a polite, worthy man who talked to me, seemed, by his air and bearing, half-professor, half-magistrate. Another, bland and well-groomed, resembled a Paris notary, the sort of man who assumes a soft voice and a sentimental air at the signing of a marriage contract. I met others, last year, in London and in the country. With their white bands and black gowns, and the tone they take in the pulpit, one might take them for judges. They are, by education, marriage, *mores* and function, laymen, a little graver in bearing than the rest; their attire, outside church, is the same excepting for the eternal white tie; nor is the moral difference much greater than the physical one. The essential point is this: priest and laymen are on an equal footing, or separated at most by a single step: such was the principal achievement of the Reformation.

Returning to my hotel, I read, in the *Friday's Gazette,* the following proclamation: "We, Victoria, Regina; considering very seriously and very religiously that it is our indispensable duty to apply ourselves above all things to maintain and augment the service of Almighty God, as also to discourage and suppress all vice, profane practice, debauchery and immorality — we do prohibit and forbid by these presents all our faithful subjects of what condition or quality so-ever, to play, on the Lord's Day, at dice, cards, or any other game whatsoever, in public or private habitations, or elsewhere, wherever it may be, and by these presents we require and we command each and every one of them to attend, with decency and reverence, at Divine Service on every Lord's Day." *

Order to all magistrates to: "take effective means to prevent persons keeping taverns or other public houses from selling wine, beer or any other liquor, as also from receiving or keeping guests in their houses during the course of divine service, on the Lord's Day."

This order is not strictly observed: the doors of taverns are closed during the service, but one can get in, and drinks are served in backrooms. Even so, here is a vestige of former Puritanism altogether shocking to the French mind. Forbid people to drink and amuse themselves on Sundays? But, to a French peasant or workman, that is what Sunday seems to be made for. Stendhal says that here, in Scotland, in the really "Biblical" countries, religion ruins one day out of seven, and destroys one-seventh of man's

* Retranslation from Taine's French. E. H.

12

potential happiness. But he is judging the Englishman, the man of the North, by comparison with the Southerner, who is enlivened by wine, but not besotted by it, who can decently give his instincts free rein, and whose gladness is romantic, poetic. Here, the temper is different, more violent and more militant: pleasure is a brutal and bestial thing: I could quote a score of examples. As an Englishman put it to me: "When a Frenchman is drunk, he chatters; a German, he sleeps; but when it's an Englishman, he fights."

Other vestiges of Puritan severity — a few examples: on the stairs leading down to the Thames are notices warning you to be decent; at the railway stations there are large, chained Bibles, for travellers to read while waiting; in Hyde Park, a tall, sallow, bony fellow hands me two printed pages about Moses' bronze serpent, with applications to the present day.

"You, too, reader, have been bitten by fiery serpents. To cure yourselves, raise your eyes to Him who was raised up as a sign of Salvation."

Other indications point to a country dominated by an aristocracy. The gates of St James's Park bear the following notice: "The park keepers have orders to refuse admittance to the park to all beggars, any person in rags, or whose clothes are very dirty, or who are not of decent appearance and bearing." *

At every step one feels very remote from France.

Three million five hundred thousand inhabitants; it adds up to twelve cities the size of Marseilles, ten as big as Lyons, two the size of Paris, in a single mass. But words on paper are no substitute for the effect on the eyes. You have to spend several days in succession in a cab, driving out north, south, east and west, for a whole morning, as far as those vague limits where houses grow scarcer and the country has room to begin.

Enormous, enormous — that is the word which recurs all the time. And, moreover, rich and well cared-for, so that they must find us neglected and poor. Paris is mediocre by comparison with these 'squares', 'crescents', 'circuses', and the endless rows of monumental houses built of massive stone, with porticos and carved fronts, lining the very wide streets. There are fifty as wide as the

* This is retranslated from Taine's French and may not, of course, be the exact wording. E. H.

*rue de la Paix*. There can be no question but that Napoleon III demolished Paris and rebuilt it because he had lived in London. In the Strand, in Piccadilly, in Regent Street, in the neighbourhood of London Bridge and a score of other places there surges a bustling, thrusting crowd such as our busiest boulevard gives no idea of. Everything here is on a larger scale; the clubs are palaces; the hotels are monumental; the river is an arm of the sea; the cabs move twice as fast; watermen and 'bus conductors run a whole sentence into a single word. The people are sparing of words and gestures, the last atom of value is extracted from every action and every minute: a man produces, and spends, twice as much here as in France.

From London Bridge to Hampton Court there are eight miles, almost three leagues, of buildings. After those streets and quarters built all of a piece, in blocks, and to one design, like a hive, come innumerable houses built for their owners' enjoyment, cottages set in lawn and trees, and in every style, Gothic, Greek, Byzantine, Mediæval or Renaissance Italian, or in a mixture of every variation on these styles. As a rule they are built in rows, or in groups of five, six, twenty all identical and visibly built by the same contractor, like so many examples of the same vase or bronze. They turn out houses as we turn out Paris fancy-goods. What a multitude of easy, comfortable, of wealthy households! The whole implies large profits from quick turnover, an opulent free-spending middle-class very different from our own, financially straitened and looking twice at every penny spent.

The most modest houses, built of brown brick, are pretty by reason of their cleanness: the window panes are polished like mirrors, there is almost always a small garden, green and full of flowers, and the façade will be covered by a creeper or climbing plant.

All the surroundings of Hyde Park are covered with similar houses, but larger and handsomer and which, in the midst of London, still keep a look of the country. Each stands alone in its square of lawn and shrubbery: two floors in impeccable taste and immaculately maintained; a portico, a tradesman's bell and a visitor's bell; a basement for the kitchen and servants, with a service staircase· Very little moulding or ornament; no outside shutters; large, clear windows letting in ample light; flowers on the window-sills and the peristyle; stables in a separate building, so that the smell and sight of them be out of the way; all outside walls dressed with white stucco, shining, glossy; not a splash of

*Fig. 2  London Bridge*

15

mud or dust anywhere; the trees, lawns and servants all groomed like articles in an exhibition of model products.

And how well this shell represents the creature dwelling in it! First, the Teuton, loving nature and needing a semblance of the coutryside about him; next, the Englishman, requiring privacy in his own home, on his staircase as well as in his room, and for whom the promiscuity of our great Parisian hives would be intolerable, so that even in London he designs his house like a small, isolated, closed castle. Simple, however, and feeling no need for outward show; but, on the other hand, very particular as regards neatness, cleanliness, order and comfort; and separating his life from those of his inferiors.

There is an astonishing number of such houses in the West End. About six thousand francs rent *; five or six servants; the master spends between thirty and sixty thousand francs a year.

There are ten such fortunes and such kind of lives in England for every one in France.

The same impression when you visit the parks; both taste and scale are utterly different from ours. Saint James's Park is a real piece of country, and of English country: enormous ancient trees, real meadows, a lake peopled by ducks and wading birds; cows, and folded sheep graze the eternally fresh grass. There are even sheep on the narrow grass verge all about Westminster Abbey. These people adore the country: you have only to read their literature, from Chaucer to Shakespeare, from Thompson to Wordsworth and Shelley, to have proof of this. What a contrast with the Tuileries, the Champs-Elysées, the Luxembourg! As a rule a French garden, in the style of Louis XIV, is a drawing-room or gallery in the open air, a place to stroll and converse in company. In an English garden, the kind they have invented and propagated, one is better alone, so that the eyes and soul can converse with nature. We have made a park to this design in the Bois de Boulogne, but there we made the mistake of building a group of rocks and waterfalls; its artificiality is at once apparent, displeasingly out of place, and English eyes would have perceived this.

Regent's Park: this is larger than the Jardin des Plantes and the Luxembourg gardens together: I have often noticed that our lives

* The rate of exchange was about 23 francs to the £. E. H.

seem to them narrow and shut-in; they have a greater need for air than we have, a greater need for space. English people I used to know in Paris left their windows open the whole time, even at night; hence their need for movement, their riding and walking expeditions in the countryside. Stendhal pointed out in this connection that an English girl covers more ground on her feet in one week, than a Roman girl does in a year. Northern men, with their athletic temperament, need plenty of air and exercise.

Regent's Park is in a backwater; the noise of traffic is no longer to be heard, London is forgotten, the place is a solitude. The sun was shining, but the atmosphere was still full of humid clouds, perambulating watering-cans which, every quarter of an hour, let fall their load of rain. The wide, damp meadows had a charming softness; there was a small, monotonous sound from the dripping of rain from the trees into the still waters of the lakes.

I went into a hot-house: splendid orchids, some with the velvety opulence of the iris, others flesh-coloured — of that indescribable shade, delicious, melting, vibrant with light, with which living flesh palpitates, a woman's breast. One's hand reaches out to touch, yet hesitates, afraid. Beside them great palm-trees rear their foliage in the moist, warm air.

A singularity, from our point of view, is that there are no keepers. Anyone who wishes may enter; yet no damage is done. I can well understand their laughing at our public establishments and festivals with their accompaniment of municipal guards. It is the same in their railway stations: everybody is free to go on to the platform, meet their friends at the carriage doors; they are surprised and shocked at the way we are shut up in waiting rooms, parked, led here and there like sheep and constantly in charge of an official.

Returned as far as Piccadilly on foot: 'London weather' again, a small, continuous rain, and black mud underfoot. F——, who has just spent a winter here, says that there is not much snow, not more than in the centre of France, but on the other hand eternal fogs and rain nearly every day and, for pedestrians, a most execrable wallow of mud. Witness the ladies' feet and footwear: *bottines* which are veritable boots, the large feet of a wading species * and a stride and carriage to match. The same question always recurs to me: what do they do in their leisure time, on Sundays particularly? The club, often to drink port. There was a member of F——'s club who sat in the reading-room, drank a

* *échassiers* E. H.

17

large glass of wine, went to sleep, woke after half an hour and drank another, went to sleep again, and so on without ever uttering a word. Another, a great merchant and immensely rich, employing sixteen gardeners at his country place, spends his days in business, returns home at evening, hardly speaks a word, behaves like an automaton in his family. His daughter keeps herself amused by spending the whole year travelling with a governess. His sole contribution to the family life is money: this is a common trait of the English character; it is not very expansive and not very amiable.

Between Regent's Park and Piccadilly much struck by the funereal aspect of the wide, interminable streets. The road surface is black macadam; the rows of houses, always the same, are built of blackened brick and the windows gleam darkly; each house separated from the street by its iron railings and area. Hardly any shops and not one attractive, no shop-windows, no print-shops. It would all be too melancholy for us; nothing to catch and amuse the eye; pleasant loitering out of the question, you must either work at home, or take your umbrella and go to the office or committee-meeting.

Hyde Park is the largest of the parks, with a small river, wide lawns, cattle, shady places — a country gentleman's park transported to the heart of the capital. Round about two in the afternoon the principal road through it becomes a riding-school; there are ten times as many men on horseback, twenty times as many Amazons, as in the Bois de Boulogne, on a big day; tiny little girls, and boys not more than eight years old ride their ponies beside their father's horse. I have seen massive and dignified matrons at the trot. This is one of their luxuries; another is their establishment of servants. For example, I have just been visiting a family of three persons: they have seven servants and three horses. The mother and daughter go for a gallop in the park every day; they even pay calls on horseback sometimes. They economise in other ways; on the theatre for example, where they go very rarely and then only when they have free seats. All this exercise seems necessary to their health; girls and ladies ride in the park even when it is raining. Three horses and a carriage cost about £200 a year. One's conclusion, from this crowd of people on horseback, as from the houses and servants, is that the wealthy class is far more numerous in England than in France. Another indication of the same thing: the expenditure in linen, clothes, gloves, dresses — all fresh and clean. The climate is very dirty,

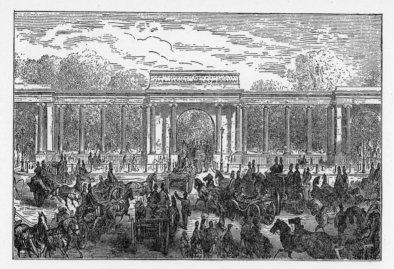

*Fig. 3   Entrance to Hyde Park*

things have to be changed and replaced frequently. Every news-paper carries the advertisements of dealers who will come to your house and buy your part-worn clothes. Immaculate appearance is obligatory for a gentleman: his suits, once past their best, go to a man of the lower classes and end up in rags on the back of a pauper. Hence one's clothes are a badge of social rank. In nothing is the distance between classes so clearly indicated as in a man's appearance. Imagine a dandy's evening suit, or a lady's pink, flowered hat: the one you will see again on some poor wretch huddled on the steps leading down to the Thames, the other at Shadwell on the head of an old hag sorting rags and rubbish.

From five o'clock to seven, dress parade. * Beauty and adorn-ment are abundant; but there is a want of taste. The colours are outrageously crude, and lines ungraceful. Crinolines too full, or the fullness badly draped, like geometrical cones or else dented; ribbons and scarves, green; gold lacing; bold, flower-patterned materials; a profusion of floating gauze; hair bunched, falling or curled. The whole display surmounted by tiny hats, much trimmed but hardly perceptible. The hats are over trimmed, the hair too shiny and clamped to the temples with too hard a line; the *mantelet* or *casaque* hangs shapeless to the hips, the skirt is mon-strously overfull, and the whole of this scaffolding is badly put

* *revue des toilettes* E. H.

19

together, badly matched, striped, fussed, overdone, loud, excessively numerous colours each swearing at the others.

In sunshine particularly, the day before yesterday at Hampton Court, among 'shop-keepers" wives, the spectacle was wildly ridiculous. There was a quantity of violet dresses, of a really ferocious violet, encircled at the waist by a gold belt. It would have made a painter weep. I said to one lady, "Your clothes here are more 'showy' than in France." "But our dresses come from Paris!" I was careful not to reply, "But it's you who choose them." *

Excepting in the highest class they get themselves up like bundles of rags. One can guess at sound bodies, well built, sometimes beautiful: but they are entirely concealed. Their physiognomy is often pure, but it is also often monotonous. Many of them are baby-faced wax dolls with glass eyes and seemingly as devoid of minds. One also sees faces the colour of raw beef-steak. There is a fundamental stupidity and brutality in these too white or too red masks of inert flesh. Some of them go to the extreme of ugliness and the grotesque, creatures with heron's feet, a stork's neck and always that great frontage of white teeth, the prominent jaw of the carnivore. On the other hand one sees women who go to the extreme limit of beauty: angelic face, the periwinkle blue eyes soft and deep, the complexion that of a flower or a child, the smile divine. Recently, at about ten one morning near Hyde Park corner, I was struck motionless with admiration at the sight of two girls: sixteen and eighteen respectively, wearing rustling dresses of white tulle, all in a cloud of muslin, tall, slender, their figures as perfect as their faces, reminiscent of those astonishing flowers one sees in exhibitions of choice blooms, a whiteness of the lily or the orchis· And in addition, a gaiety, an innocence, a superabundance of healthy vigour and simple unreserve, laughter, and the light, free movement of a bird, as if the earth did not feel their weight.

Many of the horsewomen, too, are charming: so simple and serious, with not a grain of coquetterie. They come to the park not to be looked at but to take the air: the movements are free from all affectation or pretentiousness; their hand-clasp candid, almost manly; no fussiness in their attire, the short coat well cut to the figure reveals them as well-grown, soundly built. As I understand the matter, a girl's first duty is to be in good health. They manage

* "I do not know who it was that compared the Englishwoman to a fenced field in which enemy colours meet and wage war on each other."

Souvenirs Comte Joseph d'Estournel

*Fig. 4  Hats*
*"Oh yes, my dear, the advantage is — you can wear more Flowers*
*for your Money, and the Rain don't spoil them."*
*(Punch, November, 1863)*

their horses with perfect ease and assurance. Sometime the father
or brother who is with them stops to talk business or politics with
a friend: they listen and become accustomed to weighty ideas.

The fathers and brothers in question are pleasant to look upon;
expressive, decided faces, showing that they bear or have borne
the real weight of life; less worn than ours, less prompt at smiling
and the grimaces of polite society; but more collected, more
decided, so that they often leave one with a vague feeling of
respect, at least of esteem, and sometimes of complete trust. Perhaps it is because I am aware of their way of life: yet it does seem
to me that their faces are not misleading, that one cannot be mistaken; noblemen, members of Parliament, land-owners, their
manners, bearing, faces, show them to be men accustomed to
authority and action.

A great many calls and a number of walks. What pleases me most here are the trees. Every day, when I leave the Athenaeum, I go and sit for an hour in Saint James's Park. The lake gleams softly beneath its covering of mist, and dense foliage hangs above its still waters. The rounded trees, great domes of green, compose a sort of architecture far more delicate than that of masonry. The eye is rested by shapes not clearly defined, colours washed pale. Such are the beauties, tender and touching, of the misty lands, Holland for example.

Yesterday at eight in the evening, from Suspension Bridge: the weather was fine yet all things looked vaporous; the last glow of light melted into a whitish, smoky haze; to the right, a vestige of redness; the surface of the Thames and the rest of sky a pale slaty colour. Such tints are to be seen in Rembrandt's landscapes and Vermeer's twilights. The drowning light, the air peopled by mists and vapours, the imperceptible and continuous changes in that vast exhalation which softens and erodes all outlines, shading them with blue, all leaves the impression of a vast, vague life, diffuse and melancholy, the life of the humid land itself.

I felt this even more strongly at Richmond. From the terrace one can see several leagues of country; the Thames, here no wider than the Seine, winds among meadows and between clumps of tall trees. Everything is green, a soft green almost extinguished by distance. One is aware of the peace and freshness of infinite vegetation. The grey sky over all, a low, dull dome; a whitish haze at the horizon, here and there a darkening cloud mass or the purplish stain of a downpour. From every valley rises slow-spreading mist, like muslin drawn between the groups of trees. By slow degrees the floating, drifting gauze of the earth meets and mingles with the uniform veil of sky.

What a silence in the park! Herds of deer graze the moist clearings: does come to the railings to watch people pass, showing no fear. Could there be any countryside better calculated to relax the nerves of men who toil and strive? Mighty oaks, great lime-trees, horse-chestnuts in flower are noble creatures which seem to speak together in low voices, majestic and secure. About their feet the tall, coarse grass on which the rain has left its tears seems to smile sadly and tenderly. From air, sky and all things under it emanates a kind of affectionate quietude; nature welcomes and soothes the soul left bruised and shaken by strife. How strongly one feels that their countryside suits them! And their reason for loving it. Doubtless their climate is better than ours for trees;

*Fig. 5   Scene from a London Park*

moreover they have had no invasions, no popular revolutions to mutilate or destroy them. But even so their natural taste has contributed to the preservation of their trees. Lord —— is the park ranger, and has a house which goes with that office: this is a vestige of feudal usage; here antiquities have been better respected and preserved than in France, and among these the trees must be counted.

Those of Windsor and Hampton Court are also very fine. From Kew Gardens to Hampton Court stretches a walk between gigantic horse-chestnut trees whose white and pink flowers suggest chandeliers. The foliage is so dense that it is cool beneath them in full sunshine. On the velvet lawns starred with flowers and surrounded by wistaria, are set coppices of rhododendrons as tall as two men, loaded with bee-loud pink flowers. There are so many of them, they are so magnificent, their texture is so frail and their tints so delicate, they are massed with such prodigality in vast bouquets all impregnated with light, that one stands dazzled. The effect is delicious, intoxicating, almost outside nature. A little further on, in an enormous hot-house, palm-trees as big as oaks spread their strange foliage, and banana trees unfold leaves large enough to cover a twelve-year old child. All this is one of their talents; they understand landscape gardening to admiration; I have not seen a single palace, however classic, a single cottage, however poor, where this architecture of plants was not understood. Sometimes the impression made is too brilliant; in sunshine it is excessive: the incomparable greenness is then apt to assume tones so rich and intense that they could never be transferred to canvas; there they would offend, they would be too crude. They must be perceived not by the eyes but by the soul, they are a festival of colour, an explosion of joy. And it is the superabundance of moisture which has gone to produce and maintain them, to swell and build up the plants to the perfection of their blooming; the caress and the protection of soft mistiness. Under a more ardent sky such flowers as one sees here would have hardened and dried. They are not accustomed to strong sunshine which is why under to-day's bright sun I see them burst into glory. Their tint is like the complexion of a beautiful lady; they, too, are highly evolved patricians, preserved and embellished by every refinement of art and luxury. I had much the same impression recently at an official reception, when standing at the foot of a staircase filled from top to bottom by young ladies, smiling, wearing full-skirted dresses, and trains of tulle or silk, their heads circled with diamonds, their shoulders bare. There, as here in the park, was the same remarkable impression of splendour, lustre, carried to their ultimate height, all the flowers of both civilization and nature mingled in one single bouquet and one single scent.

Hampton Court is a large garden in the French taste laid out during the reign of William and Mary, at which time our taste dominated Europe. But the English taste is not excluded. The flower beds have been close planted with roses which climb slender poles, forming columns of flowers. Every sheet of water has its ducks and swans and water-lilies opening into satiny stars. The ancient trees are propped up with iron-work, and when they die, in order not to lose them entirely, their trunks are, as it were, made into huge urns. Obviously, they are respected and loved. No railings: I saw whole schools of little girls walking and playing on the lawns, but they did not pick a single flower, and the sole protection needed by the garden is the following notice:

It is hoped that the public will
abstain from damaging what is
cultivated for the public pleasure.

I have seen whole families of the common people picnicking on the grass in Hyde Park; they neither pulled up nor damaged anything. And this is really admirable: the aim of every society must be a state of affairs in which every man is his own constable, until at last none other is required.

❊

My English friends confirm my guesses as to the size and number of large fortunes. "Take a cab and drive to Sydenham; you will pass by five miles of houses all indicative of an annual expenditure of £1500 or more."

According to official figures, in 1841, of a population of sixteen million, one million were domestic servants. * Salaries in the liberal professions are much higher than on the Continent. In Leipzig I am acquainted with a musician of the highest talent: for a lesson given at the Leipzig *Conservatoire* he receives one thaler †; for the same at the pupil's house in town, two thalers; in London, a guinea. A visit from a doctor who is not well known costs from five to ten francs in Paris; here, a guinea. A professor at the College de France receives 7500 francs; at the Sorbonne 12,000 francs; at the Ecole de Medecine 10,000 francs. At Oxford a professor, a head-master (sic) usually receives between £1000 and £3000 a year. It is said that Tennyson, who does not write much, earns 125,000 francs a year. The 'Principal' of Eton College receives a salary of 152,000 francs a year; Harrow, 157,000 francs; Rugby, 74,000 francs. Many of the masters in these schools get between 30 and 40 thousand francs; one of them, at Harrow, 63,000. The Bishop of London is paid 250,000 francs; the Archbishop of York 375,000 francs. A journalist receives 200 francs for a page of copy in the *Revue des deux Mondes;* 500 in equivalent English publications. *The Times* has paid as much as 2,500 francs for an article. The novelist Thackeray earned 4000 francs in a single day by delivering two lectures, one in Brighton, the other in London. He is at present getting £2000 a year from the magazine in which his novels are serialised, plus £10 a page. This magazine has 100,000 subscribers. Thackeray estimates his

* In 1841, population of England and Wales 16,097,786; 999,048 domestic servants (233,000 men, 766,000 women). From Porter's *Progress of the Nation.* In 1861, 147,447 male domestic servants and 1,071,201 female, total 1,208,648 (1861 census: *British Almanach & Companion, 1864*).

† about 4/- E. H.

income from writing at 120,000 francs a year. Needless to say I am setting apart the enormous fortunes of their great industrialists and noblemen, with profits or revenues of the order of £200,000 a year. Their annual expenditure is proportional. A young engineer, a younger son with his fortune to make, was telling me the other day,

"With £8000 a year one is not 'wealthy' in England, one is only very comfortable." Another, who spends his summers in the country, added,

"Look at the way our farmers live; their daughters learn French, the piano, dress magnificently."

To earn a lot consume a lot — such is the rule. The Englishman does not save money, does not think of the future; at most he will insure his life. He is the reverse of the Frenchman, who is frugal and 'abstemious'.

Where does all this money come from and how is it distributed? I shall try to obtain some statistics. Meanwhile let us take a look at one of the reservoirs from which gold flows over the whole country and to all sorts and conditions of people — the London Docks.

First the tunnel: you go down a hundred steps, and from the bottom the hole looks as high as our Pantheon. Five hundred paces long: it is a prodigious work, but, up to now, a folly serving no purpose. Little shops in the interior where children's toys are sold and a thin, tinkling music heard. Gas jets cast an unsteady light, the walls run with water: the thing is as enormous and dismal as the gut of some Babel. I am always discovering that London resembles ancient Rome as Paris does Athens. How heavy must this modern Rome, as did the ancient one, bear down upon the backs of the working classes! For every monstrous agglomeration of building, Babylon, Egypt, the Rome of the Caesars, represents an accumulation of effort, an excess of fatigue. I have never looked upon a great city, a capital or a manufacturing town, without thinking of the nations about the Mediterranean which disappeared under the pressure of the Roman machine. True, there are nowadays no slaves *de jure;* but in fact and by reason of the constraints of their station, men are often slaves.

These docks are prodigious, overwhelming; there are six of them, each a great port and each inhabited by a population of three-masted ships. Always ships, ships and more ships, lying side by side, showing the swelling lines of their prows, like handsome fishes, in their copper sheathing. One is from Australia and dis-

*Fig. 6   Limehouse Docks*

places 2500 tons; others are of 3000 or more, and they come from every corner of the world, for this is the whole world's meeting place. Most of them are magnificent; standing close under the hulls, they are leviathans, graceful and elegant as swans. A merchant, who had come to check the arrival of spices from Java and a trans-shipment of ice from Norway, told me that about forty thousand ships enter these docks every year and that as a rule there are between five and six thousand in the docks of the river at any given moment.

The wine warehouses: there are thirty thousand casks of Port in the cellars. Unloaded by a crane they appear to be moving of their own accord: deposited on a small wheeled truck which runs down a slope, they arrive in their proper place with very little effort expended. The machines work so well that they seem like living auxiliaries of the men, willing slaves. Here, for example, is a swing-bridge which weighs a hundred tons but which a single man moves by means of a crank.

Spices sector — hides and leather sector — fats and oils sector. Cellars and warehouses are colossal: beneath vaults equal in span to a mighty bridge, the crowded, busy dimness fades distantly into deep shadow: Rembrandt would have found pictures ready-made in these mysterious perspectives, in the shifting darkness of these crammed and peopled cellars, in this infinity of store-rooms swarming with workers, like an ant-hill. They roll great bales and

27

barrels calmly and without confusion. You hear the voices of clerks calling over numbers. In the middle of each cellar a 'foreman' sits at a small table, watching and making entries in a ledger. The masters, sober men in black hats walk about, supervise, say nothing. Meanwhile all about sounds the creaking of capstans and the noise of sailors scraping the hulls of their ships. So busied, dressed in working overalls, their expression serious, their faces phlegmatic or tired, they are pleasant to look upon; for one feels that they belong here and every living creature, animal or man, is a thing of beauty in his proper place.

I was seated on a bale, smoking, when a man who was passing said, without stopping, "Five shillings fine!"

"Why, is it prohibited?"

"Yes."

Nothing else. There is nothing better for action, or the promoting of action, than economy of words and gestures. For instance at Hyde Park Corner I have several times watched the policemen on point duty for a considerable time: they never speak; if there is any mix-up in the traffic, they simply raise an arm to stop the coachman, lower it as a sign for him to move on. The coachman obeys immediately, and in silence. Our steward on the steamship, many office workers and business people I have met, do likewise. When, as between an order and obedience to it, all chatter, exclamations, motions of impatience, suggestions and amendments and, in short, tumult, are eliminated, execution follows so swiftly and smoothly upon the order that they interlock in their movement like two cogs in a machine.

After an hour the mind feels cluttered with new impressions, time is required for them to sort and order themselves. I was at the corner of Shadwell Basin, watching the great slate-grey river, gleaming, breathing out mist. The North Bank bends round so as to edge the horizon with a dark fringe striped red. Several barges were passing down river, their movement as slow and supple as a sea-bird's, the dark hulls and red sails rocking to the tide. To north and south the crowded masts of shipping. There was almost complete silence, broken only by the distant tapping of a hammer, and the twittering of birds in the trees. A Dutch painter, Van der Heyden, or Backhuysen, would have taken pleasure in that plain of water, the tones of brick and tar and the horizon itself only an approximation beneath still, drawn-out clouds. I have seen nothing more picturesque in London: the rest of it is either too washed and polished, or too busy and dirty.

*Fig. 7  City Warehouse*

Near where I was is Shadwell, one of the poorest quarters. By the depths of its poverty and misery, as by its extent, it is proportional to London's enormous size and wealth. I have seen the lowest quarters of Marseilles, Antwerp and Paris: they come nowhere near this. Squat houses, wretched streets of brick under red roofs crossing each other in all directions and leading dismally down to the river. Beggars, thieves and prostitutes, especially the latter, swarm in Shadwell Street. The grating music from gin cellars can be heard from the street; sometimes the violinist is a negro, and through open windows one sees unmade beds and women dancing. Three times in ten minutes I saw crowds collect round doorways, attracted by fights, especially by fights between women. One of them, her face covered with blood, tears in her eyes, drunk, was trying to fly at a man while the mob watched and laughed. And as if the uproar were a signal, the population of neighbouring 'lanes' came pouring into the street, children in rags, paupers, street women, as if a human sewer were suddenly clearing itself.

A few of the women show vestiges of former cleanliness, or wear a new dress; but most of them are in dirty, ill-assorted rags. Imagine what a lady's hat can become after having passed for three or four years from one head to another, been dented against walls, bashed in by blows — for that happens frequently. I noticed numerous black eyes, bandaged noses, cut cheeks. These women gesticulate with extraordinary vehemence; but their most horrible attribute is the voice — thin, shrill, cracked, like that of a sick owl.

From the moment you emerge from the tunnel, the whole place is alive with 'street-boys', bare-footed, filthy, turning cartwheels for a penny. They swarm on the stairs down to the Thames, more stunted, more livid, more deformed, more repulsive than the street urchins of Paris; the climate, of course, is worse, and the gin murderous. Among them, leaning against the festering walls, or crouched inert on the steps, are men in the most astonishing rags: nobody who has not seen them can conceive what a frock-coat or pair of trousers can carry in layers of filth. They doze and day-dream, their faces earthy, livid, marbled with fine red lines. It was in this quarter that families were discovered whose only bed was a heap of soot; they had been sleeping on it for some months. For the human being reduced to these conditions there is only one refuge: drunkenness.

"Not drink!" said one desperate man, in the course of an enquiry, "I'd rather die at once." *

A passing tradesman warned me, "Look out for your pockets, sir." And a policeman advised me to keep out of certain 'lanes'.

I did, however, walk through several of the widest ones: all the houses, with one or two exceptions, were obviously inhabited by prostitutes. Other narrow alleys, and dusty yards, were foul with the smell of rotting, old clothes and decorated with rags and linen hung out to dry. There were swarms of children. At one time, in a narrow alley, I had fourteen or fifteen all round me, dirty, bare-foot, one tiny girl carrying an infant, a baby still at breast but whose whitish head was completely bald. Nothing could be more dismal than these livid little bodies, the pale, stringy hair, the cheeks of flabby flesh encrusted with old filth. They kept running up, pointing out the 'gentleman' to each other with curious and avid gestures. Their mothers watched from doorways with dull, uninterested eyes. The interiors were visible, exiguous, sometimes a single room in which the family lives, breathing the foetid air. The houses are generally of a single storey, low, dilapidated, kennels to sleep and die in. What can it be like in winter when, during weeks of continuous rain and fog, the windows remain

---

* M. de Talleyrand, in course of conversation (1834) said "The English mob (canaille) is very cowardly; victorious, it would be cruel; but thirty policemen armed with white staves are enough to make them fall back. Ours are brave and are capable of getting themselves killed" (sait se faire tuer). Vic. de Rochefoucauld. Mémoires. VI. 261

closed? And in order that each numerous brood shall not die of hunger, it is essential that the father abstain from drink, be never out of work and never ill! *

Here and there are rubbish dumps. Women work on them, sorting the rubbish for rags, bones, etc. One of them, old and wrinkled, had a short clay pipe in her mouth; they straightened up and stared at me from the midst of their muck-heap: dull, stupid, frightening faces of female yahoos. Perhaps a pipe and a glass of gin is the last thought left in their idiot brains. Is it possible that anything but the instincts and appetites of a savage or a beast of burden can survive in them? A miserable black cat, emaciated, limping, half stupefied, was watching them fearfully out of one eye while furtively sniffing and pawing through a pile of rubbish; no doubt it was right to be nervous — the old woman was watching it with a look as bestial as its own, and mumbling, and it looked to me as if she were thinking that there went two pounds of meat.

I recall the lanes which open off Oxford Street, stifling alleys thick with human effluvia, troops of pale children crouching on filthy staircases; the street benches at London Bridge where all night whole families huddle close, heads hanging, shaking with cold; above all I recall Haymarket and the Strand at evening, where you cannot walk a hundred yards without knocking into twenty streetwalkers: some of them ask you for a glass of gin; others say, "It's for my rent, mister." The impression is not one of debauchery but of abject, miserable poverty. One is sickened and wounded by this deplorable procession in those monumental streets. It seemed as if I were watching a march past of dead women. Here is a festering sore, the real sore on the body of English society. †

* In winter, 150,000 London 'paupers' live entirely on public assistance. My friends estimate the number of 'roughs' (vagrants, dangerous people) in London at 180,000.

† (statistical abstract, 1871)

Number of poor persons in receipt of public assistance in England and Wales.

| 1861 | — | 890,423   | 1868 | — | 1,034,823 |
|------|---|-----------|------|---|-----------|
| 1862 | — | 946,166   | 1870 | — | 1,079,391 |
| 1863 | — | 1,142,624 | 1871 | — | 1,086,926 |

The figures are made up on the 1st of January every year, based on the number of indigent persons on the books of assistance offices of every union and parish.

Racing at Epsom. To-day is Derby day, a gala occasion. Parliament relaxes: for three days nothing but horses and their trainers has been talked of.

We set out for Waterloo Station. A cloudless, perfectly clear sky. My English neighbours say that they have never seen such a day in London. Green fields on both sides of the road, meadows surrounded by hedges, the hedges often planted with trees. The splendour of all this green, the sheer mass and opulence of wild flowers, lustrous, golden, bursting with sap, are extraordinary. Velvet starred with diamonds, rich watered silks, the most magnificent embroideries, none are comparable for depth and richness of colour. The colour, indeed, is excessive, beyond the power of painting to convey: but never have the burgeoning and full blooming of plants, the opulence and joy of the very earth itself, anywhere dazzled and overwhelmed me with such vivid brilliance.

The Derby is a large, green plain (sic), slightly undulating; to one side are three grandstands for the public, and several smaller stands. Facing these are tents and hundreds of booths, stables improvised under canvas, and an incredible muddle of carts and carriages and coaches, horses, horsemen and private omnibuses. There are perhaps two hundred thousand people here. Nothing handsome, no elegance or style: the carriages are simply vehicles, and well-dressed women are few and far between. People do not come here to be looked at, but to look, and the spectacle is only interesting for its sheer vastness. From high up in the 'stand' the huge swarm can be seen and heard as a great stirring and muttering. But beyond, to the right a long stand of tall trees, beyond them again the undulating blue-green of the downs and the green country fading into distant indistinctness, make a magnificent frame for an indifferent picture. A few clouds as white as swans drift across the sky and their shadows follow them over the grass. A light mist, radiant with sunshine, veils the far distance; the luminous air enfolds the plain and the hills, the vast space and all the animation of this great human fair, like an immense halo.

For it is, indeed, a fair: the people have come to enjoy themselves uproariously. There are gypsies everywhere, singers and dancers grotesquely got up as negroes; booths for shooting with bow and carbine, cheap-jacks selling watch-chains with a torrent of eloquence, games of skittles, and Aunt Sally, all kinds of musicians, and the most astonishing procession of cabs, coaches, droskis (sic), four-in-hands, each with its baskets of pies and pastries, cold meats, melons, fruit and wine, especially champagne. They are being unpacked; everyone is going to eat and drink, it will restore and raise their animal spirits; noisy, full-blooded enjoyment and loud, candid laughter are products of a full stomach.

In the face of these preparations for a good blow-out, the appearance of the numerous poor is a painful sight: they try to sell you a ha'penny doll, souvenirs of the Derby, persuade you to try your luck at the Aunt Sally shies, or to have your boots shined. Almost all of them look like wretched, beaten mangy curs, waiting to be thrown a bone but without much hope. They have walked here during the night and count for their dinner on the crumbs from the vast *al fresco* banquet. Many have lain down to sleep anywhere on the ground, among the feet of the crowd, and sleep with their faces turned to the sky and their mouths gaping. Their faces have an expression of dull stupefaction or painful sharpness. Most of them have bare feet, all are horribly dirty and, what is worse, ridiculous: the reason for this is that they wear gentlemen's cast-off clothing, the women old, formerly stylish dresses and little hats once worn by young girls of family. This tatterdemalion attire, which has clad four or five bodies in succession, I always find painful to see. It is degrading: by wearing it a person admits or declares himself to be one of the off-scourings of society. In France a peasant, artisan or labourer is a man who is different, but not inferior. His working blouse or overall is his own, as my suit is my own; it has been worn by nobody but himself. This readiness to wear rags is more than a mere singularity; it denotes a want of proper pride; the poor, in this country, resign themselves to being other people's door-mats.

One of these women, wearing an old shawl which looked as if it had been picked out of the gutter, and a once stylish hat long dented, and washed out by rain, carrying a poor, livid, dirty baby in her arms, came prowling round our omnibus, picked up a bottle which had been thrown away, and drank the last drop from it. Her other child, a little girl, picked up a melon rind and began to gnaw it. They were given a shilling and some cakes. I cannot describe their humble smile of gratitude. They looked as if, like the poor ass in Sterne's tale, they were saying, "Don't beat me, I implore you; however, you may beat me if you want to." Their faces were burned and tanned by exposure; the mother had a scar on her right cheek, due to a kick in the face; both of them, especially the child, were stunted creatures and had reverted to savagery. In this country the great social mill crushes and grinds the lowest order of humanity in its steel machinery.

A bell began ringing: the race was about to begin. Three or four hundred policemen clear the course; the stands are crammed with spectators and the fields facing them are one great dark stain of heads. We go up to our seats: nothing of grandeur to be seen. At this distance crowds become insect swarms; horsemen and carriages passing and recrossing each other look like beetles and cockchafers, or great bumble-bees crawling over a green carpet. The jockeys in their red, blue, yellow or mauve stand out apart, like a group of butterflies alighted. No doubt I am lacking in enthusiasm, but I find it like watching a game played by insects.

Thirty-four starters: after three false starts they are off. Fifteen or twenty keep together in a mass, the rest are in small groups as you see them coming up the course. To the eye the speed does not look very great: like that of a train seen from a couple of miles away, when the coaches look like toys being pulled along by a child. Here, certainly, the physical impression is no more impressive, and such words as "hurricane" would be very out of place.

For several minutes, then, the brown mark dotted with red and other colours, moves steadily along against the distant green background. It turns a corner and the first group is coming our way. "Hat's off!" — all heads are uncovered and the crowd surges to its feet. A throttled cheer breaks out in the grandstands. Cold faces are now lit up with warmth, phlegmatic bodies twitch and jerk and gesticulate; below, in the betting rings, the shock of movement is extraordinary, like a sudden universal St Vitus' dance. Imagine a crowd of automata receiving an electric shock and gesticulating with all their limbs like mad semaphores. But the most curious spectacle is the human tide which immediately and suddenly breaks and spreads over the course behind the horses, like a flood of ink: the still, dark mass has melted and flowed; in an instant it spreads wide and vast, as far as one can see; now it is in front of the stands. Three or four lines of policemen form a living fence, and when necessary use their fists to keep a clear space where the horses and their jockeys arrive for weighing out and checking. There is one big moment in the race, when the horses are only two hundred paces away: in an instant the speed becomes suddenly apparent and the group of riders and mounts flashes ahead, and words like "tempest" are no longer out of place.

An unknown horse, Caractacus, has won, by a short head. The odds against him were forty to one, whereas others, very famous horses, started at three to one, two to one, nine to two: a *débacle* for betting men. The prize, with accessories, amounts to £6,775; counting his bets the owner will win about a million francs. We hear of enormous losses, £20,000, £50,000: last year a colonel shot himself after the big race, for he realised that he was ruined; had he awaited the outcome of the other races he would have won enough to pay his debts. Just as the race was starting, the owner of one of the private stands had shouted that he would lay all his takings on Buckstone. Several cabbies lost their horses and cabs, having gambled them away.

As I understand the matter these bets are to the mind what brandy and gin are to the palate, a stimulant necessary to ponderous and rugged organisms. They need violent feelings, the sensation of an enormous risk: add to that their militant, chance-taking instinct. Every bet is a duel, every big bet a danger. As for the reasons which make horses and horse-racing into a universal national passion, it seems to me that we must look for them in the rustic, athletic life they lead. The rich, and the well-to-do spend a great part of the year in the country: in such a muddy land as this the best way of getting about is on horse-back: and their temper requires much physical exercise. All these attributes of their way of living *(mœurs)* culminate in the Derby, which is their special festival.

We make our way down from the stand: the stairs and buffets are crammed to the point of suffocation; but most carriage and omnibus parties have brought their own food and the people settle down to feast in the open, in small groups. Good humour and gladness abound. The classes mingle. One of our party, P ——, met his usual coachman sitting down to eat with a gentleman, two ladies, and a child. The gentleman had employed the coachman, then invited him to lunch. The coachman introduced P ——, who received a friendly invitation to a glass of port, sherry, stout or ale. In short, on this day we are all things to all men: but only for one day, as in the Saturnalia of old. To-morrow, distinctions of rank will be as rigid as ever, and the coachman will be respectful, 'distant' as usual.

Another of our friends saw a gentleman of his acquaintance who had come in an omnibus with his daughters and his neighbours, in all eight ladies; held up near his vehicle, we were all forced to stop and eat and drink with them. Our welcome was open, cordial, jovial. The gentleman had never set eyes on me before but he invited me to visit him at his place in the country.

Meanwhile, all over the plain, jaws were working, bottles being emptied and, towards evening, the fun of the fair was at its height. Twenty-four gentlemen triumphantly set up seventy-five bottles on their omnibus — they had drunk them all. Parties bombarded each other with chicken-bones, lobster shells and divots of turf. Two parties of gentlemen had got down from their omnibus and were boxing ten against ten; one had two teeth broken. There were some grotesque incidents: three men and a lady were standing on top of their carriage, the horse made a movement and all four fell off, the lady with her legs in the air: roars of laughter. Little by little the fumes of wine were going to their heads: these people, so coldly correct in their manners, so delicate in their behaviour, began behaving very oddly. Several gentlemen went up to a carriage containing ladies and young girls, and there, against the wheel eased themselves: the mother tried to drive them off with her umbrella. One of our own party who stayed until midnight saw certain enormities which I cannot write down here. On this occasion the beast is unleashed: there is nothing exaggerated in Rubens' *Kermesse*, in the Louvre; the same instincts are involved, and given the same free rein. Only, instead of Rubens' opulence of pink flesh, imagine faces which remain serious, and well-cut modern clothes. The contrast between the natural and the artificial man is grotesque, as it is between the gentleman and the beast which bursts out in him.

On the way back the road disappeared beneath clouds of dust. Parts of the downs had been worn quite bare by feet. We were all horribly dirty and white with dust. There were drunks in the road the whole way back; at eight that night they were still to be seen at Hyde Park Corner, reeling about and being sick. Their laughing cronies supported them and the faces of spectators did not express any disgust. Nothing is barred to-day; it is an outlet for a whole year's constraint.

Towards eleven that night we went to Cremorne Gardens, a sort of *bal Mabille* where the day's madness was carried on far into the night. A crush and much shoving at the entrance; a gang of Englishmen crashed through shouting. "Make way for the Japanese Ambassadors!" Inside, especially at crossings in the walks, the press of people was dreadful, but it was possible to get a breath of air in the darker corners. All the men well or at least neatly dressed: the women were prostitutes * but of a higher rank than those in the Strand; light-coloured shawls over white gauze

* Taine uses several different words, in different contexts and some distinction may have been intended. In this case the word used is "lorettes".

or tulle dresses, red *mantelets*, new hats. Some of their dresses may have cost as much as £12. But the faces are rather faded and sometimes, in the crowd, they utter shocking screams, shrill as a screech-owl.

The most comical part, and which showed the degree of excitement, was the way they had of pinching people, especially foreigners. One of our party, a man past forty, having been thoroughly pinched, and even more thoroughly upset and offended, left the place. A woman rushed at a man who had trodden on her toes, and punched him in the back: he laughed and the whole crowd was delighted. They are certainly very good-natured; nobody lost their temper although there was good reason to, for one of our French friends was imprudently jeering and making fun of them out loud. Once you have seen this you can get some idea of the joyous rustic feasts of the 16th century, Shakespeare's *Merry England* (sic); and of the strong, young sap of that tree which Puritanism so lopped and topped and pollarded that although it grew straight it also grew rigid.

We sat down near three young women at a secluded table and offered them sherry and beer. They drank moderately. Our bookish English and their racy speech collided in a grotesque babel. One of them was very gay and wild: I have never seen such overflowing animal spirits. Another, modest, quite pretty, rather subdued, was a milliner by trade, entirely dependent on herself. She has a friend (lover) who spends his Sundays with her. I looked at her carefully; it was clear that she had the makings of an amiable and respectable girl. What had been the turning point?

Impossible to say how many of these women there are in London. Some say 50,000. There are houses full of them from cellar to attic. We escorted our three to the gate and paid their cab fares. Our own cab drove us home by way of streets, crescents and squares which I did not recognize. A sepulchral light shone over the great, empty Babylon, casting the whiteness of a shroud upon its colossal artifacts. The dense, unwholesome air seemed still impregnated with human exhalations. From time to time we saw, beneath the dying light of a gas-jet, a belated street-woman, hungry and still hoping for a customer; or a pauper in rags, his feet tied up in more rags. As we drove I thought of Haymarket at night with its strolling, lottering women; of Argyle Rooms, a

The dictionaries simply have "woman of easy virtue". The word derives from the ill-fame of the quarter about Notre Dame de Lorette in Paris. These women may have been either full-time professionals, or semi-amateurs. E. H.

kind of lust-casino, which I had visited the previous evening. The spectacle of debauchery in this country leaves one with an impression of nothing but degradation and misery. Nothing brilliant, bold and smart, as in France. In the Argyle Rooms, when a gentleman wants to dance, an usher distinguished by a plaque, and wearing a white tie, fetches a woman for him; they often dance without exchanging one word. These poor girls are often beautiful, several of them look very gentle and decent; they all dance very correctly, smile a little and never gesticulate; they are *decolletées*, but, when dancing, keep their short capes on.

As for the men, by their appearance they are prosperous tradesmen, Thames-side warehouse owners *, middle-class industrialists, or their sons, or their managers, who visit the Rooms as a relaxation from their work with figures, coal, or other trade. What they need is vulgar display, coloured glass lights, women in full evening dress, bold, loud dresses, white shawls, embroidered with red flowers and exotic birds. They are well provided with money; a bottle of champagne costs twelve shillings; the evening will cost them £6.

The tragic thing is that the man and woman both drink, that they can do nothing until they are drunk. Here brutality encounters abject poverty with stupor or drunken imbecility as the go-between. One comes away from the place in some distress, with a deep and bitter impression of the helplessness and coarseness of humanity. A human society is a beautiful edifice, but when we come to its lowest floor — what a sewer!

Civilization polishes man, to be sure, but how tenacious is the bestial instinct still!

I dare not yet pass judgment; but it does seem to me that here both evil and good are greater than in France.

* Or shop-keepers. E. H.

CHAPTER TWO

# SOME TYPES

A COUNTRY is its people: since I arrived here I have been collecting types, adding them to those I collected last year. After some experimenting I have decided that the best method is still that used by painters and naturalists: first, note the most salient features or expressions, study them in all their variations and shades, graduations and mixtures; check that they are to be found in sufficiently numerous individuals; by this means, isolate the principal characteristic traits, then compare, interpret and classify them. This is what painters and novelists do by instinct when, through the medium of a few characters, they give us a resumé of their times and environment. Thus, also, do botanists and zoologists when, choosing a few plants or animals whose characteristics are prominent, they show us a whole class in five or six representative specimens.

Take a seat on a bench beside a public walk; or take up a position, in the morning, on a railway station platform. Almost immediately French eyes, accustomed to French physiognomies, seize upon the differences; memory keeps them present to the mind although the intelligence cannot yet understand them clearly. This observation is continued every day, at table, in public vehicles, at evening parties, during social calls, in town and in country. After some time certain new types rare in France but common here detach themselves clearly from the rest; week by week they become clearer, more complete, provoke questions and suggest answers, are associated one with another, become interconnected, until at last a whole, an *ensemble,* emerges.

But now consider this: in order to describe them, we are almost always forced to refer back to their salient features, that is to their 'excesses', and such are never ordinary. The pure type, as rendered by pen or pencil, is an exception; in nature it is almost always more or less modified. But, also in nature, there are ranged about this "ideal" type a whole series of degrees and varieties; so that from it, by making certain mental reservations and subtractions, the reader or spectator can picture a close approximation to the reality.

Here, then, by groups, are the types which have made most impression on me:

1. The robust man, big and solidly built, a handsome colossus, sometimes as much as six feet tall and broad in proportion, common in the army, especially the Life Guards, a *corps d'élite*. The face fresh and highly coloured; firmly and magnificently fleshed; they might be taken for prime specimens selected for an exhibition of human beings, like vegetable-show beetroots or cauliflowers. Basically good-humoured, often also good-natured, commonly rather awkward. Their fatuousness is something altogether special: in a tight-fitting red coat, a swagger-cane in hand, they preen themselves by throwing out their chest and displaying the slim line of their loins. Under the pie-shaped cap they wear on their heads one can see the light straight parting of their heavily pommaded hair. I saw one of them, halted at a street corner, chest out, shoulders back, posing majestically before a group of street urchins. In point of mass these men are monumental: but one can have too much of a good thing and movement is so essential to animate matter!

Some other monuments — not quite so tall but even fresher and more highly shined and polished: the footmen in great houses. White cravats impeccably tied, scarlet or canary yellow breeches, magnificent dimensions and proportions; their calves, especially, are enormous. In stylish parts of the city, below the hall of the house, at about five in the evening, the 'butler' is to be seen seated, his newspaper in hand, sipping a glass of port: about him are ushers wearing their chains *, gold-laced lackeys, footmen bearing tall canes, all looking out with an indolent and lordly air at the ordinary burgesses passing in the street. Note also the prodigious burliness of the coachmen, their breadth across loins and shoulders: what yards of cloth must be needed to contain such figures! These are creation's favourites, the best nourished, the longest and most frequently rested, hand picked for physique from the whole nation. In great houses they are carefully matched: the two footmen, like the pair of carriage horses, must be exactly the same size. When they advertise for a place, in the papers, they state their dimensions: 5 ft 9½ ins; 5 ft 11 ins. They are judged by points: fullness of calves, ankles, nobility of bearing, decorative appearance, all may be worth an extra £20 a year

* *huissiers à chaine* I do not know what rank of servant Taine had in mind here: perhaps he was exaggerating a little. E. H.

*Fig. 8. Selection of English Heads*

to them. They are carefully looked after, and therefore look after themselves carefully. They eat almost as well as their masters; several kinds of wines and beers; and ample leisure. Their appearance is intended to proclaim the wealth and standing of the household: they know this and they are proud of it. Consequently their majestic stupidity has become proverbial. Thackeray drew several characters for his novels from them, and one whole novel was devoted to them. * *Punch* publishes caricatures and cartoons about them: a man-servant giving my lord notice because he has seen his lordship riding on the top of a 'bus; another, because the colour of the livery does not suit his complexion. A footman behind a carriage, so handsome that he looks like an enormous doll; 'street-boys' are sticking pins into his calves to see if he is real or stuffed.

The same well-fleshed, athletic type occurs among the gentry, I have four or five among men of my acquaintance. † Sometimes excessive eating adds a modification, for example a gentleman I saw on Derby Day: large, red face with flabby cheeks and dewlaps; full, ginger whisker, unexpressive blue eyes; enormous trunk in a light-coloured, short jacket; noisy breathing; hands, neck, temples and even the scalp were given a pink colouration by his full bloodedness. When he frowned he had the disturbing, clouded physiognomy of a Henry VIII portrait. His face and body in repose suggested a beast fattened for the butcher, so that one found oneself unwittingly calculating the weight of the carcase — 240 lb. of meat.

At about fifty, their regimen, and the port they drink, begin to deform the body and the face: the teeth jut forward, the face takes on all the marks of age and even turns into a dreadful and tragic caricature: example, seen at the review of volunteers near Hyde Park; a fat general dressed in red with the appearance of a bulldog, the brick-red face marked by purple excrescences.

Final modification of this type: it occurs among the common people, when for port is substituted bad gin. They can be seen in, among other places, the low streets down by the Thames: the faces are apoplectic and swollen, the scarlet colour so dense that it is almost black; eyes dead, bloodshot, like those of a raw lobster.

* *Yellowplush Papers.* E. H.

† *From the Matrimonial News No. 1927*
"A country gentleman of the highest class, farming his family estates worth £ 25,000. Fair colouring. Height 6 ft 2 ins. Weight 16 stone; remarkably well-proportioned; robust health."

The primal brute — brutalised.

Reduce the volume of blood and fat, but retain the same bone-structure while increasing the rustic manners; beard and moustache both enormous and wild, a mat of uncombed hair, rolling eyes, truculent muzzle, large, knotted hands. Here we have the primal Teuton as he emerged from his forests: after the show beast ('portly'), and the fattened beast ('overfed'), we have the fighting beast ('fierce'), the English bull.

All the above are quite rare, the extreme example of the type. Much commoner is the working animal, the beast of burden: big, bony body full of salients and angularities, not very well coordinated, 'ungainly', clumsy, somewhat automatic, but strongly constructed and just as capable of endurance as of effort. The type is no less common among gentry, clergy, and professional men than among the labouring classes. I can cite three examples off hand:

A tall, thin clergyman, stiff, unbending and who never will unbend: movements as jerky as a semaphor, narrow and didactic opinions, but charitable and proving his devotion in his life. The hard, strong frame was needed, if he was to endure thirty years of his apostolic trade; incessant preaching, continual visiting in the vilest alleys, long expeditions on foot in all the mud of the suburbs.

A Member of Parliament: feet, hands and shoulders of a carter; large, white teeth too close together; powerful jaw which hardly opens at all when he speaks; irregular and very prominent features; the whole person built large and rough hewn, as if hacked out with a pick-axe and insufficiently carved down afterwards. His up-to-date suit, gloves, blue tie, linen brilliantly white, all look out of place on muscles which could pull a lorry or sustain a boxing bout. His eyes are dull; few words, devoid of wit and, it would seem, of ideas. He is not a 'leader', he is simply a party member; he votes and he works. But in long night sessions, in working through a mass of papers and in checking accounts, at meetings, in Committee, at the clubs, for all such tedious and inconclusive tasks, he is well fitted, and he is excellent.

The third is an Englishman of the middle-class whom I met yesterday in an omnibus, with his family. Thirty-two years old, new clothes (twelve to fifteen thousand francs a year, I imagine), an air of solidity and resolution: a good machine, firmly set, well built, well maintained, indefatigable and regular. He was the real *pater familias* in the early stages: the face was cold, still, correct, rather heavy and rather dull. Beside him his young wife in black velvet, hat and trimmings too loud, but her person simple and graceful; very much occupied with her baby. The infant was very fair, plump, in radiant health, with full, embroidered skirts, making him both a parcel and a show-piece. Facing them sat the nurse-maid, a woman of thirty-five, obviously bent on pleasing and keeping her smile respectful.

This was a good specimen of an English household; the husband pulling his conjugal weight energetically, conscientiously and without finding it tedious. His happiness no doubt lay in having his tea beside his own hearth, with his slippers on; he will have a great many children who, not knowing what to do for a living, will emigrate and will need a constitution like his own to enable them to face 'hardships'.

To this same vigorous structure of bone and muscle add a clear, calm, active intelligence developed by a special education or by all round education; there you have the finer modification of the same type; a serious-minded man, capable, worthy to command and whom, in an emergency, you can and should trust, for he will overcome all difficulties. Put him into new clothes, too well groomed, too light in colour, and the contrast between the man and his attire is not far short of grotesque. But imagine him on the bridge of a ship, in battle, or merely in an office and in charge of twenty clerks, or sitting on a jury with power over lives and fortunes: then he will be a thing of beauty, moral beauty. He has a body to carry a soul without weakening.

The same strong growth and structure is to be seen in many of their women, far more often than in France: out of any ten girls there will be one who is admirable and five or six whom a naturalist painter would take pleasure in looking at. On horseback especially in full gallop, they are veritable Amazons, not only by reason of their skill and firm seats in the saddle, but by reason of their figures and their healthiness; the sight of them puts one in mind of the natural life, the Greek, the athletic, way of living. I met one such yesterday, in a drawing room, tall, well developed bust and shoulders, rosy cheeks, active, not too much expression. She seemed to me as well designed for life in the walks of a private park or in the vast 'halls' of a great house, as was her sister, the typical antique statue, for the free air of the mountains or the portico of a temple overlooking the sea. Neither of them could breathe in our little Parisian *appartements*. The mauve silk of her dress fitted her form from neck to hips, then fell and spread like a bright wave. To paint her as a goddess would require the

44

palette of a Rubens — those rosy reds spread upon a basis of milky white; and the flesh in sweeping lines, as if poured out and shaped in a single motion. But in this case the outline was not so exuberant, and the head was truly noble.

Lady Mary Wortley Montagu, after visiting the Court of the Regent in France, made cruel fun of our thin, painted, mannered beauties, and compared them proudly with "the bright colours and perfect freshness" of the English complexion. On the other hand one may sometimes recall Hamilton's mocking portrait:

"Mrs Wetenhall was altogether what is called an English beauty; a mixture of lilies and roses, of snow and milk as to colouring; made of wax in the matter of arms and hands, breast and feet; but the whole without spirit or expression. Her face was of the prettiest, but it was always the same face; you might have thought that she took it out of a case every morning, and replaced it when she went to bed, without having made any use of it during the day. What would you? Nature had made a doll of her from her childhood and a doll until she died remained the fair Wetenhall."*

However, even when face and form are vulgar, the whole effect leaves the mind well satisfied: a sound bone-structure with healthy flesh on it; such is the essential for any living creature. The impression made is the same as that made by a house well-built of good dressed stone with fresh plaster and new paint. One does not demand perfection in the architecture, nor even elegance. It will endure bad weather, it is comfortable and pleasant for those who are its guests; and that is enough.

Two probable causes: in the first place the special nature, the hereditary conformation of the race; secondly the habit of leading an open-air life and taking physical exercise. There was recently a reference in one of the Reviews to that 'rude, unfeeling health' which is apt to alarm delicate foreign ladies, and it was attributed to the practice of riding and to the long walks which English women take in the country. To the advantages, however, must be joined several disadvantages: the fair complexion is quickly and easily spoilt; the noses of many young women easily turn red; and they bear too many children, which deforms them. You marry a blonde angel, slender and confiding: ten years later you may find your companion for a lifetime a housekeeper, a wet-nurse, a broody hen. I have in mind two or three such matrons, broad, stiff and without an idea in their heads; red faces, china-

* As Taine gives no reference for this and I do not recognise it, it is re-translated from his French. E. H.

blue eyes, and enormous white teeth — like the tricolour flag.

In other cases the type becomes exaggerated in all its attributes; you see women who look like asparagus, or like lamp-posts stuck into crinolines. Moreover, in two-thirds of cases their feet shod in heavy 'boots' are excessively manly; and as for their long, out-jutting teeth, one cannot get used to them. Are they a cause, or an effect of their carnivorous diet?

Finally, their over-ornamented and ill-contrived style of dress completes the effect of clashing incongruities. One sees purple or poppy-red silks, grass-green dresses decorated with flowers, azure blue scarves, gold and other jewellery, all of it strapped like a harness on to gigantic harridans reminiscent of superannuated heavy cavalry horses, or on to tons of massive flesh well strapped in but bursting out of its retaining armour. In the latter style was a lady I saw in Hyde Park recently, mounted, and followed by her groom: fifty-five years old, several chins and the rest of her person to match them. Her bearing was haughty and imperious; the moment the horse broke into a trot, the whole mass shook like a jelly, and it was difficult not to laugh.

Another specimen: the children. I have been to Eton and to Harrow-on-the-Hill. As for the very little children, still in their 'nurseries' they are living flowers, rosebuds in bloom: especially in the country their chubby, cherubic cheeks, and the firm plumpness of their bodies proclaim the rich sap which will in due course make strong, stout fellows of them. From about their seventh year they are dominated not by intelligence, but by physical and moral energy. They often have a sulky, unamiable look which makes one think of young bull-dogs. For example, young H—— and little M ——, the sons of great families, seem to be, and are, no better than simple little oafs, stubbornly resistant to culture, fit only for hunting and the fisticuffs they indulge in at school.

An observer of the species told me, "An English boy is ferocious, untameable; the blood of the Norse 'rovers' flows in his veins; hence the use of flogging; in our schools it would be impossible to do without the rod."

Little precociousness or vivacity, but plenty of initiative and tenacity. (George) Eliot gives us an excellent specimen in the character of Tom, her heroine's brother. * The boys are very often churlish, a trait which has been seized on by comic draftsmen: "Charlotte", says a young fellow of eight to his eighteen-year-old

*The Mill on the Floss

46

sister, "Lend me your paint box." "No sir; you remember how you ruined it the last time." "Very well, I shall put my guinea-pig down your neck." And he is shown raising the guinea-pig to carry out his threat. The animal instincts are too strong in these boys, they are too bursting with health; books are repugnant to them, they will not and cannot learn. They like to eat, box, play cricket, ride horses.

But by the same token they are brave, enduring, bold, hardened to blows and all kinds of risks. "It is a strange thing", says the author of *Tom Brown's School Days*, "to see how much almost all English boys are in love with danger. You will find ten to join in a hunt, climb a tree, swim a stream if there is a chance of breaking a limb or being drowned; and you will not find one to play bowls, stay quiet on terra firma, or bathe where he can touch bottom." Young Tom, on his way to school, spends a very cold night on the outside of a coach, and he sticks it because he has "the consciousness of silent endurance, so dear to every Englishman — of standing out against something and not giving in." I can recall fifty small instances of this kind. By and large I am certain that in this country the physical animal, and the primitive man as nature makes him before handing him over to civilisation, is of a stronger, rougher species.

Here are a few of these instances:

Recently, when visiting breweries and two farms, I saw working and draft horses: they resembled elephants. One of the farmers had twelve, costing £50 or £60 each. These horses are athletes of their species. Glossy skins, muscular loins, colossal quarters. One of the horses, smaller, was French, and the farmer said it was not so strong and less able to stand bad weather. Now, wherever I have been I have found this same relationship between the men and horses of a country. For example, trace it place by place in the Var, at Orleans, in Normandy and in England.

Again, an able doctor here who gets a Frenchman among his patients, only prescribes half doses for him: an English dose would be too strong and would do him harm: if you ask a chemist for a purge he will give you calomel: an Englishmen often has this drug in his house and swallows a pill of it if his head feels a trifle heavy: the doctors here would be just the thing for French horses. Similarly with the wines they drink, port and sherry, very full and strong and, furthermore, blended with brandy — a practice which ruins their subtler qualities. But if they were pure the English would find them insipid: our wines of Bordeaux, and even of

Burgundy, are too light for them. In the middle-classes ale, stout, and porter are preferred, and above all 'brandy-and-water', a kind of grog which is one half spirits. In order to please them a drink must be harsh and burning; their palates need to be scratched or scraped.

The same is true of their cooking: excepting in the very best clubs and among *continentalised* English people, who have a French or Italian chef, it is devoid of savour. I have dined, deliberately, in twenty different inns, from the highest to the lowest, in London and elsewhere: huge helpings of greasy meat and vegetable without sauce; one is amply and wholesomely fed, but one can take no pleasure in eating. The best restaurant in Liverpool cannot dress a chicken. If your palate demands enjoyment, here is a dish of pimentos, peppers, condiments, Indian vinegars: on one occasion I carelessly put two drops into my mouth: I might just as well have been swallowing a red-hot coal. At Greenwich, having had a helping of ordinary 'white bait', I helped myself to more but from another dish: it was a dish of curried whitebait — excellent for taking the skin off one's tongue. Finally, on coaches and the decks of steamships many gentlemen, and even ladies, prefer to remain out in the wind and rain, certain of being buffetted and drenched: they enjoy rough weather. In my opinion all these traits indicate senses less refined and a more robust nature.

This very robust body has requirements to match. They find us abstemious: it follows that to us they seem voracious. Economists tell us that an average Frenchman eats a sheep and a half per annum, an Englishman four sheep. In restaurants you are given one roll to eat with a huge helping of meat. *Punch* carries jokes on the subject of greed among small boys. A girl looking at two pigs in a fattening pen says, "What a terrible existence! They do nothing but sleep and eat!" Her brother aged ten replies, "There is nothing in the world I should like better." An obvious exaggeration, but is is a pointer to their way of life. Van Brugh, in his *Voyage à Londres* has already given us a portrait of the gluttonous petty 'squire', unknown in France. These people have always gloried in their carnivorousness and in the fact of being well fed; this, in their eyes, was a privilege of their race, and fostered their courage. "A vigorous and valiant race," says one of their recent historians, "sound in body, proud and high hearted, well furnished with muscles which, nourished by large pieces of beef, was the wonder of their age. Friends and enemies alike described them as the most bellicose and redoubtable race in Europe. Cellini calls the English wild beasts. Four hundred adventurers, runaway London apprentices, formed into a corps of volunteers holding the garrison at Calais, were for years the terror of Normandy. When, at last, they perished, they fell surrounded by an enemy six times as numerous as themselves, and they were cut to pieces, desperate men with no care beyond the fight." *

An Englishman with whom I had some talk at the Derby did not, by this same token, altogether approve of temperance societies. By his account, these people need stimulants: he held that even in India, where he had spent five years, it would be a mistake for the English to give up drinking spirits. "Our sailors could not live without their glass of rum. We are an eminently energetic people: we need strong meats and strong drinks to keep us properly wound-up; otherwise, no 'animal spirits'. It is because of this regimen that our sailors are so brave and enduring. When they take a ship by boarding her and have discharged their pistols, they throw them carelessly down on the enemy's deck, feeling certain of finding them again after their victory."

It is possible that he was right: certain organisms are spendthrift of energy; there are chimneys which draw badly unless a big fire be built up on the hearth. Besides, the climate, the fog, their heavy manual and mental work all tend to encourage large consumption. An English workman, who alone does the work of one and a half Frenchmen and lives in the Manchester 'fog', is an engine whose furnace needs constant stoking with meat and spirits to keep the boiler going. Pitt did not find two bottles of port too much for him at dinner.

But to return to my specimens.

2. The phlegmatic: he receives impressions but they provoke no expression, much less excitement, disturbance or outburst. He is at the opposite pole to the petulant and passionate southerner. His air is cold and fixed, his gestures those of an automaton, his physiognomy immobile, his words few.

B——, having an introduction to a family, called on them. While he was talking to his hostess, her husband came in, saw the visitor the moment he opened the door, crossed the room in silence and looking the other way, sat down and, after a moment, without moving a muscle of his face said, "Pleased to see you, sir." That was all: after five minutes more he took up a newspaper and

* Froude. *History of England*. Vol. 1 Ch. XIX.

49

read it. It was not that he was displeased: on the contrary, he was hospitable and benevolent.

Account heard from a naval officer: an English Admiral, after a long battle, forced the enemy ship to strike her colours, and received her captain, his prisoner, with a single phrase, "Fortune of war." Politeness — but abbreviated, laconic.

Here is an extract of a letter from one of my friends, after he had stayed in England for some weeks:

"Shall I tell you what struck me most in this country? The torpor of their nervous system. The other day I was watching cricket being played on Kew Green; there were seven or eight youthful Englishmen throwing the balls to each other.* They must certainly have made mistakes in the game, or been clumsy from time to time. Nevertheless, during more than an hour and a half I did not hear one shout, not a single remark made in a loud voice or in a tone of reproach. They threw the ball to each other, changed positions in complete calm and as a rule in complete silence — you must have noticed that the English talk very quietly. I happened to find myself for a while in Italian company and was absolutely deafened, for I had become used to the moderate tones of English voices.

"My cabby, only the other day, took it into his head to drive me at full speed into a 'mews', thereby frightening two privately-owned horses which were being harnessed to a carriage. The groom came running out, caught hold of his horses by the bits and soothed them. Not one sharp word was exchanged between the two men. Imagine the same scene in France — the insults hurled by the lackey, proud on his master's account, the coarse remarks of the jealous plebian, etc., etc.,

"There, my dear friend, is the most significant thing I have seen in England, and the thing in terms of which I would explain English liberty. These people have water in their veins, exactly like their cattle whose meat lacks juice: compare a Saint-Leonard leg of mutton to a London one. That is why they can be allowed to forgather in meetings, stand up and bray, and print whatever they like. They are primates with cold blood and a slow circulation."

Among the people I am in the habit of frequenting here, there are two or three men who are very well educated and informed, men who think, who have written, and who talk well. They do

* This hardly sounds like cricket! However that is fortunately beside the point of the anecdote. E. H.

50

Fig. 9  *A Game of Cricket*

the honours of their respective houses, and attend to the most
interesting conversations without saying a word. It is not that
they are inattentive, bored, or absent-minded: they listen, and that

is enough for them. Questioned directly, they sum up their own experience in a sentence: that debt discharged, they fall silent again, and nobody is surprised. The explanation of such manners which will be given you is: "He is a man of few words."

Now, join to this disposition the robust, rather coarse temperament described above, and you will have a new modification of the type — the 'sluggish': slow, heavy, dull, materialistic, inapt for any refinement of culture, satisfied with some mechanical occupation, the real Flemish 'boor' of Van Ostade. Here is a brief biography which shows this character associated with a practical aptitude and a special talent.

John S —— is the son of an artisan in the vicinity of Bristol; since childhood he has worked at his father's small forge. Having a bent for mechanical things, he invented a kind of bolt for fixing rails to their sleepers, whereupon a rich gentleman of good family, who knew him, offered him the money to start a factory of his own. John consulted his father, who had remained a simple, narrow-minded artisan and refused to join his son. John persevered, applied himself to study, learnt what he needed to know of mechanics, carried his theory into practice, received the capital offered and started the factory. Last year it brought the partners £ 20,000 net profit. John is now twenty-eight, already rich, and spends his days as follows:

In the mornings he goes to his factory, inspects and supervises the workshops, takes a hand at the bench, shows a clumsy workman how a job should be done, returns home dreadfully dirty, washes, and has luncheon. Same again in the afternoon. He dines. spends his evenings sitting in a neighbouring public house where he drinks six penn'orth of beer, smokes a pipe, and goes home to bed at ten o'clock. He has been engaged to a young woman for three or four years but is still not ready to marry her: yet she is twenty-four, he loves her, he intends to marry her, he *will* marry her; but he is 'sluggish', feels very comfortable as he is, is held back by inertia, moral inertia. As for her, she waits patiently, she is gentle and submissive. He goes to see her on Saturday evenings, they take little trips together, or visit friends. Both sleep away from home for the night, and return together on the Monday morning. All this perfectly honourably: the manners and customs are here tolerant of such liberties, and nobody remarks on it.

For the rest, not an idea in his head, not an atom of curiosity; he can hardly spell. He does not read, is interested in nothing but his work. Wears a worn jacket at work and a clean one for

Sundays. Beyond that, nothing, his circle is drawn and he lives in it like a snail in its shell. However, on the advice of the gentleman, his partner, he has just built himself a fine house, but he is not at ease in it.

George Eliot has depicted the type admirably in her novels — heavy, narrow, very frequently met with in England: they remain fixed, as if chained, to an animal or manual or local existence, stick to traditions and never leave that rut except very rarely, and then only in some one respect. Consider, in this connection, John Willet, the innkeeper in *Barnaby Rudge*, by Charles Dickens; an excellent caricature: the creature is half ox, half bull; and in that dense mass of flesh a few simple ideas are, as it were, fossilized, and no new idea can penetrate.

On the other hand when your man is an intelligent and cultured gentleman, the phlegmatic temperament gives him a particularly noble air. I can recall several such, pale in complexion, with pale blue eyes, regular features, one of the finest types of the whole human species. They make a virtue of their temperament: by their way of thinking a man's principal merit lies in keeping a clear, cool head. They are right: nothing could be more useful in misfortune and danger, and that, indeed, is one of their national qualities, the gift which enables them to succeed. A French officer who fought in the Crimean War told me how, at Inkermann, a battalion of English infantry (chasseurs) wiped out two Russian regiments. The Russians kept on firing and did not give an inch; but they were uneasy and their aim was bad, whereas the English avoided all hurry, aimed carefully, and hardly wasted a shot. A man whose pulse remains normal and his judgment untroubled is ten times as strong.

The offshoots and modifications of each type are innumerable. Taking, as our principle, that in the case of the phlegmatic type gesture, movement and expression are nil, rare, or difficult, the following figures will be explicable: I am copying word-sketches made on the spot:

The 'swell' or second-rate dandy. A complete fashion plate; the very latest thing in the most correct taste as regards clothes. Whiskers, moustache and hair just barbered; the man, indeed, looks like a hair-dresser's dummy. His clear complexion and glassy eyes would suit a wax figure. Motionless attitude, restrained gestures — he must not disturb so much as a fold of his cravat. He wears his clothes as if for show. Varied, uncalculated movement, an amiable or attractive, gay or amusing, physiognomy, which alone can make this species tolerable, is altogether wanting, and all that is left is a stuffed shirt.

The rigid character, who walks as if he had a ram-rod in his body: very common among clergymen.

The big, ill-contrived machine whose cogs are rusty. The type occurs often among tall young men and also men of fifty who have spent their lives working: all the parts composing them creak at being together. Gestures and expression not being sufficiently agile, lag clumsily, then are accomplished out of place and with a discordant violence. This is especially apparent in the convulsive movement of the mouth.

The shy: expression being difficult for him, he exaggerates the difficulty to himself. If he lacks intelligence his habitual silence involves him ever more deeply in his own native vacuity. If he is very intelligent, he becomes concentrated within himself, lives solitary in a world of intimate personal feelings to which he gives access to nobody and, the more alien he feels, the more he shuts himself in. These two kinds of character are so common here it is impossible to give any idea of the number. Not only girls, but women of forty are startled and troubled at the sight of a new face; I have been told of a lady of the highest rank, accustomed to grand occasions, yet who turns mute and red when a stranger is introduced to her. There are men of education, even learned men, who have travelled, know several languages, and yet are embarrassed in company: you might live with them six months without perceiving their merits. They have neither the art nor the inclination to bring themselves forward and some considerable jolt, some urgent interest is necessary to get them to open their mouths. I know one such who stuttered in a drawing room but who, during the following days, addressed eight meetings with the greatest eloquence. This kind of awkwardness and shame, entirely physical, is peculiar to the Germanic peoples. A Frenchman or an Italian talks naturally, with ease and confidence; the Frenchman even more so than the Italian because he immediately feels himself to be his interlocutor's crony. An old historian once pointed out that of all men the French speak with least constraint or embarrassment to kings and princes.

Due to another effect of this same temperament certain English people are apt to be backward, the reverse of precocious: they do not dare to develop their qualities, and so remain longer in a purely animal or childish state. Such people are often naive, innocent, primitive. Faces, here, remain young much longer than

Fig. 10 *Railway Official and The Swell*
*Railway Official.* "*Show your Ticket, Sir — please.*"
*Swell.* "*Haw, don't want to split my Gloves — would you be kyind enough to take it yourself out of my Waistcoat Pocket?*"
(*Punch*, January 17, 1863)

they do with us, especially than in Paris, where they fade and
wither so quickly. Sometimes they remain open and candid into
old age; I have in mind as I write two white-haired old ladies
whose cheeks were still smooth and softly rosy, and an hour's
conversation with them revealed a freshness of spirit equal to

their complexion. Like all traits which are at all common, this one produces both its grotesques and its master-pieces.

The dignified lamp-post of a man; body and mind fossilised, a great many principles.

The flustered: silly, gaping look and a general air of not understanding anything.

The large, fat, lymphatic cow: white eyelashes.

The goose — female: large, silly eyes popping out of her head. Long waist and torso badly bundled up above the swell of the crinoline.

The child-girl, pink, playful, hair loose on her shoulders, a positive bird, chirping with laughter and chirruping incessantly, and with no more ideas in her head than a bird. Dickens depicted the type in Dora, David Copperfield's 'child-wife'.

The fair maiden — lowered eyes, blushing cheeks, purer than a Raphael Madonna, a kind of Eve incapable of a Fall, whose voice is music, adorable in her candour, gentleness and kindness; one is moved to lower one's eyes respectfully in her presence. From Virginia, Imogen and other women of Shakespeare and his great contemporaries, to Dickens' Esther and Agnes, English literature has always given them the first place: they are the perfect flower of England.

The thoroughly decent woman, calm, serious, never touched by temptation, and whose life is arranged so as to put away all curiosity, all evil thoughts and opportunity for doing wrong. In this class many young Quaker women are notable. Bonnet *(chapeau court auvergnat)*, white veil, the calm look of a nun. The expression it that of a person who has always lived in a moral enclosure and never dreamed of leaving it.

Since a woman's dress is a kind of self-expression, an outer appearance imposed upon the personal outer semblance, it denotes what was already manifest in the face, expression and gestures, to wit, awkwardness, want of cleverness, of suppleness and of flair. As a general rule a person's clothes, a woman's *toilette,* should express her personality; in England it nearly always does this badly. Two exceptions: the riding habit, black, close fitting to the torso, simple and without ornament, denoting boldness, agility, strength, physical well-being. And the travelling costume — the small straw hat with a single ribbon, the one-piece without odd additions, the low boots made of good leather — all indicative of a good walker, devoid of coquetterie, capable of accompanying her husband on the outside of a stage-coach, of being a real companion to a man and not a delicate and troublesome doll.

Apart from these two outfits, their dress, loud and overcharged with ornament, is that of a woman of easy virtue (*lorette*), or a *parvenue*. One is always startled at the spectacle of this paraphenalia draped on an obviously respectable young woman. On Sundays in Hyde Park such sartorial excesses on the persons of ladies and girls belonging to the rich middle-class are very shocking: hats which look like sprays of rhododendron piled up in a heap, or snow white, or fantastically small, trimmed with clumps of red flowers and enormous ribbons; dresses of purple silk, very shiny so that they reflect the light dazzlingly, or of stiff tulle on a substructure of skirts bristling with embroidery; immense shawls of black lace falling to the heels; immaculate white or bright purple gloves; gold chains, gold belts with gold clasps; hair lying in a gleaming mass on the nape of the neck. The glare and glitter is brutal: they look as if they have stepped out of a wardrobe and are parading to display the wares of a fancy-goods shop. They carry their heads stiffly, like an usher in a procession; their hair is either in a dense mass, or falls too loosely; their clothes are hung on them as if on coat-hangers. Their crinolines curve in at the bottom like a barrel, and their short capes ride up at the back in clumsy, pretentious fullnesses. As a result you do not see three pretty figures. The array of white teeth is a crude streak against the red of their lips; black, heavily shod feet are visible beneath ballooning skirts. Thus swollen up by their clothes, they rustle as they walk, their dresses going on before and trailing behind, swinging like a bell. Compared with the supple undulation, easy, silent, and serpentine, of a Spanish *toilette* and a Spanish woman's walk, a woman's movements in this country are energetic, discordant, as jerky as a mechanism.

3. Last type: the active and energetic person, capable of enterprise, of effort, of 'endurance' and perseverance, and liking effort for its own sake. The elements in such a character are numerous and I cannot yet make them out very clearly. We will examine some actual cases by way of example.

One day, as I was returning from a visit to the country, two young men asked if I would take them to the station in my 'fly' and offered to pay half the fare. Naturally I agreed to the first part of their proposal and rejected the second. We chatted. They were two brothers, nineteen and seventeen years old respectively: they had ten brothers and sisters, and they were going to New

Zealand. They proposed to stay there twelve years and return having made their fortune. They were to become sheep-farmers. I can give no idea of the lively optimism, the ardour and decision of their speech and gestures: one was keenly aware of super-abundant energy, activity, of the 'plenty of animal spirits', bursting out of them. They reminded me of greyhounds unleashed, sniffing the air and ready for the chase. According to the elder, New Zealand already has towns of ten thousand inhabitants. Starting with a thousand or two thousand pounds capital it is possible to bring back twenty thousand after twelve years' work. "You'll be about thirty", I said, "you will be returning just in time to marry."

"Yes, sir," — the reply was uttered with tremendous keenness, with an admirably youthful enthusiasm.

For the first year they will be learning the trade; then they will launch out on their own. It seems a man must be his own labourer there. They will build, chop wood, plough, harvest, pasture their sheep, and shear them, all with their own hands. So they assured me and laughed with the keenest enjoyment at the idea. The older youth told me he had some training: he had lived on a farm, knew a certain amount of applied mathematics, spoke German but no French, had travelled in France, Germany and Switzerland. His speech was abrupt and vibrant, he seemed to dart his words at you.

"Forced to try the colonies; numerous family, you know; forced to rely on ourselves." These two young men, so cheerful, bold and enterprising gave me real pleasure. It seemed to me a fine way of starting out in life. And here they have the necessary daring: the world is open to them and they are skimming its cream. England remains the goal to return to, the treasury into which everything flows. And the momentum is not lost once their fortune is made: the sons of a rich father are required to work because of their number, and because the law of inheritance gives the greater part to the eldest. In addition, whether born rich or self-enriched, there is always work to do in politics, associations, and public life, local or national. Always more work appears as the goal or term of present work. In France we make our fortunes in order to retire, rest, be idle, and enable our children to do likewise.

Now set aside youth: outwardly calmer, there remains in maturity the same need to act and be doing. In this connection, here is the sketch of a life known to me personally. Mr. W —— was the son of a small shop-keeper who had six children. His father had him educated as a practical engineer and, as soon as the young man was eighteen, ordered him, not out of harshness but on principle, to fend for himself. Many parents here think that they owe their children nothing but an education. W—— went to Scotland, found employment at between thirty and forty pounds a year. A few years later he was sent to India to put up a lighthouse: £300 a year. The lighthouse having been completed, he left there to put up another: £400 a year and £100 bonus. Back home, he worked on the construction of a tubular bridge, was in charge of the books and accounts of this undertaking, became secretary of a company in London, with a fixed fee of £150 a year. Next he married a girl who was a penniless 'governess'.

Shortly we find him secretary of a large firm at £600 a year. He goes to the office every day, works nine or ten hours at full steam. Between thirty and seventy letters to write daily and about twenty-five callers to interview, not to mention inspecting an infinity of articles and people.

At home, meanwhile, he is collaborating in the compilation of a dictionary of Greek antiquities: to this end he first had to read the Greek authors in translation and then, helped by learned friends, the promoters of the Dictionary, he taught himself to read them fluently in the original texts. He spends a part of his nights at this work: note, too, that he undertook to deal with the small articles, which are boring (for which reason nobody else would do them), but which must be dealt with. The end to be attained was the prime consideration, and to that end he provided a man of goodwill — himself. In addition to all this, he found the time to learn, and learn well, German, French and music, to cultivate his mind in all respects and be well informed about everything. He confesses that he feels a need to be up and doing; and that once, having spent two days completely idle, he almost died of boredom. He says that he enjoys travelling because every day you can stuff your mind with new facts and new ideas. He claims that this need for facts is the basis of the English character: let the machine run uncoupled to work and it wrecks itself.

The young woman he married was pretty, well-bred and well educated. Her grandfather had been a carpenter on the staff of a college. Her father, the carpenter's son, entered the college by favour, was brilliantly successful in his studies, took his finals with honours, and emerged as a *tutor* (sic). Among his pupils were some young noblemen and by their patronage he received a piece of preferment, a benefice worth five hundred a year. Moreover, he was a very good preacher and his printed sermons sold very well. Helped by his reputation he went to London, founded a chapel with the help of several rich persons, and in the end was earning £1200 a year.* He was twice married, the first time to a woman who had nothing, the second to a lady in easy circumstances, and had fourteen children by the first wife, six by the second. His sons are teachers, lawyers, clergymen, almost all of them very comfortably circumstanced. Among the daughters, several stayed at home, others went out as governesses, among them Mrs W ——, in order 'to be independant' — a phrase which is altogether characteristic and, in my view, admirable. W ——, his wife, and their three children live very comfortably. They rent a 'cottage' near London for £100 a year. Every year they spend a holiday, together, travelling. There is no doubt in my mind that they spend their whole income, and that if any provision is made for the future, it will only be in life insurance.

Here, then, is an admirable specimen of an English life: left early to fend for oneself; marriage to a woman with no fortune; a large family of children; income all spent, no savings; work very hard and place one's children under the necessity to do likewise; constant acquisition of facts and positive knowledge; find relaxation from one task in another task, and rest in travel; produce constantly and consume as much. And they ask for nothing better either for themselves or for their children.

Such a disposition of heart and mind can be explained by manifold contributing causes: here are those which seem evident to me:

The law of primogeniture, and the great number of children: as a consequence everybody is required to help him or herself and acquire, at an early age, the idea that he must be the artisan of his own fortune. But to explain the great number of children it is necessary to admit, among other causes, greater courage in the parents than in France, and especially, less sensibility. Greater courage, for they are less afraid of the worries entailed by a numerous progeny and the obligation to continue working in their old age; less sensibility, since they accept in advance the idea that their sons will have to suffer and strive, and their daughters leave them for ever to make their own lives as wives in India or Australia. Whereas a French father's dearest wish is to save his sons from the miseries he has undergone himself. As to his daughters, he stints himself to give them a dowry and could never

* Surely a curious story: presumably he was ordained in the Church of England. But he can have founded a chapel only as some kind of non-conformist. The story, indeed, is full of gaps, and vaguely sinister! E. H.

bear the idea of having half a dozen out as governesses, or of getting rid of them by exporting them.

The second cause is the climate: I always come back to this, for there is no more powerful influence. Consider the fact that the same fog, the same humidity existed — and even worse — under the Saxon Kings; and that the English race has lived in it for as long as we can follow it into the past, in its first habitat on the banks of the Elbe and in Jutland. One of my friends tells me that in Manchester last winter, the gas lights had to be kept burning constantly for five days in one principal hotel of that city. At noon there was not enough daylight to write by. The fog still continued on the sixth day, but the supply of gas gave out. During six months of the year, and on many days during the other six, this country seems to have been made for wild ducks.

After having seen London, country houses, all that is comfortable and all that is luxurious, I said to an Englishman:

"Your drawing room and your dining room are perfect; now I must see the kitchen —" meaning their industries, Manchester, Birmingham, Liverpool — "How do your workers live?"

"They work; what else could they do in such streets, and in such fog?"

The melancholy and severity of nature in this country cuts out at the very roots any possibility of a voluptuous conception of life. The ideal, under these skies, is a dry, stoutly roofed, well-heated house; evenings tête-à-tête with a faithful wife, who must be a good house-wife and neatly dressed. The rosy cheeks of well washed children in clean linen. The sight of a good, clear fire, an abundance of furniture, utensils, ornaments useful or otherwise agreeable, well set out, well polished, and whose presence reminds a man that he is protected against rough weather and worry, provided with everything his body and mind may need.

Whereas in Provence, Italy, the southern countries generally, the ideal is to be idling in the shade, on a café terrace, with a mistress, and looking out over a noble landscape, among the scent of roses, the sight of statues, and the sound of music. To appreciate and savour the beauties of light, warm air, delicious fruits and the architecture of landscape, with delicacy, it is only necessary for the senses to be receptive, open. But here the climate bottles them up and by keeping them so, blunts them.

Take an example on a small scale: at Marseilles or Milan, a poor person can buy a pound of grapes worthy of the table of the gods, for a ha'penny, and thereby acquire *the idea of exquisite*

61

*sensation;* by what conceivable means could such an idea occur
to a mind whose associated palate knows nothing beyond a bit of
meat and a glass of 'gin' or 'ale'? That way being barred to him,
man does not dream of refined, sensuous enjoyment; he would not,
even, be able to experience it, for he has become hardened, stif-
ened, has accommodated himself to the exigencies and in-
clemencies of his environment. Consequently his thoughts take a
different direction, and it is well that they do, for he would not
have the time to idle, taste, enjoy, even if he had the inclination.
Cold, rain, mud, bad weather, and ungrateful soil are enemies
against which he is obliged to struggle unceasingly. Moreover his
organism consumes more and has need of stronger refreshment, it
could not survive without spirits and much red meat. *

A poor person is not wretched in the south, the best and most
beautiful things in life are his for nothing, necessities are very
cheap, and those necessities so many fewer in the south than in
the north: abundance of food, artificial light, fire, a sound and
well closed house, new linen at frequent intervals, and so forth.
So that here the poor are painful to see: nothing could be more
dreadful than the suit, shirt or face of an English beggar; on
Sundays in Hyde Park, when a family of paupers sits down on
the grass, it is like a blemish. You must either have twenty
thousand pounds in the funds, here, or cut your throat — that is
the notion which constantly comes to my mind and I am frequenty
reminded of it by the small poster advertisement which appears
in omnibuses and announces that "Mappin's celebrated razors
cost only one shilling." The English themselves are of this opinion
and commonly say, by way of excuse, that, with them, poverty
is generally speaking, degrading. It is to some extent to avoid
falling into such degradation that the English strive so fiercely
after riches. They prize wealth so highly because it is, in their
eyes, the accompaniment to, sustenance for and condition of
morality, education and all the attributes which make a gentleman.
It is under this unremitting lash that every man goes forward,
drawing his load after him. And use turns into a need: even when
he has reached his goal, he still goes on pulling and, in default

* Taine is, of course, exaggerating: the soil of nearly all England was and
is far less "ungrateful" than that of the "southern countries". But he was
essentially an urban man and, as will appear, these prejudices did not prevent
him observing the extreme fertility of English farming land with his usual
keenness, in due course. And, of course, spirits were unknown to the poor
before the 18th, to the rich before the 17th centuries, respectively. E. H.

Fig. 11  *Basket-woman in Covent Garden*

of a load of his own, harnesses himself to that of his parish, his association, or the State.

Another motive: he has need of rugged action; his instincts are militant and it follows that he must have something to overcome, vanquish and so assure himself that he is accomplishing a difficult task. There are a thousand pointers to this state of mind: I have already noted the need for physical exercise, the long walks undertaken by young ladies, the universal practice of equitation; the cold and humid climate calls for brisk, muscular movement. To this add their innumerable pleasure yachts, their dangerous point-to-point races, and their hunting. I was told of an Ambassador who, when young, spent the whole of his summers in Scotland: on six days a week he went shooting, with a friend, in the Highlands, sleeping in the open, returning to the house on Saturday evenings but only to set out again at four o'clock on the Monday morning. Many young men and others not so young go salmon-fishing in Norway every year, or shooting buck in Canada or elephant at the Cape. As for journeys full of dangers and 'hardships', even women undertake them, and alone; I could quote fifty examples, and besides it is well known.

Now apply this need for action and striving to trade and the professions: it will supply the energy necessary for bearing the fatigues and servitudes of such labour, especially if one takes into account two circumstances which greatly lighten the principal burden of modern work, that is boredom. One is that phlegmatic temperament which eliminates brain-waves, improvisations, petty emotional distractions, thus enabling a man to function with the regularity of a machine. The other is the lack of nervous delicacy, their acquired insensibility; they are accustomed to dulled sensations and that eliminates the need for keen and varied pleasures and prevents a man from rebelling against the monotony of his work. I saw this very clearly in France when I followed, in a fabric-printing factory, the work of two English operatives among thirty French ones. They had long, cold, expressionless faces, they worked, steadily, without haste, making no more than the bare minimum of movement necessary, never showed any animation, but never relaxed; they were working as well after ten hours as they had been in the first hour.

To sum up, they have no outlet for their faculties but useful action; they live under a tyranny of manifold needs which only work can provided for; they have a natural inclination for physical and moral striving; they have no aversion to monotonous and insipid toil. In all these attributes there are the makings of strong and patient workers in any career, whether manual or liberal.

As a very natural result this character has become the ideal in England; for every nation takes the type which best manifests the national genius and serves the national needs, consecrates it, and puts it on a pedestal. That is why public opinion, the common conscience, says to every Englishman: "Work, take a hand in some useful undertaking; if you do not you are not a man and have no right to self-respect." Here, then, is another driving-force, offshoot of those already examined, yet distinct from them, and of capital importance. For it is an idea, a moral and mental convinction: now, it is a fact that in this country pure ideas, convictions, opinions arrived at by the reasoning mind are far more important and far more efficacious than they are elsewhere.

Nothing could be more rare than to find a man dominated by these things among the lively, southern peoples. It seems to me that a Frenchman, for example, reasons for the sake of reasoning; it gives him pleasure to string a series of ideas together, and if the resultant conclusion is new and has a wide bearing, his pleasure is extreme. But there he stops: he has provided himself with a beautiful spectacle to contemplate, and that of the highest order, and that is enough for him. Whereas for a Germanic, and notably an English mind, a conclusion slowly and reasonably arrived at is no more than a point of departure: it becomes a principle, a *spring of action*, one of the forces, often the greatest, governing his behaviour. He does not, like the opposite type, act on impulse, on the spur of the moment, as a result of strong feelings which reflection has left unimpaired and which find expression in a hot will to action. In his case such impulses are relegated to the background, and it is his *idea* which takes first place and determines his course of action. Having admitted as a principle that a man should make an effort of some kind, and make himself useful, he has no need of any more immediate motive for doing so.

I mentioned above the case of Mr. W——. Concerning those small articles of Greek antiquity, which he had undertaken to deal with for the Dictionary, the reason he gave for doing so was, "It had to be done." In the same spirit Arthur Young spent two years on horseback visiting every part of France in the interests of agriculture. Frenchmen to whom he explained this had difficulty in understanding. From their point of view, the thing was all very fine *in words:* but actually to leave one's family and business and undertake so long a task, with so remote an outcome, and so uncertain of success, alone, unbidden, from personal choice and for a coldly abstract idea — all this seemed to them strange.

The same causes as those cited above will explain the power of an idea, especially a moral idea, in this country. In the first place, given the phlegmatic and hardened temperament, rival influences are less powerful. There are fewer forces due to vivacity of mind, digressions and impetuosity to break the line of uniform behaviour. Furthermore, the attraction of the pleasures of the senses is less, less powerful and less seductive. Finally, when one has voluntarily set out to accomplish something; when, upon reflection the end has been judged noble; and, upon trial, the means difficult, then pride and the militant spirit lead to an obstinate persistence until the end is achieved. This is the sense of duty; and the English say that this, at all levels, is one of the essential traits of their national character.

This being established, let us examine a few types. If, at eight o'clock in the morning, you stand at the exit from a railway station, you will see people arriving from the country for their day's work; or if you walk along a busy street, you will be struck by the number of faces which manifest this type of cold, obstinate determination. They walk upright and stiff, with geometrical movements, without looking to one side or the other, undistracted from their course, entirely taken up with their own business, like so many automata driven by springs. The long, bony face, the pale complexion often with a shade that is yellowish or leaden, the rigid look in their eyes — everything, down to the tall, black hats, strong boots, rolled umbrella carried in a certain way, suggest a man who is not to be touched by ideas of pleasure or elegance, and solely concerned with getting through a great deal of work as quickly as possible.

Sometimes you may see Pitt's physiognomy reproduced — the lean, impassive, imperious face, the eyes pale but burning, and a glance that flashes like a sword; such a man is of finer mettle, but his will is none the less incisive and harsh; it is even more so, for if the others are iron, he is tempered steel. And the effect is at its height when this expression is met with in the face of a girl: this I have seen several times and speech, accent, thought were of the same kind. At the end of two minutes' conversation one was aware of the cutting edge of a knife. No doubt it is women of this kind who, by way of an outing, go alone to Alexandria or Khartoum; or who, as philanthropists, conduct parties of emigrant women from London to Australia.

Here is a copy of a note which I made after an earlier visit to this country, the substance of which has been confirmed for me by the present visit.

"If we except the handsome men and beautiful women to be

66

seen where people of fashion show themselves *, the typical Englishman or woman is, four times out of five, as follows: among women the capacity to put up with a great deal is apparent, and their faces frequently show that they have had to do so — hence a look of resignation, or dullness, or obstinacy which makes people say, 'she has made up her mind'. Among men, the capacity for a great deal of action, for sustained effort; their faces bear the mark of prolonged attention (to work), in drawn features, an absence of softness and thoughtfulness; the jaws are firmly clenched, the face impassive; 'steadfastness'."

The excess of this faculty, the excesses of this way of life are everywhere apparent, and notably among the poor. Numerous are the faces among workmen and 'day labourers' in the country which are deeply lined, very pale, worn out by fatigue, making one think of those old cab-horses one sees standing patient and inert, their legs splayed, while the rain pours down their lean old flanks. Lank, greying hair, rather sparse; the mouth hanging half-open as if the muscles had given way of their own accord; the eyes have an almost sightless look of indifference. The man is still functioning but it seems as if this must be due simply to momentum: he has become a machine. When some slight expression does return to his face, he has the look of a man waking from a bad dream.

'The wear and tear of life', the exhaustion of a creature harnessed to too heavy a burden, overdriven and harassed, is even more apparent in the women. Sometimes, in the course of visiting them, and in response to a question, one may see their lips trying to remember how to smile. But at the sight of that attempt at a smile one turns one's head away and feels a lump in the throat.

4. The strong, the phlegmatic, the hard worker: many varieties are grouped about these three types according to differences in class, education, trade or profession, sex and age; and these again are complicated by the greater or lesser degree of purity and intensity in which the typical attributes are present. But all this is no more than a sketch; it must now be verified and corrected, we must go deeper and take care never to lose touch with the living reality.

* *les beaux et les belles des promenades.*

# CHAPTER THREE

# MANNERS, CUSTOMS AND DOMESTIC LIFE

❊

PRESENT AS a guest at numerous dinner and luncheon parties, and as a visitor in country houses belonging to members of the gentry and the nobility.

Drawing-rooms and dinners are the same here as they are everywhere else: there is a certain level of luxury and elegance which is common to the rich all over Europe. The only very striking difference at a dinner or evening party here is the remarkable freshness of the women's complexions, and also their *toilette*. The colour and texture of their skin is dazzling. Yesterday I was placed beside a young lady whose neck and shoulders seemed made of snow, or rather of mother o' pearl: this extraordinary whiteness is so superlative that, to my eyes, it is not alive. Pink dress, a crown of red flowers, green trimmings, and a gold necklace, like some savage queen: they rarely have any sense of colour.

Grand affair at the house of a cabinet minister: the staircase was monumental and the rooms lofty, princely. But this is rare: as a rule their houses are not well contrived for such receptions. When the party is numerous the two drawing-rooms on the first floor are inadequate: very rich people who are obliged to maintain the dignity of their position throw open two floors of the house to their guests, and the ladies, for want of room and to get a breath of air, often sit out on the stairs.

Today numerous persons of consequence were pointed out to me, but I have no right to describe them here. Several of the girls and young matrons were very beautiful, and everybody very splendidly dressed. Several of the ladies had their hair full of diamonds and their shoulders, fully displayed, had that dazzling whiteness which I mentioned above: the petals of a lily or the sheen of white satin are nothing to it. But there were also many stork-like figures in gauze and tulle, many lean hags with prominent noses and nut-cracker jaws: ugliness, here, is uglier than with us.

As for the men, their physical type and facial expression are ill-suited to such surroundings: they are often too tall, too strong, too much the automaton, with dull or wild-looking eyes, and angular or lumpy features. I met two Frenchmen from the Embassy there; how pleasant their intelligent, cheerful, lively faces were, by contrast!

One's introduction ensures a welcome of the most perfect courtesy. The French believe, but quite wrongly, that they have a monopoly of such politeness: in this respect all well-bred Europeans are alike.

Another evening party, at Lady S ——'s. One of the girls played the piano and sang a Norwegian song; she sang it well, with much spirit and expression, which is by no means common. According to my musical friends the English are even less gifted in matters of music than we are. Consequently, on this subject, they are able to entertain some singular illusions. Thus Miss B ——, having ruthlessly flayed a sonata, her performance was generally applauded: her mother informed me, 'She has quite a genius for it'. Two of the girls present were beautiful and graceful, but with too much pink in their colouring, and too many shrill green trimmings to their gowns, which was very distressing to the eyes.

On the other hand, how simple and affable they are! On two out of three occasions when one talks with a woman here, one feels at ease, touched, almost happy: their greeting is kindly and friendly; and such calm, kindly gentle smiles! No ulterior motives; their intentions, expression, everything, are open, natural and cordial. You feel far more at ease than with a Frenchwoman; there is none of that vague fear that you are being judged, made fun of. You do not feel yourself to be in the presence of a sharp wit, a keen and cutting mind apt to cut you in four pieces at any moment; nor of a lively, demanding, petulant imagination requiring you to produce piquant anecdotes, to shine, amuse and flatter, to be ready to purvey all these nice things or be left standing, abandoned because you have no sweets to offer. Conversation here is neither a duel nor a competition: you can speak your thoughts as they are and without embellishment; you have the right to be yourself, ordinary. You may even talk to a woman on serious topics without boring her or seeming tedious; you may receive sensible and positive information from her, and discuss things with her as with a man. Here are two conversations which were noted down by me on the spot.

Dinner at 'Mistress' T ——'s; her two nieces dined with us. Very simple, schoolgirlish dresses. The elder hardly raised her eyes throughout the meal, or did so briefly and shyly. This was not silliness: after dinner I chatted with them very easily for an hour. Their silence is due to nothing but shyness, a childish modesty, the simple wild timidity of a startled doe. When you speak to them they blush. For my part I like this youthfulness of soul: a young girl should not have worldly assurance and manners too early: our French girls are flowers too quickly in full bloom.

They spend the winter and summer in the country, twenty miles from town. At least two hours walking every day; then they work, all the family sitting together, or listen to someone reading aloud. Drawing, music, visiting the poor, reading (they subscribe to a 'circulating library'). They read novels, travel books, history and a few sermons. On Sundays they go to Church and teach a Sunday School class of the village children. They are not bored and do not want to be out in the world.

Last winter they went to France, and consider Frenchwomen 'very agreeable', amiable, with cheerful, engaging manners. But they were surprised and hurt by the close and continuous watch which is kept over girls in our country. They are much more independent in England. Even in London a girl is free to go out by herself, or at least with her sister. There are, however, some excesses in this respect: Mrs. T——'s nieces censured those 'fast girls' who ride to hounds, treat men as comrades, and even smoke.

Everything about these two girls was ordinary — education, mind, character, faces; they are healthy and have the freshness of youth, no more. They were 'average girls'. But this modesty and simplicity, health and common sense are what is required to make a good wife, who will be satisfied with her household, will bear her children without being ill, will be faithful to her husband and will not ruin him with dress-makers' bills.

The principal point to notice is the absense of coquetteries: I will begin by pointing out the excesses of this quality, its unfavourable aspect. In the course of the winter I was in a Paris drawing-room on one occasion, placed between a fat, bald, flabby red-faced man, a kinsman of a highly-placed Englishman, and his sixteen-year-old daughter. The girl had a gently pretty face, but what ignorance of dress! She wore thick brown gloves, her hair was curled and tied back and not given any shine *(non lustrés)*, she had on a sort of ill-fitting cassock-like white dress, so that her figure looked like a faggot tied up in a sack. The whole evening she was as mute as Cinderella among the splendours and surpassing elegance of the beauties and dresses all about her.

Here, in St James's Park, at the Exhibition, in picture galleries, many pretty and well dressed young women wear spectacles. I need not mention a number of other, similar traits. It is quite clear to me that, compared with Frenchwomen they have much less of that feeling which makes a woman carry herself at all times and in any company as if she were on parade and presenting arms.

As a result, natural behaviour is less constrained and breaks through more readily. I was staying recently in the country thirty miles from London, and went for a long walk with the daughters of the house, which included climbing quite a steep hill. The girls, still very young, were real little goats, for ever leaping and cavorting, even when we were climbing stiff, stony slopes. Exuberance, full freedom given to the flow of sap and animal strength; nothing feminine about them. In the carriage, before arriving at our point of departure, their noisy, lively chatter, bright eyes, and above all the energy and intensity of their utterance suggested happy, English 'boys' on holiday. The youngest had a lovely colour in her cheeks, like an apple. * Both of them had strong jaw-lines and big feet. Miss Charlotte (fifteen) told me she would readily walk twenty miles. They have learnt German from their 'nurse' but do not yet know French —

"Yet you have a French governess?"

"Yes, but then we're so stupid!"

Which was followed by a burst of laughter! Certainly they are not troubled by conceit; they never dream of playing a part. Tall and well-developed, the daughters of a rich nobleman, they are still children; not one of their ideas or gestures betrays the woman. No precociousness, nor worldliness; these two things are associated, and give rise to a number of consequential qualities.

I can vouch from personal experience for the great degree of liberty they enjoy: I see many of them riding in Hyde Park of a morning with no other company than that of a servant. When staying in the country I had only been there two days when I was asked to escort one of the young girls of the household to a place a mile distant. S ——, who has spent a year here in England, finds this free and candid intercourse charming. A gentleman to whom he was introduced said,

"Come home with me and make the acquaintance of my daughters."

They are comrades, as men might be but more amiable and polite. One can go riding with them, accompany them to 'archery

* *Pomme d'api:* This apple is cream flushed with rose pink. E. H.

71

meetings', talk familiarly with them about everything, or almost everything, and joke and laugh with them without ulterior motives. Impossible even for the most conceited ass to treat them otherwise than as sisters.

Two Frenchmen of my acquaintance who were in Manchester, were dining out: at eleven o'clock they were asked to escort to their homes two girls who were among the guests. The four of them took a cab and drove for half-an-hour: they chatted gaily together, without any awkwardness or feeling of disturbance on either side.

Thanks to these manners and customs (*moeurs*), a man, however hardened and accustomed to life's ugliest side, is bound to keep some small corner of his soul open to delicate and poetic feelings. In France this is something wanting: an Englishman who has visited our country is surprised and shocked by the insolent way men stare at women in Paris, and do not make way for them on the pavement. You have to have lived abroad to realise to what extent our manners and way of talking are, in this respect, displeasing and even offensive: foreigners consider our attitude to women no better than that of a commercial traveller — fatuous, conceited, rascally and smutty.

The fact is we do not readily experience the feeling of respect: sex, social station and education do not, in France, create such wide differences as they do in other countries. Moreover, apart from the fact that among us people of all kinds and both sexes *are* more nearly equal, they also have more need to feel themselves so.

Dined out at F——'s. The ladies told me about the education received by girls here.

In well-to-do or wealthy families they all learn French, German and Italian, as a rule from childhood, from foreign nursemaids or governesses. French usually comes first: nearly all of them speak it fluently and some without any accent; I have already mentioned the only exception I have met with. They read Dante, Manzoni, Schiller and Goethe, our own classics, Chateaubriand and one or two moderns. Some of them learn a little Latin, which is of use to them in teaching their own children later on, or their young brothers.

Much natural history, botany, mineralogy, geology: they have a taste for all things natural. In the country, at the sea-side, in their frequent journeys, they have opportunities to see minerals, plants and shells, and to form collections. This fits in well with that English habit which consists in gathering a provision of facts; as a result they are more and better educated than our own girls. Another motive is that many girls do not marry and must be trained in advance for some employment. Lady M —— tells me of a family in her neighbourhood where there are five unmarried daughters, all handsome: the two eldest are thirty-five and thirty-six respectively. The trouble is they have been brought up to luxury but have almost no dowry.

A gentleman will often give his daughter a dowry amounting to no more than his eldest son, and heir's, future income for one year; furthermore he insists that the gentleman who marries his daughter make a 'settlement' on her, two, three or four hundred pounds a year, an income entirely at her own disposal once she is married, and which will constitute her 'pin-money'. This requirement discourages many suitors; besides, it is accepted here that one ought to marry for love, there must be a decided inclination. Now it frequently happens that a girl either experiences no such inclination, or fails to inspire one. Consequently many girls miss the bus and become (sic) 'spinsters'. They are to be met with in most families: but the condition of aunt is very well established. They help to bring up the children, take charge of some department of the household, the fruit bottling or the linen, make herbals*, paint in water colours, read, write, and become learned. A number of them write moral novels, sometimes very good ones: Miss Yonge, Miss Kavanagh, Miss Brontë, the authoress of *John Halifax* (sic), Miss Thackeray, and others are all well known. Talent is not uncommon among these 'authoresses some of them are of the first order, Mistress (sic) Gaskell, G. Eliot, Elizabeth Browning; the last two possess genius.

To original works we must add translations; many works in German and French have been translated, and well translated, by women. Others write for the magazines, compose short, popular treatises, join associations, hold classes for the children of the poor. It is always the same question — how to find a use for their abilities, or acquire a talent which shall be a remedy for boredom. This is true even of the highest in rank: consider the Royal Family's occupations; the Queen and her daughters present

* Albums of pressed plants? Taine can hardly mean literally herbals; much less herbaria. E. H.

water-colours, engravings and drawings executed by themselves to be sold for charity. Prince Albert was one of the best-informed, most active men in the Kingdom. Everybody undertakes something, specialises in something, works at some agricultural or scientific improvement, some work of charity, or some foundation.

So that life is earnest and all, even young girls, know that they must prepare themselves for it and provide themselves with some ability or other. N ——, who comes to England every year, was visiting an old friend, a wealthy man and father of a family. This friend told him,

"I am much disturbed. My daughter Jane is twenty-four, has no husband in mind, often shuts herself up in the library, and is beginning to read weighty books."

"What dowry are you giving her?"

"Two thousand pounds."

"And your sons?"

"The elder will have the estate, the younger a mine which brings in two thousand a year."

"Give Miss Jane five thousand."

This advice showed Miss Jane's father the way: he gave the girl £5000. Now she is married, and has a baby, she was made for motherhood and it would have been a pity had she been obliged to become a learned 'spinster' with spectacles on her nose. Suitors did not offer for her because her parents' house-keeping was on too grand a scale. But what I admire in all this is the girl's cool common sense and courage; seeing herself at a dead-end she changed her course without a murmur and set to work to study.

In not one of the London or country houses I have visited have I ever noticed a fashion journal. One of my English friends who has lived in France replied (when I told him this), that well-bred women do not read such rubbish. Indeed, there is a special Review at the very opposite extreme, the *British Women's Review*. The number I have before me contains documents and letters on emigration to Australia, articles on State education in France, and other, equally serious, matters. No fiction, no chatty column of theatrical gossip, no fashion notes, etc. Everything is serious and solid. Consider what a contrast with us! You will see, in any provincial *château*, fashion journals with coloured * illustrations, drawings of the latest thing in hats, explanations of one or other embroidery stitch, sentimental short stories, sugary compliments paid to the reader, and above all the correspondence between the

* *enluminées:* it would seem they were hand-coloured. E. H.

editress and her subscribers on the last page, a masterpiece of grotesqueness and insipidity. It is shameful that a human intelligence can digest such a diet. It is better to have an ill-made dress than an empty head.

Here are the titles of some of the articles written by women in the *Transactions of the National Association for the Promotion of Social Sciences: Education through the Workhouses* by Louisa Twining; *District Schools for the poor in England* by Barbara Collett; *Application of the principles of education in schools for the lower classes* by Mary Carpenter; *Present State of the Colony of Mettray* by Florence Hill; *Hospital Statistics* by Florence Nightingale; *The Condition of working women in England and France* by Bessie Parkes; *Slavery in America and its influence on Great Britain* by Sarah Remond; *Improvement of Nurses in agricultural districts* by Mistress (sic) Wiggins; *Report of the Society founded to furnish work to women* by Jane Crowe —— etc.

The majority of these authoresses are not married. Several of them are the secretaries of active associations of which the Review I have been quoting from is the central organ. One of these associations provides women with work; another visits the sick; another visits workhouses. All the articles are instructive and useful. The custom of holding classes, visiting the poor, conversing with men, discussion, study, personal experience of the facts have together borne fruit; these women know how to observe and to reason, they go to the bottom of things, and they understand the true principles of betterment.

"Above all and as our first aim," writes Mary Carpenter, "we must develop and direct the child's will, enroll himself as the principal soldier, the most efficacious of our co-operators in the education we are giving him." We cannot, she maintains, be corrected nor perfected but by ourselves: initiative, personal effort, 'self-government' are indispensable; the moral rule must not be applied from outside, but must well up from within us.

Whoever has read English novels knows with what precision and truth these authoresses delineate character; it often happens that a lady who has lived in the country, in a confined circle, and taken up with domestic cares, finds herself obliged to write a novel to earn her living, when it transpires that she knows the human heart better than a professional psychologist. To be well-informed, learned, useful, to acquire convictions, communicate them to others, to employ one's abilities and employ them well, all this is something. You may laugh if you like, and say that such customs make school-marms, female pedants, blue-stockings, and not women. As you wish; but take a look at our own empty idleness in the provinces, the boredom of our ladies, the life of an elderly spinster in France, given up to breeding canaries, spreading gossip, doing crochet work and going to every Church service.

Moreover, in England not all these ladies are pedants. I know four or five ladies or girls who write; they are none the less gracious and natural: most of the authoresses whose names I have mentioned are, according to my friends, domesticated women of very simple manners. I have named two who have genius: a great French painter, whose name I could give you, and who spent several days with both of them, never even discovered that they were women of talent. Not once during twenty hours of conversation did the least sign of the author appear, not the slightest suggestion of a need to talk of themselves or their books. M ——, invited to stay at a country house, discovered that his hostess knew far more Greek than he did, begged her pardon and confessed himself beaten: whereupon, as a joke, she wrote his English sentence of excuses in Greek. Bear in mind that this Hellenist is a woman of the world, and, indeed, of fashion: furthermore, she has nine daughters, two nurses, two governesses, a proportionate number of servants, a great house to run and frequent and numerous house guests. In all of which she maintains perfect order; never a suggestion of trouble or fuss, the whole mechanism seems to run itself.

Here, then, are combinations of contrasting faculties which may well give us to think. It is too readily believed in France that if a woman ceases to be a doll, she ceases to be a woman.

Conversation with a number of Englishmen on the subject of marriage: they have all lived abroad and I believe them to have been talking impartially; besides, their conclusions agree with each other.

An English girl wants to marry only for love *(inclination);* she creates a romance in her imagination, and this dream is part of her pride, of her chastity. Thus some of them, and those of the highest character, would consider that they were sinking below the requisite standard of behaviour if they were to marry without feeling the enthusiasm proper to an absolute preference. To marry is to give oneself wholly and for ever. For examples of this deep feeling, go to the novels written by women, notably *John Halifax Gentleman* and others by the same authoress. These are the theories of a pure, exclusive spirit which seems to have been out in the world without being, I will not say soiled, but tainted by it.

But in her private romance the English girl is still English, that is to say positive and practical. She does not dream effusions, does not dream of sentimental walks hand-in-hand beneath the moon, but of her share in some work. She wants to be her husband's helper and useful associate in long journeys, difficult undertakings, all sorts of enterprises, even dangerous or tedious ones. Such, for instance, as Mrs Livingstone and Lady Samuel Baker (sic); the first crossed Africa, the second went to the source of the Nile and very nearly died of it. I have met the English bishop of the Sunda Isles, a country of wild beasts and cannibals; his poor wife bears in her face the stigmata of that terrible climate. A girl of the neighbourhood (where I am staying), rich and of good family, is at present engaged in making preparations for her wedding; they include crating a piano. The man she is marrying is taking her to Australia, and she will return only once, in five or six years, to see her aged parents.

Another young lady, very frail and delicate: her husband is in the Punjab (salary £6000 a year, plus £1200 allowances); she has been two years back in Europe for a form of laryngitis which will recur the moment she returns to India. They have four young children; at two years of age they are sent back to England, for the Indian climate kills them, and there are, in this country, whole boarding-schools full of English children whose parents are in India.

Very often a 'lady', daughter of a marquis or a baronet, with a dowry of seventy-five or eighty thousand francs, marries a simple 'mister' and immediately finds herself living, of her own free will, in a state of life a great deal inferior to what she has been used to: she adapts herself to it.

The reverse of the coin is husband-hunting. Worldly and vulgar characters are by no means above this, and certain girls use, and abuse, their freedom to get themselves an establishment. A rich and noble young man is much run after. Too effusively welcomed, flattered, tempted, provoked, he becomes cautions and is consstantly on his guard. It is not so in France: girls are kept under too much restraint to take the initiative; in our country the game never turns hunter.

As a rule dowries are very small. I have been told of several families where the eldest son has from a hundred to two hundred thousand pounds; the daughters receive from three to five thousand. Consequently in order to marry they must inspire a man with passion. Many never marry, as a result of a frustrated inclination, and then they live with their eldest brother.

Every Englishman has, in the matter of marriage, a romantic spot in his heart. He imagines a 'home', with the woman of his choice, the pair of them alone with their children. That is his own little universe, closed to the world. So long as he has not achieved it he is ill at ease, contrary, therefore, to the Frenchman, for whom marriage is the end of something, a *pis-aller*. He is often obliged to wait, especially if he is a younger son, because he is not earning enough 'to maintain his wife'. He goes to India or Australia, works with all his might, comes home and marries; here the passions are deep and tenacious. When an Englishman is in love, one of my hosts here assured me, there is nothing he is not capable of doing. Thackeray has shown the intensity and persistence of that feeling very well in his portrait of Major Dobbins (sic) in his love for Amelia *(Vanity Fair)*. He waits fifteen years without hope because, for him, there is only one woman in the world.

This state of mind entails much silent agony, prolonged secret tragedies. Many young men lose their hearts in this way, and prolonged chastity, habits of taciturn concentration, a capacity for feeling greater and less diffuse than with us, carry their passion to an extreme point. And frequently it comes to nothing because their love is not returned, or because there is some too great difference of rank, or because they have not enough money to maintain a family which is very costly here. Whereupon they go half out of their minds, travel to distract their attention, go to the ends of the earth. One such who was quoted to me as an example was jilted for a rival who had a title; for two years his family feared for his reason. He went to China and Australia; now he fills a position of consequence, he has been made a baronet, and is in charge of very important business; but he is not married, and from time to time he slips away, goes off on a walking tour in order to be alone and not be obliged to talk to anyone.

I have already made it clear that young people of both sexes meet and mingle freely and without surveillance: they are thus able to study and get to know each other as much as they like during four, five months, or longer, ride and talk together throughout several seasons running, in the country. When the young man has made up his mind he begins by declaring himself to the girl, only asking for her parents' permission thereafter. This is the opposite to the French custom: in France a man would consider himself wanting in delicacy if he said one word, however vague, to the girl, before speaking to her parents. On this point the English censure us, and make fun of our hasty weddings before a notary-public. Yet C——, who is English and knows France well, admits that their love matches frequently end in discord, and our *mariages de convenance* in a happy union.

Nearly always the wife's dowry is put into the hands of 'trustees', who take responsibility for its management and pay only the income to the couple in question; as a rule this income constitutes the wife's pocket money, but out of which she has to clothe herself and her children. Her fortune thus becomes a sort of endowment, safe from anything which may happen to the husband (or his business). This precaution is taken because the law assimilates all a wife's property in her husband's, and without such an arrangement she would begin her married life absolutely penniless, she can own nothing on her own account and is, in the eyes of the law, a minor. This was one of the reasons which drove Mr Stuart Mill to protest so vigorously against the subjection of women. And they are, indeed, subjected in this country, before the law, in religion, in manners and customs, far more rigorously than with us. A woman's husband is her lord, and very often he takes that title seriously. Since the wife contributes hardly any money to the *ménage,* and her little nest-egg is set aside, the husband considers that he has the right to tell her nothing of his business. Sometimes she does not even know what he does, how he earns the money he brings home; he gives her so much a month to run the house, and renders no account of the rest. Whether he speculates, builds, sells or buys, it is no business of hers: often a woman finds that ruin has overtaken them without her ever having had the slightest warning of it. She is no more than an intendant and her business is to look after her house and her children.

More often than not she resigns herself to this rôle: by conscience and by training she is gentle and submissive. Nevertheless, as one of my friends assures me, this inequality has serious drawbacks: the husband is often a tyrant, and if he dies his widow, kept all her life in ignorance and dependance, is not capable, as in France, of understanding his business, governing his children, and becoming, herself, the head of the family.

Marriage is regarded with profound respect and public opinion concerning it is rigid. Read, for example, the kind of books and periodicals in which, in France, writers allow themselves the greatest measure of licence, for example novels and comic papers: adultery is very rarely excused; even in the freedom of private conversation between men it is treated as a crime. There are some hitches in the regard for this rule about which I shall have more to say, among the class of 'tradesmen', and among certain of the nobility of the second order, people of fashion *, who travel and whose *mœurs* are modelled on those of the continent. But in the great body of the nation, among well brought-up people, wives are almost invariably faithful.

C —— tells me that I may be here for eighteen months and frequent every known *salon* without encountering a single exception: only one is talked of in the very highest class. One would have met with more fifty years ago, at the time of Lord Byron and of Alfieri. Since then received opinion has become strict, and the Queen has worked to that end with all her might, first by her own example, secondly by her influence. She excluded ladies of questionable reputation from her court. The whole urgency and pressure of business of the Crimean War were required to make her tolerate, at Windsor and under the same roof as herself, a statesman with a reputation as a 'profligate'. Another safeguard is fear of publicity and the newspapers.

In this article our loose and easy ways shock them extremely. C —— tells me that in a Paris club he heard one man of the world say to another,

"So, my dear fellow, your wife has got herself a lover?"

·This remark seemed to him monstrous: and he is right.

A book like Balzac's *Physiologie du mariage* would shock the public enormously, and *The Society for the repression of vice* would perhaps take action against it; but probably it would not have found a publisher. As for our ordinary novels, a liberal periodical, *The National Review,* cannot find words strong enough in which to condemn them. "Ignominy without name, the morals of petty speculators and women of the streets." † They forget three things: first that such disorders are not customary in France excepting in the class of fashionable *parvenus;* they very rarely touch the rich or well-to-do bourgeoisie which has strong family traditions. Secondly, in the provinces, everybody's business is known to everybody else and the much-feared power of gossip acts as

* *fashionable* (sic).

† Re-translated from Taine's French. E. H.

a sort of policeman. Finally, the French display what foreigners hide, they have a horror of hypocrisy and prefer flaunting their vice to concealing it.

According to my friends the good behaviour of English ladies can be explained by the following causes:

1. They are more used to controlling their own behaviour, having been free since their childhood.

2. They are less open to illusions and romantic dreams, being used to the company of young men and having some knowledge of the world.

3. They are accustomed to think things over and have a fundamental common sense, because they have received a more serious education. They have studied several languages, glanced at several sciences, travelled at least in England and often abroad, heard their father discuss politics and other weighty matters with his friends. Besides which, Protestantism develops habits of reflection and reasoning. Finally, novels are all moral while, in charitable organisations, in their contacts with the poor, and their acquaintance with parish business, they have acquired some knowledge of real life.

4. They live for eight or nine months of the year in the country where they are more out of the way of temptation.

5. They have a great many children who take up their time. A full 'nursery', with its staff of nursery-maids and governesses, requires constant supervision.

6. They undertake all sorts of additional work: Sunday-school classes, needle-work schools for the poor in the country, visiting the poor, botany, mineralogy, collections of plants and butterflies, reading. Every family in easy circumstances living in the country receives, apart from *The Times* and diverse other substantial journals and reviews, numerous books sent to it by the 'circulating libraries'. Mudie's, the principal circulating library, buys one hundred and fifty thousand volumes a year: this firm took three thousand copies of *Livingstone's Journey in Africa*, two thousand four hundred of Macaulay's *History of England*. A quantity of serious books arrives in this way in the libraries of 'country seats', and is renewed from month to month. Among these books the commonest are works of political economy, natural history, history, and especially travel. Scores of these are published every year: the greatest pleasure for an Englishman, after actual travel, is to read about it: by this means he adds to his store of facts. The ladies have the same taste: all those whom I know have been

to France, Italy and Germany. A young matron with whom I was dining yesterday will spend the coming winter in Rome, the spring in Jerusalem. Those with delicate chests go to Cairo as readily as we go to Nice. During such journeys abroad they take notes, keep a diary, and when they return these are occasionally printed, while some are circulated in MS among the diarist's friends.

Thus they keep the world always at their finger tips, and I am acquainted with a number who take an intelligent and well-informed interest in the 'settlements' at Melbourne, the oil-wells of Pennsylvania, the Tai-ping rebellion in China, or the annual massacres in Dahomey. To all this must be added the great amount of physical exercise they take, and the talents they cultivate: every family has one or two water-colourists, and all the ladies of every family ride at least once a day. By all these occupations the mind is kept busy, and time filled up, which bars the way to unwholesome ideas.

Such are the auxiliaries of the moral principle, but we also take account of the principle itself. In France it is based on the feeling of honour; in England on the idea of duty. Now clearly the former is rather arbitrary. Honour does not mean the same thing to everybody: a man piques himself on being strict about one point, and thinks himself free to behave as he likes in everything else. He marks out a segment in the circle of bad actions and regards that as forbidden ground; but the segment varies, according to taste. For example, a man will be truthful in speech but not in writing, or vice versa. My honour is the thing I glory in, and I may choose to glory either in this or, on the other hand, that. Whereas the idea *duty* is strict and allows of hardly any compromise. An Englishwoman knows that when she was married she promised to be faithful, and the memory of this promise remains firmly anchored in her conscience. According to my friends the hold it takes is so strong that often, after a single backsliding, she breaks with her husband once and for all: her whole past sweeps over her like a flood, almost drowning her in grief and shame. Besides, she has not the flexibility of mind and the social dexterity necessary for reconciling her position and duties as a respectable married woman, with an intrigue: ambiguity is repugnant to her clear-cut character, the idea of sharing herself out revolts her, the necessity of living an incessant lie is intolerable to her. She therefore requires her lover to abduct her in order that she may be divorced.

❋

I shall continue to report conversations: I like nothing better than an evening passed in this wise, with one or two sincere, unprejudiced and benevolent interlocutors, men who know life and have travelled. National vanity is no bar: we talk to inform ourselves, not to compete or to shine. We do not stop short of quoting the small, characteristic fact, the precise and conclusive detail. Each of us contributes, as briefly as he can, the best from his personal experience, the choice items from long accumulated stores, his favourite dishes, as it were.

Here, then, are those of my friends: never was my mind better or more copiously nourished; I would sit questioning them and listening to them until one o'clock in the morning.

As a rule an Englishwoman is more manifestly healthy and beautiful than a Frenchwoman. The principal reason for this is hygiene: children ride, are a great deal out in the fresh air, do not dine with their parents, and do not eat sweets. Furthermore, their nerves are less agitated and their temperament is calmer, more enduring and less demanding. Nothing is more wearing nowadays than incessant wants incessantly frustrated. For example, in the Crimea, French wounded survived less often than English wounded because the latter did not resign themselves so quickly to dying. The principle holds even truer in the educated classes, especially among women: among them an unquiet or too ardent mind disturbs and taints the well of life; nowadays, a woman who wants to be healthy must accept her state of life.

On the other hand Englishwomen are less agreeable. An Englishwoman does not dress to please her husband, does not know how to make herself attractive, and has not the gift of being *coquette* and *piquante* in the privacy of her own home. * She is ignorant of many of the finer and more delicate graces. She considers all the little womanly means of arousing love and tenderness unworthy of her; and, still more often, has not the wit to invent them. She will put on pretty new dresses, be scrupulous as to her personal cleanliness, but no more; she is not attractive and one is quickly bored in her company. Imagine a very beautiful, rosy peach, moderately well-flavoured, beside an aromatic strawberry full of high flavour.

It is the same thing when we come to the other affections. B——

* This would appear to be so true that we have not even words for it. The dictionary fobs us off with words like 'dainty' and 'stylish'. If the reader does not know exactly what the French words mean, alas I cannot tell him in our language! E. H.

says they have more charm in France when they are strong and sincere. There is, in all things, the turn of hand or phrase, the manner, the subtle *nuance:* in the case of our feelings these are represented by little acts of forethought, attentions, certain words, the tone in which they are uttered, consideration, tact, all of which constantly renew and vary the sweet emotion itself.

C —— says that an Englishwoman is incapable of managing a *salon* as well as a Frenchwoman; I mean by *salon* what is meant by the word in Paris, a *salon* where one enjoys oneself. He hardly knows two or three of his countrywomen who could do it. English-women have not enough tact, quickness, or suppleness to adapt themselves to people and things, vary their welcome, understand half a word or a glance, slip in a word of praise, make every guest feel that his presence is important to his hostess. An English hostess is no more than affable, she has only goodwill and serenity. For my part I ask nothing better. But it is obvious that a woman of the world, who wants to make her drawing-room a meeting place frequented and eagerly sought by distinguished men in all walks of life, needs a more manifold and subtle talent. C —— has a great admiration for the ease with which our young matrons in France quickly learn the ways of high society. A month after her wedding a French woman knows how to receive any guest and do the honours of her house. Similarly, in the shop-keeping class, a newly-wed girl can take her place behind the counter with aplomb, at once grasps the technicalities of selling, can talk and smile and please the customers. I saw the contrast in a restaurant at Dieppe. The husband, a Frenchman, always eager and smiling, was con-stantly making the rounds of the tables, being polite to the customers, and seemed to take real plesure in serving them. The wife, English, sat stiff and serious, asked her guests, as they got up to leave.

"Havé-vo payé, Mosieur?" (sic). It never occurred to her that this question, and in such a tone, might give offence.

On the other hand my friends say that French politeness is more apparent than real, little better than an ornament, and that many foreigners are misled by it. They are welcomed by you, they think you are their friend, and are greatly surprised, three days later, to find that you have forgotten them. We make a show of being obliging but it is not convincing because there is no real feeling behind it, no natural kindness. It is no more than a matter of training, habit, a point of honour, and it is to some extent due to egoism. Our good manners are only a demonstration of our *savoir-vivre;* and we have a general feeling that we shall be done by as we do .For a quarter of an hour we give ourselves up to a pleasant atmosphere of mutual graciousness and deference; it is an agreeable interlude, we enjoy it, but in our eyes it does not mean anything. A courtesy calls for another as an anecdote calls for one in exchange. We pay, and are quits, and neither of the parties is under any more obligation to the other than that of raising his hat and smiling when they meet again.

The Englishman is more openly cordial and *serviable.* He will put himself out for a stranger who is introduced to him, run errands and take pains on his behalf. As far as I can tell from my own experience, this is a fair judgement. In the first place I have never found the English self-centred and unaccomodating, as they are supposed by us to be. Both in London and in the country I have on a hundred occasions asked my way: it has always been pointed out to me and quite often people have put themselves out, accompanying me as far as was necessary to put me on the right road. In public vehicles and trains whenever I ask a fellow-traveller to tell me when we reach my stopping place, he does so with good grace. Nor, if I begin a conversation, does he smile at my linguistic mistakes, but joins in with great good nature.

One evening recently, having walked a long way from my hotel and lost myself, a gentleman I asked to direct me insisted on accompanying me back, spoke to me in praise of France, asked me what I thought of London, and shook hands with me when we separated. Another, on a similar occasion, made me get into his carriage and drove me to a cab-rank.

The newspapers announce the arrival of three thousand choral society singers from France: they add that they must be given the best possible welcome so that they will go home with a good opinion of England. Not once has a policeman, a clerk, a cabby or conductor been ill-tempered or rude to me. But what is altogether admirable and perhaps unique in all Europe, is their manner of interpreting the word hospitality: I cannot think of the hospitality I have received here without a feeling of gratitude. The person to whom one presents a letter of introduction does not consider his obligation discharged by an invitation to dinner; he helps you with information, acts as your pilot, draws up an itinerary for you, undertakes to keep you busy and amused; he takes you to call on his relations, introduces you into his own circle, invites you to stay with him in the country, and, when you leave, gives you letters of introduction to other people. In the end you tell him, "This is too much; I should never be able to do as much for you in Paris." And you receive the same welcome from friends of your sponsor to whom he introduces you, and again from *their* friends. Sometimes, after an hour's conversation with a gentleman you have just met for the first time in your life, he will invite you to stay for a week at his 'country seat'. If you go you will be treated like a member of the family.

What is even more striking is their open-heartedness: often, after one or two days, a man will make no difficulty over talking to you of his intimate private affairs. I would sometimes ask for information about the running of a household: and my host, in order to be more exact, would quite often tell me the amount of his income, and his expenditure, the rent of his house, the origin of his fortune, family and marriage, and a number of small domestic or personal facts. Sophisticated people are more reserved in France.

We sought reasons for this difference: here is a brief summary of them: The English are hospitable,

1. Because they are bored: most of the well-to-do upper class * spend eight months of the year in the country, sometimes far from any town, very isolated: they feel the need for conversation and new ideas.

2. Because of social customs: in London people hardly speak to each other, such is the rush of life and so short the time spent there, often less than three months. There are too many people and too much business: so that the country house is their real drawing-room, the place for social intercourse.

3. In consequence of domestic customs: many children, numerous servants — in a big house well run there has to be a certain rule of reserve, and this is also promoted by the habitual stoicism of the English character. Consequently the presence of a stranger is not, as would be the case with us, disturbing a family intimacy, checking the freedom and gaiety and chatter of a family closed circle; it will not be forcing people to study their behaviour, restrain their familiarities and their impulses. All it means is one more occupied chair at table and in the drawing-room, no more: there is no change in the tone of behaviour and conversation.

4. Because of their mastery of domestic comfort and service.

---

* *Gens du monde.* People in "society" but I think the word would be an anachronism in this context; it does not seem to have been in use until later.
                                                                E. H.

The organisation is perfect and the machine working. The servants are well-drilled, the rooms in readiness, time scrupulously kept. There is nothing to be undone or redone, and above all nothing to be improvised because of a stranger in the house.

5. Out of kindness, humanity and even conscience: it is a duty to be useful, and a foreigner is so lost and ill-at-ease when he arrives in a new country! He ought to be helped.

❋

This leads us to take a look at an English household. Rules and discipline are more strictly kept here than with us. In this, as in other departments, the social fabric is loosely woven in France, firmly woven in England.

I have three households in mind: in one there are seven servants, cook, kitchen-maid, two 'housemaids', a chamber-maid, coachman and man-servant. * In the second, fifteen servants, and in the third eighteen. A male servant receives £40 to £50 in wages; and if he is not found in meals, which is often the case in London, he will be paid an extra twelve shillings a week for his food.

Every servant has his duties strictly defined. The work is shared out, and no territory overlaps or depends on another. For example, in the third of the households I have in mind there is a special man for cleaning out fireplaces, carrying coal and maintaining the fires. Two ranks of servants, lower and upper, the latter being responsible to and transmitting the orders of their master and mistress. At the head of the men is the 'butler', and of the women the first chamber-maid.† If a 'groom' (sic)** appears in a soiled coat the master will say nothing to him, but will reprimand the 'butler'. The upper servants are, as it were, sergeants, with a consciousness and the authority of their rank. Clear definition and delimitation of duties, and a hierarchy of powers, such are the proper foundations of an effective organisation.

The rest of the picture is of a piece with the foregoing. The servants in a big house have a proper value for their own dignity, and will take service only in a respectable house.

* I use man-servant for *valet-de-chambre* so as to reserve "footman" for *valet-de-pied*. E. H.

† *Femme-de-chambre:* I should have thought the head-housemaid was the chief woman servant. Taine may mean this. There is no mention of a house-keeper. E. H.

** Taine must mean page, I think. E.H.

S ——, requiring an additional 'housemaid', thought of a local girl who was not married but had a child: but before engaging her he put the proposal before his servants for their opinion. They discussed the matter and, having a good account of the girl, agreed to accept her among themselves. As a rule their behaviour is unexceptionable even though several, of opposite sexes, be young, unmarried, and living under the same roof: in his whole lifetime S —— has only had one case of immoral behaviour among his servants.

In the matter of their work, too, they are conscientious, exact, regular, always on time: they have a time-table and a rule and they keep to it precisely. As a result the domestic machine seems to run itself, and the master and mistress have no need to interfere with it: here again, S —— claims that the 'sense of duty' is fundamental in an Englishman, and that this feeling is supreme in the kitchen and antechamber, just as it is among a ship's company or in a factory; and that there is nothing like this feeling for reconciling a subordinate to his subordination.

Two circumstances, moreover, tend to lighten the burden of the subordination. Servants have their share of independence and they value it. A number of them have their own club, in London, an association whose members undertake not to stay more than two years in any one place: the object of this is to give the masters less of a hold on them. Furthermore, as their times of work are clearly laid down, the intervening intervals are their own to do as they like with. They have their own 'hall', a large room where they eat and pass their time.

In the house I have mentioned their meals are served half an hour before the family's. They have a small library of their own, with games of draughts and chess. After dinner they may go out, only one being kept on duty to answer the bell. He who would receive much, must not ask too much: the man who gives the orders should always provide for the physical and moral well-being of his subordinates. If he wants to be obeyed willingly and fully, let him be a real 'leader', a chief, always responsible for every initiative, the accepted and authorised judge of their conduct.

To this end the master of a household is, on Sunday evenings, his servants' spiritual guide, their chaplain. You will see them file into the room, the women first, the men following, soberly and gravely, and take up their places. The family and their guests will already have foregathered. The master reads a short sermon aloud, followed by a prayer, whereupon those present kneel or bow their heads, with their faces turned to the wall. Finally, he recites the *Our Father*, the others repeating it after him line by line. This done, the servants file out again, in the same order, in silence and thoughtful composure: I have watched them several times and not a muscle of their faces moves. By this community feeling and by thus undertaking a moral leadership, the master succeeds in really being a master. In France he is very far from this, from having his rightful position in his house and in the feelings of his people, or even of his children.

But let me at once note the disadvantage, the other side of the case. In the ordinary intercourse of life the English are not fluid or flexible: the classes are separated by a barrier and far from making gaps in it, they set it with spikes. For instance, Mr. N ——, an Englishman living in France, engaged a French tutor for this children. At the end of a month Mrs. N —— no longer found him to her taste, would not speak to him, and if she wished to communicate with him sent him a note. One evening, in the drawing-room, Mr. N —— went to sleep and Mrs. N —— began to read a book. The young man, not daring to take up a book and having nobody to talk to, ended by falling asleep himself. On the following day she said to him curtly: "Sir, your behaviour yesterday evening was very ill-mannered. I hope there will be no repetition of it." Some days later a young lady whom he knew was invited to the house and he went to sit next to her at table. Mrs. N —— raised her voice,

"That, Sir, is not your place. Go and sit next to your pupil."

He refused, at once left the table and the house and, citing his agreement, claimed a year's salary. It was refused. He took it to law. Mr. N —— was ordered to pay.

This reminds me of another story, dating from the last century. Lord ——, having engaged a French tutor, advised him to speak no language but French to his sons.

"I am charmed, my lord, that you have so high an opinion of that language."

"Sir, we despise it, but it is our wish that, when in France, our children shall speak it at least as well as the natives." One can just see the smiling, eager face of the Frenchman fishing for a compliment, and the expressionless face and surly manner of the Englishman as he bites the other's head off.

The lot of a governess in England is not a pleasant one: see, for example, the novels of Charlotte Brontë. Most of those I have met had turned their faces into wooden masks, and nothing could be more startling when the face in question is young. Manner, bearing, everything is artificial and made to order, composed and maintained in such a manner as never to lay the subject open for a moment. Even after several days of familiarity and away from the house in which they are employed they remain on the defensive. The habit of keeping a sharp watch and firm control over themselves is too strong; one might take them for soldiers on parade. As for the servants, their expression of humble and submissive respect is greatly in excess of anything of the kind to be seen in France. It is, in fact, unpleasant to see one man taking such an attitude towards another man.

There is the same basis of unbending self-control in the relationship between close kinsfolk. A young man, speaking familiarly of his father, will call him 'my governor'. And in fact he is, by law and custom, the governor of his house, which is his castle, and of the garrison within it. Excepting in the case of an entail he can disinherit his children, and as we have seen, his wife is subject to him.

Mr. W——, a rich landowner and a man of the old school, has, among other children, a son with a malady of the chest. The unfortunate young man, on his way home from Nice, and feeling he was about to die, stopped at Boulogne: he wanted to die in his father's house, where he had been born, but did not dare go to it without being invited, nor did he even dare ask permission. His mother, sick herself and wanting to embrace her son once more before he died, did not dare take it upon herself to go to him. The young man did not set out on the last stage of his journey until he had received a letter from his father.

Inequality of situation is another cause of coolness in family relationship. The distance between the eldest son, who will be a nobleman with an income of two hundred thousand francs, and the youngest with his five thousand francs a year, his two furnished rooms, and his days spent in a machine shop learning to be an 'engineer' — that distance is too great. Real familiarity, real ease, are out of the question. Their education may be equal but they feel the gulf between them. The case of two brothers has been quoted to me in this connection: both are at Oxford University; but the elder receives £100 a year more than the younger.

As a final cause of distance between members of a family, there is the independence of the children. A son or daughter can marry without their parents' permission, and not infrequently make use of that right: from this arise quarrels which may last a lifetime. Meanwhile every father knows that his children may escape him, may openly defy him, striking at his most sensitive place. Often, as a consequence, he will say to himself, "Since they have that right, let them pay for it." Following which line of thought some, especially those who have a legion of children, give themselves no trouble to marry their daughters: let them find their own husbands, it is their business, as it is the sons' business to earn their own living.

Here there is a great difference from our own households, in which the parents give themselves wholly and unreservedly to their children, and wherein eldest and youngest, brothers and sisters, are all on a perfectly equal footing, and almost as much so with their parents: wherein, too, familiarity and intimacy are so complete, and each member of the family finds it natural to enter, daily and hourly, by question and advice, into the thoughts and feelings of the others; wherein nothing is closed, nothing held back, every soul is open to the day, open in a hundred thousand ways to the curiosity and sympathy of the others.

The English find this astonishing: in this connection S —— greatly admires our sociability, and good character. He has often seen, in France, two or three households together under a single roof, at one table for meals, for six months in the country, sometimes for a whole year in town and country: sometimes it might be two brothers with their wives and families; or, again, the parents, with their daughter and son-in-law, or their son and daughter-in-law. Nothing could be more unusual in England. Different characters would come into collision: each married couple with its household needs its independence and its own house. We are able to melt into each other, to have all things in common; whereas they, even when they live together, keep distinct from each other, and set up frontiers. Self is stronger. Every Englishman and woman holds some part of himself or herself back, has a corner of the mind and heart inviolably private, a kind of forbidden enclosure which is respected by everyone, even by brother, father or sister, even, indeed, by his or her mother. To enter it would be an intrusion and nobody does so excepting, perhaps, the subject's lover, the husband or wife to whom his or her whole life has been entrusted and engaged.

This forbidden territory varies in extent from person to person. It may include business, that is matters of money and ambition; it may be certain deep feelings — a hope, an unprosperous love, an old and prolonged grief for someone who has died; it may include certain intimate and elevated ideas, for example a religious belief. It may even, sometimes, include everything, in which case the subject is mute and does not like to be talked to. But in any case the line which he has drawn round himself remains unbroken: no expansive moments will bring him to cross it. And if somebody else steps over it, it will be an indiscretion touching him on the raw: his nearest and dearest would as soon burgle a house. Thus a father or mother are, in England, much less well informed of their daughters' feelings, their sons' business and pleasures, than in France.

In order to bring this fact clearly home I should have to go into much detail: instead I will put forward a single feature of the phenomenon. In France a son tells his mother everything, even about his mistresses: it is an old-established custom. Madame de Sévigné received confidences from her son which she retailed to her daughter, confidences which were, moreover, excessively scabrous and which she redeemed in the re-telling by her gaiety, her marvellous lightness of touch, her *verve*. Many young men of our own times confide similar things to their mothers, or at least hint at them, and let their status as triumphant lovers be suspected. The maternal recipients of such confidences are not scandalised by them; they are much too happy at being their sons' confidantes, at being treated almost like a crony. They may scold a little; they will do little more than dismiss the naughty boy with a half-smile, a raised finger and a word of indulgent warning. B ——— considers that this would be quite impossible in England: a son would not dare do it and his mother would be shocked or revolted if he did. And it is the same for everything else: they have no knowledge of those long, long conversations, those complete outpourings of the heart, in which the difference in age neutralises the difference in sex, and in the course of which a son, who is beginning in the world, finds in his mother, who is withdrawing from it, his cleverest, subtlest guide and his most perfect friend.

The English custom of reserve leads to a kind of stoicism. There is no confiding, no letting go, even with one's nearest and dearest. * In a family which has just lost a near relation, a father or a son, there is never an outbrust of grief, no noisy crying or loud mourning. On the day following, everyone comes down as usual in the morning; all take their places at table in the usual

* The most moving and terrible example of this is, perhaps, the life, sickness and death of Emily Brontë. E. H.

way and at the usual time. There will be a little less talk than usual. One may be grief-stricken, but that does not mean one must not get on with one's job, and do it as well and as conscientiously as ever. When, after the death of Prince Albert, the Queen shut herself up in solitude and seemed to be giving up the business proper to her position, the newspapers, after letting several months go by, began to censure her conduct, and informed her that a private grief excuses nobody from fulfilling public obligations. A writer in the *National Review* praised Eugénie de Guérin, * so pure and so sad; yet, according to him, she was wrong to let her sadness appear, and even, indeed, to *be* sad. "An Englishwoman with an honest, healthy mind, would consider that 'cheerfulness' is itself a duty, and would abstain from expressing any distaste for life."

I have translated this word 'cheerfulness' † badly, because I cannot do otherwise. It indicates the opposite of despondency, a sort of smiling serenity. Nowhere is this feeling nobler and more touching to see than on the faces of old ladies. One of my acquaintance, ten years bedridden, was still tranquil and benevolent: evening and morning the children of the household were brought to her room, she knew and directed their daily occupations, kept herself informed of the household's activities in the greatest detail, worked at small tasks, read and prayed and was never for a moment idle; tedium had not drawn a single line on her brow.

Another, seventy-five years old and a great-grandmother, had the peaceful smile and smooth complexion of a nun. Two others, again, have remained present to my memory like a beautiful Dutch painting. It was in the country; a lofty drawing-room, the walls white and pearl-grey; the light colouring softened by the shades of evening. The wide central window was a deep bay; beneath it were flower-beds and beyond, through the shining window-panes, was a vista of green. A girl, beautiful, intelligent and cold, sat on a chair by the window, gravely reading a little book, a religious treatise. In the middle of the room two old ladies sat at a tea-

* Eugénie de Guérin. 1805-48. Author and mystic, born in Albi. Her grief was due to the death of her brother, G. M. de Guérin, whose *Reliquiae* she edited. The occasion of this article would have been the publication of her *Journals and Letters* in 1865, in English. E. H.

† Taine has to use the word *gaieté*, one of whose dictionary meanings is *cheerfulness*; but it is better rendered by *blitheness*. The French have no word for *cheerfulness*, an interesting example of the fact that the best translation in the world is little better than an approximation. E. H.

table, entertaining their guest. Large-featured faces, serene, decided, even commanding; in that point only were they different from Flemish portraits. Their costume consisted of black silk dresses, very full, with white lace at the throat and wrists, richly made caps with gauze veils, white embroidery on their bodices; they were Mierevelt figures. The touch of stiff opulence which is displeasing in the attire of a young woman suited their age and their seriousness. All about them were the signs of ample means, an unquestioned position, well-balanced minds, and healthy souls and a life well-lived. One of them was seventy and looked fifty, had never married and had, by means of family connections, been used to the society of the most distinguished minds in France and England. She spends the season in town, staying with friends. At home she reads. Dickens and the moderns seem to her low and too restless; she prefers authors whose tone is elevated and manner well-bred: M. Guizot, M. Mignet, *
Hallam, Macaulay, the latter rather less than the other three; Arnold, M. Stanley †, and others who write on ethics and religion as dutiful moderate liberals. In the same sprit, in the France of the 18th century, did ladies read Du Guet and Nicole.

The second old lady has four sons, all settled overseas in the consular or diplomatic services, one in Africa, one in Turkey, a third in Sweden. Every other year each of them comes to spend a fortnight with her. She does not repine at being alone and far from her sons: she is, like a Roman mother, glad to know them all "serving their country in positions of honour."

In all of which two things are, I believe, chiefly to be distinguished: the first is an energy, partly innate, party acquired, that force of character by which man becomes master of his soul, keeping himself on a firm rein, is sufficient to himself, risks and endures misfortune, grief and discouragement; the other is the existence of a hierarchy which introduces inequality, subordination, authority and order even into private lives. But every coin has two sides. As far as I can judge this same character and this rule of life create a great many tyrants, churls, people who remain mute because they are unwilling to reveal their minds, eccentrics, and people who are downtrodden. A certain number of house-

* Mignet was a French historian (1796-1884) whose History of Mary Queen of Scots had made him known in Britain. Hallam was the historian father of the poet A. H. Hallam whose death at 22 inspired Tennyson's *In Memoriam.*

† M. Stanley, the journalist, explorer and company-promoter. I think Taine really meant the other Stanley, A. P. — the dean. E. H.

holds exist which resemble the Harlowes in Richardson's novel: but on that subject the lips of an observer must remain sealed. I refer the reader to George Eliot, Dickens, and Thackeray; notably to Thackeray's portraits of Lord Steyne, Barnes Newcombe, Lady Kew; of old Osborne and of Clive Newcombe's mother-in-law.

❄

It is not easy to persuade an Englishman to talk about his illicit *amours;* for many of them this is a closed book the mere mention of which is shocking. And their writings, in this respect, are even more reserved than their talk. The reserve practised in their novels is well known: not one but can be read by a young girl. If a novelist does introduce a woman who behaves immorally, it is only to remove her as quickly as possible, with a motion of contempt or disgust; and he will have the air of walking on hot coals; scabrous detail is merely sketched and thrown into the shade or kept remote. They never depict a hussy * as attractive, she is always repulsive.

In *Vanity Fair* Thackeray was bold enough to place an adventuress among his principal characters; compare the disagreeable Becky Sharp to Balzac's Madame Marneffe. In *Pendennis* he sketched the seduction of a *grisette:* but it comes to nothing and this tale of little Fanny might have been written by a clergyman. In his respect all of them are, indeed, more or less clergymen, more or less prudes. If the matter were submitted to a naturalist for his opinion he would no doubt point out that races differ fundamentally, that one may have as little modesty as a dog, another as much as an elephant; that one may hide what another parades. Thus, for example, what we display — and exaggerate, they conceal — and attenuate. It is necessary to discount part of what we say and add something to what they say.

Nevertheless, after diverse conversations and much observation, I believe them to be more continent than ourselves: for this the following reasons are suggested:

Their senses awaken late; Tacitus noticed it long ago. † In this respect, and generally, the northerner is less precocious than the southerner; this is an attribute of race, one of the basic character-

* *coquine.*
† *Sera juvenum Venus.*

95

istics differentiating the Teuton from the Latin. Even nowadays many University Students at Jena, Leipzig, Halle or Bonn form Associations to swear vows of continence.

Shyness is very common: on this head, indeed, they are nearly all shy.

They work very hard and are spurred on by competition; they have their way to make; as a comfortable standard of living is very costly and it is necessary to earn a great deal of money, their minds are concentrated on that and imagination has no leisure.

Physical exercises provide a wholesome distraction; as a change from work they row, skate, play cricket, ride, travel, go shooting in the Highlands or abroad, climb mountains. A young man, rich and idle, spends barely three months in London, and the temptations of London are very much less seductive than those of Paris.

Public opinion is less tolerant than with us, and they are very much afraid of it.

Most of them retain their religious beliefs into maturity or to the end of their lives, which is a brake — weak, it is true, but nevertheless a brake.

An Englishman begins dreaming of marriage early and, in imagination, creates his own romance of love and domestic happiness. All contemporary literature, both verse and prose, holds him to this idea to the exclusion of any other idea on the subject. For although this pure and charming dream does not abolish brutality, it takes all glamour from mere gallantry, which is brought down to the level of a commonplace amusement, and rather a low one: a man tells himself, "There is something better than this," and the easy love affair loses its keen attraction and any chance of being taken for real, supreme happiness.

The *grisette,* the woman of easy virtue *(lorette),* the sparkling and amusingly flirtatious little woman, are all rare. There remains only the street woman, smelling of gin, repulsive and pitiable.

In addition to which, as we have already noted, married women are almost all faithful. B —— maintains that there are exceptions in the highest class, that adventures, like those of Lady Adelina in Lord Byron's *Don Juan,* do occur — in the country, in secret and with infinite precautions. But it is among the well-to-do 'shopkeepers' that accidents of this kind are more frequent because their women are idle. Not having, as in France, the recourse of the theatre and visiting, nor like the wives of gentlemen, that of patronage and the care of the poor, above the need to work, never having to cook or to sew, they wither in idleness: the great emptiness of boredom is a wide open door to seduction. As a rule, the lover is a man of the world, a rich gentleman, who deals at their shop. Even for him, excepting in the case of a few 'profligates', the situation is disagreeable. An Englishman in a state of adultery is miserable: even at the supreme moment his conscience torments him.

As for the 'kept woman', she is carefully hidden. Reserve, in this matter, is obligatory and extreme. I have been told of a young man who was out on the Thames, in a boat, with his mistress, whom he was taking out to dine. A steamship passed and he happened to see his sister's fiancé on board: upset and ashamed, he refused to go on with the evening, and rowed straight to a landing place. Yet he had not even been seen. W—— has travelled widely; I have been on terms of familiar conversation with him for a fortnight; he is twenty-eight years old and I am sure that he is sincere; nevertheless, when I tried to make him talk of the world beyond the pale of respectability, he appeared embarrassed and ill-at-ease. He assured me that he knows nothing of this world, nor of young men leading irregular lives, that he has no intercourse with them, and that a man is kept very busy in London by the duties of his profession, by his family, by sport, cricket, riding and service in the Volunteers.

At a watering-place, B—— met a clergyman accompanied by a young woman, pretty and modest; he became acquainted with them and wished to introduce them to his wife. The clergyman avoided the occasion for several days, and, finally, asked for a few words in private: he then explained that the young woman was a 'governess', and his mistress: involved in sin, he still retained his respect for marriage.

Wealthy young men who do have a mistress place her in a house outside London, where they visit her on Sunday, returning to town on Monday. Thus even in his irregularities the Englishman is attached to a hearth, a 'home'; he wants a woman who shall be his own, exclusively, and not publicly. His "little place" is a real household. As a rule his mistress is a farmer's daughter, * or a governess. The latter, daughters of poor clergyman, often pretty and well-bred, lonely in a strange household where they are something between servant and guest, are exposed to peculiar temptations. Many such unions last a long time, some for a lifetime. Sometimes, after he has known you for long enough, the lover may invite you to dinner. "Come and meet 'my little girl', she is a

* See, e.g., George Eliot's *Adam Bede*.

perfect 'lady'!" You may encounter a young person busy with her household, modest and well-behaved, and you must talk as if you were in the house of a read lady: a too lively word would shock her. She does not play the *gamin,* the *garçon,* the pal, as she would in Paris. S ——, who has lived among us, claims that for one of these irregular *ménages* in England, there are three in France.

Very few high-class prostitutes *(lorettes).* This species which, latterly, has swarmed and flaunted it in Paris, has but a meagre colony in London: I am referring to those women who have a *salon,* their own carriage, are to be seen in the *Bois,* and whose adventures are reported in the lesser newsprints; women who have been compared to the *hetairai* of Athens and to *cortigiane* of the 16th century. Nevertheless, there are a few; it is a continental import. I have seen three or four, very well known, in Hyde Park, who were pointed out when they appeared, although sufficiently distinguished by the coarse insolence of their *toilettes.*

One of my friends has visited one of these women; she is at the top of her profession, entertains lords and sets them to cards. Her guests smoke in her house, and cross their legs — all awkwardly and clumsily enough. High spirits, witty naughtiness, sparkling gaiety are necessary ingredients for the seasoning of such an evening: but here they are wanting. B —— added, laughing, "My first visit cost me a guinea in concert tickets; I found this method of gaining experience too costly for a mere 'esquire', and sent the lady my card, with a sonnet, and P.P.C. at the bottom."

Some of these women drive their own horses admirably — but put them all together and they do not compose a demi-monde in serious rivalry to 'society'. Here, the gulf which separates virtue from debauchery is deep and sheer; there is no ladder from one to the other, as in France. Their religion has the same quality: paradise on one side, hell on the other and no intermediate stage, no purgatory.

What remains, then, is nothing but an expression of lust, simple and coarse. Brillat-Savarin said: "An animal feeds, man eats, but only the gourmet really knows how to eat." It is very certain that in this, as in their cooking, they are ignorant of Brillat-Savarin's precepts. Throughout the day, in the Strand and Haymarket, a large number of shops and more or less respectable-looking houses display this notice: 'Beds to let'. At evening, in the same places and elsewhere, numerous figures are to be seen entering and leaving, figures which have the bearing, the look, the gravity which is peculiarly English. The mature man, the young man of the respectable classes, on that evening he is supposed to be travelling, or at his club. He does not make himself conspicuous, does not offer his companion his arm: his expedition is secret and anonymous and represents no more than an escape of the beast which everyone of us carries within himself.

Two merchants in a large way of business, mentioned to me in this connection, arrive at a certain great city, go to a certain place, each carrying forty pounds sterling, shut themselves up in it, do not leave the house night or day, and occupy the intervals in drinking: this is what sailors arriving in harbour call firing a broadside. Their families believe the two businessmen to be in the country. After eight days they are informed that their eighty pounds had all gone; and they leave.

The appetites, in this race, are violent and dangerous: see them for example, as depicted in Fielding's and Smollett's novels; and their scandalous eruption during the carnival of the Restoration. To bridle them, public opinion, religion and conscience are not excessive forces. For they have need of all their strength to keep this Caliban in check: he is far more savage and far uglier than the merry, jovial satyr of France or Italy. So that they are right to push severity to the point of prudishness: the more damaging the flood is apt to be, the more necessary it becomes to watch and strengthen the dykes. For those whom it sweeps away wallow in mud and viciousness such as are inconceivable to us: examples of this are to be found in Smollett's *Miss Williams,* in Mackenzie's *Man of Sentiment* and in Alfieri's *Memoirs.* Today no novelist would dare touch such raw truths, even with the tips of his fingers. I myself have personal knowledge of several such, but it is better not to write them: one may change details and circumstances, but there remains the risk of injuring the families of those concerned. Sometimes a coachman or a lackey plays the leading role, as in Alfieri. In such cases the parties are sent to Australia while the family hides itself in London, or abroad.

Bear in mind that their young women are free and left to care for themselves, that they are frequently without a dowry and obliged to contrive marriages for themselves. What opportunities for sliding down the slippery slope, and how powerful the brakes, interior and exterior, need to be to hold them back!

For example, a young woman, daughter of a clergyman, goes riding every day with the young squire of the parish, goes for walks with him, begins to get herself talked about; 'flirtation', the art of fishing for a husband, is not uncommon; Thackeray described it in *Vanity Fair*. In playing this game, a young woman gives a man a great many holds over her, and a very cool head is necessary, to avoid giving them all.

In the 'middleclass', intermediate between gentry and persons employed in manual occupations, many a girl permits herself singular liberties: for example, she will call on the young man she prefers in his own lodgings. On this point I have personally been told details of a scabrous nature, by a person concerned, which have no counterpart in France. No doubt the girls of our own *petite bourgeoisie* are more carefully watched over; but by the same token, they are more nearly intact.

And the things that are done to get husbands! One often sees advertisements in the press to the following effect: "any reader wishing to offer himself as a suitor (to the advertiser) may, in the first instance, receive a photograph, in full evening dress, deposited with the editor." Two young Mancunians of our aquaintance caused a note of the same kind to be inserted in a newspaper: they declared their matrimonial disposition and begged the ladies interested to walk, at a certain time, past a certain café. They themselves took station in a café opposite and, at the stated time, three young women, quite pretty and respectable, walked up and down before the place in question and finally stopped in a marked manner, in front of the specified door.

In this country and class a woman has need of a man in order to subsist; her own work will not enable her to provide for herself; set this female poverty beside the brutality of the men, and there remains no mystery about the lamentable Haymarket marchpast. My English friends admit that, in London, the number of these poor girls is enormous. They let themselves go and give up all effort to recover their position: they are without the springs of character and intelligence, the ingenuity and expedients of a Frenchwoman. They do not know how to be thrifty and save, how to buy, or get themselves given, a little place of their own, how to become haberdashers, dress-makers, dealers in toilet articles, as they do in Paris. They are aware of their degradation, consider themselves lost, spend what they earn from day to day, take to drink and die in the workhouse.

I do not know how it is, but, whenever I consider this English society, always, beyond the human head and the splendid torso, I find myself aware of the bestial and muck-fouled hind-quarters.

CHAPTER FOUR

# EDUCATION

A VISIT to Harrow-on-the-Hill; I have also been to Eton. Harrow, Eton and Rugby are the principal establishments for secondary education in England and correspond roughly to our great *lycées*. There are about 800 pupils at Eton, and 500 in each of the other two, between 13 and 18 years of age. But between these schools and our *lycées* the difference is enormous and no other comparison could make the contrast between the two peoples so clear. * I am told that I can safely take Harrow as a specimen.

It is a free and private establishment not subsidised by the State, founded in the past by a legacy and consequently endowed with an hereditary (sic) estate yielding an income. In some cases the income from such estates is very large. In the case of Harrow it is small (£1100). Great or small, it is managed by a council of trustees (sic) (governors) recruited by election. Harrow has six, great noblemen or landowners of the neighbourhood, who have authority to make considerable changes and to appoint the 'head-master'. But the principal part of the machine is the company of house-masters: † each of these teaches a subject — Greek, Latin, Mathematics, etc. — and, in addition, boards and lodges from ten to thirty boarders in his house. As a rule the boys are two to a room, but each of the older boys has a room to himself. House-masters with only about a dozen boarders give them their meals at their own family table. Where they are more numerous they eat at two tables presided over by ladies of the master's household. Thus the boy, when he first arrives at school, finds himself in something like his own paternal household, the more so in that English families are numerous. He has a home of his own, dines within three paces of a lady, is, in short, a person among people. He lives in a natural, whole environment and is not, as with us, subject to a barrack-like communism.

Another difference: in France a *lycée* is a large, stone box into

* See, in this connection, the admirable report by MM. Demogeot, and Montucci: *De l'Enseignement Secondaire en Angleterre et en Ecosse.* 1868.

† *professeurs maîtres de pension.*

which you enter by means of a single hole provided with an iron gate and a porter. Inside are a few courtyards like playgrounds, occasionally a wretched stand of trees but, on the other hand, a great many walls. Since the said box is always in a large town the young man who once passes its iron gate is confronted, inside and out, by nothing but bricks and mortar. Whereas here the school is a small town by itself, with numerous ways open to the country. At Eton I noticed that the walls about the big central courtyard were covered with roses, creepers and honeysuckle: beyond lie lush meadows where monster elms spread their age-old branches; near them, a river, green and gleaming, on its waters swans, on its islands grazing bullocks. The stream turns and flows towards the horizon in a green vista.

The countryside, at Harrow, is not so pretty, but there is no want of green grass and foliage and fresh air. The school owns a field of five or six hectares, * which provides room for the game of cricket. I met small boys in black jackets, older boys in black swallow-tail coats, and all wearing a little straw hat not only in the town, but outside it, along the hedgerows and beside the pond. You can see from their muddy boots that they are often out on the roads or in the damp fields. Thus, whereas, with us, adolescence is spent, as it were, under a cloche of artificiality, through which penetrates the moral and physical reek of a great city, here it is spent in the open air, without any kind of sequestration, the boys being free of the fields, waters and woods. Now it is a most important advantage for the body, imagination, mind and character to be able to develop in a wholesome and tranquil atmosphere in conformity with the blind requirements of their instincts.

On the whole, then, human nature is treated here with more respect and is less interfered with. Under the influence of an English education boys are like the trees in an English garden; under that of our own, like the pleached and pollarded trees of Versailles. Here, for instance, schoolboys are almost as free as undergraduates. They are required to be present in class, for study, † and for dinner, and to be in by a certain time at night, but no more. The rest of the day is their own, and it is up to them to employ this leisure as they please. The only task which must be done in their free time is a certain amount of "homework" but this they can do where and when they like. They may work in their own rooms or elsewhere. I have seen boys studying

* 12 to 14 acres. E. H.
† *répétitions.* E. H.

in the bookshop, others reading seated on a balustrade. They please their own taste, wander where they like. They go for runs in the country, fish, skate, bathe and go birds-nesting. They are to be met with in the streets, at the pastry-cooks, or in the sausage shop. They are masters of their time and also of their money, treat themselves to snacks and buy things to decorate their rooms. It seems that if they run into debt, their small matter of privately owned furniture or furnishings is sold by auction. * Initiative and responsibility: it is curious to see babies of twelve raised to the dignities of manhood.

A maximum of eight hours work a day; it is more likely to be six or seven. With us it is eleven, which is unreasonable. An adolescent needs physical exercise: it is against nature to force him to be all brain, a sedentary book-worm. Here, athletic games, fives, football, running, rowing and above all cricket take up a part of every day. Moreover classes end at noon two or three days a week to make time for games. Pride plays an important part; each school tries to beat its rivals and sends teams of players and oarsmen, picked out and trained, to play and row against the others. Harrow beat Eton last year and hopes to be victorious again this year. While I was there eleven of the biggest and most skilful boys had to maintain the honour of the school against eleven players who had come from London. There were two standard bearers who stood, flag in hand, to mark the limits of the field. Hundreds of boys lined both sides of the field, keeping their distance and greeting every fortunate stroke with applause. The business was taken seriously: the adversaries belonged to a famous 'cricketers' club; their strength, coolness and address were admirable. Certainly the boys have a perfect right to become passionately interested in a game which they see grown men making the main object of their lives.

And there are, in point of fact, gentlemen in this country whose ambition and regimen are those of a Greek athlete; they adopt a special diet, abstain from all excesses of eating and drinking, build up their muscles and follow a careful system of training. As soon as they are ready they set out to obtain the prize for rowing or cricket at all the principal athletic games meetings in England, and even beyond it, in America. I have been told of a team † of eleven cricketers who actually went to play in

* See, for full details of their lives, *Tom Brown's School Days*.

† As this was before France had taken to sport and adopted English words, Taine has to use such words as *"bande"* of cricketers. E. H.

Australia, as formerly athletes went from Punt or from Marseilles, to Olympia. There is, then, nothing surprising in it if adolescents become enthusiastic over games backed by such authority. The chief (sic) of the cricket eleven and the captain of the rowing eight are more important people in the school than the best 'scholar' (*humaniste*) in the classes.

Here then, thus early, are the seeds of the spirit of association, an apprenticeship in both obedience and command, since every cricket team accepts a discipline and appoints a leader. But this principle is applied very much more widely; boys and youths together form an organised body, a sort of small, distinct State with its own chiefs and its own laws. The chiefs are the pupils in the highest class ('sixth form'), more especially the fifteen highest pupils in the school ('monitors') and, in each house, the highest pupil. They maintain order, see that the rules are obeyed and, in general, do the same work as our ushers. * They prevent the strong from bullying the weak, are arbitrators in all disputes, take a hand when a small boy gets into some kind of trouble with a villager or a shop-keeper, and punish delinquents. In short, pupils in England are governed by pupils; and each one, having first been subject to authority, comes in due course to wield it. During his final year each is enrolled on the side of the rules, the law, and it becomes his business to see that it is respected; he learns its value, and adopts it of his own free will, instead of kicking against it, which is what a French schoolboy would not fail to do.

Consequently when they leave school and begin their adult lives they are less inclined to consider the rules absurd and authority ridiculous. They reconcile liberty and subordination, are nearer to an understanding of the conditions in which a society can exist and the rights and duties of a citizen.

In addition to this general training, there is a more particular one. The older boys form themselves into 'debating societies', in which questions of ethics and politics are discussed; the head-master is only their honorary president. After the young orators have spoken, the audience votes; minutes of the speeches are kept; such a society is Parliament in little. Furthermore three of the oldest boys publish a review — *The Triumvirate*. Their object is "to arouse in their schoolfellows broader ideas of patriotism and interest them in their country's affairs." They belong to the Conservative opposition party, discuss the French Alliance, the

* *maîtres d'études*. E. H.

election, the electoral laws. A good deal of commonplace notions and some turgidity of style; but good sense is not wanting. For example, on the subject of the suffrage, which they want to broaden, but only up to a point, they appeal to their young readers' own experience: they, during their holidays and in the country, must have seen that the villagers and shop-keepers of the class it is proposed to enfranchise are sufficiently intelligent and well-informed to vote sensibly; thus the argument put forward is practical, drawn from facts, and not from some pompous theory.

I have just been reading an issue of this review; there can be no doubt that our own pupils in rhetoric * are very far from having reached this standard of political education and information. There is something more to be said: all these boys, or nearly all, are religious; they would be shocked by any remark wanting in reverence and in chapel they sing seriously. Since Arnold's time the object of their education has been to turn them out as *Christian gentlemen.* Most of them are practising Christians, take Holy Communion and, of their own accord, say their prayers at night. Thus, when they take their places in the world, they do so as defenders, not as opponents, of the great ecclesiastical establishment, the national religion.

From whatever point of departure I begin, I come to the same conclusion: in England there is no wide separation between the boy and the grown man; school, and the great world, are on the same footing with no wall or ditch between them, so that the one prepares for and leads to the other. The adolescent does not, as in France he does, emerge from a forcing-house, from a special atmosphere. He is not disturbed and disorientated by an abrupt change of air. He has not only been cultivating his mind, he has been undergoing an apprenticeship for adult life. Not only has he ideas, but what is more they are appropriate to the world he is being received into. In politics and in religion he finds, at twenty years of age, forms and structures for which his tastes and faculties have been adapted in advance. In this way it is easier for him to escape scepticism, he is more quickly schooled to the world, and will have less groping to do before he finds a use for his capabilities.

All the boys I saw in their class-rooms, in the fields and streets, have a 'healthy and active air'. Obviously, at least in my view, they are both more childish and more manly than our own boys: more childish in that they are fonder of games and less disposed

* The highest class in a *Lycée.* E. H.

to overstep the limits of their age; more manly in that they are more capable of decision and action and self-government. Whereas the French schoolboy, especially the boarders in our colleges, is bored, soured, fined-down, precocious, far too precocious. He is in a cage and his imagination ferments. In all these respects, and in what concerns the formation of character, English education is better; it is a better preparation for the world and it turns out more wholesome spirits.

"When", says the author of *Tom Brown's School-days,* "I formed the project of writing this book I endeavoured to represent to myself the most common type of a little English boy of the upper middle-class, such as I had witnessed in my experience; and I faithfully maintain this type from the beginning to the end of my story, while merely striving to give a good specimen of the species".

The book thus conceived enjoyed an enormous success. Youths and grown men, all recognized themselves in the book, and we may make use of it ourselves while recognizing, with its author, that Tom's portrait, if not actually flattering, was certainly bene-volently drawn.

Neither Tom nor his father were much concerned with educa-tion properly so-called. The father, wondering what last words of advice to give his son, reflects:

"Shall I tell him to mind his work and say he's sent to school to make himself a good scholar? Well, but he isn't sent to school for that — at any rate not for that mainly. I don't care a straw for Greek particles, or the digamma; no more does his mother. What is he sent to school for? Well, partly because he wanted so to go. If he'll only turn out a brave, helpful, truth-telling Eng-lishman, and a gentleman, and a Christian, that's all I want."

And when Tom, after several years, asks himself what he went to school for, he comes, upon reflection, to this conclusion:

"I want to be Al at cricket and football and all the other games, and to make my hands keep my head against any other fellow, lout or gentleman. —— I want to carry away just as much Latin and Greek as will take me through Oxford respectably. —— I want to leave behind me the name of a fellow who never bullied a little boy, or turned his back on a big one."

Remarkable words, and they do sum up very well the ordinary feelings of an English father and son: learning and the cultivation of the mind come last; character, heart, courage, strength and physical address are in the first rank. Such an education turns out

Fig. 12   *A Healthy and Amusing Game*
*Flora. "Good gracious, Reginald, what have you been about?"*
*Reginald. "Oh nothing! We've only been playing at being Tom*
*Ayers and the benicia boy!"*   (Punch, May 5, 1860)

men capable of great moral and physical strivings, with all the advantages, but likewise all the disadvantages, of that particular orientation of body and soul.

Among other undesirable consequences there is this, that the rougher instincts are developed. "Games take first place," said an Eton master, "books second." * The boys, like Tom, glory in being fine athletes, and spend three, four, even five hours a day in noisy and violent physical exercise. When running ('Hares-and-hounds'), they wallow for hours over ploughed fields and through sodden meadows, fall in the mud, lose their shoes, pick themselves up as best they can. At 'Football', the groups hurl themselves against each other; the boy who happens to be underneath bears the weight of the whole mass; his arms and legs may be put out of joint, his collar-bone broken. At cricket, the big, heavy ball is flung with such force that a clumsy player who gets in its way will be knocked down by it. Almost all the games usually entail some cuts and bruises; the boys glory in not feeling them, and, as a natural result, are no more reluctant to inflict than to suffer them. A boy thus becomes pugnacious, a boxer. The author of *Tom Brown* says that to fight with their fists is the natural and English way for English boys to settle their quarrels. All the men I have met did so when they were at school, and it is still common there. This duelling — for it is a kind of duel — has its rules, its proper place, its audience and its seconds. Each combatant has two helpers who sponge his face and make a knee for him to sit on in the intervals between bouts; these bouts are repeated often for as long as half an hour. The principle laid down is that one must go on so long as one can still see and still stand up. At the end of the fight there will be black eyes, cheeks swollen and bruised, sometimes a thumb out of joint or a split lip.

Unfortunately the school's official institutions have the same tendency: in addition to lines, being kept in, and prison, † use is made of flogging. In some schools if a boy's name appears three times in the punishment roll, he is made to take his trousers down for a beating. This morning, at Harrow, four boys were beaten (fourteen strokes each, not hard enough to draw blood). In all colleges this amiable office is performed by the head-master. It would be very difficult to find school-masters in France to accept a salary of a hundred, or a hundred and fifty thousand francs at that price. In principle the cane ** may be used on any boy, even the oldest: but it is hardly ever used excepting on the little boys and middle school boys. The strange thing is, it is not unpopular:

* Demogeot and Montucci. p. 22, op. cit.
† I do not know what this means: it is literally prison in the text. E. H.
** Taine calls it a whip. Perhaps it was. E. H.

fifty years ago the boys at Charterhouse, upon learning that there was a proposal to replace beating by fining, revolted against the proposal with cries of, "Down with fines! Long live the whip!" and, on the following day, renewed acquaintance with their beloved rod.

School-masters with whom I have discussed this matter do not consider this form of punishment humiliating and say that it develops a stoical courage in the boys: in their opinion, blows are the most natural form of repression. Provided received opinion does not regard flogging as shameful, and that the victim does not feel insulted by it, all is well. Apart from the 'head-master', the older boys responsible for discipline have the right to inflict the same punishment, to which end, in some schools, they carry a cane and make use of it.

I come now to a very shocking institution of which I must say something, that is, 'fagging', the obligation which the little boys are under to be the servants of the bigger ones. At Harrow, Rugby and certain other institutions it has been modified and softened; but it remains bad in itself. For it is a school for bullying and by it English boys are urged along the way to which they already incline, in the direction of all those excesses entailed by their energetic temperament — violence, tyranny and harshness. A lady of my acquaintance who, it is true, is of foreign origin, could not bring herself to expose her son to 'fagging' and sent him to a *lycée* in Paris. According to official investigations, * the little boys are valets and slaves. Every big boy has several who are obliged to run his errands, sweep his room, clean his candle-sticks, toast his bread and his cheese for him, call him in the morning at a stated time, be present at his games often for two or three hours a day, run and fetch his ball, to be at his orders all the time he is working, and to put up with his whims.

"At Westminster College (sic), the life of a first-year scholarship boy is a servitude so continuous that it is impossible for him to find the time necessary for his studies. It is a sober fact, says one witness, that from the 1st January to the 31st December the young scholar has not a single moment of his own time which is not subject to interruption. At three-thirty in the morning two of the youngest, appointed according to a rota, get up to light the fire, heat water, and call those of the older boys who have given them orders to do so. Often the older boy, called at four, does not

* Demogeot and Montucci, op. cit. p. 49. See also *Tom Brown's School-days.*

109

actually rise until seven-thirty, and has to be warned of the time every half hour. Every small boy has to carry out this task two or three times a week." *

Add to this all the chores to be done during the day, and at evening.

"The older boys like tea: it has to be made for them two or three times in an evening, but coffee is not, therefore, neglected ... Kettles have to he refilled every few minutes."

One witness says that when, on Saturday evenings — when Westminster boys are allowed out — his son arrived home from school, he was so exhausted by lack of sleep that he wanted only to go straight to bed. In order to maintain a punctual and minute obedience the older boys employ terror. "Blows and kicks are no more than commonplace amiabilities among them, and do not count among the regular punishments. —— The first grade of real punishment consists in systematic face-slapping; the patient (sic) has to stand with his arms at his sides and hold out his face to receive a dozen slaps, right and left. —— Another time he may have to place his hand palm down on the table; the back of his hand is then beaten with the blade of a wooden knife, sometimes until it raises a weal." Next in the scale comes the bastinado (bastonnade), then the two kinds of "tanning". The boy is beaten on the thigh † with a fives racket, which breaks the skin and draws blood. Or he places his foot on a sink set as high as a table, and the executioner, taking a run of two or three steps, kicks the part of the body thus exposed. "I have heard tell," says the reporter, "of two or three cases in which the boys were so cruelly bruised that they were long forced to refrain from taking part in games and other exercises." Tom Brown is tossed in a blanket and thrown so high that he strikes the ceiling. One day, having refused to sell his lottery ticket to some big boys, he is seized and held in front of the fire and roasted (literally) until he nearly faints. This actually happened, the novel merely copied an authentic fact. Moreover, equally revolting incidents are to be met with in the lives of Cowper, Lord Byron and Sir Robert Peel.

The features of their system which have just been cited are, no doubt, its blackest and since, in matters of reform, the English are persevering, the picture is tending to grow brighter. But, even supposing the reforms accomplished, the impression remains very disagreeable. For, by and large, a school conducted on such lines

* Presumably from Demogeot and Montucci, op. cit. E. H.

† gras de la jambe. Thigh? Calf? Bottom? E. H.

110

is a sort of primitive society in which force reigns almost un-checked, the more so in that the oppressed make it a point of honour never to denounce their oppressors. The masters intervene as little as possible: they are not, as they are in France, the stand-ing representatives of humanity and justice. Very rarely, and only in some schools, may they be appealed to or the advice and aid of the oldest boys sought. The weak must fend for themselves, and must suffer in silence. And consider what a temptation it is for a vigorous young man to possess power and the right to use force! It is not good to give a free rein to the instincts of domi-nation and bullying. Use leads to abuse, appetite grows with what it feeds upon, and a man is stimulated to strike more blows by the blows he is already striking. No man should ever be given the chance to turn despot and hangman.

On the whole, education, on these terms, is not unlike that of the Spartans: it hardens the body and it tempers the character. But, as far as I can make out, it often produces (merely) sports-men and louts.

Needless to say the cultivation of the mind is bound to suffer from such a regime. "Seeing that these young people are ready to sacrifice everything for cricket; seeing that they devote to it a number of hours and an enthusiasm out of all proportion to what they devote to their work; seeing that they talk, think and dream nothing but cricket, it is not surprising that we should find many people attributing the wretched intellectual results we obtain to this mania for *muscularity*." *

A vice which is unknown among us and which is connected with this predominance of physical over moral values, is gluttony, and notably the taste for wine: hence drunkenness is a failing as-sociated with flogging. Some boys stuff themselves with food, and precocious drunkards are to be found among them.

English education is not such as would be necessary to counter-balance these gross tastes. There is nothing in it to attract the mind, and it can hardly be considered by the boys as anything but so much forced labour to be got through. The literary element is very small, the technical element predominates. The principal object arrived at is a good knowledge of Greek and Latin and the ability to write verse and prose in these two languages cor-rectly. And, in fact, by virtue of a good memory and much practice, the cleverest boys succeed in this.

* Article in *The Museum*, 1867, by Mr. Farrar, Master at Harrow, quoted by Demogeot and Montucci.

In one respect, knowledge and handling of Greek, they are greatly in advance of our *lycée* pupils. I have before me the exercise book of a prize-winning school-boy in which scenes from Shakespeare are very well translated into Greek iambics in the style of Sophocles. But in other respects I think they are behind us. Their Latin, prose and verse, is less elegant and pure than the better compositions of our boys in Rhetoric classes. They do not seem really to know any history, but retail legends of Curtius and Regulus as authentic facts. They utter dissertations upon chivalry and the Middle Ages, in vague generalities, as used to be the case in our old *Université*. They seem to have no sense of the differences in *mores,* feelings, ideas and characters brought about by the passage of centuries. They do not appear to have read, like our own bettter pupils, the works of any good historian, a Thierry, a Michelet or a Guizot. They have, in general, few ideas: if we except present and practical questions of contemporary politics, a boy at the Rhetoric level in a Paris *lycée* has more. They have read many classical texts: but the explanations of these given to them are wholly grammatical, positivist. No attempt is made to expound the beauty of the passage in question, nor its delicacies of style, nor the pathos of the situation described by it; nothing is said of the author's method of obtaining his results, nor of the nature of his talent, the cast of his mind. Anything of the sort would seem to them vague. The master does not talk to his pupils as a critic addressing persons of taste; he makes no attempt to refine their response to literature; he makes no commentaries on the great writers of their own country.

The same is true in mathematics; * they teach rather its formulae, than its spirit. They are still using Euclid as their geometry text-book, and it is learnt by heart and recited by heart: reason and reasoning take a back seat. "Too often this teaching tends to produce only hellenists and calculators."

Whereas a young Frenchman of nineteen is, if he be intelligent and has applied himself, provided with a good general education, a great number of embryo ideas, a few half-formed ideas all his own, a decided preference for this or that author, for one style rather than another. He will have the beginnings of some theories, some vague opinions about beauty, history, philosophy, and at the very least a feeling that there exist vast questions of major importance concerning which he ought to have an opinon. This will be all the stronger in that scepticism is all about him in the very

* Demogeot and Montucci. *Ibid* 119-121.

air he breathes and that, as a rule, he will have lost his religious beliefs and that there is no universally imposed or accepted doctrine to check the free wandering of his mind so that, if he wants to come to rest in a port, he is obliged to find a harbour and invent an anchor for himself.

Here, however, several distinguished Englishmen with whom I have discussed the matter said that they considered their school, and even university education, as no more than a preparation, a system of exercises, a 'training' of the attention and the memory, and no more. "When we had finished with school and university," they told me, "we were obliged to re-educate, or rather to educate, ourselves, and to acquire by reading whatever we know of philosophy, history, political economy, natural science, art and literature." A beginning has been made in remedying these defects and in enlarging the circle of teaching: but it is still very narrow, still has Euclid and Sapphic verse as its centre, and it follows that the mind, less quickly adult, attains only later to a whole and balanced view.

A final detail which completes this sketch of the difference between the two countries: on an average the cost of keeping a boy at Harrow is £200 a year. How many fathers, in France, could devote five thousand francs a year to the education of a son? In France a civil servant, or a man belonging to one of the liberal professions, as they are called, usually earns 3000 francs a year at thirty, five thousand at fifty: and as a rule his private means are very small. In compensation, it will cost him not more than 1000 francs to keep a son at college *, four hundred at a small seminary; and State scholarships are numerous. One may, I think, reckon that a classical education is five times as dear in England as it is in France. They themselves recognize that one of their national vices is the habit of excessive spending. Only 8,500 primary schools are assisted by the Parliamentary subsidy for education; in France the same subsidy would wholly maintain 25,000 schools. It would give primary education to 1,500,000 French children, instead of 950,000 English ones. Mr Arnold calculates "that costs of maintaining and administering French schools are, taking account of proportional values, a quarter of what they are for English schools."

At Oxford, where I am going tomorrow, and at the universities in general, B —— tells me that the average undergraduate spends £300 a year: however, £200 is enough; and few, by strict

* *Lycée;* good secondary school. E. H.

economy, live there on only £100. The author of *Tom Brown at Oxford* quotes the case of a very poor student who managed on £75, but only because his lodgings were free, and at the cost of being despised. In France, any medical or law student who had £75 (1875 frs.) a year, and lodgings, would be very comfortably off. There are many with no more than 1500 frs. and it would certainly never occur to the richest of students to despise a fellow-student who happened to be poor.

Well, I am at Oxford and provided with a 'fellow' (agrégé) who answers all my questions with the greatest good-nature in the world. We are in a garden full of flowers; nearby, separated by a wall, is a handsome kitchen-garden. Both belong to the professor's house. Impossible to conceive of a more pleasant and poetic residence for a scholar. But I will revert to that: just now I want to get down our conversation.

Oxford is a collection of twenty-four colleges; that is, distinct, independent foundations each one having, on an average, an income of £15,000: Magdalen College has £45,000 or more. In addition, the town has a university of teachers which is a centre for all the colleges.

A college is composed of (1) the 'head' in receipt of from £1000 to £3000 a year; (2) 'fellows' — £200 — £300 (3) 'tutors', a kind of invigilator-supervisor of studies, paid partly out of college revenues and partly by the students, £400—£500; (4) 'scholars', students who, by merit, have won scholarship or bursaries of £50—£120; (5) students (undergraduates) properly so called, paying fees, and to the number of from forty to eighty. The remainder of the establishment's income is used to pay servants, cooks, the porter, etc., and also the officers who administer college property. *

The University is a corpus of professors analogous to our Collège de France. An undergraduate is not obliged to attend their lectures. Most of the professors are paid between £500 and £600 a year; two or three chairs are worth less than £200; on the other hand, others may be worth £1000, and certain professors of theology receive as much as £1700. One of them, the 'regius' professor receives £2300 a year. In some cases a canonry, or the diaconate of a cathedral, is attached to a chair,

* See notes at the end of the book.

bringing in from £1000 to £3000 in addition to the use of a large house and garden. But they are obliged to live generously, to entertain a great deal, to contribute to all sorts of charities, etc.; so that, like the bishops and many other high public functionaries, they spend all their stipend.

There are about 1300 undergraduates at Oxford *, and 1200 at Cambridge; there are also students at London. But as a general rule, this highest education is for the aristocracy, the rich, for a small minority, in the first place because it is expensive (£200 to £300 a year, but the temptation to spend more is great), secondly because it is an intellectual luxury (pure mathematics, Greek, Latin) and delays a young man's beginning upon a profitable career.

Each undergraduate has two or three rooms in a college, which can thus be considered a kind of hive. They are obliged to attend chapel at eight in the morning and to dine in 'hall' at five in the afternoon; to be in their college by nine at night and, in general, to attend a 'tutor's' conference every morning and a lecture in the afternoon. Infractions of this rule are noted and punished, especially if they are repeated.

To return to college after nine o'clock constitutes a misdemeanour; after midnight, a serious one; to stay out all night, very serious indeed. Punishments are, in certain colleges, by fines of from five shillings to £1; in others a *pensum*, more or less long. More often punishment takes the form of a reprimand from the Head, gating, being temporarily sent down, and finally being sent down for good. This detail is important: for it will be seen that the schoolboy has more freedom, the student less, than with us. An adolescent does not, when he becomes a young man, pass from cloistered discipline to complete independence: the process is gradual. At school be has already become accustomed to being left to himself in certain respects; but at University he is still not left entirely to himself. This is an excellent precaution: the habit of freedom is a moral guarantee against the abuse of freedom; surveillance is a physical guarantee.

Another check: Oxford and Cambridge are small towns. The young men are not, as they are with us, cast among the temptations of a capital city, reduced to a sedentary and cerebral life without the necessary counter-poise of physical exercise, and led to seek amusement at the theatre, in cafés, on the boulevards and in the strong stimulants of the great world. There is no debauchery at

* See notes.

Oxford; University Officers patrol the streets after nine o'clock and may enter any tavern or public house. Libertines go to London or to the neighbouring villages; my friend and informant estimates that half the undergraduates are pure. The principal fault is the taste for wine: fifty years ago drunkenness was general here, as throughout the upper classes; now here, as in the whole upper class, it has become rare.

A final favourable circumstance: the undergraduate, like the schoolboy, remains a good Protestant; he is religious, or at least feels a respect for religion. Out of one hundred young men whom my friend had the chance to question, only two declared themselves to be free thinkers; seventy belonged to the 'Broad Church' party, the remainder to the two variants (of Anglicanism) called 'High Church' and 'Low Church', the first of which favours fine ceremonial and pompous ritual and is near to Puseyism,* the other being altogether Calvinist and somewhat iconoclastic.

An undergraduate's studies last three years; during the first year nothing much is done but to revise and go over whatever was learnt at school. The first two examinations are primarily grammatical and linguistic; they entail an acquaintance with two or three Greek and Latin authors, Greek and Latin composition in verse and prose, and some questions on the Bible and the Gospels. The third deals in the same subjects but more profoundly studied, considered from a fresh point of view, from the critical, historical and philosophical points of view. Thereafter the undergraduate has a choice between four final examinations, one in mathematics, one in physical and natural science, one in letters and the ancient languages, and the fourth in modern history, legislation and political economy.

An undergraduate who fails to pass goes to another college and starts over again; should he fail a second time it is usual to leave the University.

There are two kinds of undergraduates: 'class-men' who aspire to honours, well worth having and which lead to valuable places in the University, the Church and elsewhere; and 'pass-men' who, as in France, are a majority, have no ambition beyond getting a *degree*; they do little more than attend their 'tutor's' lectures, and not those of the professors, and confine themselves to a minimum of study. †

* Taine gallicises this word as *puséyisme* which suggests that it was understood in France. E. H.

† See notes.

*Fig. 13 Inside the Sheldonian, Oxford*

The distinguished men who are the product of this education are for the most part mathematicians (notably at Cambridge) or humanists. But in the last ten years this established order has been flagging; contemporary ideas and modern sciences have been making their way in. New Chairs have been founded, and others have broadened their field of study and teaching. See, for example, the writings of Stanley, Jowett, the famous book entitled *Essays and Reviews*. Max Müller, the Sanscrit scholar *(Indianiste)*, occupies a Chair of the history and philosophy of languages, here at Oxford.

But all this is only the bark: what of the timber? The thing that matters is always the ethical content, morale, cast of mind, the dominant inclination of the men in question. How do these young men live, and what are their inclinations? To find an answer one should spend six months here: in default of personal experience, however, here are three or four accounts of their manners and *mores* which my friends tell me are true to life. *Pendennis*, by Thackeray; *Tom Brown at Oxford;* and a short, quite entertaining novel, illustrated by the author, called *The Adventures of Mr Verdant Green.*

The first point to note is that Oxford and Cambridge being meeting-places for young men of family, the tone and manners are appropriate to the character and position of their denizens. An English University is in many respects a club for young men of the nobility and gentry, or at least of wealth. Many newly rich men send their sons to University solely in order to enable them to make connections among the best people. Some of the poorer students, of low origin *, toady to their noble or gentle fellow-undergraduates who, later, may be in a position to give them a 'living'.† Not even the established usages of the University itself fail to promote this distinction of rank: in certain colleges under-graduates of noble birth eat at a separate table, wear special clothes, and enjoy certain small privileges. Imagine, if you can, anything of the kind happening at a French seat of learning!

The author of *Tom Brown* shows us, at St Ambrose's, a group of poor students called *servitors,* a sort of semi-scholarship holders, on whom their rich or noble fellows look down from a great height. In France, at the Ecole Polytechnique, the students do not know the names of bursary holders; those names are known only to the committee whose members are on their honour to keep them secret: such are the delicacies of the egalitarian spirit. Whereas here rank and fortune are greatly considered. The author of *Tom Brown* says that the lackey spirit and the worship of money are the most general and shameful evils at Oxford, as in the rest of England, and later, writing of his hero, says that sad to say his instinct was already teaching him that poverty is a shameful thing for an Englishman and that if you do not know a man really well you should always give the impression of assuming him to be the owner of an unlimited supply of ready money. "If", says one of the characters in the book, "the Black Prince were here, he would change his motto from *Ich dien* (I serve) into 'I pay.'"

Many of these young men have £500 a year and more to spend, and moreover get credit from tradesmen. They make it a point of honour to spend lavishly, cut a figure: they own horses, dogs, a boat on the river; they furnish their rooms with costly

---

* *Roturiers.* In justification of "low origin" cf. Jane Austen's "of low origin, in trade, and only very moderately genteel". This state of mind was probably not yet quite out of date in Taine's day, but nearly. E. H.

† cf Trollope's *Framley Parsonage.* E. H.

and elegant objects. "London wine-merchants supply them with liqueurs at a guinea a bottle, and wine at two guineas the dozen. Their cigars cost two guineas a pound; pineapples, hothouse fruits, and the rarest preserves figure at their suppers." They treat themselves to *gourmet's* dinners. They drive about Oxford and its neighbourhood scattering money at every tavern. "In the daytime they hunt, ride point-to-points and play billiards until the time when the doors are shut, when they are ready to take a hand at vingt-et-un, and to go on playing cards in their rooms, to an accompaniment of punch and other hot drinks for as long as any of them can still sit up in their chairs and play."

They are very little troubled by the work they are required to do. It is, especially during the first year, of the slightest. "Twelve two-hour tutorials a week, the New Testament, the first book of Herodotus, the second of the Aeneid, the first of Euclid: in addition two hours work a day: no supplementary work in the form of composition, verses or anything else. A tolerably fair scholar has no need to do any preparatory reading; he has already done all that in school, and knows it by heart." *

Thus, the undergraduate has even more leisure than our own first-year law students. Under such conditions a young man must be naturally very studious or very ambitious to do any reading at all, qualities which are given to very few. The others follow their bent, and it is here that the difference between the French and English temperaments is most clearly to be seen.

In France our temperament is precocious: the imagination of the school-boy, kept for long hours of boredom at his desk, becomes heated; the dangerous air of a great city penetrates to him; the conversation of his seniors and a literature which is too free does the rest. He is too often foolish enough to think that there is honour in playing the man before he is of an age to do so. Then, suddenly released and left unchecked in a great capital, he is exposed to the infection of example, finds all the convenience of anonymity, and in every place of public resort temptations spread out before him. Furthermore, in this respect, accepted opinion is not in the least strict, enjoining only prudence and good taste. Tolerant of escapades, it condemns only drunkenness, gross debauchery, and low entanglements which may degenerate into marriage. A mother once said to me, "When my sons go to Asnières, I know it, but I pretend not to." Our worldly morality

* Source not given for any of the foregoing quotations. E. H.

requires us to show tact, moderation and foresight, in this as in all things, but no more.*

The young man is ignorant of the fact that there is no worse way of wasting his strength, that such intercourse degrades the heart, and that after ten years of such a life he will have lost half his will-power and purpose, that all his thoughts will have an after-taste of bitterness and sadness, and that the spring of his being will have lost its temper. True, he learns about life, but very often he also loses all energy, all warmth of heart, and all power to act, so that at thirty he is good for nothing but to be a clerk, a provincial, a dilettante or a *rentier.*

Whereas here, as far as I can judge, a man remains more nearly intact, in the first place because he is subject to discipline, † more watched over and less tempted, and in the second place because public morality, written and spoken, is stricter. A book like Henry Murger's *Vie de Bohème* would be set aside and classed with the old, picaresque novels, and considered to be a picture of knaves, rascals and semi-sharpers. In the three novels of Oxford life I have mentioned extreme decency is maintained. There is a brief glance, in *Tom Brown,* at a group of wealthy *viveurs* each of whom has a mistress on the side, kept in a village; but they are censured even by many of their fellows. In the case of each of the three heroes we are shown a stirring of the heart, a budding passion ('calf-love') for a *grisette:* but they all stop, or are stopped, in time: and even the *viveurs* themselves admit that the seduction of an innocent girl is the act of a cad.

Two derivatives from these maxims tend to support them. The first is the precociousness of love and marriage: they fall in love early, often at no more than twenty, and often wed a few years thereafter. The other is the lively, popular, almost universal taste for bodily exercise. In this respect the universities are a continuation of the schools. Cricket, rowing, sailing, owning dogs and setting them ratting, fishing, hunting, riding, driving four-in-hand, swimming, boxing with gloves on ('sparring'), fencing and, of recent times, drilling with the Volunteers, these are, for them, the most interesting occupations. They do not go very well with serious reading: Plato, in his *Dialogues,* long ago declared that the lives of an athlete and a thinker are incompatible. According to a learned foreigner who has had a long experience of Oxford, if

* Asnières is a suburb of Paris. Presumably it was a resort of illicit pleasure. E. H.

† See notes.

*Fig. 14   Brawl between Town and Gown, Oxford*

subtle philology and elevated philosophical speculation have difficulty in acclimatizing themselves at Oxford, it is because the undergratuates eat too much and make overmuch use of their muscles. *

But sport is an excellent outlet for the strong and superabundant sap of youth, and at university, as at school, the spur is rivalry. Each college has its boat, its eight rowers and its coxswain, all hand-picked and long trained. Training begins five or six weeks before the races. It consists in rowing from five to twenty miles every day, dining early on a great deal of meat, stale bread and very little wine; tobacco is rationed; a maximum of two pints of beer a day; no pastries or ices; no late supper and early to bed. Such was the rule imposed on *Tom Brown*. During the first days the whole body is upset; during the last the oarsmen suffer agonies of thirst. During the actual race the effort is so enormous that there is a risk of bursting a blood vessel, and when it is over several feel sick and giddy and are unable to speak. All Oxford is present for the race, both town and gown. When the race starts an excited, absorbed crowd follows the boats, running and shouting, out of breath, jumping over ditches, their feet in water, stumbling and falling all along the banks of the river. The description of the race must be read to get any idea of the seriousness and enthusiasm of the competing crews. The last minute before the starting gun is solemn.

"Short minute, indeed! you wouldn't say so if you were in the boat, with your heart in your mouth, and trembling all over like

* See notes.

a man with the palsy. Those sixty seconds before the starting gun in your first race — why, they are a little life-time . . . For the first ten strokes Tom was in too great fear of making a mistake to feel or hear or see. His whole soul was glued to the back of the man before him, his one thought to keep time, and get his strength into the stroke . . . Isn't he grand, the Captain, as he comes forward like lightning, stroke after stroke, his back flat, his teeth set, his whole frame working from the hips with the regularity of a machine?"

The fanfares sound, the cheering swells to a thunder, embroidered handkerchiefs wave in the breeze. That evening the crew has a feast in the great hall of the college: there are speeches, applause, toasts, singing in chorus, a glad and glorious uproar. It is obvious that such a triumph must be as highly prized as the palm at antiquity's Olympic Games. And the interest is still very much greater when, in the month of March, the race takes place on the Thames between the crews of the two Universities; for two days nothing else is talked of in London.

Doubtless the cultivation of the muscles carried to these lengths entails a certain roughness in their manners. 'Town and gown' come to fisticuffs in the streets on occasion. But by way of compensation this gymnastic and athletic life dulls the senses and calms the imagination. Moreover when thereafter the moral and mental attributes and life develop, the soul finds itself housed in a stronger, healthier body. The young men one sees walking about here wearing their singular traditional costume (a short, black gown and a sort of flat *shako*) are full of sap and strength, of a fresh and handsome bearing, well muscled and articulated, and, in my view, their faces freer from trouble and fatigue than those of our students.

In the past twenty years a gradual movement of reform has been at work and several features of my description require modification. In most Cambridge colleges 'Fellows' are now allowed to marry; dissidents * and Catholics are admitted to the schools. The passion for rowing has somewhat abated; students of different social classes are less unequal; in some colleges the undegraduates' expenditure on food and drink is watched over and restricted. Oxford is ceasing, little by little, to be an aristocratic club, an athletics gymnasium, an Anglican ecclesiastical preserve; it is becoming a modern school, a lay and liberal academy. †

* Nonconformists, etc.

† See notes.

At two o'clock I attended a ceremony in the great hall of the University. The costumes were grotesque, like those worn at our own major distributions of prizes. Speeches in Latin, which recalled the rubbishy anachronisms of the Sorbonne. A set of verses in English, read aloud by the student-laureate: the subject was Sir John Franklin, and the lines rhetorical in style. Five or six distinguished strangers (foreigners?) received the honorary degree of Doctor of Laws, *in jure civili;* but they pronounce it *in ioure çaïvaïlaï*. An Englishman quoting Caesar's *Veni, vidi, vici,* but pronouncing in this same way, *Vénaï, Vaïdaï, Vaïçaï,* my neighbour informed him, "Julius Caesar could never have pronounced such a phrase."

In the afternoon there was a session in a museum, a vast, more or less Gothic building which is not yet finished, with experiments and readings in the physical and natural sciences. There were flocks of ladies walking about the place, in loudly coloured, vulgar *toilettes;* several of them, young and *décolletées,* were wearing spectacles. However, only a few of the details are disagreeable; taken as a whole, town, buildings and countryside, it is all admirable. I have already walked about the town and did so again today at twilight. What a number of colleges! And each with its chapel, its high, crenellated walls, its diverse architecture, something from every age, Gothic, Tudor, 17th-century. Then there are the vast courtyards with their statues and fountains; balusters stand out against the tender azure of the sky at the tops of the buildings, windows are delicately trellised with lead, or divided into four panes by sculptured crosses in Renaissance style; there are pulpits of carved stone and, at every bend in the street, tall, conical steeples — so many noble shapes in such a small space!

The place is a natural museum where the works and inventions of six centuries have accumulated. The stone of the buildings is all the more venerable for being worn and flaked away. And how content and easy one feels among all these ancient things! The more so in that here they are not merely ancient, not neglected or ruinous as they are in Italy, but piously preserved, restored; and they have, since their foundation, been in the hands of rich, reputable and intelligent guardians. The walls are clad in an ample drapery of climbing plants; honey-suckles embrace each pillar; wild flowers dress the coping of every wall; lawns of rich, fine turf, scrupulously cared for, spread their green carpet even under the very arcades below the galleries; behind the chevet of a chapel appears a garden of flowers with thousands of roses in full bloom.

At one end of the town is a walk sheltered by immemorial trees beneath whose branches run two swift streams; and beyond, the eyes rest delightedly on meadows opulent with grasses and plants in flower and seed. Impossible to conceive of a more magnificent vegetation, a richer verdure, rich yet tempered by the stipple of colours provided by buttercup, daisy, dock in flower and grey-tinted grasses.

The countryside is in all the glory of its freshness. Let but the sun emerge and the whole land smiles with charming gladness; one might think of it as a shy and lovely maiden, glimpsed laughing beneath her veil as it is pulled aside. Meanwhile the light of day was waning, a vague whiteness hung above the meadows, and under that soft gauze the river flashed darkly. A silence fell, broken only by the melodious chiming of Christ Church bell. Could there really be a town but a hundred paces away? How sheltered and withdrawn is study here, and how poetic!

Visit to Magdalen College; I cannot grow tired of admiring these ancient edifices festooned with ivy and blackened by time, these crenellated towers, mullioned windows, above all these vast, square courts whose arcades form a walk similar to that one sees in Italian convents. Of an afternoon they are, but for one or two passing undergraduates, deserted; there can be nothing more sweetly tranquil than this architectural solitude, poetic, intact and without ever a hint of abandonment, ruins and death. Herds of deer graze peacefully beneath mighty elms; a long walk, bordered by the most beautiful trees, winds between two rivers. Oxford is built on low ground, formerly a swamp, hence the freshness and the incomparable opulence of her verdure.

At Worcester College a considerable sheet of water, where swans glide, washes in slow small waves the fringe of flower-starred lawns. On all sides great cedars, massive yews, oaks and poplars rear their boles and spread their foliage. From branch to branch clamber honeysuckles and wistarias, and trail to the ground. The great garden of St John's and the small garden of Wadham are masterpieces of a unique kind, higher than art itself. For nature and time have wrought them; can any human art produce a thing so beautiful as a group of perfect trees three centuries old?

Surely not: yet one returns and, beholding Oxford's architecture again, changes one's mind; this, too, is three centuries old and seems rooted in earth as rightfully as the trees themselves; the colour of the stone has adapted itself to the climate, and age has

124

communicated to these buildings something of the majesty which belongs to natural things. One is not aware of any mechanical regularity, any official imprint: each college has developed of its own accord, each age has built in its own style; on the one hand Christ Church's grandiose quadrangle with its lawns, fountains and staircases, on the other, over there, near the Bodleian, a pile of buildings, or carved porches, high belfried towers all flowered and embroidered, and column-circled cupolas.

Sometimes the chapel is a little cathedral. In some colleges the dining hall, sixty feet high and its walls lines of arches, is like the nave of a church. The Council Hall, completely panelled with ancient wood, is worthy of our own old Capitular chambers. Imagine the life of a 'Master' or a 'Fellow' in one of these monuments, beneath these Gothic carvings in wood, lit by Mediæval or Renaissance windows, in the midst of luxury, but austere and in perfect taste: prints, engravings, books, all admirable. At evening, coming down the stairs, with light flickering over great, dark shapes, one seems to be moving against a stage set...

Nothing is wanting here, neither the beauties of art, nor nature's freshness, nor the gravity and grandeur of history. A little while ago, when I was visiting colleges, I was told the names of former scholars, students for ever celebrated: Wycliff, the Black Prince, Sir Walter Raleigh, Pym, Hampden, Archbishop Laud, Ireton, Addison. In each building the 'Guide' points out the dates of founding and founders' names, subsequent embellishments and restorations.

All these men of the old days seem living yet, for their work has survived them and endures. The wisdom of past ages lingers, written in Latin words upon the walls. Above the dial of a clock * are engraved these solemn words: *Pereunt et imputantur*. And this is no dead or sleeping town: today's labours are completing and enlarging those of the yesterday: contemporary men, now as then, contribute their building and their gifts. When, at the Bodleian, one has seen the manuscripts and precious books, and portraits by Van Dyck, Lely and Kneller, one finds, further on, a recent gallery of original sketches and drawings by Raphael and Michelangelo, in which all the vitality, all the feeling for the nude, all the superb paganism of the Renaissance bursts out in incomparable frankness: the collection cost £7000; Lord Eldon alone gave £4000.

I visited the houses of several professors, some of them re-

\* Possibly a sun-dial. E. H.

sembling our own old mansions (hôtels), others modern and charming, all with gardens, flowers, views noble or smiling. From the walls of the oldest houses portraits of former occupants of the house and office look down upon every modern comfort. I compared them with those of our own men of learning — a kind of cage on the third floor in a big city; with the wretched lodgings of the Sorbonne. I thought, too, of the dreary and dilapidated aspect of the *Collège de France*. Poor Frenchmen, who are poor indeed, and live like men encamped! We belong to yesterday, ruined generation by generation — by Louis XIV, Louis XV, the Revolution and the Empire. We demolished the past, and all had to be done over again. Here the new generation does not break with its predecessor: reforms are superimposed upon institutions; and the present, resting upon the past, continues it.

# CHAPTER FIVE

# THE COMMUNITY AND THE GOVERNMENT

✥

A NUMBER of short visits to places thirty and forty miles from London. One ought to try and see the local districts, the parishes, for it is not possible to understand the social fabric properly until one has studied three or four of its component threads in detail. As usual, I met with the most perfect kindness and hospitality.

The same countryside again: meadows separated by hedges, with occasional tall trees. The country is one sheet of green: one's eyes are satiated with it, and it is the strongest impression I shall bring back from England.

From the top of a high hill which we crossed, I was told you can see forthy miles in every direction: nothing but flat verdure; no forests, a few thin stands of trees; beet, lucerne, hops, peas, gentlemen's parks tufted with trees, hollows where brimming, yellow streams flow slowly, watery meadows where ponderous cattle graze and chew the cud. The fresh green grass, incessantly reborn, springs everwhere superabundant. Translate it into meat and dairy-produce, and compare that to the bread, wine and vegetables which form the principal food of our own peasantry. In this respect and many others the English are much more like the Dutch than the French.

A Paul Potter or a Ruysdael would find subjects for paintings here. Beauty is not wanting in this sky, overcast, full of grey, or almost black, clouds lifting and spreading against a still background of white vapour. Here and there between us and the horizon, the view is obscured by a downpour of rain. All the colours are pale, gentle, melting subtly into melancholy.

We passed wild, deserted 'commons' with an occasional horse grazing in solitude. This is the primal soil of the land, full of gorse and brambles. Generation by generation it has been reduced, and civilisation, like a rising tide, has eaten it away and left only strips and tatters. What labour has been needed to turn it into pasture and market-garden! What patient effort to make it man's own!

This they have accomplished, and each century of history has seen more wild, rough pasture turned into enclosed meadows by thousands of acres. It was more beautiful in its primal state: its coarse and thorny vegetation, its dull or sombre tints were better-matched with the aspect of the English sky. The cultivated land, nature civilized, bears all too visibly the imprint of man's industry; it is too rectilinear; the colours are false or ill-matched; the foliage of turnips is of a green shot with purple, a harsh colour; the finer plants shine under the sun, too dazzling and too fragile in colour, so that you are aware that they are here by artifice. The whole countryside seems to be a fodder-factory, the mere anteroom to a dairy or a slaughterhouse: picturesque ideas must give way to the utilitarian. And it must be admitted that there is as much worth in the latter as in the former: after all, man lives on mutton chops, and the spectacle of an ungrateful soil transformed into a good wet-nurse is also a fine one.

Walk in the country and visit two villages. There was a downpour every other hour, recalling an English saying: "When it is not raining, take your umbrella; when it is, do as you please." But in sunshine the effect of this humidity is charming: the grass has a fresh newness which is delightful. Drops of water run down each stem, shining like pearls. Suddenly a whole meadow will burst into light as the emerging sun touches it, and its drifts of white and yellow flowers turn luminous.

Yet still the sky is part covered by spreading vapours: here and there the clouds darken, turn purple and, a quarter of a league away, melt into rain again. This exchange between moist heavens and moist earth is constant, and the contrast between the splendid colours of the land and the confused tints of the sky, is strange. Your eyes follow the changing tints and vague motions of the ubiquitous misty exhalation as it drifts and tears against the hedges, like muslin. A light breeze bends and sways the foliage of tall trees; and you stand listening to the slight sound of rain drops falling upon their pyramidal heads.

Some of the cottages are very poor, built of wattle and daub (pisé), with thatched roofs, the rooms too low and too small, the windows also too small, the interior walls too thin. Think of a large family crowded into two such rooms in winter, with clothes drying on them, baby linen hung up to air, and a roaring fire: during the long periods of rain and snow, they must live in an unwholesome atmosphere, breathing their own bodily emanations.

Many of the mothers have haggard faces blotchily red, and a

wasted, exhausted look; they have too many children and are all overtired. The tenant of one of these cottages was a day-labourer, married, father of six children, and earning twelve shillings a week. He is usually taken on by the year or half-year. A cottage like his costs between three and four pounds a year. His face was drawn, strained, sad and humble. My introduction to these people was performed with consideration and courtesy; they were asked to excuse us for troubling them, and to allow the visiting French gentleman to see the cottage. They at once consented, smiling kindly. I hastened to say that I had seen many French cottages less well furnished. Whereupon my companion said that was some consolation: the poor day-labourer did not appear to be of his opinion.

However, his little house was clean: the blue-patterned plates were ranged in good order above a dresser. The iron fireplace was tidy. I had already seen cottages of this class elsewhere; almost always, at least in one room, there is an old carpet on the floor. There is often wall-paper, chairs of well-polished wood; small, framed prints; always a Bible and sometimes a few other books — works of piety, modern novels, how to rear rabbits, and so forth. In short, more articles of use than in our own poorest cottages. Furthermore, they are better maintained — no broken doors, hanging shutters, broken windowpanes, stagnant puddles, or manure heaps all over the place. The floors are well-swept, nothing is left lying about. Probably untidiness and dirt are unhealthier in this climate than in ours, and people are obliged to be neat, careful and regular in their ways, as in Holland.

The village has only four hundred souls. Yet the little inn was decent, gleaming with cleanliness; one would have no hesitation in staying a night there, and one would be comfortable. We visited the carpenter's house, and the carter's. Both were at tea with their families: there was butter on the table. Their houses are red brick and roofed with tiles. Beside one of them was quite a large garden full of vegetables, well cultivated, with rows of fine strawberries, and bee-hives in one corner. Both houses had small flower gardens, with roses, a creeper, climbing plants, all very pleasant. The rooms were rather low but sufficiently airy; the small, diamond-paned leaded windows let in ample light. A brick path scrupulously washed led to an out-building: the privy was as well kept and clean as in a middle-class house. Two bedrooms on the first floor. A few books — *The Whole Duty of Man*, a *Murray's Guide*, a family Bible, five or six volumes of history.

Not a speck of dust on the windows, not a splash of mud on the floors anywhere, not a hole or tear in their clothes.

A number of other people of the same social station passed up and down the street, and their clothes were the same. True, it was Sunday. But on the whole my impression was that they are better found and more careful of their appearance than French peasants. The pride, glory and superiority of our peasantry is in the possesion of land: they prefer to be in all things abstemious, to deprive themselves of comforts, in order to own their own few acres; and they save on their well-being to acquire them. Moreover, that acquisition constitutes a fund: in the event of sickness or famine they have a sure recourse on their own doorstep.

Whereas here, by all accounts, the rural worker is as free-spending as an urban workman, as lacking in foresight and as exigent in matters of comfort. There only has to be an accident and they at once become a charge on the parish. *

Visited a farmer who cultivates a hundred acres. The cleanliness in his house was altogether Dutch; I have seen nothing better in the regions of Utrecht or Amsterdam. The farmer's wife told me that every year the inside walls are whitewashed, that the stone flags of the floor are scrubbed once a week: I felt quite ashamed to walk on them and soil them.

Another farm, again of one hundred acres; the farmer pays £1000 a year in rent and also tithes and taxes. Similar cleanliness and good order.

A third farmer we called on has three hundred acres and also pays £1 an acre rent; but only because it is poor soil, for his neighbour on the far side of the hill pays £800 for four hundred acres. The domestic arrangements inside the farmhouse were as comfortable and pleasant as those of the largest and finest farms in La Beauce and the Paris region. The house was old, with a high porch in front which serves as an entrance hall. Here and there about the yard were handsome pines and ornamental trees. A pretty, green garden about one wing of the house. The principal room was furnished with antique pieces. The staircase of solid wood, and a sideboard both date from the 16th Century. The hearth was immense, capable of burning an entire tree-trunk, a

* "After careful thought I prefer the condition of the rural day-labourer in France, Spain and Germany, who, by sobriety and thrift, ensures, before all other satisfactions, the ownership of a strip of land and a humble dwelling ... I have long perceived that the over-riding need for comforts in English working men bars the road to ownership and independence."

Le Play. *La Réforme Sociale.* 11. 35.

real Yulelog; it is provided with a double, wooden screen which, in summer, closes the opening and, in winter, is a protection against draughts. Some quite good prints on the walls and a fair number of books in addition to the family Bible.

The farmer has twelve enormous and superb horses and a steam-engine for threshing the corn. Among other sources of profit he sells eighty fat pigs every year. His face I found intelligent, decided, serious and calm. He was neither surly nor garrulous. His wife appeared to be a capable and methodical housekeeper. One would have to be English and live with them for a year to discover what they have in their heads. In *Adam Bede* George Eliot painted a farmer and his wife: they are characters done in minute detail and high relief; I am told by my friends that they are in every way excellent, and strikingly true to life.

We went to see a fourth farm: six hundred acres, and about £600 a year rent. This time I was astounded: we were introduced into a cool and lofty drawing-room. Long curtains held back by gilt loops; two elegantly framed looking-glasses; chairs in good taste. In the middle a table with a number of handsomely bound books. In short, the country drawing-room of a Parisian with a private income of twenty-five thousand *livres*. Adjoining the room was a conservatory full of flowers,* giving on to a pretty country-side of sloping meadows and distant woods.

The farmer's wife came in: she was a woman of thirty but looked twenty-six and was wearing a dress of narrowly striped grey silk; one or two rings on her fingers, her hands perfectly white, the nails pink and cared for, her figure admirable, tall and slender as a Diana, extremely beautiful, full of cheerfulness and high spirits, without a trace of awkwardness, and conversing very well. I heard later that she rides and plays the piano, but is nevertheless an excellent housekeeper. She goes to the kitchen every morning, gives her orders, supervises what is done and sometimes makes a little pastry herself. On one occasion when there were guests and her cook was away, she prepared and cooked the dinner with her own hands. Apart from a few *nuances* in manners and language, she is a lady; and at heart she is altogether so. My escort praised her highly, but added that in numerous other cases a similar education and similar tastes are apt to make a woman dissatisfied with her condition; and that there are, nowadays,

* This feature of English domestic architecture was apparently new to Taine. It was, in fact, new to the English at that date. Taine calls it "a kind of green-house, a glazed parlour full of flowers." E. H.

many farmers' daughters who are stylish, spendthrift, and idle, consequently *déclassées* and unhappy.

"Since you have begun," B —— suggested, "you may as well finish the job."

So, twelve miles further on, we stopped at a model farm. No central farm-yard: the farm is a collection of fifteen or twenty low buildings, in brick, economically designed and built. Since the object was to put up a model, it would not have done to set the example of a costly edifice. Bullocks, pigs, sheep, each in a well-aired, well cleaned stall. We were shown a system of byres in which the floor is a grating; beasts being fattened remain there for six weeks without moving. Pedigree stock, all very valuable. One bull and his family were Indian and reminded me of Buddhist sculptures. Steam-engines for all the work of the arable land. A narrow gauge railway to carry their food to the animals; they eat chopped turnips, crushed beans, and 'oil cakes'. Farming in these terms is a complicated industry based on theory and experiment, constantly being perfected, and equipped with cleverly designed tools. But I am not a competent judge of such matters, and amused myself by watching the farmer's face: he had red hair, a clear complexion but marbled with scarlet like a vine leaf baked by the autumn sun; the expression was cold and thoughtful. He stood in the middle of a yard in a black hat and black frock-coat, issuing orders in a flat tone of voice and few words, without a single gesture or change of expression. The most remarkable thing is, the place *makes money* (ital. sic), and the nobleman who started it in the public interest now finds it profitable. I thought I could see, in the farmer's attitude, in his obviously positive, attentive, well-balanced and readily concentrated mind, the explanation of this miracle.

We set out for home and all about us night was falling over the countryside. Trees grew indistinct and vanished in a grey cloudiness; strange, yellowish tints spread over the meadows. The murky air grew thicker, enveloping even the very hedges of the road and drowning everything beneath its soft, dense covering. In this gloaming, which suggested a painting by Rembrandt, I went over in my mind those things which had made most impression on me. And first came the children's faces, so fresh and full of health, so vigorous and plump, even in the poorest cottages. One, still in his cradle, had been sleeping with one arm thrown out; his little, button-nose was almost transparent under the light, his mouth looked like a cherry and his cheeks like two fat roses. The flesh would yield to the finger if you touched it, and the petals of a dew-drenched flower have not more brilliance. In my view this leaves our southern types far behind; in them man is, almost from infancy, completed, finished, stable in a definitive shape once and for all. But here one is aware, as in a Rubens, of the continual growth and change in life and its fragility, and its delicacy; and, at the same time, the sap of life, its inexhaustible and spontaneous renewing of the human substance.

I remember a little boy of four years old, who leant against a wall, astonished, mute, hiding his big, shy eyes, putting a finger in his mouth and letting us stroke his hair without saying a word; in another moment he dared raise his eyes and look at us as if we were strange animals, then suddenly shy again, hid his cherub's face with both arms. You can watch the play of feeling beneath their clear complexion as you can watch the colours change over the face of their meadows.

My friends told me the village I had seen was a fair specimen, and that the domestic interiors I had visited should give me an exact idea of the comfortable average for the whole class; but that in some districts, for example Norfolk and Lincolnshire, I could see finer farm-houses. Since then, and also by reference to official documents, * I have come to see that this judgment was inexact. The evil aspect is greater than I had realised: the poor are becoming poorer and poorer. Great holdings are on the increase, small holdings are disappearing. † At the end of the last century Arthur Young was writing, "I do not know a single cottage to which a bit of land is not attached." Furthermore, under the open-field and common system, the poor villagers had each some poultry and a pig on the common. But by means of 'enclosure-acts' the commons have been continuously reduced **; thus the peasant can no longer have recourse to his own small supplies of meat, and having sold his strip of land is left with nothing but his two arms, which he now hires out.

In the purely agricultural districts it seems that the wage is from seven to eight shillings a week, and not twelve as in the district I visited. To eke it out the villagers hire out their wives'

* First and second *Reports* of the Commission on the employment of children and women in agriculture. 1868-69.

† For the best account of this I know see that isolated work of belated genius, Flora Thompson's *Larkrise to Candleford*. E. H.

** According to Fawcett, *Manual of Political Economy*, Enclosure Acts since 1710 had taken about eight million acres of land from the commons and given them to the great landowners of the neighbourhood. H. T.

and their children's arms as well as their own. They are to be seen in groups, hoeing root-crops, the cultivation of which is being constantly extended. Agriculture, having increased the scale of its operations and become a scientific industry, is, on the other hand, introducing the rule of work, the monotony, the poverty and misery of manufacturing centres into the countryside. The children waste away, remain ignorant, and become vicious; in one district of Lincolnshire out of four hundred cottages, two hundred have only one room where the whole family sleeps pell-mell.

Two *Punch* drawings which I saw recently, on this subject. A landowner is showing Mr Punch over this stables, which are admirable. "Yes, Mr Punch," says he, "handsome, clean stall, well aired, plenty of light, drainage, perfect ventilation, the best water and the best feed possible, and good treatment, that's my plan." They move on to a cottage. A single room, almost bare; three chipped plates on a plank, a battered kettle, two garments hung up to dry: the distress and squalor are horrible. A wretched man in rags, with a dented hat, is trying drearily to warm himself at a tiny brushwood fire. His hollow-eyed wife is crouching with two children on a truckle bed. On another is a young girl and a little boy. On a mattress in one corner, a young man. They are all emaciated and cringing. Mr Punch is saying to the landlord "Your stable arrangements are excellent! — Suppose you try something of the sort here! Eh?"

Here, then, the ulcer and the cure are shown together.

And in contrast I think I can say that in the case of our own four million landowning peasants, prosperity, especially during the last twenty years, has been on the increase. The vices of our State are different, political, and are due to the instability of the Government and the want of permanently established and lasting liberties. But every State has its hereditary diseases: one can only point out the symptoms, show that they derive from the organism itself, and apply some temporary palliative to the sores; major surgical operations, advocated by certain people, rarely result in anything but making the patient worse than ever.

Having made further enquiries into the matter, I think there can be no doubt that the class of agricultural labourers is, in this country, the most wretched and the most backward of all. * A *savant* recently told me, "As regards intelligence and ideas the

* Brit. Alm. & Companion. 1864. Resumé of census of 1861 on the various trades and professions). Out of 20 m. inhabitants of England and Wales, there are:

*Fig. 15   The Cottage*

*Mr. Punch (to Landlord). "Your stable arrangements are excellent!*
*Suppose you try something of the sort here! Eh?"*

*(Punch Almanac, 1861)*

distance between them (the agricultural labourers) and our
'mechanics' is as great as it is between the mechanics and men
like myself."

Two acquaintances who have lived in France add to that that

> Landowners:   male 15,131
>                     female 15,635
> Farmers & )     male 226,957
> Graziers    ): female   22,778
> Agricultural        )    male 914,301
> labourers working ) : female   43,964
> for hire          )
> Shepherds )
> working    ) : Male 25,559
> for hire   )

The total number of persons employed in agriculture in some way or other
and working actively in it with head or hands is —

> Males     1,631,652
> Females     378,802
>                 2,010,454.

The total for males and females for 1956 is 1,042,000.   E. H.

135

the French peasantry is greatly superior: they praise especially their frugality, the habit of being sufficient to themselves, their hard work and their passion for land. According to these same two acquaintances, the English peasantry is very different, improvident, spendthrift, a constant burden on the parish or private charity. Even if an English peasant had a bit of land, like ours, he would not be capable of getting a living from it *; in the first place for want of thrift, and then because he is dull, has no ingenuity; and also because the soil of England is of indifferent quality and requires much improvement, which calls for capital investment. So that it really only lends itself to large-scale exploitation, stock-raising and grazing.

According to a clergyman who has lived in Devonshire and other counties, an agricultural labourer's wages are between eight and nine shillings a week, sometimes ten, but he would have to be very strong and very skilful to earn twelve. Now, as a rule such a man will have six children: impossible for eight people, or for that matter five or six, to live on such pay. So that these workers cannot manage without resort to public assistance or to private charity.

Moreover the women of this class, and of the working class generally in England, are wanting in address: they have not, like Frenchwomen, the trick of good management, orderly minds, the habit of bargaining, the art of making a little go a long way and something out of nothing. They cannot repair or turn a coat, make the best of a dish; quite often they cannot cook. One of my friends, who is on his parish committee for outdoor relief, had an allotment of fifteen shillings a week paid to a family in which there were fourteen children; neither the mother, nor the eldest daughter could make soup, roast a joint, or make any kind of a dish; they were accustomed to buy new bread, butter, tea and ham at the village shop, and always the dearest. Every member of the family could hoe a field; not one could cook a chop.

To this must be added the fact that since the agricultural revolution, eating habits have changed. Fifty years ago meat was a luxury to the rural poor, and they only ate it once a week. In winter they had only salt meat. Now they want fresh meat every day. so that England, which produces so much, is nevertheless forced to import more from Denmark and Holland; in 1862, for

* An obvious injustice, since before "the common was stolen from off the goose" the English peasantry did make a living from their land. The whole passage is, of course, special pleading, retailed by Taine. E. H.

Fig. 16   *The Pig and The Peasant*
Peasant. *"Ah! I'd like to be cared vor half as well as thee be!"*
(Punch, September 19, 1863)

example, three thousand head of cattle on the hoof entered the country by way of the Thames. *

To sum up, agricultural labourers live partly on alms; and the very burdensome 'poor-rates', together with very liberal private charity, are barely sufficient to support them. †

Now let us look at the good which is the counterpart of this evil. I have already made two expeditions of the kind I am now engaged on at forty or fifty miles from London, and in both cases, as where I am now, the number of gentleman's parks is astonishing. There is a constant succession of them all the way along the road; in some places they form a continuous line until one gets to London. Not only are the most ancient estates kept in

* Mrs Grote, *Collected Papers.* p. 73.

† *Fortnightly Review.* 1st Jan. 1871: "In the greater part of England an agricultural labourer's wages vary between 10 and 12 shillings a week. His rent costs him 1/- a week. It is impossible to live on this with a wife and only two children." Grote, ibid. p. 76: "Not one agricultural labourer can live and keep his family on his wages only; they subsist in part on their earnings and in part on alms."

being by virtue of the law of primogeniture; but in addition almost every self-made rich man's ambition is to own an estate, establish his family in it, and enter the ranks of the local gentry. It is in this direction that the bulk of England's 2,500 millions of annual savings is spent. * The money is used less to relieve the poor than to enrich the rich. But in compensation the rich are natural-born leaders, benevolent, and recognized as such. In my friend B——'s circle there are about forty families composing the local society and managing the whole district, at their head a marquis whose park covers seven hundred acres, four baronets, a lord (sic) and several members of the House of Commons. A clergyman with whom I went for a walk told me these gentlemen are almost "the fathers of the people".

B—— himself is the near kinsman and heir to a great nobleman whose estate he manages; he will one day have an income from this estate of £40,000 a year. Meanwhile, on behalf of his kinsman, he supervises the property, directs the work, builds healthy cottages for the work-people, subscribes to charities and public works and while improving the estate, serves his country's good.

It would be hard to find a single one of these great landowners who does not freely give of his money and time for the common good. They sit on the bench of magistrates, are 'overseers', 'justices of the peace', chairmen of committees and useful associations. One of them, whose fortune is thirty million francs, and whose brother is as rich as himself, has a one-million-franc share in an undertaking whose object is to provide London with drinking water. There are forty shareholders, each with a million-franc share. By way of relaxation from business and Parliamentary duties, this gentleman has built a church, which we visited: very pretty, in excellent Gothic style, with stained-glass windows, wood-panelling, a carved pulpit; in short, a little gem set among ever-green laurels. He has endowed it and pays the incumbent's stipend. †

---

* Presumably francs, i.e. £100 m. E. H.

† Mr. Cobden having ruined himself, his friends opened a public subscription which brought him in £70,000. Having ruined himself a second time, a second subscription raised £40,000. On one occasion Miss Burdett Coutts gave the Bishop of London a blank cheque to build a church: it cost £40,000. Another time she founded and endowed a bishopric in China. I am told of a duke who contributed £40,000 to his Party funds for election expenses. Another lord, whose income is £40,000, told a friend of mine that he spends £20,000 in pensions, gifts, subscriptions and the maintenance of public and private buildings.

Beside the church he has established a free school; among other things singing is taught there, he has provided a piano and gives little concerts, taking pleasure himself in hearing the children sing. As he believes in the good influence of music, he sends the master all over the country to propagate this institution. In another village I visited the local gentlemen subscribed to rent a two-roomed cottage to provide the villagers with a sort of club in which to spend their evenings; out of the fund subscribed they pay the rent and provide books, newspapers, fire, light and a woman to keep the place clean. But arrangements are being made such that ultimately this club will be self-supporting out of the contributions of its members. Man is so made that he does not appreciate a pure gift; it is necessary, therefore, that he bear part of the expense and willingly co-operate in the promotion of his own well-being. In the first room are books and newspapers; in the second they play draughts and chess, smoke, and talk. The object of the club's founders is to offer an alternative to the village inn. They understand human nature, and they know that gregarious instincts must be supplied with an outlet and the need for company catered for. These instincts and that need will in any case find satisfaction somewhere; so we should try to ensure that that satisfaction be innocent and, if possible, beneficent.

For instance, the villagers do no work on Sundays, and when the weather is dirty, cold and dark they naturally go to a place where there is fire, light and entertainment; and that place, twelve months in the year, is the public house. So give them a public house which is not so dear and where, instead of gin, they drink tea; thus they can fill their leisure time and not go home drunk. *
For the same reason one of my friends in London is a member of a Society to Secularise Sundays: it demands that Museums be opened on Sundays, concerts allowed, and also public 'lectures': drunkenness is more effectively combatted in this way than by means of sermons.

In addition to this intelligent and active charity, there are all sorts of consideration and attention given by the rich. A lord lent his park here for the last 'archery meeting' and himself presided over the occasion. His little opening speech, both serious and jesting, his respectful gallantry, gave great pleasure to the ladies.

* I doubt whether rural workers drank much gin. Flora Thompson shows them drinking beer very moderately and entertaining themselves with singing. Tea was probably much dearer than ale at the time. The arguments Taine retails here seem to me to apply only to industrial areas. E. H.

We visited Sir John ——'s park: it is crossed by a path open to the public who can visit the park without asking permission. I have also seen Lord (sic) Marlborough's park at Blenheim, where the entrance gate bears the following inscription — "The Duke of Marlborough requests people crossing the park to keep to the path and not walk on the grass." The park gate is always open and anyone at all, the villagers and their wives, may stroll in it for an airing.

Sir W. B —— is master of the local hounds at his own expense, and many small squires and farmers follow the hunt. The lady of the house where I am staying knows all the village women in the parish; she always greets them graciously and offers them her hand to shake when she takes me into their cottages; their response is cordial, even affectionate, and it is easy to see that there is no distrust and hostility between the classes. The inferior party is not envious, it does not occur to him to covet the position of the rich gentry; he is more inclined to consider the local gentleman as his protector, and takes a kind of pride in him, especially if the gentleman belongs to an old family long established in the neighbourhood. In such a case the family counts, like the most ancient and beautiful trees, as one of the ornaments and glories of the district.

Recently, while travelling by train, I was chatting with some 'life guards', positive giants in stature and very good-natured, decent men. They told me proudly, "All our officers are noblemen." After some questions about their pay, which is 2/- a day, they told me that about a third of their number are married men. I asked if widows had a right to a pension. "No, but private contributions provide them with one."

All this is a vestige of the best part of the feudal spirit. The suzerain provided for his vassal, and the vassal was proud of his suzerain.

This spirit is all the stronger in that, even to-day, the population of England is distributed in a feudal pattern. Everywhere the cottages are grouped about one or two 'country seats', modern country houses in the place of former castles and whose masters, albeit in new terms, play the part of the old barons. In every parish, even the most remote, you find two, three, five, six families whose hereditary estates and chosen residence are there, and whose patronage is both accepted and active. It is the ancient patronage of the armour-clad lord of the manor, but transposed from the physical to the moral plane, applied no longer to matters of war but to matters of peace, exercised no longer by the sword but by the mind, authorised not by a superiority of weapons, but now of education. And the business nowadays is not to range men in battle order against an enemy, but to diminish ignorance, poverty and vice. For that purpose, as for the old one, leaders are needed, local chieftains who are accepted, tried and capable: and those leaders are the land-owning gentry of the parish, the county. As long as three centuries ago the traveller Poggio could write, of this country, the following words big with a truth pregnant with consequences:

"Among the English the nobles think shame to live in the towns; they reside in the country, withdrawn among woods and pastures; they consider him the most noble who has the greatest revenues: they give themselves to the things of the fields, sell their wool and their cattle, and do not consider such rustic profits shameful."

Poggio found the contrast between this rural life of the English nobility and the urban life of the Italian nobility, very great. It is not less so for a Frenchman, and although the revolution sent many of our noblemen back to their own estates, that contrast is still striking. The city is not, as it is with us, the favourite place of residence. Apart from the great manufacturing towns, provincial cities, York for instance, are inhabited almost solely by shop-keepers: the *élite*, the nation's leaders, are elsewhere, in the country. London itself is now no more than a great business centre: people meet there, for three or four months during the summer, to talk, amuse themselves, see their friends, look to their interests, renew their acquaintances. But their roots are in their 'country seats': there lies their real motherland, in the small circle of dear friends, family centre, the place where they pursue country sports, receive guests on long visits, where their actions are effective, and where, at every turn, can be seen evidence of their own well-doing or that of their ancestors; where, too, familiar faces in the village street, the familiar shape of a hill at the end of a road leave upon the mind a friendly impression of 'home', of one's own place. It is there that they take an active interest in the parish and hope to fill its small offices. And having done so to fill them zealously, conscientiously and with enjoyment.

During the London season the Sunday night trains carry away a great number of land-owners who are going forty, eighty, a hundred miles to attend committee meetings, deliver 'lectures', hold meetings, fulfil the duties of their unpaid offices on the bench, the council or in the Church. Moreover, they are expected to be first in opening their purses as the feudal barons were expected to be in the forefront of the battle. B —— tells me that subscriptions of various kinds cost him a tenth part of his income, and that his neighbours are in like case. To that must be added the poor tax which, in this part of the country is 3s. in the £ of all income derived from land rent, and in certain districts is 7s. in the £. Voluntarily, or by legal obligation, the 'property classes' lend a hand with real courage in bearing the public burden of poverty. *

Naturally, a class of this kind is a closed society and its limits are strictly maintained. Aristocratic institutions have, like others, their disadvantages. In all his writings, Thackeray has described this system and made fun of it; the system, that is, of social enclosures, and the efforts made by those of a lower class to get in and by those of the upper class to keep them out. For example, a person like the elegant and intelligent farmer's wife of whom I was writing above is not in society: she is not invited to 'archery meetings', and several ladies B —— has named to me and whom, on this score, he disapproves of, avoid greeting her in order to stop, in advance, all access to a possible familiarity. Doubtless those English people who have lived abroad and have open minds are above such wretched manifestations of false pride, and they frankly recognize its folly and [condemn its] excesses.

* The whole of the foregoing passage is in some respects unreliable: it is obvious that Taine had heard only one side of the case and that his information was misleading. The greater part of the burden of Poor Rate had been taken off the shoulders of the country gentry by the Act of 1834. For reliable information in this connection see Nicholl's series of books on the English, Irish and Scottish Poor Law (1856) and the Report of the Royal Commission on the Poor Laws (1910). On the other hand Taine gives a picture (amply supported) by such evidence as the *Punch* cartoon (see P. 35) of rural poverty which is in conflict with, e.g. Dr G. M. Trevelyan's view of this period in his *Social History of England* (Longmans, Green Ltd., 1944). Dr Trevelyan regards the period Taine here deals with as one of relative prosperity to be followed by real rural poverty in the middle 'seventies, (see rising Poor Tax figures for 1860—1870—50 % up in ten years); and he claims, contrary to Taine, that the English agricultural labourer was better off than the Continental land-owning peasant. See, *e.g.* pp. 538 *et seq. op. cit.* As regards the taxation of the well-to-do, Taine has the following footnote to this passage. E. H.

Footnote. — For the past 20 years the middle and upper classes have paid 124 million sterling in the form of taxes on property and income, without counting death duties, tax on occupied houses paying more than £ 20 rent, stamp duties, etc., new burdens weighing almost exclusively on the class of land owners, business men and men in the liberal professions. Moreover, during the same period there have been reductions in the taxes on sugar,

But as regards the rest, under a cover of reserve, it is always perceptible. In their heart of hearts and perhaps without even admitting it to themselves, they believe, or are inclined to believe, that a tradesman, a financier, a man of business, constantly obliged to think of profit and details of profit all day long, is not a gentleman and never can be. He has not the requisite education, ideas or language. "What should a tradesman or a farmer talk of if not of matters to do with his trade? The mind, engaged in coarse occupations and set in coarse habits, itself becomes coarse." According to this opinion, feelings, also, become debased: the man who deals in money or business is inclined to selfishness; he has not the disinterestedness, the large and generous views, proper to the leaders of a nation; he is unable to forget his own small interest and think of the great public ones. And only on those terms has one any right to command. Consequently, and until he has proved the contrary to be true, the tradesman, the business man is made to keep his distance, and his family cannot be received by the reigning families.

The latter, then, are the ones who are at home, and it is they who must take the first steps towards adopting a newcomer. When a rich man buys an estate it is not his place to put himself to the expense of entertaining or to inform the neighbourhood. If, in mind, character, and manners, he is a gentleman, this will be known within a fortnight and the neighbouring families will then

cocoa, molasses, coffee, raisins, butter, cheese, eggs, bricks and other buildings materials; entering the country free and untaxed are cereals, live-stock, and foreign food-stuffs from every land on earth.

*Quarterly Review*

From *Statistical Abstract for England and Wales for 1856 to 1870:*

poor-tax, in round figures:

|      | Total        | Used in outside relief |
|------|--------------|------------------------|
| 1860 | £ 8,033,000  | £ 5,454,000            |
| 1861 | 8,252,000    | 5,788,000              |
| 1867 | 10,692,000   | 6,959,000              |
| 1870 | 12,044,000   | 7,644,000              |

"Apart from the enormous permanent revenues derived from foundations and applied to the relief of the sick and infirm, it should be noted that a rich Englishman always has his hand in his pocket. In the first place he pays all sorts of legal dues for the maintenance of paupers; in addition he subscribes to various public charities, agricultural shows, etc. He helps poor servants and subordinates, and relations unable to earn their own living. He gives alms in the streets and when on the road. When the plate is taken round after a public dinner or in church, he puts money in it . . ." etc. etc. See Mrs Grote *Collected Papers*, p. 53. This author, like many others, concludes that the poor should have fewer children.

call on him. But even when adopted he will not yet have the privileges of the others: for instance, he would not be elected as Member of Parliament and if he were to stand as a candidate the public would say, "He is too new, he does not yet belong here." He is planted, as it were, but has not taken root. His son perhaps, or his grandson, might be adopted, but not himself. To represent a constituency it is necessary to be attached to it by every interest and every habit, to have been involved in it for several generations. The primary condition of recognized leadership is long-established residence, and all strong aristocracies are local. Thus, for example, in France during the Revolution, only the Vendée followed its gentry, and that gentry was provincial, hunting squires who lived at home in constant intercourse with their peasants.

I have been trying to get a real understanding of that most essential word 'a gentleman'; it is constantly occuring and it expresses a whole complex of particularly English ideas. The vital question concerning a man always takes this form: "Is he a gentleman?" And similarly, of a woman "Is she a lady?" In both cases what is meant by a positive reply is that the person in question belongs to the upper class. This class is fully recognized as a fact: a workman, a peasant, or a shop-keeper would not try to cross the line of demarcation. But how do you recognize that a person belongs to the upper class? In France we have not got the word because we have not got the thing, and those three syllables, in their English sense, sum up the whole history of English society. The gentry, the squires, barons, feudal chiefs did not, as under Louis XV, become simply privileged individuals, ornamental parasites, troublesome, unpopular, odious, proscribed and then later, only half-restored to consequence, their minds and spirit superannuated; finally, and henceforth devoid of influence, maintained in the State rather as a tolerated memorial of the past than as an effective element. No; here they kept in touch with the people, opened their ranks to talent, recruited to their number the pick of the rising commoners; and they have remained the ruling class, or at least the most influential class in both parish and State. To that end they have adapted themselves to their time and their new rôle. They have made themselves into administrators, patrons, promoters of reform and good managers of the commonwealth; they have become well-informed and well-educated men, men who apply themselves to work and are capable and who, as citizens, are the most enlightened, the most independent and the most useful of the whole nation.

On this pattern has the idea 'gentleman' been formed, a very different thing to the idea *gentilhomme*. Gentilhomme evokes thoughts of elegance, style, tact, finesse; of exquisite politeness, delicate points of honour, of a chivalrous cast of mind, of prodigal liberality and brilliant valour: these were the salient features of the French upper class. Similarly, 'gentleman' expresses all the distinctive features of the English upper class, in the first place the most apparent, those which appeal to the simpler minds — for example, a large private fortune, a considerable household of servants, a certain outward appearance and bearing, habits of ease and luxury; often enough in the eyes of the common people and especially of the servant class, these outward semblances are all that is necessary. Add to them, for more cultivated minds, a liberal education, travel, information, good manners and ease in society.

But for real judges the essential quality is one of heart. Speaking of a great nobleman in the diplomatic service, B —— told me, "He is not a gentleman." Thomas Arnold, when travelling in France, wrote to his friends, "We see few here whose looks and manners are what we should call those of a thorough gentleman ... A thorough English gentleman, — Christian, manly and enlightened, — is more, I believe, than Guizot or Sismondi could comprehend; it is a finer specimen of human nature than any other country, I believe, could furnish." Make ample allowance for the exaggerations due to national pride, and we still have here a very instructive document. For them a real 'gentleman' is a truly noble man, a man worthy to command, a disinterested man of integrity, capable of exposing, even sacrificing himself for those he leads; not only a man of honour, but a conscientious man, in whom generous instincts have been confirmed by right thinking and who, acting rightly by nature, acts even more rightly from good principles.

In this idealised portrait you will recognize the accomplished leader. To it must be added specifically English features — complete self-mastery, constantly maintained *sang-froid,* perseverance in adversity, serious-mindedness, dignity of manners and bearing, the avoidance of all affectation or swaggering. You will then have the model which, copied as nearly as possible or at least aspired to, produces the man who commands obedience here. And a novelist has drawn him for us in a book entitled *John Halifax, Gentleman;* it is about a poor, abandoned boy who ends by becoming the respected 'leader' of his neighbourhood. Here, to give the tone of the book, is a brief quotation: when, after many difficulties, John attains to easy circumstances, buys his house and sets up his carriage, his son cries, "At last, we are gentlemen!" — "We have always been so, my son."

Now let us glance at the appearances: for they are pointers. B——, my host, who has been married for a year, wanted a cottage of his own. This cottage is charming, indeed elegant, provided with all the refinements of cleanliness and neatness, well-being and luxury. It is built of brown bricks, with numerous gables, sharp-pointed roofs, and almost all covered with creeper. It is set in a small park of velvety lawns, rolled every day, two or three superb clumps of rhododendrons, six feet tall, thirty feet in diameter. Cut in the lawns are beds of bright coloured exotic flowers, well disposed groups of trees, a tree-lined and covered walk in which the young couple can stroll alone together. And, beyond the enclosing hedge, a view of trees with openings upon glimpses of the eternal verdant panorama. A real love-nest.

Inside the house, pink or white wall-paper, light-coloured paint — lilac or creamy yellow; small-patterned tile or parquet floors, and a great many small-paned windows reminiscent of the Middle Ages. There is a good piano in the drawing-room and several handsome books — wedding presents — Tennyson, a prayer book, and others bound in blue velvet, in wood carved in gothic style, in tooled and gilt morocco leather, all carefully illustrated with that neat pencil work peculiar to English artists and some of them decorated on every page with coloured paintings and arabesques. Not an article in the house but it bears witness to a studied and even meticulous taste. Everywhere are *jardinières*, filled with rare flowering plants; inside, as outside, a wealth of flowers. This is the prettiest element of English luxury, and one they understand as a gourmet understands food.

The same understanding and care are applied to everything; there is not one article but bears witness to care and thought for comfort. 'Oil-cloth' and carpets from top to bottom of the house: the carpets serve to keep in the warmth, the 'oil-cloth' on which one actually walks, can be washed and keeps the carpets clean. In my bedroom the table is of rare wood; on it, a square of marble, on the marble a round mat of woven rushes, all this to carry an ornamental water carafe capped with a drinking glass.

One does not simply put a book down on the table, there is a little rack on it especially placed to hold books. You are not provided simply with a candlestick and candle which you blow out when you want to sleep. The candle is in a wide lamp-glass equipped with an automatic extinguisher. There are other even more striking details, and one has to stop and think for a moment before grasping the use of them. Sometimes all this apparatus seems rather a nuisance; it is taking too much trouble merely to be comfortable. In the same way I have seen travelling English people provided with so many kinds of field and perspective glasses, umbrellas, canes and iron-tipped sticks, capes, woollens, waterproofs and great-coats, with so many necessaries, utensils, books and newspapers, that in their place I should have stayed at home. As one goes from England to France, and from France to Italy, so needs become fewer, preparations simpler, life itself becomes simpler and, so to speak, more naked, more left to chance, less encumbered with inconvenient conveniences.

B —— has fifteen hundred sterling a year, three or four horses, two carriages, six servants, a gardener — the same establishment would call for approximately the same outlay in France.

We have visited seven or eight gentlemen's parks, large or medium sized, almost all very fine and two or three really admirable. The perfect meadows shine under the sun and are richly covered with buttercups and daisies. The oaks are ancient and often enormous. Embanked and cared-for streams run in the little valleys and are made to form small lakes on which swim exotic ducks. Here and there, surrounded by a belt of gleaming water, rise small islands covered with rhododendrons flaunting their rose-pink sprays of flowers. Along the walls rabbits start from beneath our feet and, at every turn is a new vista of the undulating plain, dotted with clumps of trees, its whole scale of greens softening towards the blue of the horizon. What freshness, and what silence! You feel relaxed, rested: this natural beauty receives you with smooth caresses, discreetly, intimately; it is a person, having its own character, its own accent, the affectionate accent of domestic happiness, like a beautiful wife who has decked her person for her husband's pleasure and comes to meet him with a sweet smile.

Every original work, a garden quite as much as a book or a building, is a confidence revealing deep feelings. In my opinion these gardens reveal, better than any other work, the poetic dream in the English soul. The same cannot be said of their houses, vast machines, more or less Italianate or more or less Gothic, without any clear-cut character: one perceives that they are spacious, comfortable and well-kept, no more. They are the houses of rich people who like their comforts and know how to get them and who, sometimes and often enough unfortunately, have indulged in architectural whims. Many of their stylish cottages, topped or overburdened with gables, look like toys made of painted cardboard. All their imagination, all their native inventiveness has gone into their parks.

The one which covers seven hundred acres has trees in it which two or even three men could not encompass with outstretched arms, oaks, limes, planes, cypresses (sic), yews, which have freely developed the fullness of their growth and forms. Isolated or in groups on the soft, rich meadowland they stand, their opulent pyramidal shapes or vast domes given ample room to spread, and often drooping to the very grass with a breadth and freedom which must be seen to be believed. They have been cared for like children of rich parents; they have always had full liberty to grow, all their needs catered for, nothing has ever checked their growth or hindered their luxuriance; they breathe the air and consume the soil like rich noblemen to whom that air and soil belong by right.

In the midst of this setting of living emeralds is a still more precious jewel, the garden itself. Great massifs of rhododendrons spreading and rising to twenty feet, all their flowers open; their red or pale violet petals shine softly in the sunlight, loud with hornets. * Bushes of azalea, great sprays of roses all in flower, beds of flowers opaline and azure, colours of velvet, colours of flesh. A cunning skill has so managed the succession of plants that the late bloom to replace the early so that, from beginning to end of each season, the vast basket of flowers is always in beauty. Here and there a great sycamore of noble bearing, or an alien beech with coppery foliage sustain with deeper chord or sudden discord the prolonged concert of delicious harmonies. Truly it is a concert for the eye, a brilliant and magnificent symphony of full tones which the sun, like some mighty orchestra leader, sets vibrating in harmony at a stroke of his bow.

Even in the remote outskirts of the park, and beyond in the forest itself, or on the 'common', one is aware of the near neighbourhood of these gardens. Beautiful plants have scaled the walls

* Hardly likely: Taine perhaps meant some commoner and less spectacular insect by *frelon*. E. H.

so that suddenly, among wild pine-trees, you come upon rhodo-dendron, pink and smiling, like an *Angélique de l'Arioste* in the middle of the Ardennes forest. All the vistas are suave: the ground rises and falls under a dense covering of heather; here and there the uniform colouring is relieved by the bright, charming green of bracken which, dense in places, draws green patterns on the endless carpet of old rose. Beyond this, again, a line of pine trees shuts off the horizon and the rise and fall of the heath vanishes into a pearly limbo of pale mist, shot through and through with warm light.

The house itself is a huge mansion, indifferently pleasing, massive, the interior modernised. The furniture of the ground and first floors, recently bought to replace the old furniture, cost £4000. Three drawing-rooms, sixty feet long and twenty high, are furnished with tall looking-glasses, good pictures, some excellent engravings, and bookcases. In front of the house is a conservatory where they spend the afternoons in bad weather and where, even in winter, there is an illusion of spring-time. The rooms for any young girls among the house guests are fresh, light, virginal, papered white or blue, each with an assortment of pretty, feminine knick-knacks and delicate engravings, well suited to the amiable tenants of these rooms. For the rest, feeling for the picturesque in decoration and the overall plan and arrangement is less developed than with us: for instance, less attention is paid to matching of colours and articles of furniture. But grandeur and simplicity are not wanting, and there is no taste for overcrowding or bric-à-brac. They like large, bare surfaces and empty space, and the eyes are rested, there is room to breathe and walk about without fear of knocking into articles of furniture.

Great attention has been given to comfort, notable in all that concerns sleeping, washing and dressing accommodation. In my own room there is a carpet covering the whole floor, oil-cloth before the wash-stand, matting along by the walls. Two dressing-tables, both with two drawers, the first provided with an adjust-able looking-glass, the second with a large pitcher, a small one, and a medium-sized one for hot-water, two porcelain basins, a brush rack, two soap-dishes, a carafe and glass and a bowl and glass. Below this a third toilet table, very low, with a pail, another basin and a large shallow zinc basin for one's morning ablutions. In a cupboard, a towel rail with four different kinds of towel, one very thick and fluffy.

Another, and indispensable cupboard or cabinet in the room,

which is a marvel. Linen mats under every vessel or utensil; these alone, in an occupied house, must entail a permanent laundry. Three pairs of candle-sticks and candles, one set fixed to a small portable table. Wax and paper spills in pretty little tubs, pincushions full of pins, porcelain candle extinguishers and metal candle snuffers. Every attribute of the bed white, downy, perfect.

A servant waits on you in the room four times a day. In the morning to draw the curtains and blinds and open the inside shutters, take away shoes and clothes, and bring a large jug of hot water, and a linen mat for standing on; again at noon and at seven in the evening to bring water and so forth, so that the guest can wash for luncheon and dinner; and at night to shut the windows, turn down the bed, prepare the wash-stand, replace towels and other linen. It is all done with gravity, silence and respect. These trifling details must be forgiven me: they are necessary in order to bring home to the reader the nature of an Englishman's needs, the kind of luxury he tends towards. What the English spend on service and personal comfort is enormous, and it has been laughingly said that they also spend one fifth of their lives at a wash-basin.

A number of these great houses * are historical: only by seeing them can one realise what inheritance from generation to generation can accumulate in the way of treasures, in a great family. I have been told of one in which, by a clause in the entail †, the owner is obliged to spend several thousand pounds a year on silver ware. After having crammed all the sideboards, they resorted to having the banister of the staircase made of solid silver. In the late Exhibition I saw a whole museum of valuable curios and *objets d'art* loaned by Lord Hertford. In 1848 the same nobleman, talking to a Frenchman who was a friend of his and was in serious difficulties, said,

"I have a place in Wales which I have never seen but they tell me it's very fine. A dinner for twelve is served there every day, and the carriage brought round to the door, in case I should arrive. It's the butler who eats the dinner. Go and settle down there; as you see, it will not cost me a farthing."

Naturally, beautiful things tend to accumulate in wealthy hands. Miss Coots (sic)**, Lord Ellesmere, and the Marquis of Westminster

---

* Taine calls them *châteaux*. E. H.

† *Une clause de l'institution*: literally "in the appointment (of the heir)". Whatever is meant, perhaps *entail* will serve. E. H.

** Presumably Miss Burdett-Coutts. E. H.

own picture galleries which would do honour to a small nation. At Lord Ellesmere's, in three rooms as lofty as the Louvre gallery, are a quantity of Poussins, the best Flemish painters, and, above all, three medium-sized Titians, *Diana and Acteon, Diana and Calypso,* and *Venus rising from the waves,* of a warm golden colour and a most opulent and vivid beauty. At the Marquis of Westminster's, two galleries and four enormous rooms, one hundred and eighty-three pictures and a whole *cortège* of busts, statues, bronzes, enamel and malachite pieces; six large Rubens, three Titians, a Raphael, two Rembrandts and a quantity of Claude Lorrains chosen from among his best works. And these palaces are only quoted as specimens, it would take too long to give an idea of the whole number.

In the course of another trip I saw Blenheim Castle, near Woodstock, property of the Duke of Marlborough. It is a sort of Louvre, and was given by the nation to the great general, the first duke. It is built in the style of that time, heavily ornamented. Several of the rooms are as lofty as the nave of a church; the library is a hundred yards long; an interior chapel contains the first duke's monument. There is a gallery of family portraits, another of porcelain, and several galleries of pictures. The park is two miles in circumference. Magnificent trees, a wide watercourse crossed by a monumental bridge, a column bearing the first duke's statue. There is a private room containing, under the name of Titian, twelve copies, the Loves of the Gods, voluptuous, life-sized figures: they were presented to the victor of Louis XIV by the princes of Italy. The apartments contain paintings by Reynolds, five or six large Van Dyck portraits, a Raphael Madonna and ten Rubens in which sensuality, passion, boldness and genius pour out a whole river of splendours and enormities. Two of these are Bacchanals: a colossal female faun has thrown herself down on the ground and sits stooped above her dropping dugs, and her two young, lying on their backs and glued to her nipples, are sucking avidly, the whole a great jumble of palpitating flesh; above, the dark torso of Silenus throws into relief the dazzling whiteness of a strapping, hoydenish, writhing nymph; nearby is another Silenus, bronzed and enormous, laughing a drunkard's laugh, dancing with all his heart and might so that his paunch is bouncing about, while a beautiful young woman, resting on her hip, displays the long, undulating lines of side and breasts. I would not dare to describe the third picture, the most vivid of all, of a sublime grossness, the very sap and flower of irrepressible passionate sensuality, the whole poetry of drunkenness unrestrained and bestial satiety; the title, *Lot and his two daughters*. But I am forgetting myself; these memories, like a gust of warm air, have made me digress. The conclusion I have been aiming at is that these great hereditary fortunes are as if designed to preserve these and all treasures of beauty. After a number of generations a great house and park become a casket of gems.

From which flow consequences, some bad, as touching the individual, others good, as touching the State.

Acording to S ——, who is a cosmopolitan and well-connected here, the law of primogeniture, especially in the case of noblemen, entails a number of evils. Very frequently the eldest son, spoilt even at school by flattery and complaisance, turns out a spendthrift or cranky fool. He travels without learning anything, brings home the worst habits of the Continent, goes in for a racing stable, or is endlessly bored. If the aristocracy were not renewed by recruiting from the most talented commoners, its members would soon become useless, narrow and even pernicious, as they do elsewhere. Moreover, the inequalities between children entail embittering contrasts. Here, I am less concerned with noblemen, who can push their younger sons in the army, the Church or in politics, than with the merely rich: in such families the younger sons must suffer at the constraint which casts them unprovided, or ill provided, into the chances and battle of life, exiles them overseas, delays their marriage, and condemns them to ten or fifteen years of subordination, toil and privation, while their eldest brothers, born to independence and wealth, have only to take possesion of a great house and a park which is all ready and awaiting them. However, the idea of all this is less painful to them than we are apt to think: they are accustomed to it from childhood, and as it is an ancient, legal and national custom, they tolerate it and indeed accept it as if it were one of the necessities of nature. Besides they are not afraid of work, and their pride teaches them that there is something finer in making their own way than in stepping into an inheritance.

That being granted, consider the advantages. An Englishman nearly always has a great many children, the rich as well as the poor. The Queen sets the example, with nine, and reviewing the families I know personally; Lord ——, six children; the Marquis

*Fig. 17  Well (?) Brought Up*
*First Juvenile.* "May I have the pleasure of dancing with you, Miss Alice?"
*Second Juvenile.* "A, no — thanks! I never dance with younger sons!" (*Punch*, May 23, 1863)

of ——, twelve; Sir W ——, nine; Mr S ——, a judge, twenty-four, of whom twenty-two are living; a number of clergymen, five, six, ten and up to twelve. A certain ecclesiastical dignitary has only four sons, but the expenses of his office and the charities he subscribes to consume all his 50,000 francs stipend. The bishops, many high officials and large landowners also spend their whole income.

As a general rule people here do not save much: a doctor, lawyer or 'landlord' has too many public and private calls on his purse — taxes, subscriptions, his children's school and travel bills, entertaining, horses, servants, domestic comfort. They have no idea of exercising restraint, they insist upon having every comfort, and on cutting a figure. They would rather do more work than reduce their standard of living. Instead of retrenching, they over-spend their incomes and, at the end of the year, are lucky if they have managed to make both ends meet. Too much work and too great spending — my English friends admit that this is one of England's vices.

Now, consider once again all those younger sons, well brought up, well trained, provided with a good general and a good special education, and awake, from earliest youth, to the fact that they can count on nobody but themselves. They are accustomed to well-being and luxury and have the memory of the paternal 'country-seat' always before them: what sharper spur to achievement could there be? It is like a sword at their backs, pricking them on to work. Not to attain to their father's level is to fail. A target is set up for them in their eldest brother's fortune, it is that which they have to equal. Considered from this point of view the law of primogeniture combined with the habit of living well is a system of training. They hasten away to the Indies, to China and Australia, skim the cream of the world, and return home to found a family. There is, in London, a whole quarter which is qualified as "Australian", inhabited by people who made their fortunes in Victoria or Melbourne. This rule eliminates the weaklings, who fail: but the spirit of enterprise, initiative and energy, all the forces of human nature, have free play. The men gain strength from striving, the *élite* of the nation is renewed, and gold pours into the country in a stream.

There is another advantage; only, it is true, in the eyes of a philosopher, or an artist, nevertheless it is one. Without an aristocracy, a civilisation is not complete: it is wanting in those independent, generous, broadly developed existences, freed from all petty cares and capable of beauty in their course, of making life a work of art. Somebody has written, "Down with the castles, and up with the cottages!" I believe it would be better to cry, "Up with the castles and up with the cottages!" Proudhon wanted to see all France covered with small, neat houses, in each house a family, half-rural, half-urban; about each house a smallholding and a garden, the whole country being thus parcelled up. A land of work, equality, ease and kitchen gardens. * From the historian's point of view it is a market-gardener's desire, and how ugly the country would be if there was nothing but vegetables! I do not own a park, but my eyes take pleasure in beholding one; the only condition is that it be accessible and well managed. And it is the same with the lives of the rich and mighty; they are to our ordinary, small lives as parks to little gardens and utilitarian farms. And just as a great park provides immemorial trees, velvet lawns and delicious fairy lands of massed flowers divided by romantic walks, so lives richly endowed maintain certain elegances of manners and *mores,* and certain refinements of feeling; make possible, too, a broad, cosmopolitan education and at the same time provide a nursery of statesmen.

One of the greatest industrialists in England, a radical and a supporter of Mr Bright, told me, talking of electoral reform, "It is not our aim to overthrow the aristocracy: we are ready to leave the government and high offices in their hands. For we believe, we men of the middle class, that the conduct of national business calls for special men, men born and bred to the work for generations, and who enjoy an independent and commanding situation. Besides, their titles and pedigrees give them a quality of dash and style, and troops will more readily follow officers who have that. But we do absolutely insist that all positions of power be filled by able men. No mediocrities and no nepotism. Let them govern, but let them be fit to govern." †

The aristocracy have profited by recent experience. They know that during the Crimean War a wave of public anger nearly swept them away. They realised that they must set their own house in order. They yielded to public opinion and are themselves directing the necessary reforms. It may safely be said that for the last thirty years they have been ruling not in the interest of their class but in the interest of the nation. Since 1822 they have stopped eating the national cake; the rich and the well-to-do now pay the greater share of taxes. The principal changes in the budget have had the effect of making life easier for the common people. To sum up, then, England is becoming a republic wherein the aristocratic institution is engaged in turning out the requisite supply of Ministers, Members of Parliament, Generals and Diplomats, just

* Roughly, in fact, our own subtopia. *O tempora, O mores!* E. H.

† "Qu'ils gouvernent, mais qu'ils aient du talent." E. H.

as a Polytechnic school turns out the requisite supply of engineers. Many aristocrats are men of no ability: then leave them unemployed and let them sit at home and consume their revenues. But, from their whole corpus, it is possible to select the necessary general staff; and there is nothing more precious than a good general staff.

Besides the general staff at the head of the nation's business, there is another to direct the nation's conscience instituted according to the same principles and arriving at the same result, by which I mean government in the hands of the most worthy, respected, steady and perfectible. I am referring to the clergy. We will begin by examining the sentiments which sustain it.

It is Sunday: the servants are excused from waiting at table, and the guests serve themselves; thus, as far as possible, they remember the Sabbath day to keep it holy. And such biblical behaviour is noticeable in many ways: for example, there are no newspapers on Sundays, and only one train, the railway being otherwise at a standstill. In Scotland, the Duchess of ——, who wished to set off at once to go to her dying mother, could not obtain the special train which she was ready to pay for.

We go to church for the afternoon service. The vicar, a tall, lean man of forty takes as his text the life of John the Baptist as told in the Gospels, briefly recounts the story and draws the appropriate conclusions with cold common sense. Clear pronunciation, grave delivery, no emphasis; a sound, lucid argument, developed in a serious tone must always be valuable instruction for the public, and especially for a village public. Before and after the sermon he reads the service, and the small congregation sings hymns, accompanied by the organ.

Everyone's bearing and attention are exemplary. The music is a solemn recitative, a trifle monotonous but never squalled or brayed like our plain-chant. The liturgy and the hymns, translated or adapted from the Hebrew, are eloquent, elevated and imposing: the Hebrew style, with its combination of disjointedness and sublimity, goes well into English. It has been softened and clarified in translation; but the English language is, of all languages, best able to convey the grandeur and adapt itself to the abruptness of Hebrew, for it has the same power to express

156

intense and powerful feelings, a passionate and profound veneration.

For example, the words "Mon Dieu!" in French are slurred and uttered almost flatly; whereas, in English, "My God!" is a cry or sigh highly charged with aspiration and solemn anguish. The more I read the 'Common Prayer Book' the finer I find it, and the more appropriate to its work. Whatever be a country's religion, church is the place where people come, after six days of toil, to refresh and renew their own sense of an ideal. Such was the Greek temple under Kimon, such the Gothic cathedral in the time of St Louis. In accordance with the differences in the nature of religious feeling, so do the ceremony and the edifice itself differ; but the important point is that the feeling be revived and strengthened. And in my view that is the case here in England: a farm-hand, bricklayer or sewing-woman leave the church service fortified with a number of noble impressions adapted to the instincts of their race, a vague and general feeling of an august presence, a superior order, an invisible justice. Moreover, a man of education can take his place beside them and is not put off by grovelling superstitions. Here are no fussy ornaments, painted dolls, no primping parade of posturings, processionals and mechanical, superannuated rites the meaning of which has been forgotten by the congregation. The walls are almost bare, the hymns and service in the vernacular tongue, and the celebrant indulges in no genuflexions, his bearing is that of a magistrate; and apart from the surplice he is dressed as one. As Joseph de Maistre put it, he may be defined as a gentleman charged with the duty of giving you a straight talking to. * The ceremony is an ethical meeting (sic) at which the chairman does his talking from the pulpit instead of the platform.

In the sermons, as in the religion itself, dogma always takes a back seat and attention is chiefly paid to the means and will required in order to live a good life. Religion as such, with its emotions and great visions is hardly more than the poetry which informs ethics or a background to morality. It is the extension into infinity of a luminous and sublime idea, that of justice. A person of thoughtful mind can accept all of it, at least as a symbol; and in this way, without renouncing his own personal interpretation, can remain in touch and communion with the simpler-minded men who sit beside him. On the really fundamental point, which is the ethical or moral feeling in question,

* "un monsieur chargé de vous tenir des discours honnêtes" E. H.

all are in agreement and it follows that all rally round the church and its incumbent, their pastor, with assiduous, obvious and unanimous respect. *

The clergyman, then, has authority. Note, moreover, that he is a gentleman, often by birth and fortune, almost invariably by education. The bishop of London receives £10,000 a year; one of the two archbishops £15,000; an ecclesiastical dignitary at Cambridge £7000; the Dean of St Paul's, London £2000, and the Dean of Westminster £3000. Literature and learning are titles to these great stipends: Greek will get you a bishopric; such was the case of Dr Thirlwall, author of a very good history of Greece. The average stipend, obtained by adding together all stipends paid by the Church and dividing by the total number of churchmen, is £140 a year. An ordinary 'living' is worth between two and three hundred a year. The least are £80 and there is said to be one worth£10,000. The Chancellor, Lord Campbell (sic) has the distribution of seven hundred livings; the rest are in the gift of private persons, the heirs of their founders. In addition, and quite often, the incumbent has private means. Many good families have a son in holy orders and such men often have a personal fortune, sometimes a very large income as well as their wives' dowries. Many pious and well-born girls hope to marry a clergyman.

In short, the clerical condition constitutes a career, like the magistracy with us, entailing marriage, a sober life, preoccupation with morality, a very good education, and elevated sentiments; but not asceticism, celibacy and passive obedience.

Most of the clergy are graduates of Oxford or Cambridge: those I have met all read French, and had a solid foundation in Greek, Latin, mathematics and general education. They have read Shakespeare and Tennyson; they are not ignorant of the diverse points of view in the interpretation and history of their Church. One of them explained to me the details of the successive editings of the Prayer Book, and assured me that it would have been better to keep to the first edition. Another showed tolerance for the Nonconformists, but censured the pride and vanity of the tendency among the people to interpret religion for themselves and produce their own private doctrine. On which subject consider the tone adopted in Church periodicals: it is firm, but not violent. A whole

* That Taine's principal contacts were with the upper classes is very clear here: not a word of the Nonconformist sects who were far from unanimously respectful! E. H.

158

section of the Anglican Church holds broad-minded opinions ('Broad-church'). Liberals like Mr Milman, independent-minded seekers, bold exegetists like Mr Stanley were not prevented by their views from being preferred to high places in the Church, to wit, deaneries in the capital. All of which indicates an average of mental and educational quality which is quite high — very high when compared with that of the equivalent class in France.

As to the manners, *mores* and appearances of this class, they are those of a 'gentleman', a gentleman in easy circumstances if the 'living' is adequate or the incumbent has private means. In any case their being married means that their houses have those comforts and amenities a wife always ensures. Several of the clergy in this district keep a carriage, horses, have many servants. In the case of one of their number the house, small park and domestic arrangements are all as spruce and good as my host B——'s. In the case of another, who lives six miles from here, the standard is only a little lower. I do not know whether I happen to have been lucky, but it has never seemed to me that their manners and tone were prudish. Not long ago, in Venice, I was dining at a *table d'hôte* in company with a gentleman, his wife and four daughters; he was serious, but no more so than most Englishmen; on the third day he told me he was a clergyman, and we went together to see *Marie Stuart* at the theatre.

Thus, then, by their manners, ideas and education, and sometimes by birth and fortune, they are fitted to mix with the country gentry and nobility. They are not peasants with the muck only half scraped off them by Seminary training, crammed with superannuated theology, set apart from the world by their condition and celibacy and lack of breeding; they are kinsmen and equals of the ruling class. The clergyman sitting down to dine with the squire is the director of morality in company with the director of politics, allied equals obviously superior to the men they lead, accepted by the latter as such, and, as a rule, worthy of their position. When I visit the village with the vicar he goes into the villagers' cottages, pats the children's heads, enquires how they get on, admonishes the naughty ones, says a word against drunkenness, and discusses people's business with them. He is their natural guide and philosopher. His wife teaches the poor children in school; people in want go to the vicarage for help, or a bottle of good wine and other little luxuries for the sick. A clergyman I met in London was in the habit of taking bands of 'Ragged-Schools' * children for a

* *Ragged Schools* — See below. E. H.

day in the country. He took two thousand on one occasion: it was at one and the same time a treat, and a sort of new year procession, with flags, bands and so forth. They stayed out in the fresh air from seven in the morning until evening; they ate and drank; the whole thing cost about £100 made up by voluntary subscription. The object was to provide the poor little creatures, who live in slums or in the streets, with a day of fresh air and good cheer.

Spiritual guides, and temporal guides — in both aspects the upper class does its duty, and, in parochial as in national life, its ascendency is well-merited and unchallenged.

Back in London: I have been trying, in vain, to get exact information and some figures concerning the fortunes and number of people composing the county aristocracy. According to Porter there were in 1844, 123,000 men and 322,000 women with private means in England and Wales. The population was then sixteen million. It is now twenty million (1861) and there has been a great increase in wealth. *

In 1849 the number of people owning horses as a private luxury was 140,000 of whom half had two or more horses. In 1841 the number of people employing male servants was 112,000, of whom half had two or more men-servants. Now, my friends tell me that ownership of a horse or employment of a man-servant indicates an annual total expenditure of twenty to twenty-five thousand francs a year. I presume, according to these figures, that

* In 1866 incomes deriving from trade, professions and industry, as declared for Income Tax, showed:
  133 persons with incomes of £50,000 or more
  959 „ „ „ between £10,000 & £50,000
  14,623 „ „ „ exceeding £1000
Incomes derived from funded money:
  101 persons with £4000 or more
  1943 „ „ £1000 to £4000.
The land of all England was owned by about 50,000 people (Pop. 20,000,000) and about half of it by 150 proprietors.
The National income in money (rent, dividends, salaries & wages) was estimated at £814 m.; 235,600 persons were in receipt of £300 per annum or more, 1,262,000 of £100 per annum, or more. The National wages bill for manual labour was about £325 m. of which £53 m. in agriculture, £155 m. in mines and manufacturers, £62 m. in building, transport and food-handling trades, £54 m. in public and domestic service. It is hard to indicate a modern equivalent value for the gold £ of 1866, but certainly the figures can safely be trebled. E. H.

*Fig. 18   West End Street*

the number of rich or well-to-do families in the country is of the order of 120,000.

Consider the foundations of such a social constitution as this of England: it consists in the number, wide distribution, fortune, old establishment, ability, local residence, probity, usefulness and authority of the whole upper class, one hundred and twenty thousand families. All the rest is secondary. For eighty years our publicists in France have been arguing about constitutions. I know some of them, and those among the most eminent, who want to transplant the English or the United States Constitution to France, and claim that the nation would need only two years to get used to it. One of them assured me, "It can be compared to a locomotive: all you need is to keep it filled up with water and it will immediately replace the stage-coach."

And, in point of fact, almost the whole of Europe has tried or actually adopted the English system: monarchy, more or less limited; upper and lower House, elections, and so forth. And look at the outcome — in Greece, grotesque; in Spain, lamentable; in France, fragile; in Austria and Italy, uncertain; inadequate in Prussia and Germany; successful only in Holland, Belgium and the Scandinavian countries. It is not enough simply to import the locomotive: if it is to move, it needs a road to travel on. But we should really abandon such comparisons with machinery, for the Constitution of a nation is an organic phenomenon, like that of a living body. Consequently that Constitution is peculiar to the state in question, no other state can assimilate it, and and all it can do is to copy its appearance. For beneath these, beneath the institutions and charters, the bills of rights and the official almanacs, there are the ideas, the habits and customs and character of the people and classes; there are the respective positions of the classes, their reciprocal feelings — in short, a complex of deep and branching invisible roots beneath the visible trunk and foliage. It is these roots that sustain and nourish the tree, and if you plant the tree without the roots it will wilt and fall to the first storm of wind. We admire the stability of British government; but this stability is the final product, the fine flower at the extremity of an infinite number of living fibres firmly planted in the soil of the entire country.

Suppose there were an insurrection, like the Gordon riots, but better led and strengthened by socialist proclamations: suppose, moreover, (an impossibility) a gun-powder plot which, at the same time, completely destroyed both Houses of Parliament and the Royal Family. Still only the visible summits and peaks of the government would have been carried away and the rest would remain intact. In every parish and municipality and in every county there would remain those leading families about which the rest of the people would rally, noblemen and gentlemen who would gather up the reins and take the initiative; men, moreover, who are trusted and would readily be followed and who are by their rank and fortune, by the services they have rendered and by their education and their influence, natural leaders, born captains and generals who would rally the scattered troops and immediately re-form the army. This is the very reverse of the situation in France where burgess and artisan, noble and peasant are separated by distrust and discord, where broadcloth and corduroy do, indeed, live cheek by jowl but with fear and rancour in their hearts, and where the only leaders are officials, strangers to each district, immovable yet provisional, to whom is given a superficial obedience only and not intimate deference, leaders who are tolerated or submitted to, but never really adopted.

Thus, then, English government is stable because the English have a supply of natural representatives. The full weight of this very simple statement will only be apparent if we stop and think what it means. What is a representative? To represent a person or a community of persons, large or small and of whatever size, is to *render them present* at a place where they are not in their proper persons; it is to make decisions, issue orders, and do, on behalf of and in the place of those represented, all those things which, being absent, or through ignorance, inadequacy or any other impediment they cannot do but by substituting the effective will of their representative for their own ineffective one. Such, for example, is a manager, a proxy, a trustee; a captain entrusted with the command of a ship, or an engineer entrusted with the building of a bridge. Thus, in public as in private life, my representative is that man whose decisions rest upon my firm adherence. Whether that adherence take the form of a vote or not is of little importance: votes, counted suffrages, are merely signs, indications. The essential thing is that the adherence be real and lasting, whether written down or not, whether noisily manifest, or mute. It must be a constant condition of the essential being, the inner mind, an energetic and persistent disposition of mind and heart. In this, as in all the moral sciences, * it is the *inner reality* that counts.

In which connection it is important to note this: that those legal indications by which the adherence we are discussing is supposed to be made manifest, are not infallible. Universal suffrage, or any other electoral device may attribute a majority of suffrages to a name or a list of names, but that majority does not prove firm adherence. Forced to opt for one name rather than another, one list rather than another, concerning which he has no clear and personal opinion, an ignorant man does not really exercise an effective option, and almost the whole nation is composed of ignorant men. The twenty thousand peasants and workmen and small tradesmen we lead to each polling station go to it like a flock of sheep; they know the candidates only by hearsay and hardly even by sight. All of us know citizens who vote by casual chance, saying, "One's as good as the other." In any case the preference expressed is not firm and decided, consequently it is weak and vacillating. The voters are therefore apt to abandon the man for whom they have such a very slight and indifferent preference. And consequently their government, whatever its policy, lacks roots. A gust of hostile opinion, a street riot can overthrow it and set up another in its place. And that having been done, there are many who will again say, "One's as good as the other." Their wilting affection for their man is often no more than commonplace tolerance, and never stiffens into a determined choice.

* I suppose we should now say "as in all psychology". E. H.

Thus it follows that all our political establishments, republic, empire or monarchy, are provisional, like great sets of painted scenery which, turn and turn about, fill a stage to vanish or reappear as the occasion warrants. And we see these scenes demolished and erected with a shrug of indifference. We are inconvenienced by the noise and the dust and the unpleasant expressions of the bought and paid-for applauders; but we resign ourselves to this discomfort. For what can we do? Whoever and whatever our official representatives may be, and by whatever means chance or election gives them to us, the public will is never firm and decidedly behind their actions. They are not our real and effective representatives, but our society has none better to offer us; we must keep them, for if we go further we may fare worse. The upper class cannot provide them since with us, in France, an egalitarian envy makes us accept our rich men and our nobles only sullenly. As for imitating America and setting up an intelligent democracy wherein every bricklayer and peasant is as well-informed and politically educated as a school teacher or country-town solicitor in France to-day, it will take a century and more to accomplish that. And meanwhile, by way of preparation, we might try the vote at two removes, the first electing to the *commune,* * the second to the capital of the administrative district. † Yet these are but faint hopes and doubtful expedients.

But in a country like England the representatives, being natural, are effective. The adherence which supports them is not shaky, but firm. They, and not other men, are the people the country wants to have at the head of affairs; and wants them unhestitatingly, decidedly, resolutely. Each parish, each district, knows its own Member. A farm-hand is as quick to recognize him as a man of education. For these leaders are like the five or six great trees of the locality, recognizable by their bearing and figure; all, even the children, have rested in their shadow and profited by their presence. In default of enlightenment or fine discernment, then self-interest, custom, habit, deference, and sometimes gratitude would suffice to procure them a majority of suffrages. For the grip of tradition, sentiment and instinct is tenacious. There is no stronger attachment than — attachment. So that these men are destined to rule, and a voting paper, or a raised hand do

* *Commune;* very approximately, parish. Taine seems to be proposing a system whereby the *commune* council would constitute an electoral college sending representatives to the † Administrative district; *chef-lieu d'arrondissement.* This, in Paris, is a Ward, but elsewhere a division of a *Département.*
                                                                                    E. H.

no more than confirm a tacit assent. Even at the time of the rotten boroughs Parliament was representative of the people's will, as it is to-day although the number of people having a vote is rather small. And it will still be so in ten years' time, if the Reform Bill extends the suffrage. In my view changes in the law relating to the suffrage do no more than perfect the system in detail, without affecting fundamentals. The important thing remains the same, public assent. And, enfranchised or not, the labourer and the 'shopkeeper' agree in wanting a man of the upper classes at the helm. Whether or not they have legal means of expressing this adherence and directing it towards this or that individual candidate, in either case it is given to the ruling class in general. And once the pilot is elected, whether by themselves or by others, they faithfully do as he bids them; so that, by their mute adherence he is given a stronger title to feel himself their delegate than would be the case in France where, however, all their votes would have been counted.

A stronger title and also a better one. For a man is not given the skill of a pilot simply by being elected to take the helm: election confers power, but it cannot confer ability. Long training, and special study are required to make a lawyer or an engineer; how much more so to make a statesman, to vote with discernment on great public questions, to distinguish the opportune and the possible, to take a long view of a whole question, to have a valid and motivated opinion on the degree of extension which ought to be given to the suffrage at a given moment, on the transformation apt to be wrought by instituting share-cropping or smallholding in Ireland; on India, the United States, the several and diverse European powers; on the hazards and future of commerce, industry, finance, foreign alliances and the rest. You do not succeed at this kind of work by means of abstract principles, leader-writers' slogans, or vague notions acquired in college or Law School, which is the usual equipment of the politician in France. The effect of such tinted spectacles as these is either nil, or it is misleading. Nor do the education of a barrister, the routine of a chief clerk, limited, localised and merely technical experience of any kind, add much to their range of vision. It is not by such means that a man learns to be far-seeing. The training which procures such vision is very costly. It includes travel, a knowledge of languages, meeting men of learning, and politicians abroad; it includes the acquisition, among the people of other lands, of terms and means of comparison; and the observation of manners, customs, institutions, Government, public and private life not only in one's own country.

Thus many Members of Parliament use their holidays to go to the Continent, and make investigations which may last as little as a fortnight, as long as six weeks. They go to France, Spain, Italy or Germany in order to refresh, correct and broaden former impressions of those countries; and not just once, but five, six, ten times. They wish to keep themselves well informed, to follow the movements of public opinion. By this means their judgment never becomes backward in its terms, and their chances of being exact in their information are multiplied. Let a cloud form in the political sky above Denmark, Poland, Rome or the United States and they are almost immediately on the spot, to return with reliable information.

Abroad, they obtain introductions to eminent or notable men, and invite them to visit England; glance through, and extract the substance of, their minds, as if they were books. They will often note down the details of such conversations and, upon their return, pass these notes round the circle of their friends and acquaintances. I have read some of these manuscripts and there can be nothing more informative. And to information of that kind they add all that their eyes can teach them: one will visit our farms, examine the manures we use, the machines and the cattle, make notes of figures and statistics and, upon his return publish, or deliver as lectures, a series of essays on the state of agriculture in France. Another will be inspecting the Paris manufactories, while his wife covers the technical schools.

As well as statesmen, almost all rich or merely well-to-do people do the same kind of thing. I know some who, having several children and earning no more than twelve thousand francs a year, yet set aside a thousand of this moderate income for an excursion abroad. No young man of good family but makes a tour of the Continent, any complete education must include some travel and a residence, more or less prolonged, abroad. During the vacations barristers, lawyers, teachers and professors pour by their hundreds into Germany. Many, of course, see nothing but appearances; you cannot put a quart into a point pot. But all of them bring home some ideas, or at very least, some notions of foreign parts which are less false, some prejudices less gross.

All this information combined creates a public opinion which is more enlightened on important subjects, less incompetent in matters of politics, more judicious, nearer to the truth and more accessible to good advice. It follows that the statesman whose clear-sightedness and vision have discerned the right path is supported and encouraged. The crew acclaim the captain; and it often happens, even, that the crew go out of their way to seek a captain and place him on the bridge.

What is even more important is that such an education is the best way of ensuring that men of suitable capacity will be available when sought. Common to the whole upper class, the men of large mind reveal themselves by their reaction to it. And gifted men will not, therefore, come to nothing for want of an adequate and appropriate general education; on the contrary, receiving precisely that education most apt to foster their gifts, their talents or genius can attain its full stature. And as their position, fortune and connections exempt them from too long an apprenticeship and from petty money worries, their qualities are made available to the community while they are still young. Such, for example, were the younger Pitt, Canning, Sir Robert Peel, Lord Palmerston; and, at the present time, such are Mr Gladstone and young Lord Stanley. It is, no doubt, very unfortunate that hereditary wealth and early consequence should fall, so unfairly, to a whole class and, as necessarily follows, therefore to a certain number of rascals, a few brutes, and a great many ordinary, mediocre people. But that is the price which must be paid to form an *élite*. The institution is rather like a racing stud-farm: out of one hundred horses, perhaps six will turn out to be good racers; out of a thousand, you may get one of the very first order. And remember that without capable leaders a State cannot prosper and that an emergency may, for want of a great man, mean the collapse of a nation. Is it possible to pay too high a price for an assured provision of capable leaders, and the frequent chance of a great statesman?

Let us see the machine at work: "It is a distinctive feature of our country," says the *Edinburgh Review* *, "a feature of which we are proud, that we conduct our business ourselves and without intervention by the State."

For example, out of thirteen million, two hundred thousand sterling spent on public education in twenty-one years, only four

* July 1861.

million two hundred thousand was contributed by the State: the rest was furnished by subscriptions. There are swarms of societies engaged in good works: societies for saving the life of drowning persons, for the conversion of the Jews, for the propagation of the Bible, for the advancement of science, for the protection of animals, for the suppression of vice, for the abolition of tithes, for helping working people to own their own houses, for building good houses for the working-class, for setting up a basic fund to provide the workers with savings banks, for emigration, for the propagation of economic and social knowledge, for Sabbath-day observance, against drunkenness, for founding schools to train girls as schoolteachers, etc., etc. It is enough to walk the streets or glance at any newspaper or Review to understand the number and importance of these institutions. My friends tell me that almost all of them are seriously and conscientiously managed. An Englishman rarely stands aside from public business; for it is *his* business, and he wishes to take a hand in its management. He does not live withdrawn; on the contrary he feels himself under an obligation to contribute, in one way or another, to the common good. They do it in the same spirit as, in France, a respectable, ordinary man feels himself obliged to attend regularly at his office or counting-house and do his work there conscientiously: he would lose his self-respect, would regard himself as a rascal and what is worse a fool, if he delegated that work to others, and let himself be involved in trouble or be duped and robbed, by a salaried manager.

C —— took me to a meeting of a society for the education and reform of juvenile vagabonds. This association maintains about a hundred young men between sixteen and twenty years of age, some of whom have police-court convictions against them, the rest introduced to the association by their parents, people of the poorest class, in the hope of saving them from the bad company and preventing them being turned into thieves. They are housed, clothed and fed, taught a trade (cobbler, printer, toy or furniture making, etc.). The lads of the second group had the privilege of forming a brass band from their number, and they provided music in the courtyard while we were waiting for the proceedings to begin. Their faces were dull and not very pleasant. They wore a grey and blue uniform. A penitentiary, although it be privately maintained and well run, is never a place of pleasure. This establishment was founded by a Mr Bowyer, a kind of lay St Vincent-de-Paul, and bears the title — 'Preventive and reformatory

Institution'. Visitors are asked for subscriptions and given a very instructive brochure. By reference to it I learn that "the expenses of maintenance for each young man in the establishment are, on an average, about £17 a year; whereas the maintenance of a convict in Halloway (sic) prison is equal to a curate's stipend (£75), and depredations committed by a London thief and pickpocket can hardly be put at less than £300 a year."

Conclusion: it is sound economy to pay to train your delinquents in this establishment, rather than let them grow up in the streets. English charity is justified by figures.

Fifteen of the lads were leaving, the day I was there, for Australia, by their own wish. Their fares were being paid for them, and the meeting had been called to mark the occasion. They were placed among the audience on three benches and listened to the speeches. The Earl of ——, a member of the House of Lords and a very rich landowner took the Chair, and opened the proceedings: timid manner; small, shrill voice; high, pointed collar emerging from a badly cut coat. He looked more like a retired shop-keeper than a great nobleman. After a few awkward words he read several very respectable letters from young men formerly trained by the Institution. One of them, a lumber-jack in primaeval forests, had thought at first that he would never become accustomed to the loneliness, but now he works happily from dawn till dusk. Yet he has nobody to talk to excepting for quarter of an hour every day to the woman who brings him his provisions.

Then, there was a speech by an orator-bishop, accustomed to deliver the same kind of speech every day. "You have been reared here, sheltered from temptation, like plants 'under glass'. This was to give your good instincts time to take root. Now you are going to be planted out in the open, and left to fend for yourselves; those roots must take hold and grow. To that end, do not trust in yourselves but in Jesus Christ, who is your only friend, who will be your help in loneliness and among temptations." A good delivery, fatherly and grave, without oratorical tricks or literary turns; he suited his language to his listeners. The Protestant religion is efficacious here; Robinson Crusoe's Bible is still the lonely, forest-bound 'squatter's' companion.

The third speech, by Mr S ——, M.P., was mainly addressed to the audience. Twenty-five years experience have convinced him that emigration is very salutary, in the first place because it removes young people from the danger of contagion by evil example, thereafter and above all because it stimulates the development of English qualities — energy, the habit of self-reliance, the taste for hard work, and action, all of them being inclinations which, having no outlets in the London streets, would, at home, be turned against society and used for evil ends. A sound, pertinent argument, free from rhetoric; that is rare in France. He concluded by proposing a vote of thanks to the bishop, which was carried unanimously, all the ladies and even young girls in the audience raising their hands, as well as the men.

From there we went on to visit a 'ragged school'. This is a large, brick building whose rooms are airy and well kept, and I could not help comparing them with the exiguous rooms of our equivalent school in Paris. * Unfortunately these rooms were empty, the children being on holiday that day, and the friend who was escorting me was obliged to leave me. "It doesn't matter," he said, "there is another 'ragged school' near here, in Brook Street. Go and see it."

"Alone, without being introduced?"

"Certainly. They'll be very civil."

So I went and, in fact, a gentleman who was on his way out took me in, introduced me to the 'master', and showed me over the whole place which is very well found and, in addition to a school, comprises a *crèche*, an infant school and, on the top floor, a dormitory for the oldest children. During the day the beds are folded back against the walls; during the night they can, by a mechanism it would take too long to explain here, be isolated from each other and watched over.

In the workshops young boys were doing basket work and making small wooden models for the drawing schools. They were made to sing, mark time and march past for me. Certainly, it is right that they should be kept busy and taught: for their faces make one uneasy, they had the expression common to all juvenile detainees. The big room for the youngest children was almost full and yet there was no bad smell. Almost all of them had shoes and their clothes were not too ragged. Several of the little girls were holding very young babies. The cleverest and most docile children become monitors and are given a few 'pence' a week. All, of both sexes, are taught to read, write, count, sing and drill. The mistress teaches the girls needlework; she was a pretty young woman, very lively and good-humoured, whose happy face and

* Ecole des Frères, near Notre Dame, for instance.

cordial manners are clearly excellent in such a place: she is paid twelve shillings a week, and the 'master' twenty-five.

As I see it an establishment like this, especially in a poor quarter of the city, is a means of moral disinfection. According to published statistics the number of juvenile delinquents in London has fallen from 10,194 in 1856 to 7850 in 1866. There are 25,000 children in the London 'ragged schools', 300,000 in those of all Britain. Only three of these schools are Government-assisted, all the rest are paid for entirely by private subscription. For people are aware that schooling is more important than policing in contributing to the safety of the streets.

Evening conversations about the various analagous societies; I was told of too many to remember them all and shall name only a few. An establishment has just been founded in London, a sort of club, where governesses and other respectable ladies in employment whose characters are vouched for by good references can, when they come to London for shopping or lessons, get a good meal, find a fire, a library, have tea, and meet their acquaintances. Another private establishment houses eighty young girls of the poorer classes; it is to keep them out of the way of temptations. Work is found for them, and besides, living in common is cheaper. The expenses are at the rate of £10 a head. Then there is a society for selling Bibles: they are sold rather than given away because if given away they would not be valued. The ladies forming this Society were too remote from the common people to be able to make contact with them: they therefore had the idea of appointing go-betweens, poor, respectable, zealous women who act as their agents and hawk the Bible even in the worst quarters of the city, make the acquaintance of workmen's wives, gather them together in a room of an evening, teach them needlework and housework, etc. At the present time there are a hundred of these 'Bible-women' at work. Last year one of them sold 419 Bibles and 501 New Testaments.

Temperance Societies: these exist all over England. Recently I saw some young women members of such societies in the street, ten carriages full of them, on their way to a meeting. They undertake never to taste spirits; some of them are so scrupulous they will refuse to take a doctor's prescription containing alcohol, or even the wine at communion. I saw a poster put up by the 'Total Abstinence Association' announcing the place and time of a meeting and the programme: several bands, tea at four o'clock, a walk in the park, exhibition of a collection of carpets, divine service in an attractive church, speeches by leading members, reduced prices for tickets to all members of temperance societies. This preposterous mixture of incongruous motives and 'attractions' is typically English.

Many of these Societies are corresponding members of each other, or even affiliated: for instance, most of the 'Mechanics' Institutes' and 'ragged schools' are associated with a savings bank: this is to teach thrift and its advantages to children and young people. The larger societies have their own journal, review or magazine, and special publications: such, for example, as the Wesleyan Association, the Ragged Schools Union, the Society for the Propagation of Social Science, The Society for the Propagation of the Bible, etc. All these are in addition to those leagues whose object is some legal reform and which are as transitory as their object. The most famous of these was that which set out to abolish the tax on imported grain ('anti-corn-law') and of which Cobden was the leader. The facts about it are to be found in the works of our own Bastiat: enormous subscriptions, meetings, travelling orators, public lectures, small popular treatises, massive learned works, universal and incessant propaganda. The machine was admirably contrived to rouse and change public opinion.

Here, in England, suppose a man has a good idea: he communicates it to his friends; several of them agree that it is good. Together they put up some money, publish the idea, draw sympathisers; and subscriptions come in, publicity increases. The snowball grows larger and larger, crashes against the doors of Parliament, pushes them half open and, in the end, either opens them completely or breaks them in. Such is the mechanism by which reform is obtained; it is by this means that men manage their own business for themselves, and it should be borne in mind that all over England there are small lumps of snow in the course of becoming snowballs. Many collide and are broken up, or they melt away *en route*. But new ones are constantly being made of their remains, and the spectacle of the human swarms obstinately shoving and pushing them along is a very fine one.

Seeking to explain this zeal we may adduce the following reasons: 1. An Englishman needs to be doing something; his own business attended to, he still has a surplus of energy to give to public business. Besides, many people of independent means are not employed in any business. It is this same need for action which is responsible for their many journeys and other difficult undertakings: for example, Miss Nightingale was not pious or mystical after the manner of a Sister of Charity when she set out to reorganise the Crimean War Hospitals; her only motives were humanity and a very active spirit. 2. The Englishman is rich and, moreover, provides for the future not, like a Frenchman, by thrift, but by spending more. For instance, he prefers to leave his children less money in his will if by doing so he can give them a better education; and rather than deprive himself of a trip abroad, will work an extra hour a day. By the same token, he gives and gives readily, a part of his time and money towards consolidating and improving the community which harbours him and will harbour his posterity. A man with a proper understanding of his own interests will work to maintain the roof of the great public edifice as conscientiously as the roof of his own small private house. 3. Tradition, the antiquity of 'self-government', and the wide diffusion of the knowledge of political economy. The Englishman is accustomed to take a long, broad view of political and social matters. He knows the disadvantages of letting a roof go unrepaired, the effect of leaks, the dangers of a rotten beam. As he is sensible, thoughtful, and accessible to reasonable arguments, he keeps a sharp eye, as it were, on the roof tiles and is ready to pay the tiler's bill on the nail. 4. He is able to do all kinds of tedious jobs without suffering boredom, such as attending meetings and auditing accounts. He has less need of entertainment than a Frenchman.

Visited St Bartholomew's Hospital. Income £40,000 not counting private gifts. Many other hospitals bear the inscription: Maintained by private subscriptions. The governing board meets once a week. The treasurer, although overburdened with work, is not paid. Six hundred patients, but they can take eight hundred. The building is enormous and includes a library, collections and an anatomical museum. The young doctor who took me round, and who has lived in France, told me that here a student can see cases all day long; whereas in France, unless he is an *interne* or *externe*, he cannot see them after ten in the morning. The beds of five or six paces apart, far more widely spaced than in France. Perfect cleanliness. The place seems to me very well equipped and run. Enormous kitchen, where all the cooking is done by gas. There is a vast room fitted up as a larder, for storing meat. In addition to the nurses *(infirmières)* there are 'nurses' (? Sisters) in charge of them, all of them former nurses themselves and for the most part respectable, middle-aged women: they do no night-nursing. Fifteen to twenty shillings a week, but they do not get their meals in. They are as highly praised as our own Sisters of Charity. Thus, the lay conscience can be as effective as religious fervour.

A great many fractures, and a large number of ingenious devices for supporting the broken limb, holding it in the air while still allowing certain movements to be made without hindering the knitting of the bone. Above all a large number of patients suffering from *coxalgia* *, neuroses † and scrofula attributed to impurities in the blood, bad food, and an impoverishment of the human substance. Their livid, haggard, worn faces were dreadful. My young medical escort admitted that excess of work and gin is enormously increasing the amount of madness in England.

Here, the patients are not concerned to ensure that their bodies will not be used for dissection, which is their principal worry in France. The use to be made of their bodies is kept from them. Besides, their minds are already vacant, their intelligence extinguished. They are in the same state as the streetwomen here. The soul of a Frenchman has a finer temper and does not lose its power of recovery so soon.

My young physician handed me over to a clergyman who was a friend of his, a philanthropist and a man of education, who took me with him to the St Luke's workhouse. As everybody knows a workhouse is a sort of asylum with something of a prison about it. Associated with the Poor Law administration, it is one of the distinctive features of the English social constitution. It is an English principle that an indigent person who alienates his liberty has the right to be fed. The community meets the cost of this, but imprisons the paupers in question and puts them to work. And as these conditions are repugnant to the poor, they keep out of the workhouses for as long as they can.

The one I visited had between five and six hundred inmates, old people, abandoned or otherwise helpless children, and men and women out of work. The latter class was the least numerous, thirty or forty women and a dozen men. In winter they will be in an even smaller minority. The workhouse also gives outdoor and domiciliary relief; that week it had assisted 1,011 people. The cost per head of inmates is three to four shillings a week.

We went through about seventy halls, rooms and cubicles; also the laundry, brewery and bakery. There are carpenters' shops,

* A disease of the hip.
† *Neuroses:* perhaps not in the modern sense. E. H.

174

cobblers' shops, and an oakum picking room; a nursery for the smallest children, schools for girls *, public rooms for the old men, and others for the old women; rooms for sick women, for confinements, for sick men, for sick children, and for lunatics. Also, of course, dormitories, refectories, sitting rooms, promenades etc. The whole place was adequately clean and wholesome; but I gather that other workhouses are a great deal less pleasant. The children sang — out of tune, but they looked healthy enough. As for the lunatics, the sick, and the old, I found them, as usual, far more worn than in Italy or France. A human scarecrow is far more pitiful in Holland, Germany or England than in the Latin countries. Yet I think they are quite well cared for: three meals a day, meat three times a week — the sick get meat every day. The bread was excellent. The food and cooking looked very adequate. Sheets are changed once a fortnight. The public rooms are airy and there is a fire in all of them. The old people get tea, sugar and newspapers. There are a few books to be seen — natural history, religion, or morality; Chambers's Magazine, a Bible; texts from the Scriptures hanging on the walls. One touching detail; there was a vase of fresh flowers on the table.

But what the place needs is a man who would stop and study it, whereas I was there only as a visitor for a short time. Nevertheless I saw enough to realise to what extent the English concern themselves with the community's paupers. The public mind is constantly on the alert about these 'Workhouses' and other useful institutions, and is kept informed by the associated societies, newspapers, reviews, and even by novels which, when dealing with such subjects, are virtually *résumés* of investigations or enquiries, and popularisations of the dry facts. I have read such novels, for example, on life in prison. All this serves a useful purpose.

Last week I was shown over Pentonville: it is a 'probation' prison, where convicts are kept nine months before being deported and where, according to their more or less good conduct, they obtain a proportionate reduction of their sentence. The place is an admirably contrived hive made of iron, so ingeniously designed and built that it might well be shown in an exhibition of modern machinery.

I have tickets for the review of the Volunteers, which takes place this afternoon. This is another spontaneously formed institution, entirely voluntary and founded upon concern for and

* Or, probably, for prostitutes. E. H.

understanding of the common weal. "In the event of an invasion England would not have enough soldiers. Then let us provide her with soldiers, to wit, ourselves; and with soldiers properly equipped, brigaded and drilled." Having reached which conclusion, they enrolled themselves, providing uniforms and weapons out of their own pockets, all without interference or help from the Government. In six months they numbered a hundred and thirty thousand and they expect to reach two hundred thousand. Among my own acquaintances are a painter, who is a private, and a barrister, who is a captain, in the Volunteers. On an average they drill for an hour and a half a day. But for some time they have been training for the grand review by doing an hour and a half every morning and three hours every afternoon. They often get wet through, but make a joke of their discomforts. An officer of my acquaintance who fought in the Crimea tells me that they are already well enough trained to fight a campaign. They have been supported by a flood of private subscriptions, the big men helping the little men. The Duke of —— has just sent 2000 of his miners to the review, by special express train. Almost all the young men of rich or well-to-do class have joined up. They have a club with the motto 'For hearth and home' and the ladies encourage them.

The march-past took place in Hyde Park. An immense grandstand enclosed the parade-ground and beyond it the windows of every house were crowded with people, and even the roofs were covered with spectators. Street urchins and gutter-snipes had climbed every tree and hung to the branches in clusters, singing in shrill voices. The superb Life Guards formed a living fence, and the Queen, in an open carriage, was greeted with thunderous cheering. Red uniforms stood out against the green of the grass for as far as one could see; at last the long, grey column of the new militia appeared. As far as I could judge they carried out their manoeuvres well; at the very least they appeared to be equipped in a throughly practical manner, without superfluities or fancy ornaments; they were obviously not for show, but for use.

It would be impossible to give any idea of the meetings called, arguments expounded, enquiries initiated, letters written to the papers, all provoked by the various feelings aroused by the Volunteers. It is obvious to me that 'self-government' entails, among other advantages that of bringing the whole thinking potential of the nation constantly into play.

The better informed I become and the more I think about it,

*Fig. 19  The London Crossing-sweeper*

the more convinced I am that this same *self-government* is activated not by this or that institution, but by certain very strong and widespread 'sentiments'. It is stable and enduring because respect for certain things is profound and universal. And it is, on the other hand, active and progressive because, apart from those things, everything else is open to argument, checking and change by individual initiative.

One of my friends knew Vincent, the printing operative sent out by the 'Trades-Unions' to harangue the people. Vincent once summed up his oratorical expeditions as follows:

"I am able to say whatever comes into my head, to attack everyone and everything, excepting the Queen, and Christianity. If I were to speak against them, my listeners would stone me."

Apart from these two inviolable sanctuaries public respect covers, albeit in a slightly lesser degree, the two great edifices around them. Christianity is respected and, by extension, the Church, the clergy, the individual clergyman. The Queen is respected and, by extension, the constitution, the hierarchy, the nobility and gentry. No doubt many working men are *secularists*, imbued with doctrines analogous to those of M. Comte, and soured by the monstrous inequalities of fortunes and profits. But on the whole the nation is conservative, and adopts reforms without plunging into revolutions.

The classes here are not divided as they are in France. No *coup de main* is to be feared, whether from the Throne on the one hand, or from the mob on the other. There are no alternative, available systems of government which can be thought of as substitutes for the existing system. Broadly speaking the whole population is in agreement on the main lines, and all bow down before the Law. Among a hundred supporting examples I could quote, here are two, taken from opposite ends of the scale. The Queen and Prince Albert enclose themselves within the limits of their function as constitutional monarchs and never dream of overstepping those limits. They are willing to confine themselves to the rôle of moderators, and to follow where Parliament and public opinion lead. They have no party of their own in Parliament, never intrigue against a Minister, not even against one whose person and ideas are displeasing to them; they accept their position honourably and in all its implications. *

Now for the second example, a street scene recounted to me by one of my friends, who had just come from Manchester. A street-girl in a rage had thrown a stone through a window, breaking the glass: a policeman arrived, took her very gently by the arm, and asked her to accompany him to the police-station.

* This section seems to have been written before some which appear earlier in the book. Cf. ref. to the Queen's mourning. E.H.

"Come along now, it's no good resisting, you'll only get a night in the cells anyway."

She refused to go, sat down on the pavement, then lay down, saying,

"Drag me there if you like."

A crowd collected; all her cronies arrived on the scene and urged her to go with the policeman.

"Come on, Mary, my girl, don't make a fuss, go with him, you did wrong."

The policemen sent for other policemen and Mary was taken away. No uproar, no shouting, no resistance; for it is felt that it is reasonable to obey the law. My friend added that here, when an arrested man starts to struggle, the people on the spot ask what it's all about and if they consider the policeman within his rights, lend him a hand. In the same way, whenever there are disturbances all classes provide volunteer constables. On the whole, whereas we *suffer* our government, the English *support* theirs.

An establishment which is so firm in the saddle can stand assaults on it: speeches, meetings and leagues cannot overthrow it. It follows that criticism has the right to be incessant, energetic, and even violent. The stability of the constitution makes it possible to allow the citizen complete freedom to check, verify and supervise its workings. And in fact this checking, verification and supervision are being exercised the whole time, openly and frankly. There is not one question of home or foreign affairs but it is dealt with very thoroughly in fifty newspaper articles, handled and examined from every point of view, and that with a power of reasoning and argument and a thoroughness of documentation which one cannot help admiring.

To get a real idea of what this means one should read the principal newspapers for several months. *The Times, The Saturday Review, The Daily News, The Standard* and the political and economic sections of the principal Quarterlies. They very often reach a high standard of eloquence: good sense, virile argument, full information thoroughly checked and derived from the best sources; complete frankness even to the point of rudeness; a hard and haughty style proper to a militant conviction; cold and prolonged irony; the vehemence of concentrated passionate feeling; indignation and contempt flow freely. In France such polemical writing would infallibly lead to duels and rioting. Here, however, the cooler temperament blunts the effect. It is accepted that a politician should not react to invective, even when it is personal, and it is not done to come to fighting over a scrap of paper. It is recognized that the clamour and tocsin of the Press never issue in a resort to arms, but only in meetings, protests and petitions.

On the day I arrived in London I saw a number of sandwich-men in the streets. The message they carried was as follows: *Enormous usurping of the people's rights! The Lords are adding £450,000 of taxes to the budget without the nation's consent!* (They had just added this sum in the course of rectifying the budget which had been passed by the Commons.) *Fellow country-men, a petition!* A few days later I was in Clerkenwell, a remote quarter of the city, and I read an advertisement of a meeting on this same subject in a local newspaper. Nothing more: but this plain speaking and perpetual public meetings are enough. We may put it like this: the newspapers, and public meetings comprise one great universal parliament and a great many small ones dotted about all over the country, which prepare the ground for, supervise, and complete the work of the two Houses.

We went to 'Parliament House': although its architecture is a constant repetition of a rather feeble motif and shows no great originality, it has the merit of not being Greek or Southern. It is Gothic, suited to the climate and therefore satisfying to the eye. The palace is magnificently reflected in the gleaming waters of the river. From a distance its clock-tower, its myriad spires and stone carvings stand softened against the mist. The soaring and twisted lines, the complex bones and sinews of the building, the clover-leaf and rose patterns in carved stone diversify the planes of this enormous mass, which covers four acres, and puts one vaguely in mind of a tangled forest. In default of genius, the architects at least showed good sense. They seem to have had in mind certain Flemish town-halls, and lofty capitular chambers which alone, by the variety, delicacy, elegance, boldness and multiplicity of their shapes, are capable of satisfying the Nordic soul — and the modern soul in general.

One of the halls, Westminster Hall, which is used for great political trials, is immense and of the greatest beauty: 110 feet high, 290 feet long, and 68 feet wide. The carved beam supporting the roof is said to date from the eleventh century. In all the other rooms carved wooden panelling eight feet tall clothes the walls: above them tooled and gilt leather, red and brown hangings, and stained glass. Lamps hang from the ceiling on long, shining chains. The whole effect is rich and sober. In default of light and sunshine they have recourse to colour, like Rembrandt, and to the contrast between high-lighted salients and shadowed hollows, to strong reds and rich blacks, the sheen of polished wood and leather, and to stained glass which does violence to the daylight, but certainly varies it.

The Lords have a handsome chamber for their meetings, comfortable, and appropriate to its purpose. Red leather chairs, dark, carved wood-work, gilded Gothic decorations in old gold; it makes a general impression of sober opulence. The peers present were not numerous: I was told there are sometimes only five or six. They mostly absent themselves excepting on great political occasions. Besides, debating in this House is, as a rule, pointless, since how its Members will vote is known in advance. The principal peers present were pointed out to me, and named, with details of their enormous fortunes: the largest amount to £300,000 a year. The Duke of Bedford has £220,000 a year from land; the Duke of Richmond has 300,000 acres in a single holding. The Marquis of Westminster, landlord of a whole London quarter, will have an income of £1,000,000 a year when the present long leases run out. I am told that the Marquis of Bredalbane can ride thirty-three leagues * in a straight line without quitting his own lands. The Duke of Sutherland owns the whole county of that name in the north of Scotland.

There were three bishops in white surplices present. But the appearance of the assembly was hardly impressive. One Lord had the face of an old, diplomatic hack, another looked like an amiable but worn-out librarian. The Minister who was on his feet suggested an intelligent solicitor. A few youthful peers were dandies, and had their hair parted in the middle. Others, vastly bearded, looked like commercial travellers. Lord C —— alone had the tired, keen, refined look of an artist. Their manners are very simple, one might take them for worthy burgesses meeting at their club. They keep their tall, stove-pipe hats on their heads, speak from their own seats, without fuss, and in a conversational style. This absense of affectation is excellent. A frogged uniform, such as our peers and senators wear adds a pomp and circumstance which, weighing upon the mind, make the subject's thinking as official as his appearance. The British House of Lords is engaged in business, not phrase-making.

From ten o'clock to midnight I was at the House of Commons. Here manners are even easier. The House was crowded and all the Members kept their hats on, some of them having it tilted far

* The French *lieue*, league is 2½ miles. E. H.

back and pressed down. Several wore grey hats, fancy trousers and coats, and lounged, almost lying down on their benches; one at least was draped right over the back of his seat, and two or three were quite unbuttoned and untidy. They walk about, come in, go out and stop to chat with a bored and easy air. I must say that any club where the members behaved in this fashion would be very indifferently respectable.

The Ministers were pointed out to me, Lord Palmerston, Mr Milner Gibson, Lord John Russell, Mr Wood, The Secretary for War and Mr Gladstone. A number of peers came into the gallery and sat down near us, including an immensely rich young duke. They all had badly tied cravats and the duke's overcoat was threadbare. Then there was silence in the chamber below us. The Members, crowded on the benches, have not even a table to write at. They take notes with the paper on their knees, and if they drink a glass of water in the course of a speech, put it down on the seat where they were sitting. They speak standing, from their seat, in a natural style and with few gestures.

There can be no doubt that such a small chamber, arranged as this is, is inconvenient and even unhealthy, too hot in summer and during night sittings; a man who spends much time in it must soon be worn out. But this very simplicity indicates that the Members are men of business who prefer not to stand on ceremony but to get on with the job. Whereas a special elevated tribune for the speakers, set apart and isolated like that of our own *Corps Legislatif*, encourages theatrical eloquence.

The question before the House was the encroachment of which the Lords had been guilty in passing a finance bill without the assent of the Commons. They say this sitting was one of the most important of the year; the House was crowded and attentive. After Mr Seymour had spoken, Mr Horsman rose. His pronunciation was very distinct, his style both moderate and convinced, expressive of energy but without emphasis. His argument was that the Lords is not simply a body of privileged persons; although not elected, the peers, he said, represent the people. They, too, are 'country-gentlemen', they, too, own land and shares in industry. They have the same interests, the same education and the same ideas, consequently they are as well situated as the Commons to decide the general interest. Election is only one of the means of selecting the nation's representatives; there are others, for example the possession of a certain office of dignity, which is the case of the bishops: heredity, which is the case of the Queen and the lay

peers. Besides, since 1832, the Commons have had a marked
preponderance, and a second chamber was necessary to keep a
check on them, or there would be a danger of falling into pure
democracy *, etc., etc.

Rather long-winded, and he repeated himself. However, he made
an impression: shouts of "Hear, hear!" greeted almost every
sentence. † After him Mr Bright spoke on the other side of the
question; he is an accomplished orator. But I had been seeing
altogether too many new things of recent days, my nerves are
not as tough as a Member of Parliament's, and I was obliged to
leave the House.

How does a man become a Member? B——, who has a place
in the Government, nevertheless admits that the method is crude,
and frequently dirty. The candidate hires an hotel or an inn, keeps
open table, decorates it with his colours, stands treat, has his
supporters brought to the poll in a carriage, pays for bands,
barkers, election agents, and speakers who go round the public
houses to talk in his favour, not to speak of bullies, on occasion,
or men willing to throw apples at his opponent. The scene of an
election is rowdy, often brutal; the people become like a penned
bull which suddenly feels itself almost at large. It is admitted that
elections are costly: the law tolerates a certain expenditure and
does not consider that there has been corruption so long as the
amount spent is below a certain figure — four or five hundred
pounds. To cover these expenses a political Party collects a fund;
I am told that the Duke of Buccleugh on one occasion contributed
£40,000 to his Party's funds. But over and above these authorised
expenses there are others, much larger. It is estimated that an
election may cost a candidate four, five, six thousand pounds or
even more. To persuade a voter to take the trouble of going to
the poll, he has to be given some positive advantage — a job or
the promise of one, a number of good dinners, copious quan-
tities of ale or wine, and sometimes even cash down. As a result
of an enquiry it was found that at Wakefield, Mr Leatham had
paid £30 for a vote, £40 for another. A third voter had tried
to conceal the bargain made by selling the candidate a three-
shilling hair-brush for £40. The official expenses of this election
were £461: the secret expenses, £3700.

In another election the agent, seated in one room, received the
voters and agreed a price for their vote, passing them on to

* This word was, of course, still more or less pejorative in 1865. E. H.
† Which Taine renders "Ecoutez! Ecoutez!" E. H.

another room where a second agent paid them the agreed sum. Agreement and payment being thus separated, each agent could plead that he had not engaged in that bi-lateral operation which constitutes making a bargain. But only an artist can give you the living picture: read the accounts of elections in, respectively, Thackeray's *The Newcomes* and Eliot's *Felix Holt the Radical*. By and large, it is local influence which counts, and that is based chiefly on ownership of land, wealth, long residence, old family, the extent of patronage within the power of the candidate, his notoriety and his social position. And from all I have seen of the upper class here it seems to me that these roots are sound, healthy and vigorous despite the mud and the worms among which, like those of every human plant, they have to be plunged; and despite the fact, too, that a great deal more drainage is still needed to purge the mud, and a great deal more attention to exterminate the worms.

"It works well": i.e., the machine works well. It does not break down, and there is no sign of it threatening to do so. Not only does it work, but it adapts itself to the times, rearranges and reforms its wheels and cogs. What is very much more, it is apparent from the way in which it works that it is susceptible of being very thoroughly overhauled, and might in due course include an indefinite extension of the suffrage, further limitation of the Lords' prerogative, the abolition of the Church's monopoly, and all without any violent upheaval but by a gradual and tactful adaptation of the old parts of the machine to new uses. The ruling classes keep themselves well informed, they are constantly in close touch with developments, they are continually sounding the depths and testing the current of popular opinion; and they have a keen sense of what is necessary and what is possible in the matter of change.

I was present recently at a sitting of a Parliamentary Committee. The Committee was set up to report on whether the British Museum — which is at once a library, a museum, and a natural history collection — should stay as it is, or whether some part of its collections should be moved to another place. Seven or eight members sat round a table in a lofty room open to the public. They were questioning expert witnesses: there was a naturalist, then the Crown architect, next the curator of Kensington Museum, and others. Notes were taken. The general tone was even, moderate; there were occasional smiles, it was all rather like an informative private conversation. And that, in fact, is what it was. But the question covered the smallest details and called for exact answers; they dealt with, among other things, the manner of setting out the collection of animal specimens, the number of specimens, the advantages of showing the male, female and young in a single group, the number of visitors, their age and class, the days when visitors are most numerous, the number of square feet of floor space in the building, the use and arrangement of the rooms, etc. This, surely, is the way to be well informed, this use of enquiry and counter-enquiry, with figures, details, precision, the collection of all the relevant, positive documents.

Recently Lord Stanley made a speech on the subject of India which was conceived in the same spirit, based on information and opinions provided by the generals garrisoning the country and the officials who administer it, these being quoted in context so that the speech became a *résumé* of the actual experience of thirty or forty distinguished and competent men. What a guide, and what a corrective is experience! And what a fund of common sense one needs to learn to trust it implicity! How much art and skill are entailed in reducing it to principles and then making proper use of them! In short, how very far we are, in France, from having a good political education!

# CHAPTER SIX

# GLIMPSES OF LONDON

❂

I HAVE been elected a member of the Athenaeum Club for one month. It is an important and very exclusive meeting place, well situated, where one can dine or read, almost a palace, and surrounded by other, similar establishments, all reminiscent of our own *place Louis XV.* Peristyle, view over the park, very lofty rooms, servants in breeches, very numerous, zealous and silent; every refinement of modern luxury used with taste and good sense. The library contains forty thousand volumes, and there is a superb reading room: all the Reviews in every language, all the latest pamphlets, arm-chairs moving on castors, wonderfully comfortable summer or winter. At evening, very soft lighting, like stars set in the ceiling, throws a vague luminosity on the dark panelling and woodwork. Every need is foreseen and catered for, all the senses soothed by the thousand small attentions of an ingenious, all-inclusive and exact forethought. Nearby is another, similar meeting-place (rendezvous), the Travellers' Club; how well they understand how to be comfortable!

Yesterday evening I read, at the Athenaeum, an essay by Macaulay in which he names Galileo, Locke and Bentham as the three originators of the greatest modern ideas: if, for *greatest,* one substitutes *most fruitful,* then the paradox becomes a self-evident truth. It is by recourse to experience, the taste for facts and minutely exact observation, by the accession and reign of induction in the realm of reasoning that man has been able to get the upper hand of nature, reform society, better his condition, adjust his environment to his needs, organise himself into communities, erect institutions and create masterpieces of good organisation, clever arrangement and comfort like that which I was profiting by as I read.

Letters of introduction and a pass into the British Museum. *
I shall say nothing here of the Greek sculpture and Italian drawings; nor of the National Gallery, the gallery at Hampton Court, the pictures in Buckingham Palace and at Windsor and in private collections. Only this — that the British Museum

* i.e. to the Reading Room. E. H.

contains an immense number of historical documents and marvellous objects, a complete *résumé* of five or six high civilizations represented in their fine arts and crafts, and each one differing greatly from the one I am now engaged in studying, so that nothing could better serve to bring out both the good and bad in it. But I should require a whole book to deal with that.

The library contains 600,000 books; there is a huge Reading Room, circular and topped by a cupola, so arranged that no reader is far from the central bureau or has the light in his eyes. The surrounding shelves are filled with reference books, dictionaries, biographical collections, classics in every field, very well arranged and which one can consult on the spot. Moreover, on every table there is a small map or plan to show the order and position of these books. Each desk is isolated, you have nothing but the wood of your desk under your eyes and are not disturbed or bothered by the stares of a neighbour. The chairs are of leather and the desks are covered with leather too; all very neat and clean. Two pens to each desk, one quill and one steel. There is a small book-rest so that you can have a second book conveniently to hand, or the book you are copying from.

To get a book you write the title on a form which you hand in at the central bureau: a library clerk brings it to your own desk, and that very quickly; I tried this out and proved it, even with very rare books. You are responsible for the book until you have got the form back. There is a special place for ladies which is most considerate. What a contrast with our great library at the Louvre, with its long, narrow room, the light shining into the eyes of half the readers, all the readers crowded round a single table, the name of books shouted out loud, and waits of as much as an hour for one's book at the central bureau! It has very recently been reformed on the pattern of the British Museum Reading Room, but still it is not so convenient.

But on the other hand ours is more liberally run, open to whoever wants to use it. Here, you have to be a 'respectable' person, and cannot use the Reading Room without good references. They say, however, that this does not keep anyone out, that very shabby looking people get in, men in workmen's clothes, and even people with no shoes to their feet; their referees are clergymen.

The subsidy for the purchase of new books is seven or eight times as big as ours. When shall we learn to use our money to good purpose?

In other respects they are less successful here, for example at Sydenham Palace, * which contained the Exhibition before last and is now a kind of museum. It is, like London itself and so many things in London, enormous. But how can I convey the impression of this size? All ordinary sensations relating to size have to be raised in scale here. The building is two miles round, and has three storeys of a prodigious height. You could put five or six buildings like our *Palais de l'Industrie* into it, easily. It is built of glass: the main block is a huge rectangle, rising to a dome in the middle, like a hot-house, and flanked by two tall Chinese-style towers. From either end extend long buildings at right angles, enclosing the park, fountains, statues, booths, lawns, groups of tall trees, exotic trees, and collections of flowers. Glass everywhere, glittering in the sunshine. On the horizon a wavy line of green hills, all drowned in that luminous vapour which melts colour into colour and gives the whole countryside an expression of tender happiness. And, always the same approach to the problem of building and landscaping: on the one hand the park, and vegetable architecture — well understood, appropriate to the climate, and beautiful; on the other hand the building itself, a monstrous great pile devoid of style and bearing witness not to their taste, but to their power.

Inside are: a Museum of Classical Antiquity — plaster facsimiles of all the Greek and Roman Statues in Europe; a Museum of the Middle Ages; a Museum of the Renaissance; an Egyptology Museum; a Ninevite Museum; an Indian Museum; a reproduction of a house in Pompeii; a reproduction of the Alhambra. The Alhambra decorations were copied by mouldings, and the moulds are shown, in a neighbouring room, by way of evidence. In order that nothing should be missing, there are hideously daubed copies of the most famous Italian paintings.

There is a gigantic tropical hot-house, with ponds, fountains, swimming tortoises, large aquatic plants in flower, sphinxes and Egyptian statues sixty feet tall, specimens of colossal or otherwise strange trees, among others the bark of a Californian sequoia four hundred and fifty feet tall and one hundred and sixteen feet round the base: the bark is mounted upon an interior scaffolding so as to give some idea of the tree.

* The Crystal Palace on Sydenham Hill to which site it was moved after the Great Exhibition. Destroyed by fire in 1936. E. H.

There is a concert hall with the floor sloped about a centre so that the seats are in tiers, making it look like a Coliseum.

Out in the gardens, latterly, they had life-sized models of ante-diluvian monsters, megatheriums, dinotheriums and others. Blondin goes through his performance there, at one hundred feet from the ground.

I will pass over the rest. But does not this agglomeration of incongruous curiosities put one in mind of the Rome of the Caesars and of the Antonines? At that time, too, they built pleasure palaces for the sovereign people, circuses, theatres and baths where statues and paintings, animals and musicians and acrobats, and all the treasures and singularities of the world were gathered together. There were pantheons of riches and curios, bazaars in which the taste for novelty, variety and monstrosity replaced any feeling for simple beauty. True, Rome supplied these collections by conquest, England does so by industry. Which is why, in Rome, the statues and pictures were looted originals, and the monsters living beasts, rhinoceros or lion, which tore men limb from limb. Whereas here the statues are plaster casts and the monsters made of cardboard. The spectacle, here, is second-rate, but of the same kind. A Greek would have felt very ill-at-ease in such a collection; and would have judged it good enough for a race of powerful barbarians trying to refine their taste and not having much success at it.

The same impression is left by this year's great Exhibition which, like its predecessor, is typically English, a product of the industrial and mercantile spirit, since exported to the Continent. The building is enormous and so, too, are its contents — and that is the best one can say for it. At the entrance there is a monumental fountain spurting perfumed water and resembling pastry-cook's work, decorated with angelica — the sort of wedding-cake one sees at lower-middle-class weddings. Jewels, porcelain, and *objets d'art* are ugly, over-bright, crude in colour, and wanting in taste. For example there are small sailors, lancers, Highlanders, soldiers of all branches of the army, made of silver and no better than children's toys. What man of sense would want to put such things on his mantelpiece? Then, the eye is offended by massive lustres, their ornamentation complicated and exaggerated. They fancy themselves successfully achieving a rich style with great lumps of valuable material — gold, enamel, diamonds, brooches costing ten thousand pounds sterling; what they actually achieve is a heavy, crude ostentation.

Again, notice among the objects for decorating a staircase, the sculptured figure of a Negress; it is entitled *A Daughter of Eve*. The intention is psychological, perhaps moral: the figure may mean something to abolitionists or to their adversaries, but certainly to nobody else. Beside it, by way of contrast are Saint Gobain glasses, a Gobelin copy of Titian's *Assumption*, the City of Paris (municipal) dinner service, by Christofle, an Egyptian girl, in bronze, clad in jasper, by Lerolle — these things revive one and raise one's spirits; it is like returning to subtle *cuisine* after stark roast-beef.

The final impression left by these modern jubilees is a melancholy one; in them all the faults of the industrial system, which is becoming that of all our civilised States, are revealed. Twenty pianos and organs playing together, and all playing a different tune. One of the pianos can imitate an organ, triangle, flute, drum, the whole orchestra; the pianists are hired prestidigitators, showing off. What would an Athenian, a contemporary of da Vinci, a Madame de Sévigné, have thought of this cacophony?

Nor is the charivari of colours and shapes any less stunning: the effect is comparable to that of the four immense pages into which *The Times* small advertisements are crammed. Here, and there, competition is fierce. All are clamouring the qualities of some product, some drug or medicine. Everyone tries to devise some refinement to flatter a desire, a whim or a mania. Everyone has turned specialist and is more and more deeply involved in narrow specialisation. Genius is expended in making and selling some special set of horse-brushes. If the fashion for crinolines weakens, whole populations of steel-workers are thrown out of work and starve. The mind becomes narrower, men grow hot after gain, work too much, acquire too many needs. Taste grows degraded and elaborate. Everybody becomes plebeian, proletarian or shop-keeperish, sharp, hard, anxious and unhappy. To make money — such, nowadays is the daily concern, the all-absorbing idea — and in this country more than in any other. How right they are to retain their upper class, with its independent fortunes, its well-filled leisure, its superior culture, its perspective view. Even in politics a counter-weight is useful and even so, despite this counter-weight, England's politics are becoming those of a shop-keeper who retires behind his counter, closes his shutters and announces that brawls in the street outside are nothing to do with him.

Last Sunday and the Sunday before that, there were open-air

preachers in Hyde Park, each with a Bible and an umbrella. They were private persons who felt the need to communicate their religious ideas to the public. On another Sunday I saw, at forty miles from London, on the village green, two men in frock coats and top hats, singing hymns. I am told that this is not unusual when the afternoon sermon has been a good one — they bring away a surplus of religious fervour from the service and seek an outlet for it.

The Hyde Park preachers had long, thin faces, nasal voices, and they kept casting their eyes up to to Heaven; they had an audience of about a score, sharing in the edification. Zeal is very lively, especially in the case of 'dissenters'; their young men are recruited for the work. One will take up a position at a certain cross-roads every Sunday and give away pious tracts; another gathers together a dozen or so lightermen every Thursday and lectures them on the Bible. There are still women preachers among the Methodists: it is said that one of the most disting-uished authoresses of our time began as one of these. Even in Paris we sometimes feel repercussions of this eccentric piety: there was, for example, the Rev. Reginald whose bills, advertising his ser-mons, bore in big letters the message "Come to Jesus now" (sic).

The Methodists hold, indeed, that "now", in a moment, at one touch of grace, the most obstinate sinner can be converted. The Rev. Reginald used to mount the pulpit, preach to his text, and then produce one of his followers, a fat, strapping young man, as an example and visible proof in support of it. The young man would then speak on his own account — "Yes, brethren, I was a great sinner, but the Lord's grace touched me — etc., etc." A thoroughly English notion: produce the actual evidence, the solid testimony, the living specimen, like a zoologist, in support of a mystical doctrine.

On still another Sunday, at eight o'clock in the evening in a university town, I came upon two gentlemen, and a man of the middle class, who were preaching: they do this every Sunday. The first, who was not more than twenty, was obviously in an emotional condition; he was trying to overcome his shyness and was using a great many gestures. "Jesus Christ came for us, sinners; let us take thought for ourselves, miserable sinners — etc., etc." After this beginning the second opened his Bible and read a passage about the people of Jerusalem besieged and reduced to famine by the Assyrians; the latter, terrified by an Angel of the Lord, hastily decamped; two lepers, the first to dare go outside the walls,

191

found the enemy's tents full of provisions, and ate and drank with delight. This is like the Christian who has only to get outside the walls of sin to find all he has need of in the Lord. The Christ is our comfort, our refuge and our safety. This was followed by a story of a sailor, about to put out to sea, and answering a gentleman who had expressed anxiety over his danger. "Yes, my father died by drowning, also my brother, and my grandfather." "Then why do you go to sea?" "Sir, how did your father die?" "In his bed." "And your other relations?" "In their beds." "Yet you are not afraid to go to bed, and you are right. For there is one salvation for the Christian, whether at sea or in bed, to wit, Christ."

The third preacher, a lean, hollow-cheeked man, with a harsh, violent voice, seemed to be possessed. But as his theme was the same, I left them after listening for quarter of an hour. There were about fifty people listening to them, men and women, for the most part well dressed. A few muttered from time to time, or smiled ironically, but most of the men and all the women paid serious attention and seemed much edified.

I entirely approve scenes of this kind:

1st — because 'they give vent' to a strong passion, an intense conviction which needs an outlet and, in default of one, might turn to madness, melancholia or sedition.

2nd — they are moral and may have a good effect on a few consciences.

3rd — they remind the man in the street that there are sublime ideas, serious beliefs, and sincerely zealous souls in the world. Men are only too inclined to think that indifference and entertainment are the goal of life.

These lay preachers are the vestige of the old puritan spirit, the dwarfish survivors of a great fauna, now almost extinct. The fundamental religious feeling is still there. According to G——, who completed his education here in England, the majority of young men, even those whose minds are alert, have no religious doubts whatsoever. What is now the rule with us, is the exception here. In chapel they sing the hymns seriously and with all their heart. Three-quarters of the newspapers and books published censure "French scepticism and German freethinking" with every appearance of conviction, meaning by that both the heresy which denies and the heresy which affirms. And even grown men here believe in God, the Trinity, and Hell, although without fervour. Protestant dogma is very well suited to the serious, poetic and moral instincts of this people. They do not have to make an effort to maintain their faith in it; on the contrary, it would call for an effort to reject it. An Englishman would be very upset if he could not believe in an after-life; in his eyes it is the natural complement of life on Earth. In every great crisis of his life his thoughts become solemn and tend towards ideas of the *Beyond.* And in order to have some idea of the mysterious country divined by the aspirations of his soul, he makes use of a kind of map, a very ancient one, Christianity to wit, explained for him by a highly respected body of geographers, that is, the clergy. There are several possible ways of interpreting the map, and the official geographers therefore allow a certain latitude to personal opinion. Not being constrained, then, the Englishman is not dissatisfied, and it does not occur to him to distrust either map or geographers. On the contrary, he would be very annoyed with any importunate person who tried to *unsettle* the opinions he has adopted in this matter. These opinions are formed, immutable, deep-rooted; they are a part of his education, his traditions, the great public corpus, which includes himself. He accepts Protestantism and the Church *en bloc,* with the British Constitution. In Protestantism he finds a rule of conduct, an exhortation to justice, a call to 'self-government' within his own mind and spirit. The Church, for him, is an auxiliary of the State; it is the moral health department, an office for the good administration of souls. For all these reasons respect for Christianity is accepted by public opinion as a duty, and even as an aspect of ordinary seemliness of behaviour. An ordinary Englishman would be very reluctant to admit that an unbeliever could be a good Englishman and a decent, respectable man. And anyone who, having had the misfortune to lose his own religious faith, endeavours to undermine that of other men, is censured.

"Intellectual poltroonery", wrote the *Edinburgh Review,* * is the only kind of cowardice which is common in this country, but it dominates us to a lamentable extent. Most writers suffer from scruples and alarms concerning the tendencies of their own books. The social penalties attached to unorthodox opinions are so harsh and so ruthlessly applied, that here philosophical criticism and even science itself too often mutter in ambiguous whispers what ought to be proclaimed from the house-tops."

Not only is the free and aspiring flight of the mind severely checked by this, but a meticulous rigourism frequently impairs

* April 1848.

freedom of speech and action. M. Guizot tells us in his *Mémoires* that having said, in company, "Hell is paved with good intentions", he was reproved by a lady: *Hell* is too grave a word to be used in ordinary conversation. Certain expletives, for example "Goddem!" * are monstrous and no degree of excitement or impulse can excuse them. A young Frenchman whom I met here was rowing a number of people in a boat; he made a clumsy stroke, the oar missed the water, and he fell over backwards, rapping out the unfortunate expletive. The three ladies lowered their eyes, horrified, and stared in embarrassment at the water; one of the Englishmen was frankly amused, but the other two turned as red as innocent young girls.

This religious prudishness frequently leads to hypocrisy. I know a big London businessman who visits Paris twice a year on business. When there he is very gay and amuses himself on Sundays like anybody else. His Paris host paid him a return visit in London and was made very welcome. On Sunday he came down and went into the drawing-room where he began making a few practice shots on a small ladies'-size billiards table they had there. His host came burstling in, highly alarmed, and at once put a stop to this. "What a scandal, if the neighbours should hear of it!" The next time the merchant went to Paris he took his wife and daughters with him: no more gaiety, no more relaxing of reserve, and no more amusing himself on Sundays; he was stiff, buttoned-up, exemplary. His religion is a uniform. This is an example of that 'cant' which made Lord Byron so angry. But during the past twenty years it has been on the decline. The philosophy of M. Comte, German exegesis, the conclusions to be drawn from geology and the natural sciences have been insinuating themselves, slowly but persistently. Free thinking and investigation are resuming their rights: they are not breaking any windows; but they are opening doors.

As continued observation provides me with more facts, lines of thought begin to converge. There is no greater pleasure, when travelling, than to see new facts as they are acquired fitting into those one has already collected, adding themselves, like so many new touches of line or colour, to the picture one has started. Here

* Taine tells his readers this means "God damn me!" E. H.

194

are those of the past week which belong with my observations on the aristocratic régime and the feelings which it inspires.

A lady of the middle class, but whose manners are good and appearance distinguished, goes into a cheese-shop in Brighton. The shopkeeper, in his soft, obsequious voice, enquires,

"What kind of cheese do you 'patronize', Madam?"

The point here is that it is an honour for a commodity to receive aristocratic sanction. Thus, cake boxes or pomade pots bear the inscription "As used by the nobility and gentry."

B —— visited France during the *Exposition* and was greatly astonished by the liberties French soldiers take with their officers. A captain of the *Guides* was reading a notice stuck to a shop-window; two soldiers behind him leaned forward to read it over his shoulder. "In England," B —— told me, "that would be impossible: there is such a thing as rank." In his notes on a visit paid to Calais in 1839 Dr Arnold has a similar remark. "I perceive here a fusion of ranks which may be a good thing, but I do not know that it is. Well-dressed men speak familiarly to persons who unquestionably belong to the lower orders."

As a Frenchman I cannot help feeling a little shocked when, as yesterday, I heard a distinguished, greatly respected man of forty, say 'milord' (sic), that is, *monseigneur*, to a stupid sulky little boy of ten, who happens, however, to be the son of a marquis.

S —— recently dined in hall, at Trinity College, Cambridge. There were three hundred people present and the meal was served on silver plate. There was a small, separate table for under-graduates who are noblemen, and they wore a distinctive costume. At the Universities, and even in schools, the young nobles have flatterers who are called 'tuft-hunters'; these are commoners who, by services rendered and demeaning themselves, are trying to lay the foundations of their fortune. A nobleman always has a living or a place of some sort in his gift, and may, later on, gratify his former toady with it.

It is customary to make the country's three or four most disting-uished doctors baronets. During the last reign there was one who was particularly illustrious and there was a move to give him a peerage. He refused it. "And he was right," said the Englishman who was telling me this story; "a man who has held out his hand to receive his guinea could not properly be a peer of the realm." As a Frenchman, of course, I think quite the contrary, but the incident and the comment on it are none the less characteristic.

"In England," says a novelist I have just been reading who is a very good observer, "people are much too disposed to adopt the opinions of their superiors in rank and to let themselves be led by them." The exact opposite to what happens in France.

A conversation with Thackeray: I am able to mention his name because he has since died, and in any case the ideas informing his conversation appear in his books. He confirmed to me, in person, all that he had written about the *lackey*-spirit. I told him a little anecdote in my own experience. At a meeting for charity the speaker demonstrated the importance of the cause in question to his audience by reference to the fact that the marquis of ——, 'a person in such a situation', was their chairman. Thackeray told me that insipidities of this kind are very common; he greatly admired our French equality, and said that here people of consequence are so accustomed to see lesser men on their knees, that they are shocked when they do encounter an independent character. "I myself", he told me, "am now regarded as a dangerous character."

"Intelligence (wit) and talent," Stendhal wrote, "lose twenty-five per cent of their worth on arrival in England." And, in fact, the best places are all taken by people of birth or great fortune. Artists and writers remain in the second rank, excepting for five or six extremely eminent. They are received in high society but only as 'lions', that is as curiosities. A few, owing to the moral or political character of their writings, are more highly thought of and attended to, men like Stuart Mill, Macaulay, Carlyle, Dickens, Thackeray, Tennyson; this is because they contribute, from a distance, to that work considered the most important of all, the management of the nation's business and directing of its sentiments. But according to what my friends here tell me the part played by the rest is inconsiderable when compared with the position of a writer in France. The excellent journalists who, three of four times a month, write a masterly article in one of the newspapers do not sign it and are unknown to the public. They are, in fact, what are called 'literary hacks'. Their article is read at breakfast as the slice of bread-and-butter which accompanies the tea is eaten: nobody asks who wrote the article, any more than they ask who churned the butter. And if, next month, the article and the butter are not so good, then you change your newspaper as you change your grocer. Mr X ——, the famous Crimean War and Indian Mutiny correspondent of *The Times*, is nobody here and is starving to death as director of a small paper.* Not a single journalist has ever become an M.P., much less a Minister, as happened in France in 1830.

Nevertheless, in this, as in religion, a gradual change is occurring here, and the day will come when the highest places will go to talent.

❊

I have been glancing through a large collection of bound volumes of *Punch*. This is England's best satirical journal, and compared to French periodicals of the same kind it is very instructive.

Not a single drawing dealing with prostitutes of any kind, whereas in our papers they are innumerable: that is one of our faults, it would be better not to display our vermin as we do. Gavarni once said, "I hate whores because I love women," and in a hundred drawings he makes fun of women of easy virtue. But his light ladies are very pretty, his fun provokes only a sophisticated smile, and after one has been seeing his drawings in the print shops year after year, an unwholesome impression is, unwittingly, left on the mind. I must ask the reader to forgive me for this brief digression into moralising: my excuse is that it is true. Every sight we see, every emotion we experience, leaves some small permanent mark on us, and these marks added together comprise what we call our character. After ten, twenty or thirty years we are left, in the matter of *galanterie* (of our attitude to sex), with a certain fund of weakness, curiosity, or at very least of (culpable) tolerance, and a vague idea that unconventional behaviour should have its place in the sun quite as much as the received convention, the rule.

*Punch* has not a single drawing on marital infidelity, yet we all know how numerous such drawings were in France, especially about fifteen years ago; they are less numerous nowadays, but one still sees them. Here, on the contrary, marriage is honoured, and what are represented are its sweets, its affections, its intimate poetry. For instance — "Saturday evening. Arrival of the husbands' steamer" — The jetty is covered with women, most of them young, their faces radiant with joy; and the children are dancing with pleasure. What a welcome! By way of contrast, see what a

* This was William Howard Russell. *The Times* subsequently allowed him a pension of £300 a year. E. H.

French draftsman makes of the same subject — the arrival of the husbands' train at Treport or Trouville; they are depicted as grotesquely caricatured breadwinners, or they are shown as tyrants or as cuckolds.

The same sentiment is apparent in *Punch's* conjugal scenes. Augustus, during the first month of his marriage, undertakes to make the tea. The scene is set in a pretty seaside cottage; he and his bride, their arms round each others' waists, go to the window to contemplate the calm sky and the beauty of the evening. Meanwhile the kettle boils over, the dog howls, and the maid comes rushing in to see what has happened. The fun is gentle; the artist envies the absent-mindedness of the happy couple he depicts for us.

Instead of illicit love, they deal with legitimate love. Hence they have a whole series of subjects our draftsmen hardly ever touch upon. A large number of drawings represent the little wiles and strategems of the young man and girl who are almost or quite decided on marriage. In France we have no such drawings because we have no such subject. Theodore and Emily are at the seaside, and sheltering behind a breakwater, believe themselves invisible; Theodore, on his knees, has his nose squashed against the hand the lady has yielded to him. They have forgotten the turning mirror of the *camera obscura* which has been focussed on them for the past ten minutes for the edification of the spectators. Edwin and Angelina have arranged to meet at the end of the jetty; but he has taken the left jetty, she the right; they can see each other, separated by a hundred yards, but with three miles to walk if they are to come together. A young lady, an expert horsewoman, has just jumped a hedge and thicket, leaving her rival entangled in them behind her: "That gets rid of Miss Georgina, I hope, and here I am in the same field as Augustus." And, indeed, there is a horseman in the distance. Two lovers, on horseback, riding along the front at Brighton; the air there is much better than London fogs: "At least, that is their opinion!" The irony is benevolent, one can almost hear the artist wishing he were in their place. That wish is perhaps evident in the fact that he has drawn them as smart as he could, well-bred and elegantly dressed. The young girls in these drawings, particularly, are charming. And we are shown Mr Punch as a lover, in ecstasies at the sight of their fair tresses: "It is too much!" he seems to say, "Don't be so pretty!" And here is a whole flight of them, eighteen of them, beside an inlet at the seaside, depicted in various attitudes, some stooping over a drawing, others embroidering, gathering shells, laughing: "the Sirens' Grotto."

Note that they are decent, respectable girls and so is the drawing: riding, or shown in a high wind on the jetty, nothing is ever uncovered, and if they touch their skirts it is to hold them down. For the same reason gallantry is always shown as respectful; the suitor carries the girl's easel, or wipes her little brother's nose. He is not a conquering lover but rather, submissive; it is the girls who scold and lead. Sometimes, it is even the girls who make the first move: in this connection 'Fast girls' are made objects of satire. One of them slips away from a game of croquet to chat with a young man. Another contrives a tête-à-tête by means of a game of chess. Or it is mama who is shown opening the campaign: here is a very dignified matron surrounded by her three daughters, casting her line in ecclesiastical waters, her object a young, rich, well-connected clergyman staying in her house. "I am very glad, dear Mr Cecil Newton," she says, "to find you orthodox. There is no need for me to express the hope that you have no leaning towards the wretched heresy which prescribes celibacy of the clergy." And his air of being already hooked, his sentimental and edifying grimace, the sly look he is sliding towards the three pretty "baits" are very comical.

In any case, in these drawings, as in their novels, it is marriage which always appears as the goal on the horizon: no question of any intermediate halt. Now, according to Shakespeare, "All's well that ends well." So, with our young couple married, let us visit them in their home.

Here, again, the drawings are not disagreeable, not bitterly satirical: there are no prematurely aged and ugly *bourgeois*, no ugly, scolding, tyrannical children, like those which Daumier draws so freely and with such obvious hatred. Here, the artist nearly always considers that a child is beautiful and pleasing. There is a commotion in the 'nursery'; two groups, one of little boys and one of little girls, have harnessed themselves in teams of four, and are cavalcading round the room to the sound of a trumpet; but their cheeks are so rosy and all these little folk are so happy! Two little girls in a garden are offering grandmamma their skipping rope to use, with the utmost seriousness. Here is another little girl; she has found the scissors and is solemnly cutting her little brother's hair off; he wanted to be bald, like grand-dad, you see. Christmas Eve, in a large drawing-room, decorated with holly and lanterns. They are dancing, and the smiling grandpapa stands up with his grand-daughter, a baby of six who is holding up her dress and curtseying with a merry twinkle.

Incidents, and sometimes accidents, but in either case the constant, intimate sweetness of domestic life.

True, father is shown as having his troubles: six, eight, ten children, often succeeding each other at yearly intervals. He is fifty years old, thin on top, has something of a paunch, and the latest little blessing just arrived. There is a swarm of them already and this new arrival may not be the last. And meanwhile the house is so encumbered with aunts and grandmothers, that *"pater-familias"* is relegated to the staircase, where he bolts his dinner sitting on the stairs. A Frenchman would be mopping his brow in like case: so very much happiness ends by becoming a misfortune! What a burden such a brood would be!

And then they must be taken to the seaside, housed, fed, clothed, educated, their health attended to, their pleasures catered for; above all they must be kept in obedience and concord. Truly, such a family, increased by menservants and maids, comprises a small state of which the father is expected to be the head, magistrate and sovereign arbitrator. I have myself known such families: living in the country, fifteen miles from the nearest town, they may number thirty people, masters and servants included; add to that fifteen or twenty houses, inhabited by their tenants, within range of the manor house, a dozen horses in the stables, and a home farm. Their butcher's meat is from their own beasts, slaughtered on the estate. In such conditions a modern gentleman does not differ greatly from his ancestor, the feudal baron. True, such cases are quite rare: but vestiges of the same kind  of authority are to be found in the  ordinary middle-class citizen, the London paterfamilias. He is no weakling relegated to the second rank, as in our French comic drawings. He is aware of his responsibility, he directs and administers.

For example, (here he is in *Punch*), having resolved to introduce hydrotherapy into his family: and we see his poor children, in long chemises, oil-cloth caps, come shivering and miserable one by one to the cold shower, while father wields the rough scrubbing-brush.

Again, winter having arrived, the whole household needs hard-wearing, sensible footwear: here is the shoemaker, and under the paternal eye, he is fitting the small feet of a whole family of despairing little daughters into enormous, hob-nailed boots.

Fig. 20   *Aquarium*

*Tom (who has had a very successful day) presents his sisters with
a fine specimen of the cuttle-fish (Octopus vulgaris).*

(*Punch Almanac,* 1860)

Father wants a week at the seaside: as he finds the constraints
of hotel life trying, the drawing shows him setting up house on
the sea-front. Two bathing-machines provide sleeping accommodation; cooking will be done in the open; aunt, children and mama
are all working away, and even the grown-up son is peeling
vegetables as he smokes his cigar. Meanwhile, father stands
watching them with a satisfied but sardonic expression, supervising and directing their efforts. From the mere look of him it
is clear that none will try and thwart his will: his bearing, look,
the hands clasped behind his back or thrust into his pockets, his
gravity and coolness, the scarcity of his words and gestures, all
are eloquent of the feeling of unquestioned and rightful authority
which he enjoys. Exaggeration, fantasy, caricature, I grant you;
but this is a document none the less instructive for all that: it
gives us an insight into the life of an English family, and enables
us to guess why they have, and how they rule, half a dozen or
a dozen children.

Next, portraits of servants: since this class is very numerous
and there are many servants in any family in easy circumstances,
artists depict them frequently. And one aspect of their lives shown

us is their afflictions. In an aristocratic society their position is a very low one, and they are degraded to some singular tasks. Here is an old lady walking in the park, accompanied by her dog and followed by a tall manservant: "John Thomas." — "My lady?" — "Carry Beauty, the poor darling is getting tired." The same scene, but this time played between a little girl of sixteen and her maid, or her governess: the latter is already carrying a dog under each arm, but the little patrician is complaining, "Oh, Parker, you ought to carry Puppet, too! He's going to get his feet wet!"

Pouring rain: a thrifty nobleman, nice and dry in his carriage, is saying to his servants, drenched to the skin on the box, "Good Gracious, Thompson! Haven't you men got an umbrella outside?" — "No, My Lord!" — "Dear! Dear! Dear! Then give me those new hats inside!"

From many small points observed I believe that servants in France get fewer comforts but more consideration; at least they are not kept at such a distance. The human being remains more nearly intact and is not so utterly extinguished by the livery. This fundamental difference is always cropping up, the difference which divides the land of hierarchy from the land of equality.

Another aspect of this class depicted by the artist is their absurdities: as a consequence of the aristocratic institution every class in society has an inferior class beneath it, is obstinate in maintaining the distinction, and will not suffer itself to be assimilated to it. Thackeray has given us a vivid picture of this oddity, which was that of the French court under Louis XIV. Here, it is as lively a force among the servants as among the gentry. Now, there is nothing more grotesque than vain pride in a lackey. Here we have one of my lord's servants giving my lord notice because he has seen my lord riding on the outside of an omnibus. Here, again, is a footman consenting to carry a scuttle of coals up to the nursery: "If madam asks me to do it as a favour, I shall not raise many objections; but I hope madam doesn't take me for a scullerymaid."

Being handsome, well dressed, well-fed and having an easy life, they think themselves gentlemen. They are dainty, take good care of themselves, and give themselves tremendous airs. One, riding in the carriage, is shown consulting his betting note-book. Another, summoned to get up behind the carriage, lounging languidly, refuses. "If madam does not find it too hot for her, I certainly find it too hot for me." "Jane," says a young bride to her ladies'-maid, "I was surprised to see that none of you rose when

Fig. 21 *Very Careful*
*Economical Peer (with feeling).* "*Good gracious, Thompson!*
*Haven't you men got an umbrella outside?*"
*Thompson.* "*No, my lord!*"
*Peer.* "*Dear! Dear! Dear! — Then give me those new hats inside!*"
(*Punch,* June 23, 1860)

I came into the kitchen just now." To which the maid, tossing
her head with a saucy air, replies, "Really, madam? Well, it was
we who were surprised that you should have come into the kitchen
while we were at breakfast."

But you need to see the faces, expressions, gestures: when I
seek for words to convey them I can find none, unless perhaps
in English. Only the language of a country can render the things
proper to that country, for instance the crabbed and shrewish
face of the servant who, for want of beauty, has been left an old
maid, and the complacency, solemnity, majesty and servility of
the footman who knows himself to be a handsome fellow.

Amusements: these are nearly all athletic. One has only to
glance through these volumes and albums to realise how com-

pletely national is the taste for horseflesh and for dangerous riding to hounds. In two out of every three numbers you will find something depicting misadventures or incidents of horse-riding. Constant fun is made of timid or clumsy horsemen; and of distinguished foreigners who hesitate at a jump, seeing no pleasure in breaking their necks. There are drawings of fox-hunting, in winter, with jumping over leafless hedges, and with little boys and girls following hounds on their ponies. Young girls jump hedges, ditches and five-barred gates, gallop thickets and go hell-for-leather through swampy bottoms. Tall, slender, and with firm seats, they clear every obstacle, putting novice horsemen to shame. Stout, wide-backed mamas trot in groups of horsewomen under the supervision of a riding-master. We see whole families, from the grandfather aged seventy down to his six-year-old granddaughter riding together by the seaside like a tribe of centaurs. Here is Miss Alice, aged eight, mounting her father's big horse and offering her pony to her mother who is a little nervous.

It is obvious that they all have a need for fresh air and exercise. We see them on a trip through mountain country, old women and young wrapped in rugs and waterproofs, riding on the outside of the coach with their men, the inside being left for the dogs, who take their ease there. Or they are depicted strolling on a jetty beside the sea in rough weather, rejoicing in the wind which disorders their hair and the rain which drenches them. What we have here is a primitive instinct, analogous to that of a greyhound or a race-horse. They need muscular exertion and wild weather under the open sky to whip up their blood. I have known young Englishmen living in Paris who leave their windows open all night and every night throughout the winter. This kind of thing makes us understand their passion for all kinds of exercise in the open, for cricket, fishing and hunting.

The whole sky is dissolving in water, the countryside looks like a lake: yet here is an old gentleman in a waterproof still obstinately fishing. Or another scene: the river is frozen; a countryman with a pick is cutting a hole in the ice and letting his fish-hook down into the hole to catch a pike. Neither difficulty, expense nor danger can stop them. They make journeys of five hundred miles into the Highlands to fish for salmon, stalk deer or shoot 'grouse'. Keen amateurs set out from London, with their hunters in horse-boxes, to follow hounds. B —— tells me that where pheasants are preserved, reared, guarded, fed during the winter, etc., every bird shot costs the landowner between forty and fifty francs.

*Fig. 22   A Fact*

*James. "If you please, ma'am, here is MASTER Carlo! But I can't
see MISS Floss nowheres!"   (Punch, August 18, 1860)*

But of every three sportsman there will be one who, by the end
of his life, has broken an arm or a leg. There is an endless supply
of jokes on that subject: a gentleman on horseback questions his
neighbour about the horse he is riding, as the animal seems rather
restless: "Oh, she's well known! She's broken more collar-bones
than any other horse in England." An effeminate young gentleman,
shown at the railway station setting off for some stag-hunting is
asking his tall, burly companion, "Are you taking a single ticket or
a return?" "I'm taking a return because I know the horse I'm
going to ride. But you'd better take a single ticket, and an insurance ticket." * The prospect is disagreeable, but not invariably,
since for men of a certain temper difficulty, ordeals and perils are
exciting. Many Englishmen take pleasure in putting themselves
to the proof, in hardening and training themselves to surmount
some obstacle: hence, for example, the 'Alpine Club' and other
similar clubs. The qualities of a horseman and an athlete are, in
their eyes, a proper part of the virile character ('manliness'). So
that accepted ideas reinforce instinct, and affectation pushes them
in the same direction as their own nature.

* At English railway stations one can by paying extra, buy a life-insurance
ticket. H. T. I think these tickets covered you against being killed in a
train accident, rather than stag-hunting! E. H.

Jacquemont, in India, remarked that even there they gorge themselves on meat and spirits, then gallop for two hours under the terrible sun of that country, all because that was the fashion, the done thing, or out of sheer bravado, so that they need not think themselves timid or effeminate; and they would do it though it killed them — which, indeed, it did.

The same character is apparent in the majority of little boys. The artist shows them precocious, indeed, but not in our style — not precocious in malice, wit or the senses, but in boldness and vigour. The 'street-boys' depicted are no *Gavroches:* little and thin though they be, their fists get more work than their tongues, and a witticism is less apt to please them than a feat of strength. Here are two of these pygmies trying, in winter, to shove a snow-ball twice their own height into position so as to block a doorway, and, half-frozen though they be, are clearly in their element. Nor are rich children any less tough and adventurous than poor ones: we are shown two tiny boys trying to unmoor a boat and put to sea. Their pleasures are rough and noisy: they paddle up to their knees in creeks or inlets; they catch octopuses which they bring, spitted, into the drawing-room. They learn to box when still very small, and box with the gloves on in front of their mamas. We are shown father visiting them at school, and anxiously enquiring about their progress. "Oh, not too bad. I can thrash three of the other boys already, and Fred here can thrash six, including me." Another infant, mounted on a pony the size of a Newfoundland dog, is preparing to jump a small stream and replying to the groom's objections with, "My horse and I can both swim."

B —— tells me that from childhood onwards they are constantly told, "You must be a man." They are brought up to the idea that they must never cry, never show any sign of weakness, that they are expected to be brave, enterprising and to protect the weaker sex. Here, for instance, we have a very small boy telling a stout lady frightened of a herd of bullocks, "Don't be afraid, keep behind me." Another, six years old and mounted on his hairy Shetland pony is calling to his sisters on a balcony, "Hi there, girls! If you fancy a ride on the sands, I'm your man."

Most frequently made fun of in small boys, by English comic artists, is their gluttony: Emily has offered her small brother everything she can think of to amuse him, her paint-box, piano, books, but he grumbles, "Hi! I don't call that amusement. What I want is figs, cake or a large chunk of toffee. That's what I call amusement!" Naturally, the draftsman makes the physical type

206

match the moral character. He does not draw them refined or delicate, but rough and robust. And, moreover, their natural bravery is, of course, exaggerated: we are shown two little boys on a donkey preparing to jump a ditch which is giving pause to a gentleman on horseback. An urchin of five, with his hands in his pockets, is saying to his uncle, a strapping young man well wrapped up for the street but thinking of night-prowlers, "I say, Uncle Charles, if you don't feel easy about going back alone, why, I'll see you to your door."

Subtract the deliberate exaggeration from the caricature, and you have the characteristic as it is, or at least as the English see, or try to see, it. With that as our data, and having applied the requisite corrections and confirmed the result by observation, we have the thing as it really is.

Among the supporting 'documents' we may refer to, since they depict the nature, breeding and temper of these people, there are some ready to hand. The common people, especially farmhands, sailors, farmers and petty country squires are, in this country, great, strapping fellows or loutish giants: their whole appearance is redolent of brutal strength. You can see that they take pride in being well fed. Here, for instance, is a picture of an old country gentleman and he looks like a fatted hog who has not forgotten his grandfather the wild boar. Further on is a portrait of an English juryman: he is setting out for the court, crammed to bursting with food, having eaten like an ogre, added to which his wife is filling his pockets with food. This has reference to the fact that juries are locked in until they have reached agreement so that in the end it is famine which will make them unanimous; nothing could be more horrible than emptiness with such a stomach as that!

Holiday time in a coal-mining area: fisticuffs are the principal pleasure. Here is a daughter returning home with her father, who has had his arm broken; she is telling her swain, a massive oaf, to go and take his turn at bashing someone. Two sailors, at Balaclava, stout and burly fighting animals, are humbly addressing their officer, "Excuse us, your honour, but could John Grampus and me have a day's shore-leave to go to the trenches and shoot with the soldiers?".

But the most significant of all these artists' characters is the Englishman's ideal type, John Bull, as he is depicted in political cartoons: here, as chosen by themselves, is their true representative. In this portrait which, for them, is a summing-up, they show us the base and essence of the national character. As a child he is a stout, fleshy young fellow in the manner of Rubens, or rather Jordaens, but with the scowling expression of a bull-dog. As an adult he resembles a grazier: fifty years of age, burly figure, prominent belly covered by a vast waistcoat, strong top boots, a low-crowned hat, and a cudgel in his hand. But age has in no way detracted from his strength: in a bout of wrestling or boxing he could face the most formidable opponent. Imagine a figure typifying distinction: then imagine the exact opposite; it is the latter impression which John Bull leaves on one. Short neck, massive chin, heavy jaw — the whole machinery for mastication strongly developed. His starched collar frames his shaven chin and reaches halfway up his cheeks, and his side-whiskers are shaped like mutton-chops. So that the lower part of the face is like that of M. Prudhomme. But the joyous or savage look in the eyes, the beetling and formidable eyebrows, the whole expression of the face are indicative of the strong, animal sap of the man, and his choleric temper. Very low forehead, no intelligence, his ideas few and simple, and those ideas proper to a tradesman or a farmer. On the other hand one can distinguish common sense in him, and energy, a fund of good humour, honour, application and tenacity — in short the very attributes of character which enable a man to make his way in life and which render him, if not exactly lovable, at least useful. There are better men than that in England: but one would not go far wrong in taking John Bull and analogous types as representative of the aptitudes and inclinations of the average Englishman.

At the opposite extreme is to be found the artist-type. The superiority which French drawings give him, over the ordinary middle-class citizen, is well known: here, by a notable conjuncture, the opposite is the case. Musicians appear as performing monkeys introduced into a drawing-room to make their noises. Painters are depicted as bearded artisans, ill-paid, ill-clad, ill-bred, pretentious and only one step higher in the social scale than photographers. As for the latter, they are illiterate working-men, unable to speak their own language correctly, and at best figures of fun. Thackeray frequently combatted this fault in English accepted ideas. Clive Newcome, one of his characters, the son of a colonel but a painter himself, is astonished to discover that in Paris aritsts are the equals of people in good society and that Delaroche and Horace Vernet dine with the King. In France no publicist would ever have been required to prove that the art of painting is an occupation quite as liberal as the profession of medicine or law. Probably, in the eyes of the gross John Bull I have just been describing, a painter is not a gentleman since he works with his hands when painting. He is not 'respectable' since he has no regular source of income and artists' studios are said to be haunts of dissipation. So, clearly, he is a kind of workman who does not know how to behave. A painter, in short, has the same rank as a bachelor house-painter and, like him, is probably a pillar of the nearest public-house.

The political cartoons* look as if they were drawn by John Bull himself. The drawing is hard, exact, without suppleness or finesse, and the satire sour and harsh: a bull-dog's notion of merriment. Moreover, everything is subordinated to the practical effect: matters of State — war, a change of government, a political situation — have to be expressed in terms of some familiar scene of daily life, so that even the most obtuse brains can understand it.

In drawings touching on manners the various types are very well observed and grasped by the artist, executed in a lively style, and giving clear and vigorous expression to the moral by physical means. In that respect these people are Hogarth's successors. In their frontispieces, on the other hand, and in the borders and marginal sketches of their almanacs, fantasy, a high-spirited burlesque, an eccentric and inexhaustible imagination, wild masquerades, droll processions, gracious or monstrous figures, in short original romantic and comic invention are such as to put one in mind of Dickens and even, sometimes of Shakespeare.

To complete our looting of this collection [of *Punch* and other publications] we must also take note of two tragic cartoons. They are concerned with pauperism: it is to be seen everywhere in England, at least in glimpses. A prize-winning farm-hand: the poor wretch, lean, supplicating humbly, in rags, is kneeling, his hands clasped and his head crowned with roses. Behind him in a long line stand his wife and six children looking as wretched and famished as himself. The chairman of the committee, plump and well-dressed, is solemnly handing him his reward: a hammer and a stone. Let him break up the stone and distribute it to his starving children. The assembled company are smiling: handsome gentlemen and beautiful ladies sit contemplating, with cold curiosity, as if he were an animal of some inferior but unknown species, the lamentable-looking clown who produces their bread.

Second, cheap clothing, a sweat-shop: twenty skeletons sit

* Still, no doubt, in *Punch*. E. H.

209

sewing at a bench; the proprietor, a paunchy tradesman with hard eyes and stupid dew-laps, is supervising their work with a cigar in his mouth.

These two prints, among the others have the same effect as the sight of some hideously squalid 'lane' such as are to be found in the vicinity of Oxford Street, after a long walk among the palaces, mansions and comfortable middle-class houses of the West End and the City.

Introduced to John H—— a young and very agreeable 'barrister'. He has chambers in the Temple, a sort of hive inhabited by lawyers and apprentice lawyers, and where the great number of small, furnished apartments give the impression of a *Quartier Latin* or a *basoche*.* Four associated corporations (Inns of Court) comprise the institution; each has a hall where the members dine and a law student's principal obligation is to dine in hall six times a term † for three years. A year's course of work with a 'lawyer' gives a student the right to plead cases without having followed a course of lectures. There are six teachers and the passing out examinations are optional. This, then, is not a great law school, similar to ours, and set up to teach theory before anything else. Similarly, there is no equivalent here of our *Ecole Polytechnique;* an Englishman wishing to be an 'engineer' enters an engineering firm and learns his trade while practising it, like an art student in a painter's studio. This want of organised higher technical education, this omission of important preliminary theoretical courses of training, this dependence on experience, is a remarkable and very English feature. But in any case a systematic course for the teaching of law here would be very difficult to devise. For there is no code of laws as with us, based on implied philosophical principles, but a mass of statutes and precedents more or less disparate and sometimes contradictory, which the future man of law is expected to assimilate by a long, personal grind. Furthermore there is no historical school here, such as the German one, where a subtle understanding and a broad, all-embracing vision are applied to explaining the gradual adaptation of the law to

* *basoche:* there is no English for this word; in 1870 usage, although it formerly meant a corps of law clerks, it was humorously pejorative, as who might say "a den of pettyfoggers", or "a lair of attorneys." E. H.

† If he is a member of a University, three times a term.

customs and *mores* and thereafter its conception and generation, range and limits. That which has to take the place of missing philosophical and historical theories is usage and, very often, routine.

A certain number of these lawyers, 'barristers, solicitors, attorneys' earn £20,000 a year; I was told of one who earns from £30,000 to £35,000.

We went to see some cases tried at Westminster. There is a jury in civil, as well as in criminal cases and its business is to find in matters of fact, which are distinguished from matters of law. But in civil cases a jury is only used if the parties to the case ask for one, in which event they pay a certain sum of money. We sat through three cases. In the first a woman was bringing an action for divorce against her husband; divorce has ceased to be an aristocratic privilege and no longer entails exorbitant costs. * These now amount to between £25 and £30 and are thus within reach of people with moderate incomes. It is well worth reading the accounts of these divorce cases which are frequently published in the newspapers † because they give an insight into one of the vices of English conjugal households, to wit the tyranny and brutality of the husband.

The part played by barristers here is very remarkable and quite different from that which they play in France. They not only plead their client's case, they also carry out the functions of examining magistrates; ** for in the course of the sitting they submit the plaintiff, the defendant and each witness to an examination and cross-examination. Turn and turn about the two pleaders set about their man, try to catch him out, try to make him contradict himself. It must be excessively disagreeable to be a witness in England, and the quarter-of-an-hour he spends in the witness-box is extremely unpleasant. The whole burden of the case falls upon the barristers, and the judge is there only to check and control them, prohibit certain questions, and act as moderator to the two champions, as the queen is moderator to the political parties in Parliament.

* Prior to 1857 divorce was only obtainable in the U.K. by an Act of Parliament. A Divorce Court was set up by the Matrimonial Causes Act of 1857, so that divorce for the ordinary citizen is exactly one century old. The jurisdiction of this court was transferred to the Probate, Divorce and Admiralty Division in 1873 by the Judicature Act. As Taine published his Notes in 1871, it was evidently a case under the Act of 1857 which he witnessed.

† *Gazettes.* E. H.                                                                                 E. H.

** *juges d'instruction:* this difference still, of course, exists. E. H.

The very active and versatile part he has to play must greatly enhance the importance and sharpen the wits of an advocate. In France they are too often mere phrase-spinners whose utterances decline into a rhetoric which the presiding judge is obliged to check; whereas here they are expected, like our examining magistrates, to understand and manipulate human nature. Three or four I have seen have such piercing eyes, an utterance so sharp and vibrant, gestures so abrupt and decided, that they seemed to be most admirably cunning, veritable foxes. I should not want to fall into their hands.

The woman, the plaintiff in the divorce suit, went into the witness-box to be interrogated; it is a small box with an iron grille, isolated from the court but well placed to be seen from everywhere: my escort told me she was of low degree, had a common accent and was wearing hired clothes. But her answers were informed with that persevering attentiveness and energy which I have noticed so often in this country. She was constantly on the verge of tears, yet forced herself not to cry. She was asked whether she had not struck her husband with the tongs, and if it was not she who had sometimes started their disputes. She did not answer "No" point blank, as a southern woman would have done; she lowered her head, thought for a half minute, then, sure of her memory, having checked and verified it, replied "No, never," with certainty. The tone of voice was that of complete conviction and its expression, on the word *"never"*, very fine.

Accounts of criminal trials here must be read if you would have any idea of the exalted part played by their judges, and of the equally exalted spirit in which they play it. You will never see, in an English judge, any sign of the spirit of persecution, of the feelings proper to a policeman, of the desire to avenge society, of the instinct of a hunter determined to track down and lay hands upon the quarry. "The principle of English law", says an article I am engaged in translating, "is that a man must be held to be innocent for so long as he has not been proved guilty. The burden of proof is wholly upon those who are prosecuting him. The accused, contrary to the practice in France, may refuse to speak; he is not obliged to accuse himself. Under no pretext whatsoever are the officers of the court, high or low, allowed to extract his secret from him." *

* In France, then as now, however, an accused did not appear in open court at all until it was established that he almost certainly was guilty. After the police have arrested a man the case goes to the *juge d'instruction* whose

In conformity with this spirit of the law, when the judge pronounces sentence he does so with the authority and impartiality of a conscience which is absolutely convinced. He uses neither declamation nor invective. He does not dissimulate the weak points of the prosecution's case, nor exaggerate the degree of certainty of guilt. His terms are measured; he conveys his carefully matured opinion in exactly chosen words and when, finally, to the sentence of the court he adds a moral censure, the gravity and nobility of his accents become admirable. It has often seemed to me that if Justice herself had a voice she would speak so. The man under the judge's robes has effaced himself in order to become simply the instrument of truth and law. Confronted by such a towering ascendancy even the man convicted must humble himself and subscribe to the justice of his sentence. I know no spectacle so solemnly apt to inform the hearts of men with veneration for the law.

relationship to the police is like that between an American District Attorney and the police. But the *juge d'instruction* is not simply a prosecuting official; he is virtually an official detective as well as a law officer. He will examine all witnesses, many times, in his office, confront them, confront the accused with them and so forth. He will make the documents in the case available to defence counsel. His examination terminates when he either dismisses the case *(non-lieu)* — in this function he is a sort of Grand Jury — or hands it on for trial, which he will only do if he is satisfied that the accused is, in fact, guilty. The case is then tried by three judges — the President of the Assize Court and two Assessors, and a jury of seven ordinary citizens. The whole case is managed by the President. This judge examines the witnesses using the papers in the *dossier* compiled by the *juge d'instruction*, so that the witnesses are, as a rule, merely repeating in open court what they have already told the J.d'I., though the President may put new questions. Counsel and jury may question witnesses, but only through the Court — i.e. the President not only allows the questions, but repeats them, or tells the witnesses to answer. Thus a French counsel does not address witnesses directly but says, "Will the Court ask the witness—— etc." After all the witnesses have been examined and cross-examined if necessary, the Prosecuting Counsel (Attorney General) makes a speech for the prosecution. Then the defence counsel makes a speech for the defence. Then the President sums up, much as an English judge does; among other things he will instruct the jury to give the accused the benefit of any doubt. Until a few years ago the jury retired and came to its decision alone; now the jury and President and Assessors consider their verdict together, each having one vote; in principle the President sits with the jury at this stage only to guide them on points of law. The verdict is arrived at by ballot, and a majority decides it, unanimity not being required. In murder cases the jury and judges thus sitting together have to decide on the degree of murder also, by answering a series of questions which the President will have propounded at the end of his summing-up. E. H.

But there is always some evil cheek by jowl with every good. I am told that this manner of applying the law protects the individual at the expense of society, that legal proof is too difficult to furnish, and that many guilty men are acquitted.

Good society does not patronise the theatre in England, with the exception of the two opera houses, which are luxurious and exotic hot-house flowers. There, the price of seats is enormous and evening-dress obligatory. As for the other theatres, their patrons are drawn almost entirely from the lower and lower-middle classes.* There is no longer a national school of play-writing in England; playwrights simply translate and adapt plays from the French. This is very strange, for manners in this country are peculiar and could very well be put on the stage. Moreover, it is obvious from their novels that they understand and can convey character. They have never been wanting in satirical high-spirits, and during the last century they had some excellent comic writers and admirable actors. How, then, does it happen that whereas Paris has a native comic theatre, London has none? Is it because there are no comic characters in England? It seems to me that there are more here than anywhere else, precisely because types are more clear-cut here and developed to extremes. Is it because their prudishness inhibits laughter? It does not inhibit or prohibit anything but indecent humour, and decent humour is in no way constrained. Is it because English reserve has eliminated manifold gesticulation and lively, natural expression from their exchanges? But it is a situation which creates interest, and sober-faced protagonists can perfectly well be involved in the most piquant action The thing is an enigma, especially for the reader who has just put down a novel by Dickens or one of John Leech's albums of drawings.

This evening we went to the Olympic, a small theatre more or less analagous to our Palais-Royal. The first play was a parody of *The Merchant of Venice*, full of puns and skits; but one has to be native to a country to appreciate its vulgar clowning. The other play, *Dearest Mamma*, is copied from *La Belle Mère et le Gendre*. One of the actors, Addison, plays the part of the old uncle with astonishing zest and truth. Imagine a fat, bald, cheery old fellow, pleasantly spherical in figure, tight and cosy in his

* *Le peuple et la demi-bourgeoisie.* E. H.

214

long frock-coat, easy to get on with, enjoying his freedom as a widower, systematically good-humoured, fully occupied in not upsetting "his equilibrium", eating his five meals a day and taking his three walks for the sake of his health; imagine him humming a little song for any or no reason, letting out a sort of whistle, like an elderly blackbird, at the end of every sentence, falling asleep in any available armchair and, hardened by the frosts and storms of marriage, simply nodding his head, closing his eyes and finally snoring at the onset of every dressing-down he has to submit to. Physically and morally the type is recreated with extraordinary completeness; likeable and eccentric, clowned throughout yet perfectly natural; a perfect performance.

Shakespeare is sometimes produced still. I have seen Macready in *Macbeth*, he was powerful and dramatic in the part, especially in the madness scene when, confronted by the ghost of Banquo, he gasps and pants with horror and, with a hoarse cry, crashes to the ground like a mad bull. The audience still laughs when Hamlet, in the grave-yard, says that great Alexander's dust serves today to stop a hole in a wall. But our way of seeing has changed too much; we no longer have the naivety of the sixteenth century; the illusion is disturbed by such frequent changes of scene; we cannot believe in armies represented by six actors and in the battles which take place on the stage. Even in England well-bred people must be revolted when they see Cornwall tear out Gloucester's eyes on the stage. As I see it, Shakespeare is now more effective read than acted: at least, I find I understand his characters less well when they are shown me through the instrumentality of an actor.

The cost of living in London is not too high provided one confines oneself to essentials. A young 'engineer' friend of mine spends a total of ten francs a day: his dinner, beer, roast beef, potatoes, asparagus, pastry * and cheese costs him two shillings, and his lodgings, which are very clean, comprise a bedroom and sitting-room. B ——, who is over here to read Arabic manuscripts, has, near the British Museum, a handsome room, breakfast and service for a guinea a week. Both of them had to pay more in Paris. One can rent a whole house in the neighbourhood of Regent's Park for £100 a year. On the other hand the moment it comes to

* A pie or tart perhaps. E. H.

215

living more luxuriously the prices are enormous. Four Frenchmen who spent three days at a smart hotel had a bill for eighteen hundred francs. * At another hotel in the fashionable quarter, a bedroom, sitting-room, dressing-room, service and candles cost eighteen guineas a week. Lord S —— smiled incredulously when my friend Louis T—— told him he had shot thirty-six roebuck last year on a moor *(chasse)* in France which he had rented for two thousand francs. All the pleasures of luxury, such as the opera, hunting and shooting, and making a smart appearance are reserved to the very rich; yet another aspect of the separation between rich and poor.

Our laundry did not come on the day it was due, nor on the next day, nor the day after that. Finally it was reclaimed unwashed. It appears that there were two consecutive holidays this week and the laundryman tells us that his laundresses have been drunk all week.

Since I got here I have seen three women drunk in the streets. Two, near by Hyde Park, in the most handsome street in the city, were obviously women of easy virtue of the lowest class, with ragged shawls, broken boots, idiot smiles, stumbling in their walk and babbling in their speech. The third, a decently dressed woman of fifty, was reeling about in the midst of a small crowd, admitted that she was drunk, and said that it was because she had been drinking at the Exhibition. I believe this vice to be very rare among well bred women; however, extreme boredom, or grief may lead some to it, and Eliot used such a case in the story entitled *Jane's Repentance.* †

On the other hand drunkenness among the people is terrible. During the last few days I have twice been down to Chelsea and both times came across men lying dead drunk on the pavement. My friend who lives in that district often finds working girls and

---

* £6 a day per head; say £18 or £20 of our money, allowing for the depreciation of the £ in the last hundred years. Sounds like a clip-joint!
E. H.

† *Times,* November 23, 1870. "A lady in the vicinity of London, who takes great interest in *the recovery of ladies from habits of intemperance,* continues to receive into her family one lady from the *higher classes,* requiring help in this respect. A vacancy now occurs. Address Hon. Sec. of the Ladies Total Abstinence Association, No. 33 Baker St." This advertisement opens up some odd prospects.

women in the same condition. A philanthropic clergyman of my acquaintance tells me that eight out of ten working men are drunkards.* In London they earn high wages, between £1 and £2 a week: their meals paid for, they go out drinking and may continue three or four days together, on brandy-and-water (sic) and other spirits. The drunkenness produced by these spirits stupefies a man, making him melancholy and often driving him mad. Hence *delirium tremens* and other alcoholic diseases. According to an article in the *Ragged Schools Magazine* there were eleven thousand spirits shops in London in 1848, whereas there were only four thousand butchers and bakers. Thirty thousand people are arrested every year in the London streets for being drunk. It is reckoned that the fourteen principal gin-palaces are patronised by two hundred and seventy thousand customers every week. In Glasgow, one in every ten houses is a gin-shop. † Statistics show that in Manchester about £1,000,000 per annum are spent by working men on drink; in Glasgow, about the same figure; Newcastle, £400,000; Dundee, £250,000. In Preston one hundred and forty-one working men were kept under observation and it was found that on an average they spent 22% of their earnings on spirits, rather more than £11.10.0 a year. Forty-one of them spent between 25% and 75% of their earnings. Twelve belonged to a Temperance Society and abstained from all strong liquors. And there, in fact, lies the remedy and the fervour, propaganda and usefulness of these associations is readily understandable. I have noticed their posters in many streets; they show a drunkard, lying inert, stupefied and surrounded by small imps removing his heart and brain in shovelfuls, while the principal devil stands over them holding up a bottle of gin, with the punning slogan, 'My Best Spirit'.

---

* *Ivrognes:* but probably Taine's informant meant, rather, "heavy drinkers".
E. H.

† In a recent article *The Times* pointed out that Lancashire is among the counties where education has been most neglected, basing the statement on the fact that at most weddings the register was signed with crosses instead of signatures. Mr Wilson, a Liverpool clergyman, in a letter to the same newspaper, stated that it should not be concluded that all the people who signed with a cross did not know how to read, "considering that in one case out of five, one of the parties is under the influence of alcohol when signing the register and signed with a cross because his or her condition made writing their name impossible." *Journal des Débats. 1871.*

# CHAPTER SEVEN

# FACTORIES AND FACTORY HANDS

I AM now in Manchester. During the journey I read various newspapers and reviews, and among other things three or four articles on France, their tone being against the government, condemned as being despotic and leaving no share of public business in the hands of individuals. The authors argue their case as if Frenchmen were Englishmen; they unwittingly imagine themselves transported to France, realise how uneasy they would feel there, how their own habits and customs would be outraged, and how much constraint and annoyance they would suffer under our system of government. But these constraints and annoyances, looming so large to them, are small matters to us, and most French citizens would be far more uneasy under the opposite regime. To take part in public business means shouldering an additional burden of work, serving on five or six committees, writing or listening to reports, submitting to hear twelve speeches on the same subject in as many days, digesting statistics and the results of enquiries — all very tiresome occupations. We delegate them to the Government, and if the Government be a despot, it is also a manager. It imposes certain shackles on us, but it relieves us of a great deal of trouble. We let it take its perquisites, rob us even, like a bailiff given a blank cheque, while we criticise it aloud and, beneath our breath, remind ourselves that if it becomes positively insupportable we always have the remedy of showing it the door.

True, this is poor reckoning: for after years of carefree tranquillity we wake up to find ourselves ruined and involved in bad bargains. Besides, ridding ourselves of a Government always entails scenes of violence. Finally, since a house cannot manage without a housekeeper, we are obliged, after every such brawl, to take the first that offers, which is troublesome since he is often worse than his predecessor.

Dull, flat country for the first hundred miles of the journey; thereafter the hills begin and the landscape acquires some character. High, rounded hills swimming in mist; sometimes, when the sun emerges for a moment, a pale brightness passes over the green land like a fugitive smile, but very sad and touching amid the universal mourning of the sodden fields.

We were coming to the iron and coal country, with signs of industrial activity everywhere. Slag-heaps like mountains, the earth deformed by excavation, and tall, flaming furnaces. Manchester: a sky turned coppery red by the setting sun; a cloud, strangely shaped resting upon the plain; and under this motionless cover a bristling of chimneys by hundreds, all tall as obelisks. Then a mass, a heap, blackish, enormous, endless rows of buildings; and you are there, at the heart of a Babel built of brick.

A walk in the town: seen close-to it is even more lugubrious. Earth and air seem impregnated with fog and soot. The factories extend their flanks of fouled brick one after another, bare, with shutterless windows, like economical and colossal prisons. The place is a great jerry-built barracks, a 'work-house' for four hundred thousand people, a hard-labour penal establishment: such are the ideas it suggests to the mind. One of the factory blocks is a rectangle six storeys high, each storey having forty windows: and inside, lit by gas-jets and deafened by the uproar of their own labour, toil thousands of workmen, penned in, regimented, hands active, feet motionless, all day and every day, mechanically serving their machines. Could there be any kind of life more outraged, more opposed to man's natural instincts?

At about six o'clock the factories discharge an excited, noisy crowd into the streets, men, women and children swarming in the turgid air. Their clothes are soiled; many of the children are bare-footed; the faces are drawn and dismal; a number of them stop at the gin-shops; the rest scatter to their lairs. We follow them: what dreary streets! Through half-open windows we could see wretched rooms at ground level, or often below the damp earth's surface. Masses of livid children, dirty and flabby of flesh, crowd each threshold and breathe the vile air of the street, less vile than that within. You catch glimpses of a vestige of carpet and washing hung to dry. We pushed on towards the suburbs, coming to a more open space where rows of small cheap houses have been built by speculators. The black streets were paved with ironstone slag. Lines of red roofs were ruled against the universal grey of the sky. But at least each family has its own home, and the fog they breathe there is not so contaminated. These are the privileged, the fortunate ones. And it is now summer time, the finest days of the year! And we wondered what their lives must be like in winter, when the fog descends to drown, choke, engulf the whole of the visible, natural world. And we felt for a moment all the fearful weight with which this climate and this industrial system press down upon men.

Walks and visits in the rich quarter of the town. Here and in Liverpool, as in London, the English character can be seen in their way of building. The townsman does everything in his power to cease being a townsman, and tries to fit a country-house and a bit of country into a corner of the town. He feels the need to be in his own home, to be alone, king of his family and servants, and to have about him a bit of park or garden in which he can relax after his artificial business life. From this derives the plan of immense streets, silent and devoid of shops in which each house, surrounded by a plot of green, is isolated and contains only a single family. Furthermore, beyond Manchester lies Bowden, a sort of public villa with a superb park belonging to Lord Stamford who has given the use of it to the public: magnificent trees, rich lawns, herds of half-tame deer lying among the bracken. How men emerging from factory and office must feel all the sweetness and calm of these natural beauties! For in this city there are no others: even to walk in the rich quarter of the town is depressing. Ten, fifteen, twenty houses in a row built to the same design, one after another like drafts on a drafts-board with mechanical regularity. The well-mowed lawns, the little iron gates and painted façades and symmetrical plots are reminiscent of nice, clean toys. The ornamentation of the houses is in bad taste, capitals, Greek columns, balusters, Gothic roofs and other forms all borrowed from times and places equally remote, all of it fresh and neat and incongruous, an equivocal and trumpery luxury like that of a newly rich self-made man who, trying to look smart, looks bedizened. It is a fine thing to work and an excellent thing to be rich: but to work and be rich are not enough.

But they are powerful: there is the compensation. The life of the head of an industrial or commercial house can be compared to that of a princeling. They have the capital sums, the large aims, the responsibilities and dangers, the importance and, from what I hear, the pride, of a potentate. And like such a potentate they have their agents and representatives in every quarter of the world; they are obliged to keep themselves informed from day to day of the condition and resources of both neighbouring and distant countries. They risk their profits in vast new undertakings;

they have to keep a whole population of operatives orderly and content; they are in a position to play benefactor to thousands of men; they are the generals and rulers of human toil. Quarter of a million sterling, half a million sterling, such are the figures they deal in, the order of their buyings and sellings, the values of ships chartered or goods warehoused. They send out men to reconnoitre this or that part of the earth; they discover outlets or sources of supply in Japan, China, Australia, Egypt or New Zealand. They promote sheep-farming, tea-planting, or cotton-growing in new countries. Business, in terms such as these, brings all the faculties into play.

The warehouses of finished cotton goods and other fabrics are Babylonian monuments. One of them is two hundred yards long and the bales of cloth are handled by steam-driven machinery. A cotton mill may contain as many as three hundred thousand spindles. According to one of my friends, an engineer, and basing the calculation on official figures for the imports of raw cotton and exports of manufactured cotton goods, the district of Manchester did, during two years, make a gross profit of five hundred million francs a month: at the time of writing the monthly gross profit is two hundred and fifty million francs.*

We visited the Shaw Spinning Works and the Platt works, where cotton-spinning machinery is made. Platt's produce twenty-three thousand spindles a week; their production has been as high as thirty-five thousand. They employ four thousand eight hundred operatives, their annual turnover is thirty million francs and it is said that Platt's profit last year was five million francs. When you go into the workshops you stand dazed; you are confronted by a gigantic and orderly jumble of activity, a labyrinth of wheels, cogs, moving leather belts, a whole edifice of motion and action which, from floor to ceiling and storey to storey, is toiling and turning at a dizzy velocity like some obstinate and indefatigable automaton. Eighteen great forges flame and thunder in a single workshop, each flanked by two smaller ones, while swarms of workmen are busy among shadows shot with a warm red glow. At Sharp's, where locomotives are built, seven or eight hundred artisans build a hundred locomotives a year, each costing seventy-five thousand francs. It is necessary to have seen all this to realise

* According to Mr Chadwick (Brit. Alman. & Comp. 1863) the capital invested in buildings, machines and raw materials for cotton in Lancashire, 1858, was £52 m., 28 m. spindles and 300,000 looms. Wages paid to 400,000 operatives were £205,833 a week, that is £10,653,000 a year.

the power inherent in fire and water. You see pillars of cast iron like the boles of forest-trees, iron-cutting machines which rip off shavings of iron, drilling machines which bore holes in sheets of iron as thick as your thumb as easily as if they were made of butter. There are steam-hammers so precise in their action that they can crack a nut without damaging the kernel, monstrous chisels and colossal forges. I saw eight men standing in a line and thrusting a tree of red hot iron as big round as my body into a great maw of fire.

But here man is an insect and it is the army of machines which holds the attention. At the sight of all these creatures of steel, strangely shaped, laborious and industrious, and amid the thunder of their furious haste, one thinks of the subterranean dwarfs and giants of Scandinavian mythology. Of all those deformed monsters who, in mountain caves, forged trinkets and weapons for the gods. But today it is for the insect man that they labour, it is he who commands their toil. And sometimes, seeing the disproportion between servants and masters, one is apt to forget at what a price he holds that command.

If you look at a geological map you will see, about Manchester, a wide area coloured black: this is the coal-bearing district, and towns spring up in it like gigantic mushrooms. There are seven or eight new ones round Manchester, each of forty to eighty thousand souls, for example Oldham, which I have just visited. My French engineer friend tells me that a thousand kilogrammes of coal here cost from 5 to 8 shillings. In Paris the price is 23 francs, 15 to 18 francs at Roubaix and 36 to 40 francs in the Vosges. The same black-tinted area on the map about Birmingham and Glasgow, with the same consequences. Add to this a clay soil to provide material for bricks; and here, as in London, a great estuary to give an outlet, a natural harbour, in this case Liverpool, capable of receiving entire fleets of ships. On top of all this put a hard-working and prolific population, and the whole astonishing agglomeration of products, buildings and men becomes understandable.

My friend mentioned two other features which, according to him, explain the prosperity of the big firms. On the one hand the capital invested is enormous and in industrial strife between several nations victory goes to the big battalions. Secondly, their organisation is good: their workmen apply themselves and copy the models given them exactly; the foremen are assiduous and always punctually at their posts; the machines are of excellent quality and their productivity can be estimated and valued exactly. Operatives, foremen, machines, office workers, salesmen, all work with regularity for as long as they are required to do so, like a well-adjusted and well-oiled mesh of gears. The master comes in every day and spends four hours in his counting-house and workshops to keep an eye on the whole organisation: and that is enough, the discipline and steadiness of his subordinates does the rest.

We set out for Liverpool: the name refers to a former marsh, and in fact the flat and sodden land, impregnated with sea-fogs and broken up by stagnant waters, seems made for teal rather than men. In some places the primaeval landscape survives, and one sees uncultivated sandy wastes *(landes)*, russet-coloured peat-bogs, open country without fences or hedges stretching to the indistinct line of pale green on the horizon. Heavy, purplish clouds and the incessant exhalations of sea and wet soil fill the space between the lowering sky and the endless plain as they do in Holland.

There is a large, Greek building more or less in the centre of the town, a sort of temple with a gilded ceiling and columns of imitation jasper. It is a concert hall, with a horribly crude organ making a hideous row inside. Facing it is a library, the gift of a private citizen, which cost £50,000. But there is no point in seeking beauty and elegance here. Liverpool, like Manchester, is a monster: monumental counting-houses and warehouses, immense streets of houses overburdened, as in London, with arcades, columns and pilasters, whose sole effect on the spectator is to leave him with an impression of overwhelming clutter. Half a million inhabitants and the port is the busiest and most crowded after London.

Alongside the docks the cotton warehouses form a kind of cyclopaean rampart, unending and monotonous; it is the store-house of almost all the cotton in the world. But the aspect of the docks themselves overwhelms all other impressions. The Mersey, as wide as a sea bay, extends westward, bearing ships inward and outward bound. Over six miles of its length canals open into it, carrying shipping into the basins, which are lined with stone and put one in mind of rectangular, aquatic streets multiplied and ramified into a whole town. Here ships are loaded, unloaded and repaired. Their crowded masts appear like a leafless, winter-bound forest extending as far as the eye can see and barring the whole horizon to the north. Yet vast and manifold though they be, these docks are inadequate for the multitudes crowding to use them: in groups and lines the ships wait at the mouths of each canal, waiting for a mooring. And a line of new docks is being built for them at Birkenhead, on the opposite bank of the estuary.

The spectacle of the Liverpool docks is, I think, one of the greatest in the whole world. Some of the ships are of 3500 and even 4000 tons. There is a steamer here one hundred yards long. One ship lying at anchor, the *Great Britain*, was about to sail for Australia with twelve hundred emigrants. If you go down the steps of a dry dock to the level of the ship's keel, you realise that the hull of a ship is forty or fifty feet tall. The vessel's swelling flanks, covered with copper sheeting, have the gracious lines of a wild-fowl asleep upon the waves.

From Birkenhead one can see the whole port across the enormous spread of the river; its yellow-gleaming surface is almost flat calm under the light mist. Steam-boats wallow up and down stream, meet and pass, with a stiff, mechanical motion, like black crabs. Sailing-ships glide down river, bowing, supple, beautiful as swans. The ninety-gun man-o'-war *George*, with both sails and steam, arrives in harbour like a sovereign, all that crowd of shipping making way for her. On the far shore the endless line of masts and rigging bristles against the sky, behind it the colossal heap of the town.

We visited more workshops, among them the Laird yards where iron ships are built. They are said to have built two hundred and fifty in the last thirty years: fifteen hundred workers, monstrous forges and other tools, and the yard provided with canals by which water reaches the basins. We saw a steamer on the stocks in the principal yard, a paddle-steamer 350 feet long, which is being built for the London to Ireland run: its speed will be twenty knots. It will cost between eighty and a hundred thousand pounds, will take six months to build and the uprights of the framework which contains the boilers are as thick as a man's body.

Always the same impression: enormousness. But are work and power all that is required to make a man happy? After dinner Mr B ——, a great merchant, remains at table with his guests, and they all drink port for three hours at a stretch without saying anything. Another of these wealthy businessmen goes to the country to relax his nerves as soon as he can get away: he is deeply absorbed in breeding pigs. When a man is not happy in his work he seeks to escape in dreams: a place was pointed out to me where four or five preachers, mostly Methodists, go every Sunday to preach in the open air, to a crowd of people; the idea of the Kingdom of God, of a loving Christ, their tender and all-powerful friend is a refuge for the melancholy spirit.

Another refuge is drink: "This Liverpool", says a novelist, * "is a terrible town for drunkenness. Other towns may be as bad: statistics, indeed, prove it; but I know no place where drunkenness is so flaunted, so impudent, not only in the crooked side streets and mean courtyards where one expects to find it, but everywhere. I never make even a short railway journey of an afternoon without being exposed to an encounter with at least one drunken gentle-man, snoring in his first-class carriage, or in the second class, two or three drunken men singing, swearing or letting themselves be supported and guided by their pale-faced wives. The sad thing is that their wives do not seems to be affected by it and that every-one takes the matter as being quite the natural thing. The gentle-man, who is often over fifty, is only "grey" and is used to being so every night. The other, the poor man, has had a drop, or two drops, which is what all his comrades do the moment they get the chance. They see no shame in it, laugh at him a little, humour him, and are ready to take his part against anyone who might object to such a travelling companion; they have no such ob-jection, nor have their wives. They are very well used to tolerat-ing drunken suitors, to soothing and guiding drunken husbands."

At six o'clock we made our way back through the poor quarters of the city. What a spectacle! In the neighbourhood of Leeds Street there are fifteen or twenty streets with ropes stretched across them where rags and underwear were hung out to dry. Every stairway swarms with children, five or six to a step, the eldest nursing the baby; their faces are pale, their hair whitish and tousled, the rags they wear are full of holes, they have neither shoes nor stockings and they are all vilely dirty. Their faces and limbs seemed to be encrusted with dust and soot. In one street alone there must have been about two hundred children sprawling or fighting. You draw near a house, look in, and, in the half-light of a passage, see mother and grown daughter crouching, wearing little more than a chemise. What rooms! A threadbare slip of oilcloth on the floor, sometimes a big sea-shell or one or two plaster ornaments; the old, idiot grandmother crouches in a corner; the wife is engaged in trying

* The author of *John Halifax, Gentleman,* in *A Life for a Life.* E. H.

to mend some wretched rags of clothes; the children tumble over each other. The smell is that of an old-clothes shop full of rotting rags. Nearly all these houses have, as their lowest floor, a damp, stone-flagged basement. Can one even conceive of what life can be like in these cellars during the winter? Some of the tiniest children are still fresh and rosy-cheeked, but it hurts to look at their great blue eyes; for that clear, healthy blood is going to be spoilt; as they grow older they become etiolated, their flesh becomes flabby and unwholesomely livid, and you see scrofulous little faces marred by small open sores covered with a piece of paper.

As we went forward the crowds grew denser. Half-grown boys, sitting or sprawling on the pavement, gambled with filthy cards. Livid, bearded old women came out of gin-shops: their reeling gait, dismal eyes and fixed, idiot grin are indescribable. They look as if their features had been slowly corroded by vitriol. Their rags hardly hold together and here and there reveal glimpses of their filthy bodies: and these rags are old fashionable clothes, their hats once ladies' hats.

A really horrible detail is that these streets are regular and seem to be quite new: the quarter is probably a rebuilt one, opened up by a benevolent municipality: so that this was an example of the best that can be done for the poor. Two identical rows of uniform houses and pavements mathematically laid down and framing, in their unbending lines, this swarming mass of human ugliness and misery. The air is thick and heavy, the light livid and yet dim; not a colour, not a shape upon which the eye can rest with pleasure. Rembrandt's beggars were happier and better off in their picturesque hovels. And I have not seen the Irish quarter! The Irish flock to this town, there are said to be a hundred thousand here, and their quarter is the nethermost circle of Hell. No, I am wrong, there is worse than that, something lower still, notably, I am told, at Belfast, in Ireland, where, at evening, when the operatives leave their factories, the girls, without shoes, stockings or even chemises, dressed in grey, working overalls, loiter on the pavements in the hope of adding a few pence to the day's wage.

After having made careful observations it seems to me that the two types which, among factory workers, are the most outstanding and about which are grouped the greatest numbers of variations on the same theme, are as follows:

1. The *athletic*, superabundantly well fed, massive, motionless, square trunk and immensely broad and deep through the loins. The development of the muscles, they tell me, is due to drinking 'porter'. Their broad backs, deep chests and massive shoulders are a superb spectacle. Some of them are giants, being six feet tall and more. The type is most frequently met with in iron-foundries: it is there you will see these calm colossi handling huge pieces of iron in the forge. My friends tell me that I should see even finer specimens in Yorkshire.

2. The *phlegmatic*. This type is to be found everywhere but notably in cotton mills, and so far as the faces are concerned, all the workmen up here belong to this type. The complexion is pale, the eye dull, the expression cold and fixed; the movements are exact, regular and economical, so that only the necessary minimum of effort is expended. For which reason they are excellent workers: there is nothing like a machine to operate a machine.

French manufacturers tell me that French workmen work perfectly well for the first hour, less well in the second, still less well in the third and so on in diminishing progression so that, during their last hour, they can do nothing right. Their muscular strength declines but above all their powers of attention.

Here, on the other hand, an operative works quite as well during the last hour as during the first. Besides, he works only a ten-hour day, not a twelve-hour day as in France. As a consequence of more closely sustained attention, the Englishman gets through more work. In Shaw's mill one man and two children can attend to 2,400 spindles, whereas in France two men and three, four or more children are required. But in certain other respects the French operative is superior; for example, the Vosges weavers produce much finer and much prettier fabrics. The difference between the two races is always the same: the Frenchman has a natural taste for, and quickly finds the way to what is attractive and stylish: he feels a need for these qualities.

A Paris ironmonger told me that after the Treaty of Commerce a quantity of English tools, files, pincers, planes, etc. were imported into France: they were good tools, with strong handles and excellent blades, and all very cheap. However, there was hardly any sale for them: Parisian artisans looked at them, handled them, and ended by saying, *"Cela n'a pas d'oeil"* (it does not please the eye), and would not buy. A quality always has its reciprocal fault and *vice versa*. Refinement of the senses and imaginative requirements prevent a worker from being 'steady', persevering and persistent when the task is monotonous. Such a workman is unable to plod straight on like a good plough horse; he is apt to stop, go fast in bursts, become bored; he is tempted to try innovations, yield to his own fancies.

How do English working men live and what is their budget? On this subject I have some recently published statistical works, among others Mr Chadwick's; but I rely chiefly on information given me by my industrialist and engineering friends.

A good workman in an iron-foundry earns between 33/- and 36/- a week: the others from 15/- to 20/- a week. In the cotton mills a man will earn 16/- to 28/- a week; a woman, girl or little boy from 7/- to 12/-: so that a wife and children can also contribute to the family income. It is estimated that the average wage for an adult man in Lancashire is 20/- a week, that he can live on 10/-, that if he has a wife and four children his weekly expenses will be 30/-, and that as a rule income and expenditure just barely balance. A man can keep his head above water, but with difficulty. Only exceptionally able workmen can keep ahead of their expenditure. For the others, an accident, illness, or unemployment throws them into extreme poverty and misery. Five causes of misfortune hang over all alike:

1. As the climate is very bad they are forced to spend a great deal on coal, light, spirits, meat, laundry, and new clothes. Moreover the working man is spendthrift, and the English working man particularly so. At Oldham they have four meals a day, tea, coffee, a bottle and a half of ale, butter, cheese, and meat three times a day. In Manchester the iron construction fitters are famous for being the best customers for the finest and earliest vegetables.

2. As competition for jobs is exceedingly bitter every man is forced to work to the very limit of his strength; more effort is required here than elsewhere for a man to keep himself afloat; at the slightest weakening he sinks to the bottom, and that bottom is peculiarly horrible.

3. They have swarms of children, four, five, often six or more: one of my friends knows families where there are fifteen and eighteen. Add up the expenses of confinements, layettes, medical fees for mother and children. Up to the age of ten a child costs money and earns nothing. If four children survive in each family, then either the number of people employed in industry must

double every thirty years, with all that that implies, or half the population must emigrate.

4. In an industrial civilization unemployment is inevitable. For example, a market you have been counting on is captured from you by the superior industry of a rival industrial nation; or it is closed to you by famine, war or a change in fashion. Add to that strikes, and you are apt to have hundreds of thousands of workers out in the street without work or bread.*

5. They are inclined to drunkenness, and of all possible scourges, this is the worst. The climate encourages this tendency, because a man needs to warm himself up a bit, revive his body and spirits, and to forget for a while the sorrowful and harassed life he has to lead. I have just been reading the annual report of a clergyman attached to a charitable association and in this connection it is tragic.

The effect of all these causes is that few working men achieve any independence, acquire an income from savings or are able to set up in a small business. A person of my acquaintance who is in constant touch with them, and who has been living here for 26 years estimates the number of these fortunate ones at 5 % of the whole working-class population, that is one in twenty. The majority of the rest die in hospital or the workhouse, or are kept by their children. As a rule the industrial system tends to wear a population out: thus, for instance, the people of Manchester are more stunted than those of Oldham, which is a new town.

Since the majority of English working men is employed in industry and agricultural enterprises here are run like a factory, we must, if we want to compare the average of happiness in France to the average of happiness in England, compare the life of a French peasant with that of an English factory-hand. The French peasant, frugal and living according to a conservative routine, has a very narrow life: but almost always he either has or acquires a bit of land, that is to say some tangible capital resource, which gives him peace of mind and something which his imagination can enjoy working on. Besides which life as an agricultural small-holder is more natural and less constrained. On the other hand the English working man, especially in the towns, has more ideas in his head, more notions of all kinds, more intelligence in

* According to Mr Chadwick "in October 1862, of the 400,000 workers normally employed in Lancashire, more than 150,000 were workless, and more than 120,000 on part time, about three days a week. This gives an average of 210,000 persons unemployed."

social, political and religious matters, in short a wider horizon. He is accustomed to hear important topics and remote things and places discussed; he reads the newspapers, and his mind is open to curiosity. In Manchester recently a travelling biographer * delivered two lectures on Macaulay, charged an entrance fee of eighteen pence, and the hall was filled by working men. In London a free public lecture on the usefulness of geology had to be repeated.

Another cause of mental development: a workman engaged as part of a large organisation becomes well aware that he is dependent on others: it follows that he identifies his interests with those of his fellows and is drawn out of his solitude. A —— has been giving me an account of the twenty-five workmen who, each having saved £30, some years ago formed themselves into a company to manufacture machinery. For some months they had no orders. They met and took counsel together and made up their minds to persevere, each undertaking to cut his living expenses to three shillings and sixpence a week, that is to fast, and to make his family fast. A possible customer appeared, took an interest in their project, bought a machine from them and invited the public to come and see it. It was very good, their reputation was founded, they began to prosper; they expelled twelve of their number who were insufficiently able or industrious, giving them compensation, and reorganised themselves on a new basis. When they first started, each of them had taken his turn to direct the work of the rest; but now they have elected the most capable man among them as leader. Every year he distributes a few pounds per head as dividend, but most of the profit is used to increase the size of the business and improve it. It is now worth five or six thousand pounds. The director receives no fees for his services as such, and all the members work with their hands in the shops, or as overseers; not one of them has considered retiring, turning bourgeois and living idle. †

* *Un biographe ambulant:* it seems a curious trade. E. H.

† *British Almanach and Companion* 1863, p. 30.
In a report, recently published by the Rochdale Pioneers Equitable Co-operative Society, I find the names of 150 such Associations, comprising 48,184 members together possessing a capital of £333,290 and doing business, in 1861, to the astonishing extent of £1,512,117. Of these Associations 70 are in Lancashire.

The *Co-operator* for October 1862 contains a list of 300 Societies, nine out of ten founded during the past ten years, and comprising 77,000 members with a capital of £349,000. The author of this article. Mr John Plummer,

We went to Oldham where the work-people were celebrating a sort of anniversary festival commemorating the foundation of the association in which they are all united. They marched past, carrying banners: one of these, the brick-makers' standard, bore portraits of the union's founders; in the middle was a luminous eye surrounded by a slogan announcing that they asked for justice and nothing but justice. It was a tremendous stir, women and children marching beside the men and turning it into a procession. The women were neither haggard nor meagre: handsome, well-fleshed arms, bared, broad shoulders, deep chests and full breasts. The torso, as a rule, is not symmetrical, but the frame is powerful; even in the case of the thin ones the bone-structure is strong. They stood crowded round the door of the place where their husbands were eating their corporation dinner.

Here, as in all the other towns, the union's aim is to maintain and raise the level of wages. All these unions are in correspondence with each other and they have a central office in London. When one of them calls a strike its members are supported out of their own local union fund, and also by the central fund if estimates that there are 500 Co-operative Societies in the United Kingdom, with 100,000 members and capital amounting to £400,000.

The model specimen of a Co-operative Society is the Rochdale Equitable Pioneers. It was composed, in the first place (1844) of 28 workmen who having saved penny by penny, started with a capital of £28, and, by undertaking never to buy or sell on credit, by good sense, abnegation, concord and hard work, they succeeded. In 1861 they had 4,000 members, their capital amounted to £39,335, and their turnover £152,063. By that time they had opened shops, workshops, and stalls for the sale of all essentials — groceries, shoes, clothes, flour and meat — in order to have all these things at wholesale prices and do away with middle-men's profits. They owned a library of 5,000 volumes, which also subscribed for the principal newspapers and the best reviews, and which was particularly rich in works of geography, history, political economy, social and moral philosophy; it was provided with two large terrestrial globes, a microscope, a telescope, etc. They had formed a society for the care of the sick and the burial of the dead. They had donated a marble fountain to their city, subscribed to the asylum for the deaf and dumb, to the Rochdale dispensary and the Manchester Infirmary. Emboldened by their prosperity, several members of this Association founded another Co-operative Society for the purchase of cattle and corn, to provide their own meat and flour. In 1860 their turnover was £133,000 and trading showed a profit of £10,000. Another, third, offshoot Co-operative Society built, in 1854, two cotton factories, at a cost of £70,000; the Chief Mechanic is on the board of Directors. Finally, there was a fourth Co-operative Society, with a capital of £50,000 and whose object is to provide good cottages for such workmen as invest their savings in the Society.

From an article by Mr John Plummer, in *The British Almanach and Companion*, 1862, after a visit paid to Rochdale.

their motives be considered valid by the elected central committee. To build up this fund each member subscribes a shilling a week. They all undertake not to work for less than a certain wage. In return they get so much a day from the common fund in case of sickness or unemployment. There is a meeting every week and these meetings, like the statutes of the unions, are secret. The chairmen, presidents, treasurers and other officers or delegates are elected; these offices are unpaid and every member has to take his turn in one or the other.

Thus constituted these unions are very strong: their central fund amounts to several millions.* They have been able to maintain strikes lasting six months and even a year, sometimes with success. Any workman who secedes from the union, or refuses to join it, is looked upon as a traitor. He is put in quarantine,† as if he had the plague; nobody will speak to him, or answer him, and he is condemned to a moral solitude. An investigation carried out recently revealed that to these means of intimidation were added, occasionally, violence, pillage and even murder: a secret Committee, a kind of *Vehmgericht,* pronounced sentence and carried it out. Unions of this kind naturally end in dictatorship.

It is a remarkable fact that these unions do not deviate from their original object: they have no other aim but wage increases, and do not think in terms of seizing political power, which they most certainly would do in France. They are in no way political, are not even social; they envisage no Utopias, do not dream of reforming society, putting down usury, abolishing the hereditary principle, of equal pay for all or of making every individual a partner in the State. "None of that sort of thing here," I was assured by several manufacturers, "our workers don't generalise like yours, in the first place because they have some notion of political economy, but principally because they have too much commonsense to go chasing after chimaeras. What we have to be afraid of here is a strike, not a Socialist coup."

I have just been reading a very fine novel by a person who lives in these parts and is in a position to observe the people: *North and South* by Mrs Gaskell. It contains the character of a working man and the story of a strike. If the picture is a true one, (and I believe that it is), then there is, in the men of this class, a very large fund of reason and justice. They are in a permanent state of war against

* *francs,* presumably. E. H.

† i.e. "sent to Coventry". *Coventry* in this context is no doubt a corruption of quarantine. E. H.

the bosses, but on limited ground — that of supply and demand. Within this enclosed field both sides have the same weapon; the men can withhold their labour; the employers can refuse the men work. The weapon is equally harmful to both sides. Each side persists in this refusal to the extent of its strength and courage, the workers starving themselves and the employers ruining themselves: the strife, in short, is honourable and within the law.* While awaiting the outcome, respect for the law and no violence: public opinion acts as a neutral power which the workmen seek to win to their side by showing wisdom and patience. Such, in the matter of strikes, is Higden's advice. B —— tells me that many working men personally known to him follow this line of conduct. They admit that the quarrel between the workman and his employer is their own private business, and the community is not called upon to take a hand in it. The community has the right, they hold, not to be disturbed, and the employer, as well as the workman, has his rights, the right to lower his price, to defend his own interests however he can.

B —— engaged, at a very high price, a very clever English operative for his French factory, but on condition that the man's wage will be reduced by half if he allows his new workmates to know how much he is being paid.

"I understand, sir," this workman said, "business is business for the employers as well as for us."

B —— thinks that no French working man would show so much self-sufficiency or be able to consider the matter abstractly and in cold blood. Exiled to a remote township this English workman worked very well: his life was not very cheerful, he did not know one word of French and could not talk to a soul. But he had his little son with him and busied himself with this child. B —— sent him an English newspaper three times a week and spoke a few words to him whenever he inspected the factory. That was enough for the man; silent and worthy, he spent more than a year in that fashion.

Nevertheless the situation does have its effect and it cannot be

* Taine means to praise this kind of struggle in that there is no resort to violence on either side — in that sense it respects the law. Strikes were not literally lawful until 1871 and were often broken by using the army. E. H.

denied that the workmen look upon the masters as their natural enemy. The employers are making very great and praiseworthy efforts to diminish that hostility. They have founded and backed 'savings banks', 'penny banks' in which a workman can deposit even the smallest savings. They build and let them houses which, at the end of several years and by means of a cleverly contrived system of amortisation, become the property of the tenants. They set up 'ragged schools' and 'Mechanic's Institutes'. When the Queen paid a visit to Manchester, sixty thousand Sunday-school children marched past her and sang *God Save the Queen*.

The masters have to send every child between 12 and 15 years of age working in their shops to school for two hours a day. The principle behind all these institutions while it is philanthropic is not disinterested: it is the desire to reduce the workers' *improvidence*. This, I am told, is the worst vice of the English working man. The brute in man is very strong in this country: the reasonable and reasoning intelligence has difficulty in emerging. The spark of mind is choked by the dark, heavy vapours of instinct, and does not flash forth, spontaneous, lively, a thing of air and light, as among the Southern peoples. It needs help, it needs feeding to coax it into a flame strong enough to overcome the gross matter which overlays it. When this is accomplished the flame is very powerful; but nowhere is the task of civilizing the people so urgent and so necessary as it is here.

We visited several of these public education and recreation establishments. The first was Peel's Park, a sort of large, English garden in the centre of the city where the poor can sit at ease among trees and flowers. It was founded by a privately subscribed £35,000 gift and includes a museum and a library. The museum has two galleries of very good pictures and drawings on loan for six months from their owners, a natural history room containing birds, snakes, butterflies, etc., a room of antique or foreign woven fabrics, a room of industrial raw materials, specimens such as cotton, hemp, madder etc. — in short a collection of objects to instruct the mind or please the eye. Our guide, a rich business man, told us:

"All this appeals to the senses in an interesting way. It keeps our working men occupied and gives them something to think about. They must have something to amuse them; and besides, every hour spent here is an hour less in the public houses."

He drew our attention to the fact that there are no keepers in the rooms; their only guardian is the common sense and honesty of the public, and nothing is ever stolen, damaged, or even touched although there are, on an average, 2500 visitors a day.

From there we went to a free library, also set up by private subscription, and which is chiefly used by working men. It has 25,000 volumes: the librarian told us that the library is used by 10,000 readers a month; there are also newspapers there. Anyone who can produce two respectable references may take books away: between twelve and fourteen hundred people are regular borrowers. By reference to the records I was able to see that *Lives* of Nelson and Wellington, and works of theology, are the favourite reading. According to the librarian a number of his borrowers are educated men, and form collections: he told us of one working man who knows the names and characteristic appearance of nine hundred of the *coleoptera*. They are very fond of natural history and the natural sciences in general. They have a taste for facts and experimental proof which often leads them very far from the Bible to the very limits of positivism: the *Secularists* find many recruits in their ranks. They also read the political economy Reviews, and newspapers: now, English newspapers, even those of the smaller towns, are very educational, full of exact and circumstantial information, news and dispatches. It seems to me that here a working man who does not drink and spends an hour a day reading should have a well furnished and healthy mind.

We then went on to another institution, a 'Mechanics' Institute', again founded and maintained by private subscription. Six hundred pupils, boys and girls, all over ten years old. There are two kinds of teaching: for those who can afford a small fee there are classes in French, German, drawing, music, and mathematics, usually attended by the children of small shop-keepers. The other classes are free and include reading, writing, linear drawing and arithmetic: many of the children attending these, sent on by factory owners, are in rags. Draftsmanship and elementary mathematics are regarded as the most important subjects. In the highest class, which is for thirteen- to sixteen-year-olds, they are taught the Sixth Book of Euclid: for they must be able to understand their machines. As usher, the master chooses one of the boys from the class. There is a pleasant library containing a thousand volumes, and a room provided with newspapers and reviews where the pupils go to read. There are now one or several of these special schools for factory workers in every industrial town and the results obtained are giving great satisfaction. The maxim inspiring their establishment is this: that unless you educate the people they become ungovernable. Religion helps in this work; for a Protestant needs to be able to read the Bible. A great number of schools are annexed to churches, notably to Nonconformist chapels (churches of 'dissenters'): it is a general rule that a church gives rise to a school.

I have the greatest admiration for the spirit of all these institutions, and for the generous and sensible initiative of those private citizens who voluntarily and at their own expense set about improving the commonwealth, forwarding the State's business without having recourse to the State. Rich people give money for useful purposes on an enormous scale here. To take action of one's own volition, drawing on one's own purse or otherwise, to set change in motion rather than wait for it to happen is natural to them. Many of the servitudes to the State which we accept would seem intolerable to them; whatever smacks of the barracks, of regimentation, is repugnant to them. For example, at their railway stations there are no closed waiting-rooms where the travellers are folded like sheep: they wait for their train on the platform. There are no luggage tickets: every traveller puts his trunk in wherever he likes, and recovers it in due course as best he can. Yesterday the omnibus I was riding in went off its normal route and by way of a different street at the request of two ladies who asked permission of the other passengers. Furthermore, as it was raining, the driver allowed three standing passengers beyond his proper complement.

Last Sunday I heard a lay preacher in one of the squares, a poor devil of a fanatic, a sort of Bunyan with a long beard, a battered old hat and threadbare frock-coat. He stood on a milestone with the New Testament in his hand, and began to deliver a lecture. "You notice that the Apostles did not dare to bury Our Lord: it was one Nicodemus, a rich man, a gentleman, who did that. It had to be so in order to fulfil the prophecy which we find in St John." Then he read the prophecy. "Thus, you see, you must never trust tradition, but believe only in the Scriptures." He concluded with a prayer, his eyes raised heavenwards, his tone contrite. About thirty people stood and listened to him: a number of street urchins played tricks on him and threw his hat on the ground, but five or six stiff-looking people, with very worn faces, listened soberly and attentively. One bystander told me that it was wrong to make fun of the man, that he was neither offending nor insulting anybody and that he had every right to speak according to his conscience. What I found most striking was his earnestness

236

and his courage: he was indifferent to ridicule, and, having something to say, came forward and said it without worrying about anything else. 'Self-help' again, that is the key word which is so little understood in France. From the same personal impulse come forth all those associations, unions and institutions which are so numerous here, and among others their municipal institutions.

Manchester is a self-governing city, chooses and pays its own police, and rules itself with hardly any interference from the Government. It follows that the social edifice is supported by thousands of independent columns, and not on one only, like ours: hence sudden collapses, like our revolutions of 1830, 1848 and 1852, are impossible.

Our friend, the rich business man, took us to see a big workhouse outside the city. There is another, within the city, containing 1200 infirm persons; the one we visited can take 1900 but at the moment only has 350. It cost £70,000. The two together cost £55,000 a year to run, which comes out of the Poor rate. The 'Manager' gets £200 a year, the doctor £170; £20 a year and all found for the attendants. The master-cobbler who teaches the inmates his trade receives £1 a week. The governors give their services gratis.

The building is huge, perfectly clean, and well maintained: big courtyards, gardens round the building, a view of fields and tall trees, chapel, public rooms twenty feet high. It looks as if the founders and administrators of the place have taken pride in doing a handsome and useful job.

There was no bad smell anywhere about the place. The beds were almost white and provided with patterned bed-spreads. The oldest and most infirm women had white bonnets and new clothes. Everything has clearly been foreseen and planned with a view to maintaining a fresh atmosphere. There is a special room for lunatics, and another for female idiots: the latter do some hours needlework every day and during recreation periods they dance together to the music of a violin. They pull very strange faces, but they seem healthy and do not look unhappy. In another room children were at their lessons, one of the older ones acting as monitor.

The kitchen is enormous: a structure of masonry contains eight or ten boilers in which oatmeal gruel is cooked: this is the principal article of their diet. Each inmate receives two pounds of 'oat-meal' a day, a pound and a half of potatoes, half a pound of bread and, four times a week, four ounces of minced-meat or boned meat. The only drink is water, excepting in case of sickness.

We were considerably surprised: beside the rows of hovels in which the poor live, this place is a palace. One of us gravely requested our friend and escort to keep a place for him in the institution where he could spend his old age. Consider this: a labourer at Manchester or Liverpool can barely afford to eat meat once a week, yet has to work ten hours a day! Here, a person in good health works six hours a day, has newspapers and the Bible to read, as well as a few other good books and Reviews; and he can live in pure air and see trees. Yet at the time of writing there is not one able-bodied person to be found in a workhouse: the one we saw is almost empty and will only be filled when winter comes. As a rule, when a workman out of a job applies to the municipality for help he is told, "Give us proof that you are willing to work: go to the workhouse." Nine times out of ten the men refuse. What is the reason for this repugnance? I saw, today, an old woman sorting through a heap of rubbish, and picking out remnants of vegetables with her thin hands: she may have been one of those who are unwilling to give up their drop of gin. But what of the others? I am told that they will stick to their 'home' and their liberty at any price and cannot bear to be shut up and become subject to discipline. 'They prefer to be free and to starve'.

But then, the children? All those little ones, with their white skulls showing through the tow-coloured hair, crammed into a single room with their thin and haggard mothers — how can the fathers bear such a sight? They do bear it, they do not want to be parted from them, to make over their rights as head of the family, and be kept away from them in a different compartment: it seems to them that in such conditions they would cease to be men. The workhouse is looked upon as a prison and the poor make it a point of honour never to enter one.

Perhaps, too, we are bound to admit that workhouse administration is clumsily despotic and harassing; this is the fault of all bureaucracy, it treats men as cogs in a machine, and as if they had no feelings, causing them, unwittingly, to rebel. This particular horror of the workhouse has been described by Dickens,* who takes the side of the paupers.

An evening at Belle Vue to get an idea of popular entertain-
* *Our Mutual Friend.*

ment. The place is a sort of dance casino surrounded by a garden, with stage shows, curiosities, and works of trumpery art. On a dais decorated with a portrait of Wellington they acted a representation of the siege of Badajoz, with a parade of patriotism which was received with loud cheers. A little later, there was a firework display. But among the flower-beds parties of working people and small shopkeepers or others of that class sat eating, drinking and playing a game which involved kissing. Inside the building, in an enormous room, working men and their girls were dancing, taking big jumps, rather violent but not indecent; it stretches their muscles after their weeks of standing still. Many of them looked rough and surly; none sly or insolently jaunty. What, as usual, comes out in them is the athlete, akin to the bull-dog, instead of the witty rascal, akin to the spaniel and the monkey.

It costs a shilling to go in; sixpence extra for the dance hall. As Belle Vue is quite far out, at the extremity of a suburb, one must add to that the cost of getting here: there was a great number of omnibuses and cabs standing at the door. Add to that, again, the price of refreshments, and remember that as a rule the workmen who come here bring their 'sweethearts', or a prostitute, and must therefore pay for two. Now, a cotton-spinner in a factory earns 23/- a week. Here, then, is a good example of English spendthrift ways. B —— says that many working men here who earn the equivalent of six francs a day spend four on food and drink. There are men in the iron-foundries, a sort of sub-contractors *, who, in a good year, can make £150, £200, even £300. They spend it all and put nothing by. B —— claims that, apart from accidents or sickness, an English factory-hand who is hard-working and thrifty is sure to prosper, or at least to earn a fair living. But they are not thrifty. †

One of our friends having introduced us to two policemen, we spent from ten o'clock until midnight visiting the bad quarters

* *entrepreneurs subordonnés.* I do not know what this refers to. E. H.

† *British Almanach and Companion:* résumé of the census of 1861 on trades, employments and professions. Population of England and Wales, 20,066,224. The class of people employed in industry numbers 4,828,399 individuals, 3,262,510 males and 1,565,889 females. People employed in textile factories number 2,231,417; 890,423 males and 1,340,994 females. Employed in the mines 330,446, of whom only 94 females. Dr David Chadwick of Manchester, estimated that "in Lancashire, the number of persons directly employed in the cotton industry in 1859 was 400,000" and that the livelihood of 800,000 people in Lancashire is bound up with this industry alone.

of the city. There are six hundred policemen in Manchester, their average wage being about a pound a week. Our two were 'detectives'. One of them has been twenty-six years in Manchester; the other has worked in several big towns. Both were serious-minded, sensible, judicious men: they did not make a parade of expertness, spoke little and answered to the point. Their still faces and thoughtful expression inspired confidence and showed their worth. They confirmed what we had been told about the repugnance of the poor for the workhouse: according to them this institution is quite worthless and merely encourages laziness. A family with three children can, they said, live on 30/- a week, and earns that much. But most of the men marry young, often at eighteen years of age: by thirty they have six children; they drink a lot, hardly save anything; the wife becomes a bad housekeeper while becoming a good factory-hand. As a rule when a working man dies he does not leave enough to pay for his own funeral.

We saw one-night lodgings where, in a low, airless room, there were four or five beds, all occupied: a whole bed cost fivepence, half a bed twopence-ha'penny. One of the beds was occupied by a man and wife: the man's face was a painful sight, haggard, with livid patches, the rest yellow, and all lined by sickness, it looked like an old wax mask.

We visited a casino where five hundred people of wretched appearance were crowded on to greasy benches watching a stage where two frail young girls in pink gauze were dancing. The entrance fee was twopence. The audience was drinking gin and smoking, and the air, thick with the emanations of human bodies, was stifling.

Next, to a brothel. One of the policemen told us that the girls are recruited chiefly among the mill-girls. They sat in a low room downstairs and were not at all *décolletées*. Several of them were very thin and their ignoble faces had become, as it were, like those of savages. Next to a greasy mulatto woman I noticed a young girl with a pretty, delicate, intelligent face, thoughtfully bent towards the red glow of the fire. The month is July but this fire is necessary of an evening. It was the same in thieves' public houses; * we saw twenty or thirty of these dens, and there was always a heaped-up fire of red-hot coal to do the cooking and dry the washing. The men sit about playing dominoes and smoking; when we came in they said nothing but all raised bright, motion-

* *cabarets de voleurs.*

240

less eyes, the eyes of a beast of prey, and stared at us. The crude gas-light is horrible, playing upon such faces.

I have visited similar quarters of the town, similar low dens, in Paris, Bordeaux and Marseilles, but nowhere has the impression made on me been so strong. I felt I was in a nightmare, or in a story by 'Edgar Poe'. The gas-light cannot overcome the shadows in that heavy, stifling air full of unfamiliar exhalations. Nothing could be more frightening than that black darkness shot through with vacillating fingers of brightness. The symmetrical streets seem like the corpses of streets laid out side by side and for ever still. Here and there one sees wretched women trailing their faded finery, wearing their professional smile: and as they pass you are tempted to draw away, as from a haunting spectre, a soul in agony.

Every ten minutes we went into yet another foul den: coming in from the empty darkness outside, the low room, the red-hot stove, the crude brilliance of gas-light, and the vile gathering of haggard, anxious, dangerous faces, put me in mind of a vent which must surely open into Hell.

Certainly the vile and horrible are worse in this country than elsewhere.

# CHAPTER EIGHT

# THE ENGLISH MIND

I BELIEVE that I am beginning to form some idea of the nature of an English mind, so different from the French one. When I find that an idea of this kind has taken form in my mind, I carry it at once to two or three English friends, men who have travelled, and submit it to their judgment. We discuss it together, and from that discussion it emerges corrected or developed; and the next day I write it down for what it is worth.

The inside of an Englishman's head can be very fairly compared to a Murray's Guide: a great many facts, but few ideas; a great deal of exact and useful information, statistics, figures, reliable and detailed maps, short and dry historical notes, useful and moral tips by way of preface, no all-inclusive vision, and no relish of good writing. It is a collection of good, reliable documents, a convenient body of memoranda to get a man through his journey without help.

A Frenchman requires an agreeable shapeliness in every piece of writing and every article about him. The Englishman can be satisfied with utility. A Frenchman enjoys ideas as such and for their own sake; an Englishman regards them as instruments of foresight or mnemonics.

Here are two small matters of fact by way of evidence: Stevenson, the famous engineer was asked how he had invented his machines, among others the locomotive. He replied that it was done by imagining and picturing in his mind, with great precision, the diverse parts, their shapes, their dimensions, their joints and possible movements, and the whole series of changes which a change in one part, dimension or joint must introduce in the interplay of the whole movement. Thus his mind resembled a workshop: the parts were there, numbered and labelled; he took them down as he needed them, mentally fitted them and engaged them together and, by trial and error, arrived at a working combination. Whereas Léon Foucault, on the other hand, once told me that having stumbled upon a forgotten proposition in speculative mechanics propounded by Huyghens and Lagrange, he had

### Fig. 23 French Caricaturists and the English

THE FRENCH CARICATURISTS, WITH THEIR USUAL ACCURATE
KNOWLEDGE OF BRITISH MANNERS AND CUSTOMS, ARE FOND
OF REPRESENTING OUR SOLDIERS AS CONTINUALLY PLAYING
AT BILLIARDS — WELL! PERHAPS IT WILL BE FOUND THAT
THEY *DO* PLAY THEIR *CANNONS* REMARKABLE WELL!

° ° *British Officers of Distinction.* \* \* *Daughters of Albion! (The wonder-
ful fidelity of this representation will be immediately ackowledged).* o o
*Young Guardsmen! (Painful, perhaps, but too true!) The BOULE DOGUE.
(Asleep, of course.) (Punch, June 16, 1860)*

followed up its consequences which had, in due course, led him
to the idea of his governor.\* As a general rule a Frenchman gets
his results by means of classifications and by deductive reasoning;
an Englishman by inductive reasoning, by means of close attention
and memory; that is by a clear and persistent picturing to himself
of a quantity of individual facts, the accumulation of a number
of isolated "documents", which are then brought into juxtaposition.

In this connection, Carlyle's *Life of Sterling* contains a letter
which has always struck me as interesting. Sterling was in the

---

\* Léon Focault, 1819-68, French physicist. He invented, among other
things, electric lighting. Royal Society's Copley medal for researches into
comparative velocity of light in different media. Proved the rotation of the
earth with his pendulum demonstration. The "governor" in question was the
gyroscope, which he also invented. He introduced physics into astronomy
and his name survives in the electrical term *Foucault Currents.* E. H.

Antilles: a cyclone had just devastated the island, and he, and his wife who was pregnant, had nearly perished. The letter is an account of this event written to his mother. Note that the writer is a lettered man, a poet who had received a very complete education and was a master of his language. But, in these circumstances, as in any others, an Englishman's first need is to convey an exact, positive, *graphic* idea. His description is a pure 'statement of facts':

"My dear mother,

"... nearly all the property both of Susan and myself was suddenly destroyed by a visitation of Providence far more terrible than any I have ever witnessed.

"When Susan came from her room to breakfast at eight o'clock, I pointed out to her the extraordinary height and violence of the surf, and the singular appearance of the clouds of heavy rain sweeping down the valleys before us...

"A few minutes after the closing of the windows I found that the shutters of Tyrrell's room, at the south and commonly most sheltered end of the house, were giving way. I tried to tie them; but the silk handkerchief I used soon gave way; and as I had neither hammer, boards nor nails in the house, I could do nothing more to keep out the tempest. I found, in pushing at the leaf of the shutter that the wind resisted more as if it had been a stone wall or mass of iron, than a mere current of air... The rain on my face and hands felt like so much small shot from a gun. There was great exertion necessary to shut the door of the house.

"...; and then the window panes were smashed by the mere force of the gale without anything having touched them... I went into our bedroom where I found Susan, Tyrrell, and a little coloured girl of seven or eight years old and told them we should probably not be alive in half an hour...

"The house was under two parallel roofs; and the one next to the sea, which sheltered the other, and us who were under the other, went off, I suppose at about ten o'clock. After my old plan, I will give you a sketch, from which you may perceive how we were situated."

And he does so, drawing not one plan, but two, geometrically, with letters and indices.

"The a, a are the windows which were first destroyed: b went next; my books were between the windows b and on the wall opposite to them. The lines C and D mark the directions of the two roofs; e is the room in which we were and 2 is a plan of it upon a larger scale. Look now at 2.   a is the bed, c, c the two wardrobes, b the corner in which we were. I was sitting in an armchair holding my Wife; and Tyrrell and the little black girl were close to us. We had given up all notion of surviving and only waited for the fall of the roof to perish together.

"Before long the roof went. Most of the materials, however, were carried clear away; one of the large couples was caught on the bedpost marked d, and held fast by the iron spike, while the end of it hung over our heads: had the beam fallen an inch on either side of the bedpost it must necessarily have crushed us. The walls did not go with the roof; and we remained for half an hour, alternately praying to God, and watching them as they bent, creaked and shivered before the storm . . .

"The old cook made five attempts, after saving Tyrrell, to get to us; and four times he was blown down. The fifth time he and the Negro we first saw reached the house. The space they had to traverse was not above twenty yards of level ground, if so much . . ."

The same style continues to the end, exact, simple and, in appearance, cold. It is the method of Defoe and of Swift: there is no style less literary or more informative.*

The same impression persists if one compares the newspapers, reviews and speeches of the two nations. The correspondent of an English newspaper is a sort of photographer who sends his paper "films" taken on the spot: these are printed as such. Sometimes, indeed, there is a divergence between the arguments propounded on page one, and the dispatches printed on page two: and in any case the latter are singularly long and detailed. A Frenchman would want to shorten and lighten them; they leave on him an impression of fatigue; it is all too massive and piled up for his taste, a solid block badly dressed, awkward to handle; so that a French journalist is expected to help the reader, to sort out the essential for him, to pick out from the cumbrous mass the two or three anecdotes which are really informative, and to sum up the whole in one clear idea expressed in a single vivid phrase.

The difference is no less great and apparent if one compares their principal quarterlies with our reviews. In ours an article, even on science or political economy, must have an exordium and a peroration, in short, must have a proper architecture. There are

---

* In saying there is no style less "literary", Taine puts a special construction on the word, just as, for some critics, "style" means "elaboration". In fact, of course, this simplicity calls for the highest measure of literary skill in prose writing. E. H.

not many contributions to the *Revue des Deux Mondes* which are not preceded by a peristyle of general ideas. Whereas in England facts, figures and technical details predominate. Excepting when they come from the pen of a Macaulay, these articles seem to us heavy and boring; they are, as it were, admirable quarries full of massive stones not yet dressed and which, to be generally service-able, require more shaping. Similarly in the case of oratory; English eloquence is impeded by a surplus of unassimilated documentation; French eloquence evaporates in theories.

All his education urges an Englishman in the same sense. In the principal London college * B —— had a friend, a most distin-guished young man, second in mathematics, first in literature, and deeply versed in the Latin authors, notably Catullus. In his view Catullus was the most exquisite of poets; the young man knew every line of him by heart, was acquainted with all the inter-pretations put on them, had studied all the commentaries, and could almost have published his own edition of the poet. But if he had been asked to give an inclusive generalisation on the sub-ject, say six pages summing up the meaning of the poet's work, he would not have been able to do it, which he candidly admitted.

At Oxford and Cambridge studious undergraduates read all the Latin authors, even the low Latin ones — Statius, Claudian, Manilius, Macrobius, Aulus-Gellius; and they know Greek very thoroughly, having written Greek verse even at school. But they have no general ideas about the subject: they know the letter of antiquity but are ignorant of its spirit, and have no feeling for the civilization of antiquity as a whole, of the cast of mind and spirit proper to Mediterranean, polytheistic man, the feelings of an athlete-dialectician-artist. Consider, for example, Mr Gladstone's strange commentaries on Homer. Mr Grote, in his great *History of Greece* shows himself able to deal only with constitutional and political history. Only twenty years ago the universities were simply conservatories for the cultivation of Greek, Latin and Mathematics, sealed against the outside world, smelling strongly of the lamp, and very little apt to encourage the subsequent full flowering of those minds they cultivated when the latter were transplated into the open. They taught no natural sciences, no philosophy of history, and no English composition. For some years Continental discoveries and methods have been making their way into the English universities, but even today the teaching is de-signed to strengthen the mind rather than to open it, and young

*Public school. E. H.

men emerge from this training as from a course of mental gymnastics, but without any idea of mankind and the world. As to that there is one waiting for him, ready made, perfectly acceptable and which the young man has no difficulty in adopting.

Whereas in France there is no fixed framework into which the young man's mind can fit itself: the constitution, changed half a score of times, has no authority; religion is a product of the Middle Ages; old forms are discredited, new ones barely sketched in. From the age of sixteen the student becomes a prey to doubts: he drifts; and if he is intelligent his most imperative need is to contrive for himself some system of convictions, or at least of opinions. But in England the framework is there ready: religion is almost rational, and the Constitution almost excellent: the awakening mind finds the main lines of its future beliefs already laid down. It feels no need to start building itself a moral and intellectual dwelling from the ground up; at the most it may envisage the enlargement of a Gothic window, the clearing out of a cellar, or the repairing of a staircase. Less shaken, less unstrung and less stimulated, the young man's mind is active, for it is not spurred on by scepticism.

To this education undergone by the adolescent and the young man, add that by which the grown man and the same man in his maturity is influenced. In the first place, the whole of written or spoken literature is designed to supply him with facts rather than theories. I have referred above to the characteristics of their newspapers, reviews and speeches. They belong, likewise, to their books: not only to the more serious works, but to their novels, those novels which are so detailed, so scrupulously thorough, copied so closely from the life, and which are, to literature what Dutch pictures are to painting.*

We must, above all, bear in mind that domestic and foreign travelling which is the complement of their education, the occupation of their holidays, a habit, a pleasure, and almost a mania; and in addition the very widespread reading of travel books. Mr Murray paid £9000 for the copyright of Mr Livingstone's book: judge, by this price, what must have been the demand for the book and from that the extent of public curiosity. Finally we must take account of their application to business, as that is understood

* To understand this spirit read, for example, a few detailed and complete biographies, e.g. *Shakespeare and his times* by Nathan Drake; Boswell's *Life of Johnson;* Carlyle's *Cromwell's Speeches & Letters;* Southey's *Life of Wesley;* Lockhart's *Life of Sir Walter Scott.*

here, the information they are accustomed to extract from the minutes of their association meetings, the figures, documents, statistics and comparative tables they are all expected to study and understand so that they may act effectively and successfully in the circle, great or small, of their public or private interests. By way of all these channels, kept open from childhood until the end of their lives, positive information flows into the English brain as into a reservoir. Yet the availability of all these sources does not wholly explain the fullness of that reservoir: there is something more, a slope, as it were, which determines the flow of waters, the innate bent of the race, to wit their taste for facts and their fondness for experimental demonstration, the instinct for inductive reasoning and their need for certainty. Whoever has studied their literature and philosophy, from Shakespeare and Bacon down to the present day knows that this inclination is hereditary in the English, that it belongs to the very shape of their minds, that it is part of their very way of understanding truth. By the English way of looking at things, a tree must be known by its fruits, and theory judged by practice. A truth has no value unless it leads to useful applications in practice. Beyond such practically applicable truths lie nothing but vain chimaeras. Man's estate is conceived as being such that he is enclosed within a narrow circle, capable of enlargement but for ever closed by barriers, and within which knowledge is necessary, not for its own sake but as a basis for action. Learning, science, are conceived of as valid only in so far as they can be checked by experiment and justified in use.

That having been admitted, it seems to me possible to have a fair idea of the furnishings to be found in an ordinary English mind. As far as I can judge, the provision of facts carried in the head is three or four times as considerable in the case of a well-educated Englishman as in that of the equivalent Frenchman. This is so, at least in all that concerns languages, geography, political and economic questions, and personal impressions picked up abroad in contact with living men and concrete things.

On the other hand, it frequently happens that the Englishman gets less advantage out of the heavy luggage he carries, than the Frenchman out of his one small case. This fact is obvious in many books and Review articles: the average English writer, although very well informed, has limited vision. Nothing is more rare than to find, among these people, a free and wide-ranging play of intelligence in a soaring, far-seeing mind. Their prudence confines them to the beaten track, keeps their feet on the earth, keeps them harnessed to their loaded cart: excepting two or three, there are hardly any English writers who make their readers think. More than once, in England, having got to know a man I have been as astonished by the diversity and soundness of his knowledge as I have, at the same time, been surprised by his want of general ideas. Five or six come to mind as I write, all so well found in information that they had all the means to raise their minds to the point where a comprehensive view can be taken. But they have stopped half-way, have come to no conclusion. They did not even feel the need to arrange and order their knowledge into any kind of system; their ideas were all incomplete, isolated from each other, and they showed no desire to link them together in some coherent philosophical concept.

In this connection let their language bear witness: it is extremely difficult to translate abstractions which are at all elevated, into English. Compared with French, but especially with German, it is like Latin compared with Greek. For French people nothing could be more natural than this formula: *le beau, le bien et le vrai*. But if one renders it, literally, in English, it at once assumes a bizarre and crabbed aspect: *the beautiful, the good and the true*. But if it be rendered in the more usual style — *Beauty, truth, goodness*, it is no longer an exact translation.* In their library of words there is a whole shelf empty: the highest. And the reason is that they have no ideas to fill it with.

Whence they derive some advantages and suffer some disadvantages. Comprehensive ideas are outlines within which are more or less numerous sub-divisions, and once formed by the mind can be applied so that a broad view of a whole subject and of its parts can be taken. This mental operation is greatly facilitated if the mind is provided with such an instrument; and if it wishes to pass from theory to practice, it can 'organise' the material without difficulty. This word *(to organise)*, which dates from the Revolution and the [first] Empire, sums up the faculties of the French mind very well, expressing the success of the rational mind in ordering and distributing its material, the vast and happy effects

* This argument does not seem to me very profound: it is true that the "cast" of a language does depend on the cast of mind of its speakers and certain concepts are very difficult to translate with any degree of truth. It is also true that the concept 'the good, the true and the beautiful' is faintly absurd. That it is not absurd to a Frenchman, or was not once, might be due to the uncritical "literaryness" of the French mind, which Taine sees as a transcendental virtue. Is it? E. H.

of the art which consists in simplification, classification and deduction. It was cultivated by arm-chair thinkers during the 18th century: it was put into practice by their intellectual heirs in the *Assemblées* and the *Conseil d'Etat*. Its monuments are the Civil Code, the University, our military, ecclesiastic and judicial institutions, our great administrative bodies, all the principal component parts of our social mechanism. A nation which is wanting in this kind of mind will also be wanting in the kind of works it can create. Thus England, instead of a legal Code, has a mass of precedents, and instead of an *Ecole de Droit,* law students must undergo a routine of legal pettyfoggery. I often hear Englishmen complain of many similar gaps in their social system. Their legislation is so obscure that when a man wants to buy an estate in England he begins by engaging one or two lawyers who will not have overmuch time if they are given a month to investigate the vendor's title and make sure that the acquisition of the property is not likely to involve the purchaser in some legal chicanery. C —— tells me that the condition of several of their great administration offices, and notably the Admiralty, is ridiculous: disorders, sinecures, expenses out of proportion to the results obtained, delays and conflicts; the whole mechanism is incoherent because it is not constructed according to a principle. In all that they do here they can make progress only by trial and error and groping their way: they learn their business, whatever it may be, by persistent attention to it, by work and by sheer technical grind: they are purely empirical, *à la chinoise*.

But, on the other hand, when the acquisition of ready-made general systems of ideas is easy, and made early in life, the mind runs the risk of becoming lazy: such is the Frenchman's case. Often by the time he leaves school, almost invariably by the time he is five-and-twenty, he takes possession of these frameworks, these systems of thought and, as they are convenient, applies them to every subject; and thenceforth he ceases to learn anything, believing himself sufficiently well-furnished intellectually. He confines himself to reasoning about things, and frequently reasons in a vacuum. He is not up-to-date with his observation, and he is not in possession of the special information which would be conclusive. But as he is not aware that anything is wanting, he does not seek it, but goes on repeating ideas proper to last year's newspaper leader. He forgets that a man must keep his information up-to-date, must constantly be taking on more mental luggage if he is not to be caught short, unprepared for eventualities.

Not only are indifferent minds tainted with this failing in France, but the very finest intelligences are not exempt from it; indeed, I know only two men who have passed their fortieth year yet still have enquiring minds and have not failed to go on renewing themselves. Whereas, according to C——, the education of an English mind goes on almost indefinitely: even in his maturity an Englishman continues to travel, keeps himself informed; he tries, especially in all that relates to economics and politics, to keep up with external change, in the cultivation of his mind. New facts he likes for their own sake; he takes pleasure in noting them and is careful to remember them. Accumulated in this way these facts form a continuously replenished store at the back of his mind, a sort of solid layer of common sense. For although they are not knit into a system, and are not even apparent, they are there and their weight will count in any decision a man has to make. Thus provided, a man may be narrow-minded and devoid of ideas, yet still he will, by a kind of instinct, steer clear of any serious mistake or imprudence: he will be vaguely aware that the sensible and useful decision lies in this direction, and not in that. The disconnected information he will have picked up about the United States, India, China, on the effects of universal suffrage or free-trade, will incline his mind, in advance, towards the wiser party in controversy, and free public discussion will complete the work of pushing him in the most reasonable direction.

And being thus disposed, he can accept an expedition like that of Abyssinia,* but would never have tolerated our Mexican expedition. † He may wish to see the suffrage widened by degrees, but he will be reluctant to grant it suddenly to the whole adult population. In this way he is on his guard against political theories and adventures, the constitution of his country does not fall into the hands of the theorists, nor its business into those of hot-heads. Such are the effects of the public's good sense, comparable to so many streams irrigating the fields through which they flow. We have seen the common source of all of them: it is a deep pool, obscure, constantly full, constantly swollen by new tributaries — I mean tributary streams of new, positive facts which, accumu-

* The campaign of Sir Robert Napier terminating in the capture of Magdala, 1868.

† Napoleon III's disastrous attempt to maintain his puppet emperor, Maximilian von Habsburg, on the Mexican throne, where he had placed him in 1864. E. H.

lated, stored, filtered drop by drop, form an inexhaustible reservoir and overflow in a hundred salutary little trickles over the whole domain of action.

When we praise this taste for facts in the English we should remember that it is a question of moral as well as physical facts: they are zealous observers of the inner as well as the outwardly manifest life. In this connection I very recently had in my hands two long letters written to a friend by two young women both of whom had been one month married. It is a pity that discretion must prevent me from printing them here, for they might almost have been especially written to demonstrate the innate habit of, and hereditary talent for exact observation, applied in one case to physical, in the other to moral things.

The first letter gives a minutely detailed description of the writer's husband, his figure, the colour of his hair, his complexion; then his 'country seat', the rooms, their relative positions, the furniture, the park; then, drives in the neighbourhood, with full details of the fortunes and marriages of all the neighbours. The other letter describes, in detail no less exact, all the feelings which the writer had experienced from the day when she first saw her future husband at an 'archery meeting'. Both letters ended more or less identically to the effect that now the writer was the happiest woman in the world. One letter is vulgar, the other refined; one writer has eyes only for appearances; the other can look into her heart. But in both the delicate self-examination, and the ponderous descriptive catalogue, lucidity of mind and freedom from mere verbiage are equal. Nothing but facts: no general reflections; both the psychological account and the list of positive statistics are strictly documentary. It was self-evident, as I read these letters, that their writers' only wish was to inform their correspondent, the one concerning her social position, the other concerning the history of her feelings, and that any addition or generalised deductions would have seemed to them mere idle chatter.

In default of these letters, let the reader turn to contemporary English novels: the same spirit is there apparent. They are parcels crammed tight with small physical and moral facts, the latter in very great abundance and those, for the most part, precious jewels of observation. Never has any other literature succeeded as theirs does in revealing and following those feelings, that subterranean working, by which a character is formed; or the slow burgeoning and opening of a passion, a vice or a virtue; or the imperceptible gradations by which, year after year, a mind and heart, a soul, assume a certain form. The modern English novelists are alone in having understood the child, and the way in which a child becomes a man. In this connection the novels of Eliot should be read. Since Locke, psychology has been native here; and it makes its way side by side with statistics and political economy.

Exact knowledge of all those appearances by which man manifests himself; and exact divination of the inner workings of the mind and heart; — it is by these two means that the reliable foresight and sure touch required to manage all things pertaining to humanity are to be attained.

And in this richly fertile soil grow many original talents, but all of them very different in aspect to those we have in France; some have a taller, stouter growth; others are stunted and distorted. Let us first consider that talent most readily attributed to Frenchmen: 'wit'.

Wit is the art of saying things amusingly; my English friends consider it an attribute of the French temperament. Sir Henry Bulwer * asked two little French village boys, seven and eight years old respectively, what they were going to be when they grew up. Said one, "I shall be the village doctor." "Oh," said the other, "if my brother's going to be a doctor, I'll be the *curé*. He'll kill people, and I'll bury them, and in that way we'll share the whole village between us."

One day at Besançon I was listening to two soldiers talking as they lay sprawled on a bank; one of them got up, saying, "Come on, time's up; to work!" "Bah!" said the other, "stay where you are; we'll get our ha'penny just the same."

A German General recounts in his memoirs that one day, after a brush with the enemy, a captured French *hussard* was brought to him with his face deeply gashed. "Well, my poor fellow," the General said, "so you've got a sabre wound it appears?" "It's nothing. The fact is the barber shaved me a bit too close."

Even in antiquity it was noticed by one writer that the two most highly-prized qualities among the Gauls were courage and wit, † and his Latin phrase designates, very exactly, the real spirit of conversation, the talent *faire des mots*\*\*, the taste for the short, lively phrase, unexpected, ingenious, and spiced with gaiety or malice. Foreigners greatly admire this gift; and they say that it is

* Bulwer, H. *France social, literary, political.* p. 75.

† Duas res industriosissime persequitur gens Gallorum, rem militarem et arguti loqui.

\*\* The art of making spontaneous witticisms.

accompanied by taste, and that both qualities are universal and precocious among us. A little work-girl will dress well, have pretty manners and an agreeable bearing; a private soldier or a workman will be alert, smart, cut a good figure and know how to crack a joke. This is the *ingegno* of the south, easy, spontaneous and brilliant. That of the north is, by comparison, lame and late: in England the common man of the people is an oaf, at best a sensible oaf, and a young woman of the lower or lower-middle classes a caricature bedizened with loud and vulgar fripperies. A much more prolonged course of culture is required to polish an Englishman or woman, than a Frenchman or woman. Civilization is not native here, it is acquired, and its elegance, style and beauty are to be found only in the upper class. With us something of its quality is to be found in all classes, a fact which gives life in France a more pleasing texture, a more ornamental quality.

As far as I can judge, the English do not know how to entertain themselves with conversation. For a Frenchman the most agreeable moments in life are, I believe, those which he spends in intimate conversation with a few well-bred, intelligent men, after a supper. It is then that there occurs, in every man present, a sort of bubbling-up of ideas, a sparkling discharge from the mind. They think, and speak as fast as the thought occurs to them, on the highest subjects, leaping from one to another in short, vibrant phrases, and their ideas, thus swiftly released, soar in a swarm. In two hours their wide-ranging, adventurous talk will have made a complete tour of the world. Everyone present will have contributed a summing-up of his own thoughts, in sober or jesting language, indulging in excesses of thought or language, in paradox and fancy, not taking his own or others' sallies too literally, nor seeking any end but a kind of holiday for his mind. Philosophy, science, morality, art, literature, and all the treasures of human intelligence are handled not as if they were ponderous ingots or heavy sacks of gold, but as prettily coined, easily carried, well engraved money which rings and glitters as it passes lightly and with a pleasant chinking from hand to hand.

It seems that in England such small change is rare and, moreover, is not current coin. It is considered too light in its metal and is suspected of being too base an alloy. Here, they are more apt to handle the raw and ponderous metal I mentioned above. Conversation is either information, or altogether wanting. From which arise several vexations, among others being boredom: for our minds need occasional holidays, with fun and games. In Italy distractions are the opera and love, in Germany philosophy and the mind's music, in France those intellectual fireworks I have just been describing. Here, there is nothing beyond work conscientiously done, useful production, and a secure and convenient comfort in one's home. It is not enough, however, to be happy in the possession of a well-sprung carriage, a well-kept house, a regular occupation, a seat in Parliament, and the prospect of a probable place in Heaven. There are times when, among all these sources of happiness, a man finds himself yawning and feeling morose. Whereupon one packs a bag, boards a ship and follows one's nose in search of something different, some entertainment or at least a ray of sunshine.

But, on the other hand, the English are much better than we are at after-dinner 'speeches'. You may read reports of these every week in the newspapers. They deliver a great number of them at every political, geographical, economic, scientific or corporation dinner, dinners given to eminent men, or illustrious visitors. I remember one of these dinners, at which I was a guest albeit unworthy, in the company of one of my French friends, a famous explorer. Towards the end the chairman toasted the Queen, then proposed toasts to fourteen or fifteen of the company. "I have the honour to propose the health of our distinguished guest, Mr So-and-So." Then a few words of praise, admirably delivered with grave cordiality, touched here and there with 'humour'. For my part I was full of admiration for the way it was done, but above all for the way in which the speaker never appeared bored. After these words of introduction, the guest in question rose to speak — "I thank the company of gentlemen here present and our distinguished chairman for the very flattering — etc., etc." Here followed some remarks which varied according to the explorer or traveller who was speaking. The specialist on the Nile promised his help to the first expedition formed to seek the source of that river. The Polar enthusiast said that his ability to over-winter among the ice-floes was due to the hard regime of an English education and the training derived from sport. The man whose territory was Western Australia said there was ample room there for English colonists. And, of course, each speaker trumpeted his own little fanfare in honour of Anglo-Saxon energy, the propagation of British civilization, the future of humanity and the progress of science. The company applauded by tapping the table with their hands or a knife. There were shouts of 'Hear! Hear!' and two, three or four cheers. Some of the company stood on their chairs to salute the speaker by holding up their glasses; good humour spread by contagion and soon there was quite an uproar.

Against the orchestral background of this somewhat heavily scored music, the subsequent speeches formed appropriate solos. The commonplaces of which they were composed did not jar, one was not repelled by their vulgarity, nor bored by their seriousness, nor embarrassed by their solemnity: at least the English guests had all adapted themselves to the tone taken by the whole company. But my French explorer friend did not find himself able to join in the chorus: he had a quiet word with the chairman, asking to be excused from speaking. I asked him why he had avoided taking his turn.

"What I should say would be contrary to their taste: or to mine."

To him, a long sustained speech was repugnant; he saw in it a kind of affectation, especially over one's dessert. As a Frenchman he would have preferred a casually dropped *mot fin*, an easy, frivolous conversation with his neighbour at table which would, for all its light-heartedness and the speaker's mocking smile, have conveyed his thoughts on the subject in question. But in England you do not simply sketch an idea: you explain it; for they like their ideas fully and energetically developed, and are prepared, even at table, to bear the full weight and emphasis of explanation. And I suppose they must take pleasure in feeling their nerves vibrating and their will stirred by a collective emotion. Thus a dinner of this kind is first cousin to a 'meeting', and concludes more or less deliberately in a resolution, a subscription, propaganda, and action.

I read an ill-natured newspaper article which said that you cannot speak French without lying: the very language exaggerates: "A thousand thanks!" "I am enchanted!" "A charming man!" The writer forgot that the listener subtracts what is excessive. The fact is, our conversation and our written language style are full of hints, implications and fine shades *(nuances)*. It seems to me, for instance, that La Fontaine, Mme de Sévigné, Voltaire, Montesquieu and Courier cannot be effectively translated into English. Their savour evaporates, their graces fade and their liveliness grows heavy. Recently one of the Reviews here was grumbling about *La vie de Jésus*,* disliking "All these fine ambiguous phrases which seem to be saying one subtle thing, but are actually saying two contradictory things." Many Englishmen have no understanding whatever of such refinements, and they accuse our literature of falsity because their own literary sense is blunt. We, on the

* Renan's. E. H.

other hand, might accuse them of being unable to argue without coming to verbal blows. Their polemics are extraordinarily rough and rude; in France the use of such language would lead to daily duels. Fortunately it is considered here that duelling is absurd, and that no newspaper article can ever call for or justify an appeal to swords. Their debates are like boxing bouts: the combatants, after having severely hurt each other and knocked each other down, shake hands without hard feelings. After reading their newspaper for a few months you get used to it, and finally come to the conclusion that the brutality of the language is amply compensated by the candour of its tone, the strength of conviction implied, the soundness of its reasoning, the sincerity of its indignation, the constant and manly breath of eloquence which animates it.

This is not to say that they are wanting in wit: they have a wit which is all their own; true, it is not very pleasant, but it is altogether original, its savour powerful, keen and even somewhat bitter, like their national drinks. They call it 'humour': it is, as a rule, the joking of a man who, while joking, keeps a straight face. It is copious in the works of Swift, Fielding, Sterne, Dickens, Thackeray and Sidney Smith: in this respect *The Book of Snobs* and *The Letters of Peter Plymley* are masterpieces. And much of it is to be found, of a quality most native and salty, in Carlyle. It results on the one hand in clownish caricature, or on the other hand in sustained, deliberate sarcasm. It shakes the nerves or it sinks deep into the memory. It is a work of either comic imagination or concentrated anger. Its spirit rejoices in violent contrasts and unexpected travesties. It dresses folly in the garments of reason, and reason in the cloak of folly. Heinrich Heine, Aristophanes, Rabelais and occasionally Montesquieu are the authors who, outside England, have the largest dose of it. And even so, to arrive at the same result we should have to subtract something from the last three, an alien element, a French high-spirits, joy, gaiety — those kinds of good wine which are only vinted in the lands of the sun. For in its pure and insular state this 'humour' always leaves an after-taste of vinegar. The man who uses it is rarely benevolent and never happy: he feels deeply and fiercely denounces life's discords. He is not really amused by them; at bottom they make him suffer, and anger him. A continuous feeling of melancholy and anger are necessary to make a man study the grotesques of life minutely, and coldly sustain his irony. Perfect specimens of this *genre* must be sought in their great writers; yet

257

it is so native to this country that one meets with examples of it every day in ordinary conversation, in literature, in political debates; and it is the current coin of *Punch*. Here is an example taken at random from a number I have just been reading:

*Letter from a Secretary of the Treasury
to a Member of Parliament.*
*Library, The House of Commons*

Dear Sir,

Lord P —— has passed me your letter in which you draw his attention to the fact that the session is nearly over, that you have lent his lordship's policy a support as judicious as it has been constant, and that your services merit a reward in the form of a place.

In reply to your letter I must ask your permission to point out that your first proposition is the only one on which Her Majesty's government has the honour and pleasure of finding itself in agreement with you, and that, personally, I have the honour to be, dear sir,

Your very faithful and humble servant.

Do you like 'ale'? Drink it, your palate will acquire a taste for it: it is a wholesome drink and, on the whole, strengthening. It is the same with English humour.

Visited Kensington Museum, the National Gallery and later the Exhibition. The whole of English painting, ancient and modern, is well represented there; moreover, I had already seen two exhibitions of contemporary English painting in Paris. There is, of course, no better means of judging English taste in all that relates to physical beauty than a study of their painting: here, then, are its most salient characteristics.

Heroic painting is rare and poor, as likewise figure painting, whether nude or draped in the antique style or *à l'Italienne*. There are a few very artificial religious pictures. A number of enormous sentimental or historical contraptions, without substance — Hilton's *Edith Swan-neck*, West's *Death of General Wolfe*, etc. Great and noble classical painting, the feeling for a beautiful body, understood and loved, in the manner of the *Renaissance*, that tasteful and learned paganism to which David, and M. Ingres made themselves the heirs in France, has never taken root here. Their school is a branch of the Flemish, but a knotted, stunted branch, the growth of which has, in fact, aborted, but in a way which is entirely original.

Their painters derive, by way of Lely and Kneller, from Van Dyck. In the 18th century a number of them, Gainsborough and Reynolds for example, still showed the Flemish origin in their lively feeling for colour and flesh tints in landscapes and portraits. These painters show themselves men of the north who, following in the steps of the Antwerp masters, are still intent on understanding the men, nature, and physical poetry of the humid lands. Thus Gainsborough's *Nancy Parsons, Lady of Dusanville, Boy in blue;* and some other portraits, likewise his *Watering Place, The Market Cart,* and some of his seascapes: his reds are soft and pale, the tones of the blue silk and his pale yellow, melting, the whites of his pleated or creased lace collars harmonise with those of the faces, distances melt in a vague mistiness, and objects stand out from their background not by the sharpness of their outline but by the gradation of their tints, so that they emerge imperceptibly from the misty atmosphere. Gainsborough has all the riches, all the melancholy, all the delicate sensuality, and all the penetrating and subtle caresses of colour at his command.

Reynolds: *Miss Price, Lady Elizabeth Forster, Miss Boothby, Georgina Spenser, Duchess of Marlborough, Marquess of Hastings, Marquess of Rockingham, Mrs Stanhope, Lord Heathfield, The Banished Lord, The Holy Family, The Three Graces.* He is of the same school as Gainsborough, also to some extent as Rembrandt, but more modern.

Excellent engravings, in the black and white style, and in which so many 17th and 18th-century portraits have been reproduced, also show the Dutch feeling for light and shade blended in dark shading and hatching.

There is something of Flemish colour values in Hogarth's paintings, which are not so hard and prosaic as his engravings, and one can still find a trace of it in Constable, Wilkie, Lawrence and Turner.

But from the very beginning a specifically English sap began to flow beneath the Flemish bark, and it bears witness to its presence by effects which become more and more marked as time goes on. The painter ceases to be simply a painter: the soul, thoughts, the invisible inwardness of his subjects occupy his mind quite as much as the living body, and frequently more so. He shows the moral character, now in a shade of melancholy, now, again, in a profound and pensive reverie, or else perhaps in a touch of aristocratic arrogance or distinction. Gainsborough's *Boy in blue* already shows that expressive and altogether modern physiognomy in which a work of graphic art transcends the real limits of painting. His *Musidora* has such finely made feet and such an intelligent head and face that she is no longer a Bather; she is a lady.

In the same way, Reynolds is a descendant of Van Dyck, but a remote one, so refined and spiritualised that he seems to be separated from his ancestor-in-art by a whole world. His *Three Graces* have nothing of the naïve and primitive: something patrician, almost scathing, in their look and bearing enables us to recognize that they are, really, 'ladies'; despite their being dressed as goddesses one has a vague feeling that they must have their carriage, their major-domo, and fifteen footmen in yellow breeches somewhere in the background. The same painter's *Exiled Lord* is a sentimental elegy in the manner of Young. His great noblemen are no longer simply cavaliers dressed in their finery, and fit to exchange pistol shots or lead a lady up the dance, but for nothing else: this simplicity, the simplicity of true, pure *painting* was not enough for him; he has exercised his ingenuity, understood the complexity of the man beneath the appearance. He has told himself, "One can never put into a head more than one has in one's own," and, armed with this thought, has painted thoughtful souls.

And so, by degrees, the physical in their painting becomes subordinate to the moral: painting will turn into a kind of psychology, and the sensation experienced by the eyes will be treated as an accessory. The painted canvas will be no more than a foreground, a curtain behind which the mind and spirit will perceive, in the distance, ideas, purposes, lessons and studies in character and manners.

It was Hogarth who first conceived this theory and put it into practice. According to him a physical type could only be interesting if it gave salient expression to a moral type. In fact he treated painting as if he were a novelist-moralist after the style of Defoe or Richardson, and his pictures are sermons against vice. Confronted by them one forgets the painting, for one is watching a private tragedy or comedy. The face, clothes, attitude and accessories are *résumés* of character, abridged biographies. His pictures form a preconcerted series and tell a progressive story:

they are illustrations of an implied text, and by their means that text can be read chapter by chapter. Note, in his *Marriage à la mode* the grief-stricken gesture of the old major-domo who foresees the family's ruin and is leaving the room with his hands raised towards heaven; the brutal and sensual stupidity of the gallant who, sprawled in a chair, sings at the top his voice while being dressed. The mind grasps, follows the train of events and consequences, acquiesces in their inevitability, and comes to the requisite conclusion as if it had been attending to a sermon. Less conclusive but equally literary are the works of Wilkie — *The Village Festival, The Blind Fiddler, The Parish Beadle, Blindman's Buff, A Wedding:* he is a painter of life among the humble, a Teniers if you will, but a reflective, observing, thinking Teniers in search of interesting types and moral verities. His pictures swarm with ingenious *purposes*, cheerful satires; they are informative and documentary, like Walter Scott's *The Antiquary* or Eliot's *Adam Bede*. He makes you think and he amuses you, but that has nothing to do with his painting; and there are a number of others who, like him, are writers or poets out of their proper path.

Among these painters who have mistaken their vocation, one of the great ones — and one of the most out of his real element, is the landscape artist Turner. Nowhere can we see more clearly than in his work the error committed when a talent which should address itself to the senses, undertakes to address itself to the mind and soul.* The collection of his work fills three rooms. There are landscapes by him which are very fine, of a simple grandeur in which one finds a profound, and indeed even an august, feeling for nature: such are *Knighton's Bank, Frosty morning, Bligh Sands, Cattle in Water, Saint Mawes Cornwall.* But these belong to his first period. By degrees the appeal to the eye, the optical effect came to be of secondary importance to him, and the feelings and dreams of the speculative and reasoning brain became sovereign. He tried to paint mighty epics, philosophical and humanitarian: he believed himself to be the greatest of men and I have been told that he died mad. It is certainly the case that his painting became mad, more or less in the same way as Victor Hugo's prose and poetry. *Apollo Killing Python, Hannibal's Army in the Alps*

* It may be as well to remind the reader at this point that Taine, despite this extraordinary statement and what follows, was a distinguished critic and historian of painting. His point of view becomes clearer when he comes to his amusing demolition of Ruskin, below. E. H.

*During a Storm, The Flood, The Burning of Sodom, Light and Colour after the Flood, Rain, Steam and Speed in a train, Steamboat in a Snow-squall* — these and thirty or forty others carefully collected together by himself and hung according to his instructions in a place apart, comprise an inextricable slushy mess, a sort of whipped froth, an extraordinary jumble in which all form is drowned. Place a man in a fog in the midst of a storm, with the sun in his eyes and a giddyness in his head and then, if you can, convey his impressions onto canvas, and there you have something like it: these are the confused visions, dazzlements and delirium of an imagination driven mad by its own straining.

The increasing exaggeration of cerebral and mental life in our time has shifted the centre of gravity which gave art its stable equilibrium. English painters are still remotely connected with the Dutch masters by a few superficial affinities, by the small size of their canvases, by their choice of subjects, their taste for realism, and by the precision and minuteness of their detail. But the spirit has changed and their painting is no longer pictorial. Compare, for example, Potter's animals with Landseer's, the latter so carefully drawn, so intensely studied, especially his stags and dogs. The English painter does not like animals as such, simply as living creatures; and certainly not simply as forms, shapes seen in relief or splashes of colour harmonising with their surroundings. He humanises his beasts, his painting has philosophical, moral or sentimental purpose. He tries to suggest a line of thought to the spectator; he paints animals as a fabulist. And the scene in which he sets his animals makes a sort of problem picture, with the key to the enigma printed below it. For example, *Peace and War, Dignity and Impudence, Low Life and High Life, Alexander and Diogenes,* and *A Dialogue at Waterloo* — all these expressed in canine types and attitudes. The same procedure is followed by figure painters: the essence, for them, is in the anecdote, the story, the literary attribute, the representation of some aspect of *mores* which they have chosen as a subject. The pleasure of the eye, harmony, and beauty of line and colour are all relegated to secondary rôles: such is the case in the work of Maclise, Leslie, Hunt, and one of the most famous, Mulready. I have seen a score of his pictures — *First Love, The Wolf and the Lamb, Open your mouth and shut your eyes, The Battle Interrupted, The Younger Brother, The wife of the Vicar of Wakefield.* It would be impossible to find anything more expressive; never has so much effort been expended in trying to address the mind by way of the senses, illustrate an idea or a truth, or in collecting a greater mass of psychological observations onto a surface twelve inches square. What patient and penetrating criticisms! What connoisseurs of human nature these painters are! What clever contrivance, and what aptitude in rendering moral values into physical terms! And what admirable vignettes these artists might have drawn to illustrate an edition of Sterne, Goldsmith, Crabbe, Thackeray or Eliot! Occasionally one comes across a masterpiece in this *genre*, for instance, Johnson's *Lord and Lady Russel receiving the Eucharist:* Lord Russel is about to mount the scaffold; his wife is looking into his face to discover whether he is reconciled with God. This look, intensely wifely and intensely Christian, is admirable; Lady Russel is reassured, at peace concerning her husband's salvation. But what a pity it is that these artists, instead of writing, took to painting!

In the prodigious effort they have made to concentrate their entire attention on man's moral aspect, their optical sensibility has become both distorted and blunted. I do not believe that pictures so very disagreeable to look at have ever been painted. Impossible to imagine cruder effects, colour more brutal or exaggerated, more violent and gaudy discords, harder or falser juxtapositions of tones: examples are Hunt's *Two Gentlemen of Verona,* with its bluish trees sharp against the brown of the earth, and the figures' scarlet clothes; and his *Christ at night with a lantern,* the whole in a greenish-yellow atmosphere like that of the disturbed water about a swimmer as he comes to the surface after a dive. Millais' *Noah's daughters leaving the Ark:* the purple of the dress and the way it glares out against its surroundings has to be seen! Then Crow's *Pope introduced to Dryden* — light blue waistcoats, red velvet coats, and the accessories in high, sharp relief, as if it had been done for a bet. Mulready's *The Bathers* look as if they are made of china. Millais' *The Eve of St Agnes:* imagine a lady in full evening dress, *décolletée* and who, owing to the deliberate twilight effect, is tinted, like the room in which she stands, a sort of corpse-green.

As for their landscapes: blood-red poppies like holes in parrot-green lawns; flowering apple-trees in which the hard white of the petals against the blackish branches is painful to the eye: a meadow-green graveyard in full sunlight, with every blade of grass provided with a high-light and shining like a pen-knife blade. There can be no doubt that there is something peculiar in the condition of the English retina. Analogues are not wanting to confirm this: they are to be found in a score of details of their daily life, for example in the reds, purples, purplish-browns and raw greens with which they decorate the covers and colour the pictures in their children's books; in the gaudy and over-elaborate clothing of their women; and even in the sight of their meadows, flowers and countryside under a sudden blaze of sunshine. Perhaps we are bound to admit that in every country it is the appearance of natural objects which educates the eye, that tastes are formed by familiar and customary things, and that some secret affinity arranges the colours in the products of artifice in accordance with those of the natural environment. And it is a fact that here the women's clothes do by their lustre, freshness, opulence and ill-matching put one in mind of the brightness, youthful freshness, magnificence and contrasts of their vegetation and garden prospects.

One could discover resemblances, too, between their mauve and violet silks and the changing colours of the distance in their views, and their clouds; between their gauzy scarves and vapoury lace shawls, and the pale and splendid mists veiling their horizons.

But many of the effects which are harmonious in nature are displeasing in painting: they cannot be conveyed on to canvas; or at least they cannot be so conveyed quite raw. On canvas they are discordant because taken out of the context in which they were harmonious. For a number of the recourses which nature disposes of are not available to the painter, among others being full sunlight, real light, the flash of daylight on water, the scintillation of light rays on a green leaf. These are supreme values which dominate all others and relieve them of any excessive hardness of accent; and deprived of this tempering influence, the other effects shock the eye as a chord from which the high note had been omitted would shock the ear. Thus, in order to express these effects they must be transposed: no painter, no artist of any kind, is a mere copyist: even when he confines himself to interpreting, he invents. For what nature accomplishes by one system of values and means, he is obliged to render by using a different system of means and values.

Such, then, is the mistake made by contemporary English painters: they are faithful copyists, but they are *literal* copyists. When one has seen their country one does realise that most of their effects on canvas are true enough: here, indeed, is an English lawn revived by recent rain; here, indeed, are their white dawn skies, their gleaming sands at low tide, the sharp or violet-shot

264

green of their multitudinous waves. Faithfully rendered are the swollen ears above the pale gold straw of their corn harvest, the glowing purple of wild heather on a lonely common. Upon thinking it over one cannot question their exactitude: what is more, one recalls the pleasure experienced at the sight of the real landscape, and is surprised to feel displeasure at the sight of the painted one. And the reason is that the translation is no more than a transcription: to be faithful in detail they have been false in the whole. With all the conscientiousness of meticulous artisans they have conveyed the sensations of their eye, point by point, raw and unchanged, on to canvas. And meanwhile they were dreaming, moralising, following, like poets, wherever the sweet or melancholy feelings evoked in their souls by the landscape led them. But, between artisan and poet, the painter has disappeared. One cannot but praise their patience and feel that one would doubtless have been moved by the original of what they have painted: but their copy is no more than a *suggestive document*, and one readily abandons it because it is ugly.

A man has, however, come forward to justify them and to erect a theory on the basis of their practice. John Ruskin, admirer and friend of Turner, and a writer with very strong convictions, passionate, original, very able, studious and popular, is a man in whom the peculiarly English genius is very manifest. There is nothing more valuable than personal, independent and well co-ordinated ideas when, like Ruskin's, they are courageously expressed; for they make us reflect upon our own ideas. There can be nobody who has read his books, *Modern Painters*, and *Stones of Venice*, who has not been made to think by them.

Ruskin's first principle is that we ought to love truth as it really is, and the characteristic detail, with enthusiasm. He tells us that every kind of ground, rocks, clouds must be known by the painter with the thoroughness of a geologist and a mineralogist. When Salvator, he says, puts into his foreground something of which he, Ruskin, cannot say whether it is granite, slate or tufa, then there is neither harmonious union nor simplicity of effect, but merely a monstrosity. Titian, he tells us, was sound in botany, for in his *Bacchus with Ariadne* the foreground is occupied by the common blue iris, the aquilegia and *Capparis spinosa;* and the foreground of Raphael's *Miraculous draft of fishes* is covered with that kind of marine cabbage called *Crambus maritima*, all of which plants are painted with scrupulous regard for truth.

But, we are told, in order to produce beauty, truth to nature is only one means and art goes beyond it; for its proper business is to evoke superior emotions. Nor is it sufficient for it to provoke sensory pleasure. Such pleasure may be the foundation of the impression made, but it must in addition be accompanied by a feeling of gladness, then by a feeling of love for the object painted, then by a perception of the goodness of a superior intelligence, and finally by an urge of gratitude and veneration for that intelligence. No impression can in any respect be considered as an impression of beauty unless it be composed of these emotions, just as we cannot say we have any idea of a letter if we perceive nothing but its scent and beautiful handwriting, without understanding its contents and purpose.

Now here, indeed, we have the aesthetics of a man of the north, all spirit and protestantism: and all his judgments conform to this standard. The pictorial quality of a painting is of no importance to him, nor the pleasure of the eye, and he tells us that the landscape painters of the past had nothing but "mechanical and technical qualities", instancing Claude Lorrain, Gaspar Poussin, Salvator Rosa, de Cuyp, de Berghem, Ruysdaël, Hobbéma, Teniers (in his landscape painting), Paul Potter, Canaletto, "and the diverse Van-something and Back-something,* especially those who defamed the sea." Most of these professional landscape painters, says Mr Ruskin, had no other object but to display their manual dexterity; and the best act of art patronage which a monarch could perform would be to collect all their canvasses into a gallery and set fire to it.

There are a great many people who will be bound to hope that in no circumstances will Mr Ruskin ever be called to the throne.

He is equally down on Italian painting, on its spirit and its cult of the perfect, athletic body. To his way of thinking the mythological paintings and nudes of this school, which number half the total, were painted simply to pander to sensuality; they should be classed with opera ballets. Before Raphaël, art was employed to bring religion into the light; with Raphaël, religion begins to be used to bring art into the light.

Perugino's crowned queen becomes simply any Italian mother (*Vierge à la chaise*). This, he feels, was not a healthy change. The artist's motive ceased to be love of truth and became simply pride. He thought of the Madonna as a convenient subject for the display of his transparent shadows, his cleverly chosen tints, his scientific fore-shortening; and as a beautiful woman, who, if she

* Doubtless the admirable G. van der Velde and Backhuysen.

were well painted, would make an agreeable piece of furniture for the corner of a boudoir, and who could be composed by combining the beauties of the prettiest peasant girls — "That is what Raphaël thought of the Madonna."

A little further on Ruskin describes, in faith and awe, the apparition of Jesus walking on the waters before Peter, and compares Raphaël's cartoon of the scene with the real thing. He points out the well curled hair and properly laced sandals of the figures; but these men had spent the whole night on the water, in sea fog, and on a filthy deck. Their clothes are surely very inconvenient for fishing, with their cloaks trailing a foot behind them, and their fine fringes. And especially we are to notice Peter who, wrapped in his fringed mantle, is starting forward to kneel and take the keys gracefully. And then the whole group of apostles, instead of being gathered close around Christ, as must have been the case, are stretched out in a line so that they can be seen. Moreover, beyond them is a beautiful, but Italian, landscape full of villas and churches. At which spectacle our belief, our faith in the event begins to fade away; we feel it to be no more than an absurd legend, a hotch-potch of muscular arms and curled heads, Greek philosophers' heads. And all that men have imagined to help them picture this true story, so strange and so extraordinary, with its infinite severity, infinite tenderness and infinite variety, is, as by a single sweep of a sponge, wiped out by Raphaël's empty elegances.

It is, of course, easy to convict a painter, even a very great painter, if you impose on him a purpose which he never had: Raphaël was concerned to paint a group of grave and handsome men, well-built, well posed, well grouped and draped; and to do no more than that. Mr Ruskin censures him for having made St Paul a thoughtful Hercules leaning on a conqueror's sword, and adds that no artist has yet painted the real St Paul. It is certainly as well that they have not painted him: "that ugly little Jew," as M. Renan calls him, was beautiful only in his soul, and his soul is in his *Epistles*. Raphaël was right: contrarywise to literature, painting, having the living body as its object, does not depict the soul excepting indirectly and as an accessory. Mr Ruskin demands of painting the effects proper to literature. "In Turner's *Building of Carthage* the principal object of the foreground is a group of children amusing themselves sailing little boats." And this, according to him, is a most lofty thought, worthy of epic poetry: for this children's game shows the sea-faring aptitude and future greatness of Carthage. Whereas, he goes on, in analagous subjects, Claude introduces, for example, people carrying red coffers fitted with iron locks, and takes a childish pleasure in rendering the gleam of the leather and its metal ornaments.

But what if that red and that gleam serve as complements and foils, and are therefore useful values, halting and holding the eye or preparing it; what if they are used, that is, like the scale of the horn or the hautbois in a symphony? Whoever would do without that scale has no ears: has that man eyes who would do without Claude's red and Claude's gleam?

So, then, according to Ruskin we are to have the fact, the real thing, the material and physical object, with its own physiognomy and in all its detail, scrupulously conveyed intact on to the canvas, so exactly rendered and set that a scientific specialist, a botanist or geologist, would find a documentary specimen in the picture. Nothing for the *décor*, nothing for the secret requirements of the eye or the pleasure of the senses; beyond, and in compensation, the impression to be made on the moral being, the silent dialogue between soul and nature, the unheard but prolonged and vibrant reverberation of a profound *ego*, answering, like a mighty and private harp to every external touch by sounding unexpected sonorities.

For them this ego, this mighty *Me* is the principal personage of the world. Invisible, all visible things are rallied to him, subordinate to him; and their only merit is in being aware of him, in corresponding to something in him, accomplishing a representation, an expression, of some emotion latent in him.* The spiritual being is the centre at which all else finds its goal.

To have taken so dominant a place the spiritual being must be very strong and all-absorbing. And so it is, as one perceives as soon as one considers the principal features of the English character: the need for independence, the capacity for initiative, the active and obstinate will, the vehemence and pungency of passions concentrated but controlled, the harsh though silent grinding of their moral machinery, the vast and tragic spectacle which a soul entire furnishes for its own contemplation, the custom of looking into the self, the seriousness with which they have always consid-

*              *An artist*
*Who paints a tree, a leaf, a common stone*
*With just his hand, and finds it suddenly*
*A-piece and conterminous with his soul.*
*Why else do these things move him, leaf or stone?*
                    *Aurora Leigh. 303*

ered human destiny, their moral and religious preoccupations, in short all the signs of faculties and instincts which were already manifest in the pen of Shakespeare and the hearts of the Puritans. Taking only the moderns we may say that there is in every Englishman something of Byron, of Wordsworth and of Carlyle,* three very different minds yet similar in one point which is a strength and a weakness and which, in default of better terms, I will risk calling hypertrophy of the *Me*.

For a soul so constituted and disposed the proper medium of expression is poetry. They are as great in that art as they are indifferent in the others. In my view there is no poetry equal to theirs, none which speaks so loudly and clearly to the soul, which moves it more profoundly, in which the words are so charged with meaning. None, moreover, which better conveys the tremors and impulses of the inner being, whose grip is so effective, whose note so poignant; none, furthermore, which so plucks the deepest and most personal strings of our being or draws from them chords so splendid and so penetrating. It would take too long to pass their whole literature in review and I shall content myself with notice of a single, recently published poem, *Aurora Leigh*, by Elizabeth Barrett Browning, a strange work and her masterpiece. And even so I shall not have room to say how beautiful, after twenty readings, it seems to me.

The poem is the confession of a generous, heroic and passionate soul in which genius is superabundant; a pririt whose culture has been thorough, complete; a philosopher and poet inhabiting the highest regions of thought and who yet transcends the noblest of her ideas in the even greater nobility of her instincts. She is altogether modern in her education, her pride, her boldness, in the constant quivering of her taut sensibility, screwed up to such a fine tension that the lightest touch rouses in her an immense orchestra and a most astonishing symphony of chords.

The poem, then, is nothing less than a soul, the intimate monologue of a soul, the sublime song of a girl's heart, and an artist's heart drawn to and colliding with an enthusiasm and a pride as strong as its own. It sustains, through explosions and variations of the same theme, strophe and antistrophe of feminine and masculine voice, drawing always further apart, increasingly opposed one to the other, until at last, drawn suddenly together,

* Like all Frenchmen Taine assimilates Scots, Welsh and Irish to English. Perhaps I should have written *Briton* for Englishman but the word is faintly absurd. E. H.

269

they unite in a long duet of pain and delight so exalted and intense in tone that it cannot be surpassed.

Formerly the epic poem thundered and rolled over the foundation or destruction of cities and the great battles of the gods. Here its subject is the battle of ideas and passions, and the transformations of character. Not appearances, but inner realities, are its matter; and wide though the epic frame be, this inwardness is rich and great enough to fill it. The motions of a soul so full and vibrant with life are quite equal to the shock of armies meeting. In default of legends and divine apparitions, such a soul has its intimations of the infinite, its dreams and aspirations embracing the whole world, its tempestuous or luminous conception of beauty and truth, its hell and its heaven, its dazzling visions, its prospects of the ideal, each leading to a glimpse of yet another, caught not like Homer's, from the high points of a tradition; nor, like Dante's, from the summits of a dogma; but from the peaks of the most exalted modern ideas, and to be gathered together when seen from still higher, a place of sanctuary and the dwelling of a god.

There is nothing official about this god; he is the god of the soul, of a fervent and fecund soul in which poetry becomes piety, and which extends and amplifies its own noble instincts beyond itself, spreading over the infinity of nature its own feeling for the holiness of beauty.

All this is expressed in a style of an unique kind, which is much less a style, indeed, than a system of notation, superlatively bold, sincere and faithful, created from instant to instant, out of anything and everything (de toutes pièces) in such a fashion that one never thinks of the words but seems to be in direct touch with the gush of vital thought, with all its palpitations and starts, with its suddenly checked flights and the mighty beating of its wings. With it the reader soars from the depths of sarcasm and familiarity, to the heights of ecstasy. It is queer language, yet true even in its least details, and the only one capable of conveying the peaks and troughs of the inner life, the flow and tumult of inspiration, the sudden concentration of ideas, too crowded to find vent, the unexpected explosion into imagery and those almost limitless blazes of enlightenment which, like the northern lights, burst out and flame in a lyrical mind.

"Never flinch,
But still, unscrupulously epic, catch
Upon the burning lava of a song,

The full veined, heaving, double-breasted Age:
That, when the next shall come, the men of that
May touch the impress with reverent hand and say
'Behold.' — behold the paps we all have sucked.'
That bosom seems to beat still, or at least
It sets ours beating. This is living art,
Which thus presents, and thus records, true life.'

The manner is the natural complement of the matter:

"What form is best for poems? Let me think
Of form less, and the external. Trust the spirit
As sovran nature does, to make the form;
For otherwise we only imprison spirit,
And not embody. Inward evermore
To outward, — so in life, and so in art,
Which still is life.

Poetry, thus conceived, has only one protagonist, the soul and mind of the poet; and only one style — a suffering and triumphant cry from the heart.

The more I dwell upon this conformation of the English mind, this habit of turning in upon the self, this primacy of the moral being, this need to perceive that moral self first of all, and thereafter to see all nature through him, the nearer do I come to understanding the strong and manifold roots of that poem, their religion. To understand its value and authority exactly, two aspects of it must be distinguished: on the one hand the redactions of its various editors; on the other the feelings of the reader.

The editing varies from sect to sect — Quakers, Presbyterians, Wesleyans, Unitarians, Anglicans: but the Anglican Church is the most widely and best accredited. In its favour are its antiquity, its alliance with the State, its privileges and endowments, the presence of its bishops in the House of Lords, its domination in the Universities, its middle position between two extremes; that is, between the cult, dogma and spirit of Puritanism, and the cult, dogma and spirit of Catholicism. Moreover, this Church is an old and lawful compromise that suits the majority, which is attached to formal transactions, readily follows tradition, and lets itself be directed by statutes. Furthermore, the Church is rich, is one of the powers that be, has affiliations in the aristocracy, has splendid connections, and is one of the great organs of the constitution. By these tokens it has the support of statesmen, conservatives, society and all who would be known as *respectable*. Finally, the Anglican 'Prayer Book' is very beautiful; the Church's services are grave and noble, its conduct half-tolerant. It leaves the individual some free judgment. And thus authorised it can impose, or propose, its particular text, and it can be said that this text is generally accepted.

Three parties may be distinguished in this official Church: one, more aristocratic, authoritarian and attached to ceremonial, is called the 'High Church'; another, more popular, passionate and concerned with evangelisation, is called the 'Low Church'. Both being somewhat narrow and inflexible there is room, besides, for a liberal party, called 'Broad Church', which includes all the finest minds and the most conciliatory spirits, those, in short most capable of reconciling science and faith. It is thanks to them that the gulf separating lay thought from ecclesiastical tradition is ceasing to be unbridgeable.

Among several other polemical and dogmatic treatises I have just been reading *Alford's Greek Testament,* one of the best authorised commentaries on the Scriptures. It does not go so far as German criticism: the author's historical feeling is hampered by orthodox prejudice: but his concessions are substantial enough to satisfy common sense. According to him the Gospels are not altogether in agreement; sometimes, indeed, notably in chronological matters, they contradict each other. This is because their authors "were not simply spokesmen, organs used by the Holy Spirit, but only saintly men inspired by Him." For their writings they had a common basis, to wit, tradition and several fragmentary versions in writing, but this material was subject to every variety of diction, arrangement, omission and addition which any account is bound to suffer in the course of passing through several different minds in different places. Each narrator impressed his own mark on the story according to the nature and cast of his information and the gaps in it, and to the quality of his memory, imagination and feelings. The whole story is true, but as a whole rather than in detail.

Thus, then, between the divine kernel and the several human shells, there is no fixed limit: each person can cut away more or less of the outside skin of the story and, even in the Church itself, some cut away a great deal. According to Mr Stanley, being a Christian does not entail believing in this or that event in the life of Jesus, or in this or that dogma as revealed by Jesus, but in Jesus Himself, in the moral and religious spirit of the Gospels. He explains the gift of tongues in the same manner as M. Renan. He is at one with the German theologians in holding that the Gospels as we now have them were written long after Paul's Epistles. His commentary on the Epistles is written with the sensitive feeling, the free and penetrating intelligence of a modern critic dealing with Dante or Pascal. He describes Corinth, with its sea and its temples, after Pausanias, various travellers, and his own personal experience. He shows us St Paul dictating to his disciple Sosthenes, who stops him from time to time to point out something he has forgotten. We can, he says, imagine the letter to which Paul was replying unrolled in front of him so that he could refer at a glance to the difficulties raised by his correspondent, and pick out the objections, sometimes quoting them, sometimes expounding them in his own words. He analyses St Paul's style very well, a style as powerful and remarkable as the feeling which inspired it, a style which is jerky, tormented by the writer's inner turmoil, made up of outbursts in which sharp fragments of fiery thought heave and collide like lava in the flames and smoke of an eruption. Mr Stanley compares St Paul's style, in some respects, with that of Thucydides and, better still, with Cromwell's. He shows us the Hebrew temperament and oriental imagination at work in the Apostle, and in this connection reminds us of the state of mind of the prophets and psalmists; he even goes so far as to point out that the vestiges of an analagous exaltation still survive in the Moslem dervishes. In short, according to him in order to understand the evangelical age we must first of all realise that the evangelists were zealots, fanatics acting amid scenes of enthusiasm such as formerly occurred among the Puritans, or such as are to be met with nowadays in the 'Shoutings' which take place in America.

Mr Jowett pushes criticism even further. To read the New Testament he rejects the authorised version and turns to Lachmann's. The former is to the latter what Renaissance editions of Sophocles and Thucydides are to those of Dindorf and Becker, or what the Port-Royal *Pensées* of Pascal are to M. Feugère's edition. Mr Jowett does not believe that early Christian faith coincides exactly with ours. They believed that the Second Coming and the end of the world were imminent, and carried away by their conversion, lived in a kind of ecstasy, their faith being "simple and childish". Their beliefs were those of men who did not see very far into the designs of Providence and had never dwelt on future prospects. Their feelings were those of men who thought of Christ's coming as we might think of the return of a lost friend, for many of them had seen Him on earth and could not believe that He had been taken from them for ever.

If, says Mr Jowett, we consider these early Christians only in their appearances and from a worldly point of view, they leave on us much the same impression as would nowadays be made by a sect of nonconformist fanatics, poor dreamers, narrow-minded, grotesque and even dangerous. Their language is redolent of the disposition of their minds. The words justice, faith and charity are much vaguer in St Paul than with us: they correspond to more violent conditions and a play of ideas less well-defined. When St. Paul says that Adam's sin is imputed to all of us, he is being carried away by passionate feeling and writing in a particular Hebraic style: he only means to say, "we are all one man by the community of our vicious nature." And by that communion, and not otherwise, are we all involved in Adam's sin. The exaltation and zeal of the Apostle and Oriental have found expression in approximations and his similes and mental images are not to be taken for formulae. When he speaks of redemption and expiatory sacrifice he is alluding to a Jewish custom. And between the mind of St Paul, stormy, exalted, trained in the synagogue, expressing itself in exclamations, thinking in block ideas — between such a mind and the modern lucid, exact and discursive intelligence which unravels and traces a skein of well-defined ideas thread by thread, the difference is immense. It would be absurd and, what is more, horrible, to set up local metaphors as philosophical doctrines.

The reader can see for himself what must be the consequences of such writings. The advent of philology, criticism and psychology into this field means an overhauling of theology and a transfiguring of the whole dogma. The effects are already apparent. Distinguished men, historians and churchmen, have resigned their places in the Universities or the Church because they could no longer subscribe to the thirty-nine articles. Bishop Colenso of Natal, questioned by his neophytes about the Old Testament, and required to give his word of honour that it was all true, fell into a profound meditation, studied the question, read German exegesis, and ended by publishing a book which relegated the Bible stories to the status of myths. A well-informed friend of mine estimates that out of twenty-four bishops, four are in favour of Oxford liberal criticism, and that these four are supported by the great number of well-thought-of and influential laymen who approve of this criticism.

The modern spirit is also making inroads by way of other rifts in the traditional fabric, rifts due, for instance, to geology and natural history, for which the English have a great aptitude, and to experimental psychology, which they have long fostered. For what the English prefer above all is proven facts, whether object-ive or subjective, facts actual and incontestible which everyone can experience as such whether in himself or outside himself. From this very disposition theories, and even a philosophy, can derive, for example the hypotheses of Lyell, Huxley, Darwin and Tyndall, the philosophy of Herbert Spencer and Stuart Mill. Such a bent, when it is predominant, must lead the mind towards one of the forms of positivism; and, in fact, positivism, especially among scientists and men learned in natural philosophy, is not unusual here.

Among other and contemporary peoples, for example the French, the state of affairs is much the same although the proportions are different. There, too, we find a symbol, a text accepted by the majority, interpretations of it, more or less broad, accepted by various small groups, scientific scepticism favoured by a few free-thinkers and a number of learned and scientific specialists. In all this the resemblances are striking but they are superficial. Which brings us to a consideration of the second factor, the feelings and attitude of what we called the "reader" of the religious "poem", the accepted symbol. It is in this particular that the two peoples differ radically.

The Englishman has a naural aptitude for the feeling of the *Beyond (l'au delà)*. For him there lies beyond human experience, however indefinitely prolonged we may suppose it to be, a chasm, a void, a great unknown, a place of light or darkness: as to this the most determined sectaries of pure experience are in agreement with religious believers. Beyond those things which are accessible Herbert Spencer expressly allows for that something which is in-accessible, the *unknowable,* the infinite of which we know only a superficial fragment. And although Stuart Mill refrains from affirming the existence of this infinity which transcends all limits, he at least accepts it as possible. An enormous darkness, void or filled, lying all about the narrow circle of vacillating light cast by our little lamp, such is the impression commonly made by the spectacle of the universe upon sceptics and believers alike.

Such an impression entails a serious state of mind, and cannot fail to be accompanied by a certain feeling of fearfulness: man is confronted by a spectacle out of all proportion to himself, hence overwhelming; and he is disposed to respect, even to awe and wonder. And as he is thoughtful (in England), and apt to meditate on human life ('to moralize'), he has no difficulty in being aware of this great *Beyond* in the moral as in the physical world. He is readily and quickly aware that his power is limited, his foresight short, his institutions precarious, and that he is like a leaf borne along on an immense and tumultuous stream. On days of anguish, when he is mourning a death among his nearest and dearest, in sickness or in danger, when his ignorance and dependence are made apparent to him in signs vivid and terrible, this feeling becomes poignant. He turns his eyes upon the great, universal motion and the grandeur and obscurity of its government is borne in upon him. Dwelling thus upon it, he endeavours to picture it and, for want of a figure to fill the void, pictures it to himself as a government by a *somebody*, an intelligent and deliberate rule — the work, then, of a power and a mind in which are wanting none of those things wanting in himself.

Now, one more step: if, among the imperfections which he discovers in himself, the gravest, in his eyes, are his bad inclinations; if he be principally concerned with the idea of the just and the unjust; and if his conscience be alert and active, then the original feeling, defined, directed and completed, will lead to the concept of a moral God. "Begin by looking at every thing from the moral point of view," as Thomas Arnold wrote to a person who was tormented by doubts, "and you will end by believing in God." In short, the edifice having been thus prepared and its columns raised, that belief, like the keystone of an arch, takes its place at the summit of its own accord. The mysterious and infinite *Beyond* becomes a mysterious and infinite Providence; and the text of the Scriptures, the liturgy of the Church merely give formal expression to the inarticulate cry of the heart.

Such is the inarticulate elaboration, such the inner ferment by whose means the idea of God is formed and developed. The child receives it from outside itself, like a graft. But in order that this graft "take" instead of remaining in the child's soul as so much dead wood, the soul must adapt it to itself, knit it and cause its own sap to flow in it. This it contrives to do by a long labour of which it is quite unconscious. As a rule many years must pass before the junction is complete and transforms the alien scion into an acquired organ. So far as I can tell, this junction occurs naturally and effectively in an English mind, along the lines which I have just described; that is, first by an awareness of the infinite powers which press all about us, by the concentration of these vague powers into a person, and by the installation of that person on the moral throne of the world.

In this way religion ceases to be an official formula recited on occasion, and becomes a living feeling which is experienced as such. The reader who would convince himself of this has only to look into the detail of their daily lives as it appears in letters, biographies, poems and novels, in all those spontaneous documents which cannot be suspected of hypocrisy. Recently, in connection with a case at law, the newspapers published the letter which a poor sergeant, killed at Petropavlovsk, wrote to his wife, Alicia, on the eve of battle: nothing could be grander, more touching, or more deeply felt; it was the testament of a soul. Or take three novels at random: there will be two in which, at the major crises of the story, prayer is introduced; or if not prayer, at least the solemn feeling proper to a man aware that, over his head, over all heads, hovers an infinite source of justice. One may dispute their doctrine; but in the face of their feeling one can only give way; it is sublime.

# CHAPTER NINE

# A TOUR OF BRITAIN

FROM MANCHESTER to Glasgow: left at two o'clock in the morning. At dawn I was looking out on landscape still English, meadows and fields and hedges upon a soil not naturally fertile and fat as in Flanders, but worked and forced to be productive by man's industry. Past Carlisle the ground begins to dip and rise in long, high hills, which are used as pasture land. Solitude; no trees, no arable; here and there a house. The great, green swellings starred with the white dots of grazing sheep. This eternal green, for ever damp and pale, leaves a strange impression.

The approaches to Glasgow crowded with innumerable chimneys and tall, flaming furnaces; I counted sixteen in a single group. Glasgow, like Manchester, is a city of iron and coal. It, too, stands on a black-tinted part of the map, and the Clyde gives it a great port with access to the sea. One is tempted to find, in the physical character of a piece of country, a prediction of its future: the green earth, flocks and herds, dairy produce, the cold and humid climate produce men who are carnivorous, energetic, obstinate and hard-working; coal, iron, the neighbourhood of the sea, and rivers providing harbours, invite man to turn industrialist and trader.

Three hundred and seventy-five thousand inhabitants. But the aspect of these great hives is always heart-breaking. Children swarm bare-footed in the mud; women in rags, flesh showing through torn dresses, giving the breast to their infants at street-corners. The climate is worse than at Manchester. We were at the end of July and the sun was shining, yet I was glad of my coat. Fortunately, the human body adapts itself to its environment: I saw fully grown girls lying on the grass by the promenade, without shoes or stockings; and there were little boys bathing in the river. Moreover, certain features of their moral character compensate nature's disadvantages. It happened that I put up at a hotel for 'commercial gentlemen', and for twenty-four hours, notably during meals, had occasion to see scores of them. Their physiognomy is a mixture of the landowner, school-teacher and shoemaker. Whereas our own commercial travellers look like something between a wag and a military man. Now, in matters of business and commerce the former character is apt to be more successful than the latter: nor is the difference thus indicated confined to the commercial travellers of the two peoples.

By steamer, and in the luminous mist of early morning, we made our way down the Clyde, among masts and rigging, to the sea. We steamed along an irregular and deeply indented coast, from bay to bay. These almost land-locked bays are like lakes, and each sheet of water gleams within an amphitheatre of green hills. Every swell and ridge of the shore is dotted with white villas. The water is peopled with ships: I was shown a height from which one can sometimes count as many as three hundred in view at one time. A warship, a three-decker, swam in the distance, like a swan among gulls. This great, wide-open space, teeming with life opens the soul: your chest expands splendidly and gladly do you breathe in the cold, brisk wind. But the effect on nerves and heart is not that of the Mediterranean; this air and scenery, instead of encouraging to ease and pleasure, urge to action.

A little boat drawn by three horses took us up the Crinan canal between two grass rides. On one side are rocks covered with scrub, on the other steep slopes, rust red and grey; here, at last, was colour, pleasure for the eye, shades composed harmoniously. There were wild roses on the banks and among the bushes, and some delicate, white tufted plant which was charming.*

Leaving the canal we embarked in a steamer again, the estuary opening before us wider than ever. The sky was entirely clear and resplendent and the twisting waves quivered and glittered beneath the sun, like so much molten metal. The ship left a wide wake frothing and bubbling and sea-birds followed us tirelessly, swimming in our wake. On both sides were islands, rocks and bold promontories, all bristling in high relief against the pale azure of the sky: the scenery changed every quarter of an hour. But at each new prospect the infinite view of the sea appeared again, its almost flat plane meeting the curve of the sky in a white mistiness.

The sun sank low, we were off Glencoe, and Ben Nevis appeared, its peak marbled with streaks of snow: the gulf narrowed, and the water, now enclosed by barren mountains, had an air of

* Probably ramsons, i.e. wild garlic. E. H.

drama. Man is not welcome here, nature has remained wild and untameable; the landscape is lunar.

We disembarked near Fort William; by a lingering, palely ruddy twilight we could still see something of the desolate landscape, peat-bog and the broken surface of the valley between two ranges of enormous mountains. The cry of some bird of prey broke the silence. Here and there we could see a few wretched cottages; I was told that the ones higher up the mountains are hovels without windows, and with a hole in the roof to let the smoke out. Many of the old people are blind. What a land of hostility to man!

On the morrow, travelling by the Caledonian canal, we passed for four hours between wild solitudes, a monotonous procession of treeless mountains and enormous humps of green dotted with great boulders. A few dwarfish sheep forage for grass on the slopes; sometimes the winters here are so hard that the sheep die. From time to time you see wild-eyed, shaggy cattle, no bigger than a donkey. Plants and animals all perish here, or grow stunted. To get anything of value out of such land it would first be necessary to reafforest it, as is being done in Sutherland. The trees restore the soil, then shelter the men who farm it, their beasts, and their arable fields.

The canal opens into a string of lakes, and there can be nothing nobler and more moving than the sight of them. Their waters, turned brown by peat, form a vast, gleaming plain surrounded by mountains. As the ship goes forward the profile, then the whole shape of each mountain are slowly revealed: the most distant, receding one behind another to the horizon, which they close, are blue. They seem gathered in session, an assembly of mighty and melancholy beings about the dark waters which reflect their forms; from time to time, above them and their lakes, the sun shines out from behind its veil of clouds.

Towards the end of the journey these solitudes become less austere. Woods appear on the mountains until at last they are quite covered with trees. The slopes become gentler, the peaks lower and rounder and the broadening valleys are tilled and carry a standing harvest. Hollows and slopes are clad in the fresh green of forage plants. We entered Inverness and were astonished to find, so near the extreme north of Scotland, on the very flank of the wild Highlands, a lively and attractive modern town. It is built along both banks of a clear and swift-flowing river. A number of its buildings are new; a church, a castle and an iron bridge. One is aware of bustling activity, cleanliness, attention to business. The window panes shine and paths are washed down; door-handles are of gleaming brass, there are flowers in every window and the poorest houses are freshly white-washed. Well-dressed ladies and gentlemen in smart suits pass up and down the streets. There are even works of art to be seen, Ionian columns, buildings of pure Gothic, and other architectural amenities, jerry-built it is true, but proclaiming a desire for improvement, an intention to do better. Obviously the land itself is poor: it is the industry, order, economy and toil of its inhabitants that makes it what it is. What a contrast with the appearance of any small town on the shores of the Mediterranean — neglected and dirty, and with the townsmen living like worms in a rotten beam!

I spent a week in the neighbourhood, with a friend. Nearly all the cottages are well-kept or recently renovated. The little farms and peasants' cottages are covered with honeysuckle and surrounded by roses in bloom. True, these excessively low houses have often only one floor and are too small, for building materials are dear; true, also, the bed is set permanently in an alcove built of planks, where it gets no air, because of the bitter cold in winter. But these inconveniences, arising from the nature of the soil and climate have acted as a spur to the inhabitants.

There are books to be seen even in the smallest cottages; the Bible first of all, a few biographies, travel books, medical dictionaries, manuals on fishing, treatises on agriculture, eight to twenty volumes as a rule. Nearly all the Scottish peasants can read and do read. My hosts always shook hands with the cottage people, including the young girls, and told us to do likewise; they did not appear awkward or embarrassed. Every peasant here feels himself master in his own house, free both spiritually and temporally, responsible for his own salvation, all of which gives him a natural dignity. The rich and the gentlefolk do not shut themselves up or hold themselves aloof out of distrust, repugnance and selfishness, as they do in France: they give public lectures or readings, and subscribe to local charities and endowments. One gentleman built a church, which was shown to me; another had an iron suspension bridge erected, putting up a notice requesting users "to drive their vehicle at walking pace." The wall of this gentleman's park is only two feet high, anyone can go in and the only rule he makes is to prohibit people from doing any damage.

Between Keith and Aberdeen I came across a cheap excursion train, its carriages crammed with people. They were all on their way to a religious meeting, a 'revival' at which a number of famous preachers would be speaking. The crowd of people wishing to attend was so great that the railway company had to telegraph for extra carriages, and even so girls had to sit on the young men's knees in many of the compartments. My neighbour told me there would be twenty thousand people at the meeting, some of them coming great distances, fifty or sixty miles. While the train was waiting, the women sang hymns with an air of great conviction and serious purpose. Religious music here is always grave and sweet and never fails to give me pleasure. The carriages were all third-class, and the people shop-keepers, working folk and small farmers, all dressed like our lower-middle classes: clean suits of grey or brown cloth, often new; the faces were lively and intelligent. The race is livelier and more mentally active here than in England. They were all of the common people but they were obviously better educated than our own villagers in France.

When I reached the inn I was staying at, a Temperance Hotel, I found among the proprietress's books, moralising novels and works of piety, a treatise of apologetics in favour of 'revival meetings'. It set out to justify the shoutings, faintings, and other violent outbursts of feeling. "In the most polished circles a mother or father, confronted by a son they thought lost to them, may faint from joy, yet nobody censures their transports as unseemly. How much more allowable are the transports of a soul which suddenly feels itself saved, redeemed by Grace!"

In a newspaper article by a clergyman, I read a reprimand of Walter Scott for bringing the Covenanters into disfavour by the way he presents them in his novels.

In my opinion, Presbyterian Protestantism is the "poem" which suits these people: sad, grandiose and narrow, it is well fitted to turn a man in upon himself, to bind him to his work and make him bear his life.

Went to a service on Sunday: no pictures, no statues, and no instrumental music. The church is simply an assembly room, provided with a gallery and rows of benches, very convenient for a public meeting. And in fact divine service here is hardly more than a lecture on morality. The minister's text was, "We must work our own salvation", act, make an effort, not wait for outside help: God will help us, will give us His Grace, not because of our effort, (that is gratuitous), but in proportion to our effort. The sermon was well spoken, soberly and sensibly, without oratory. Albeit somewhat abstract, the precept was practical and calculated to stimulate thought, personal reflection, in at least some minds, especially during wintry or wet weather. To follow such an argument and pursue it further with the help of one's own reading in the Old Testament or the Gospels is an occupation to elevate the mind and set the conscience to work.

Apart from the sermon, the service comprised a reading from several chapters of the Bible, notably from St Paul, prayers in prose, recited out loud, psalms and hymns sung by the congregation. The prayers and hymns are conventionally flat and quite modern: but only in the great century of literature, from Shakespeare to Milton, did they really know how to talk to God. But the psalms, although feebly translated, are still effective by the power of their feeling, and the worshippers' lungs, and even nowadays a troubled soul with a sense of spiritual responsibility can understand their significance: they are a dialogue between the human heart and the eternal Judge, alone and face-to-face. It is by their means that in the midst of disputatious theology, and preaching, and monotonous toil, moral feeling can burgeon into a flower of poetry. And such a flower is by no means uncalled for in a religion whose practice and dogma resemble a hedge of thorns.

I noticed the rapt faces of the congregation: I am told that the Scots are even more religious than the English. Presbyterianism, rigid though it be, was apparently not rigid enough for them. In 1843 some of them concluded that the nomination of ministers by a patron was contrary to God's will, and a free Church, maintained by the voluntary contributions of its sectaries, was founded. At the present time it has an income of £330,000, has founded 700 schools, and has adherents in every village. You may measure the theological susceptibility and religious zeal of its supporters by the contrast between the apparent insignificance of the point originally at issue, and the vigour of the separation from the establishment, the speed, volume and cost of the work since accomplished. The same applies to Sabbath-day observance; compared with Edinburgh, a Sunday in London is positively agreeable.

The country all about us now is very pretty: the soil appears to be indifferent but the arable farming has none of the artificial regularity it has in England. Nature, here, is rougher and less amenable to discipline. The scenery is varied and would please a painter. Wild flowers are abundant, delicate and dainty, especially the wild rose which blooms all along the roadsides. Clear little babbling brooks cross every field. On the hillsides purple heather is spread like a carpet of silk beneath widely-spaced pine-trees. Above them are the wide skirts of evergreen forests; and, as one draws near to the mountains the horizon is closed by the brown circle of barren peaks.

Another hour's travelling and one is in a wilderness, with a climate hostile to all life, even plant life. We saw a lake the colour of burnt topaz, sleeping cold and dismal between stony hillsides dotted with a few tufts of heather and rushes; half a league beyond it was another lake, and fog rising from the ground made it even more dismal. All about, the mountain peaks were marbled with drifts of snow, which melts into streams, and these spread to form bogs. Our small, native ponies picked their way, sure-footed, up the slopes until we reached a height from which the view, as far as we could see and in every direction, was of a great circle of desolate though green-clad summits. The destruction of the woods has entailed the perishing of all other life, and a ruined countryside is more lugubrious to behold than any number of ruined buildings. On our way back, by the lake, a piper played us his instrument. It is strange, wild music, whose effect matches the aspect of the lapping, mountain-locked waters, their surface veined with moving reflections, brilliant or sombre. A single, simple theme, a sort of dance air, runs through every tune, falsely, strangely, always recurring, always shrill and sharp: think of an orange, stunted by cold, its juice turned sour.

These are the Highlands. From Braemar to Perth, one crosses them, a distance of many leagues. Solitude everywhere; one may see five or six valleys in succession innocent of life, and you may travel for an hour without seeing a single tree. Then, during yet another hour, you may see here and there a wretched, twisted birch-tree, dead or dying. If, at least, the rock was naked, revealing the geological structure in all its vigour and roughness! But no; these mountains, being only moderately high, are great, softly-rounded humps, no more, scattered over with boulders and pebbles so that they look like abandoned quarries. In winter, torrents of water tear up the heather and leave vast leprous scars on the hillsides, whitish in colour under a sun too feeble to put colour into them. A miserably poor grass forms green drifts on the slopes following the trickle of streams; the rest is covered with brownish heather. The summits of the hills are truncated, and without boldness.

Far below, down in the valley, we could see a torrential stream encumbered with boulders, fighting its way through a gorge, and slackening into stagnant, marshy pools. Occasionally you come across a cottage with a stunted cow. The lowering, grey sky completes the impression of monotonous dreariness.

Our carriage climbed a last mountain: there, at last, was a steep, bold slope, a great wall of rock; but it is the only one. Then we began to go down hill, into habitable country. First the valley bottoms were cultivated, then the hillsides; trees, then woods appeared on the slopes, until entire hills were tree-clad, forests of pines spreading their sombre cloak even to the saddles and summits. Fields of oats and barley grew larger as we progressed, and there were pretty groups of deciduous trees, houses surrounded by gardens and flowers, then every kind of farmed land covering the lower, softened hills. Here and there a park and a modern mansion. The sun came out and shone cheerfully, without warmth. The plain opened before us, fertile, abundant in promise of comfort and pleasure, and we drove into Perth thinking of Walter Scott's historical description, of the contrast between plain and mountain, and of the insults and contempt commonly exchanged between highlanders and lowlanders.

From Perth to Edinburgh the country remains pretty and varied, hillier and more broken-up than England, and also leaner. Scotland is more picturesque and her countryside, less uniform and less manageable, is not simply a meat and wool factory.

One might make a similar comparison between Edinburgh and London. Instead of a level, regular, modern city, a centre of trade, comfort and luxury, you find an ancient city full of contrasts spread over three valleys and several high hills, where the steep streets, tall houses and manifold vestiges of the past produce unexpected prospects in every part of the town. On one hill-top towers a feudal castle. From there, as you go down towards Holyrood, ancient lanes and alleys open off the street and plunge down steeply towards the lower town. There one finds lanes and closes which are mediaeval warrens, whose walls, blackened by smoke-laden rain, bear the leprous accumulations of four centuries of exposure. Here and there the walls are hung with round towers, or overhung by turrets round or square. The narrow windows, baroque or misshapen, are covered by iron grilles like prison ventilators. Shallow stairways of sweating stone wind and vanish into dark interiors among crawling shadows whose depths are suddenly revealed by a stray beam of light. The steps swarm with barefoot, tow-headed children, and men crouching over a meagre meal; such scenes recall the fantastic shapes, half-shadows, and strange guests which people Rembrandt's dark basements.

The city has a number of statues; Gothic, and especially Greek, buildings; and two picture galleries. Carlton Hill, with its colonnade and two or three little temples, is trying to be an Acropolis; and this city, learned, lettered and philosophical, calls itself the Athens of the North. But what an incongruity here is the architecture of classical antiquity! Whipped by the wind, a pale mist drifts and spreads all over the city. The façades of buildings are drowned in the vaporous atmosphere and stand palely forth in the sickly daylight. A wisp of fog or cloud hangs upon the green slope of Carlton Hill, winding in and out of the columns. The very climate seems to revolt against shapes proper to a dry, hot country; and the needs, tastes and ways of northern men are even more hostile to them.

For example, the principal temptation assailing men here is to turn drunkard, and temperance societies combat it with a mixture of Biblical notions and utilitarian arguments. To this end they post up bills showing two symbolical figures: one represents 'a man', the worker; the other 'a thing', the drunkard; appropriate advice is printed below. Sixpence a day spent on beer and tobacco adds up to so-much a year: with that sum of money you could buy such-and-such articles of furniture, or so many pairs of shoes, such a number of shirts, and, of course, the one indispensable book, "a family Bible". This calculation, and the mention of the Bible, together, are strikingly characteristic. And when, from that, you go into the Museum and are confronted by three or four big Van Dycks, a Garofalo, a Veronese, and notably by two sketches of women by Tintoretto, you feel that you are indeed at the other end of the world.

Leaving Edinburgh you have the sea framed by distant mountains on your left. As you go south they shrink to a delicate, worked border about the great spread of shining waters. Berwick slips past, cheerful and picturesque beneath its red roofs, and about its tranquil harbour where a few ships lie dreaming. Further on is Newcastle, whose coal has only to be shipped to supply all the North Sea coast; it is a town of coal and factories, black and smoky and depressing as a prison. Through all this part of the journey the country is flat and almost treeless, and without hedges, although now and again there is a wooded creek and a hamlet. From end to end of the journey the sea is in sight, for the train runs along the coast, sometimes hanging above the sea itself, sometimes enclosed in a rock-cutting. The heart swells at the spectacle of that mighty spread of gleaming water. Its clear and level plain stretches away until it joins the rim of the sky; little moving mounds of foam star its azure with their whiteness. Two or three distant ships seem to glide in it like birds. Above, the pale sky curves its great arch; and one forgets the busy spectacle of the swarming human anthill in recapturing the tranquillity, simplicity, and divine immutability of natural things . . .

. . . York, next morning. A gracious, limpid river shines softly between lines of Gothic towers; beyond, a bridge and a huddle of black-hulled boats. You cross the water by ferry. Nobody in the streets. The air touches your cheeks, as fresh as it is in the country. One lingers by ancient houses each floor of which overhangs the one below; there are low blind arcades, and massive doors studded with big nails. Grass grows in the cracks between cobbles and paving stones. About the Cathedral is a square where immemorial trees spread their great domes of foliage. Everything is green, clean, and peaceful, impregnated with the past, as in a Flemish town. The enormous and venerable Cathedral adds to this resemblance. Intact on the outside, this Gothic colossus rears taller and looms wider than Notre-Dame, massive and powerful under its three towers. The interior was stripped and looted by the iconoclasts of the Reformation, and it is whitewashed, bare and sad. Of its former ornamentation only the choir-screen remains, a lacy labyrinth of carved figurines, pulpits and pendentives, their shapes intertwined with a delicate and prodigal fancy. How charming they are, these quiet old towns! But in the speed of the travelling all these sights pass through the mind like so much stage scenery . . .

. . . Last day, York to London. A man should stick to his last to the end; so I did the nine-hour journey in a third-class carriage, in order to observe more of the common people. The two most striking types were those I had already come across: the robust man; and the man already exhausted. The first had the body and bearing of an athlete, red face, ginger whiskers, the eyes of a bull, rough movements, a sullen or threatening expression which, however, sometimes turned kindly, as when he smiled or was spoken to politely. The other, hard blinking eyes, drawn features and his cravat was so tight it seemed to be choking him; his whole person was both worn and stiffened.

I saw a number of country people: none of them had the look or ways of our own peasants, that air at once knowing, suspicious and bewildered which proclaims a different species, a descendant of men subject to the *corvée,* son of a *fellaheen,* a race intelligent certainly, but uncultivated and still so bound to the soil *de facto* although no longer *de jure*, that all their thinking is confined to it. Here, the villagers who got into my train at wayside stations were more like factory workers or semi-townsmen: and indeed a farm in England is a factory, employing operatives and foremen like any other. And from York to London the countryside confirms this idea: a rectangle of greenery enclosed by a hedge, then another, and so on, in great stretches, with monotonous regularity without any of that variety which proclaims the presence of small-holding agriculture.

In the same carriage as myself was a Newcastle family, the husband, his wife and her mother, lower-middle class townsfolk, quite well dressed in new clothes. They were on their way to Venice, for pleasure, yet they cannot have been rich since they were travelling third class. To go so far, and in so uncomfortable a way, at an expense which must necessarily be heavy, certainly shows a very lively taste for travel. And I know of modest families who spend all their surplus cash in the same way, using the thousand or twelve hundred francs they can save in a year to visit the Continent, to stay in Holland perhaps, or Norway. They put nothing by: they are satisfied if each year's work provides for that year's needs.

My three fellow-travellers were making conscientious preparations for their trip: they were studying a Murray, an Italian phrase-book, and a special guide, full of figures, for the crossing of the Alps. The mother, who wore spectacles, sat silent, respectable, impassive, enduring the hard, wooden seat with stoical patience. The wife studied the Italian phrase-book and looked up words in a pocket dictionary. Her husband was obviously a good soldier in the battle of modern life, active and vigorous, his face pitted by the small-pox, his eyes staring and ardent. What singular visitors for Venice! Still, they were sensible folk, capable of learning and who, although they may not appreciate painting, will bring back a great deal of information and many useful notions. Since being in Glasgow I have talked with a number of casual acquaintances of the middle and lower classes, a commercial traveller, a house-painter, shop-keepers, inn-keepers and so forth, and they never indulge in idle chatter. Their ideas about foreigners are not too wide of the mark; they do not jump to hasty and ill-considered conclusions; they are not indiscreet; they are not boastful; and I have always found them possessed of a fund of decent and reasonable ideas . . .

*Fig. 24  The Thames*

...London, Dover and the ship, all in the rain. From London to Dover I travelled first class. There was a semi-gentleman in my carriage who suggested a game of cards for money to his neighbours; five pounds a bet.* They refused at first, then let themselves be drawn in and, naturally, lost their money. I estimate that in one hour the man with the cards won a hundred and fifty pounds.* The most remarkable thing was the players' bearing: not a muscle of their faces moved; not one gesture or a single exclamation. Their pride concentrates and suppresses their feelings, but one could sense the attraction gambling has for them, the silent but violent passion of determination and will to win. One of them, a tall, stout man with the motionless face of a bullock, kept doubling his bet, taking out his banknotes * with the air of a prize-fighter in a boxing bout. They delight in risk and it has the same effect on their minds as spirits on their palates.

A friend of mine was returning to France at the same time as myself and we compared our findings. Which of two civilizations

* Taine says *"livres"*, but not, as he usually does, *"sterling"*. It seems likely he means five livres French, that is, roughly, five shillings. — However, perhaps he means pounds sterling, in which case card-sharping must have been a profitable trade! The game was probably 'Find-the-lady'. E. H.

is the better, the English or the French? The question is too vague; one must distinguish and divide:

Three things in England are superior:

1. The political constitution. It is stable and runs no risk, like our own, of being overturned and badly reconstructed every twenty years. It is liberal, and calls upon the individual citizens to take an active part in public life, and not simply to look on as bystanders. It puts the government of the nation's business into the hands of the upper class, which is the most capable of managing it well and which finds its natural employment in such business instead of spoiling and growing decadent for want of an outlet, as with us. It lends itself to reform without being badly shaken by it, and it does, in fact, result in good government; that is, government with the greatest measure of respect for individual initiative and which places power in the hands of the most worthy. The British three percents stand at 96; British citizens enjoy full freedom of speech and association; their Press is the best informed in the world, and their Parliament the most competent.

2. Religion. It subordinates ritual and dogma to ethics. It preaches 'self-government', the authority of conscience, and the cultivation of the will. It leaves a wide margin for personal interpretation and feeling. It is not altogether hostile to the spirit of modern science nor to the tendencies of the modern world. Its priests are married. It founds schools, urges action, and does not advice asceticism. Being thus in close touch and sympathy with the lay community, it has influence over it. The young man starting out in life, the mature man in full career, are, up to a certain point, restrained and guided by a body of traditional, popular and fortifying beliefs which provide them with a rule of conduct and a noble idea of the world. Whereas, in France, at twenty years of age we are obliged to create our own idea of the universe and make our own rule of life, which we only contrive to do belatedly, often imperfectly and frequently not at all.

3. The volume of acquired wealth and the greater powers of production and acquisition. All useful or valuable works carried out in past centuries have been and still are handed down and accumulated without loss. England has suffered no invasion for eight hundred years, and no civil war for two hundred years. Her capital, today, is several times larger than that of France. Evid-

ence of comfort and opulence is more plentiful in England than in any other country in the world. Examine the national statistics of her trade, industry, agriculture and annual increment. This is true on the moral as well as the physical plane: not only does an Englishman know better than a Frenchman how to conduct his public and private business, fertilise his land, improve his cattle, manage a factory, clear, colonise and exploit distant countries, but he also knows more about cultivating his own mind and character. If we consider only the *élite* we should, I think, find in France minds equal, in all but what concerns politics, to the greatest minds in England, and perhaps even a few which are superior, loftier, with a wider range, more philosophical, at once subtler and more broadly comprehensive. But the majority of ordinary minds, those, for example, of a country gentleman, or an average clergyman, are, in this country, both more extensively and more soundly educated. Certainly the average English brain is better furnished, and that furniture is more nearly up-to-date and complete. Above all, the number of men sufficiently well informed and capable of having an opinion in matters of politics is greater. Compare the clergyman or the English gentleman we have been studying together, with a French *bourgeois* or a French *curé;* or, for instance, take a look at their intellectual daily bread, the English newspaper, and at a French newspaper — this comparison should, especially, be made between a French and an English small-town paper. The difference between them is excessive. Now it is not the *élite* minority, but the average majority which sets the tone, dictates public opinion, and manages the community's business.

On the other hand, three things are superior in France:

1. The climate: this is too obvious: but in default of personal experience and prolonged reflection it is impossible to conceive the difference which six or eight degrees of latitude less can make in reducing the sources of bodily misery and spiritual depression.

2. The distribution of wealth. There are four or five million landowners in France, and inherited property is shared by a man's children in equal parts. Taking things by and large, our institutions, instincts and customs combine to ensure that no one man has too great a share of wealth, and that every man has at least a small share. Many of us live meanly, but almost all of us live

291

without too much of a hard struggle or too much suffering. The very poor are less miserably poor. The worker who has nothing but his two hands to depend on is not constantly aware of a horrible chasm opening at his feet, a bottomless, dark cesspool waiting for an accident, unemployment or sickness, to swallow him and his family. Our worker, having fewer children and fewer needs, carries a lighter burden; besides, poverty does not degrade him so much, nor is he so inclined to drunkenness.

3. Family and communal life. Several circumstances make these easier and more agreeable. In the first place, we are by nature more cheerful, more communicative and more apt to become attached to other people. Secondly, the complete equality — or almost complete — established by law or custom between parents and children, oldest and youngest, husband and wife, noble and commoner, rich and poor, eliminates many constraints and many tyrannies, prevents many instances of insolence, makes rubbing shoulders a much smoother operation. In a typical French domestic circle people are expansive, they lay themselves fully open, and combine together to spend their lives freely and affectionately as a group. And in the wider social circle the talk is freer, there is more mutual trust and candour, and people gather together to pass an hour in easy freedom and cheerfulness. There is less awkwardness both at home and abroad, and kindness and courtesy are improvements on English subordination. In my opinion a human being in France is less frequently apt to feel the rough and despotic hand of another human being pressing him down, and, when he does, the oppression is not so heavy. A final cause of our expansiveness: in conversation we need keep nothing back, we can go right on to the conclusion of an account of events or an hypothesis we are developing. The novel, criticism, art, philosophy, and curiosity are not, among us, subject to the constraints of religion, morality and official conventions which are imposed upon them on the other side of the Channel. In Paris our thinking is freer, marked by a disinterestedness more nearly complete. Our thinking is more abstract, less concerned with practical applications, and carried on without fear of the thunderbolts of public reproof.*

* But not without fear of official interference: Taine himself was denied his doctorate by the Sorbonne on one occasion, and more than once removed from his employment in the University, or forced to change his teaching, by government or ecclesiastical powers hostile to his positivism. E. H.

To sum up: the differences we have distinguished contribute to render the Englishman relatively stronger, the Frenchman relatively happier. The Englishman's coat is harder-wearing, the Frenchman's more comfortable. The Englishman would be wise to let out his apparel a little, for it is too tight under the arms and makes him ill-at-ease. The Frenchman would do well to avoid any sudden movement: the cloth he is wearing might easily tear. Yet it seems to me that both of them are clad to suit their tastes.

*THE END.*